An Expression of Character:

The Letters

of

GEORGE MACDONALD

An Expression of Character:
The Letters
of
George MacDonald

Edited by

Glenn Edward Sadler

William B. Eerdmans Publishing Company
Grand Rapids, Michigan

To My Father and Mother

Copyright © 1994 by Wm. B. Eerdmans Publishing Co.
255 Jefferson Ave. S.E., Grand Rapids, Michigan 49503
All rights reserved

Printed in the United States of America

Library of Congress Cataloging-in-Publication Data

MacDonald, George, 1824-1905.
[Correspondence. Selections]
An expression of character: the letters of George MacDonald
/ edited by Glenn Edward Sadler.
p.   cm.
Includes bibliographical references (p.   ) and index.
ISBN 0-8028-3762-X
1. MacDonald, George, 1824-1895 — Correspondence. 2. Authors, Scottish —
19th century — Correspondence. I. Sadler, Glenn Edward. II. Title.
PR4968.A44   1994
823'.8 — dc20

[B]   93-41107
                                          CIP

The editor and publisher gratefully acknowledge permission to reprint letters of George
MacDonald granted by the institutions and publishers listed on pp. 378-79.

Contents

IV. America and After

V. Living Abroad and More Novels

VI. Last Years — Bordighera

A Personal Note

I can first remember becoming aware of my great-great-grandfather when I was about nine years old. By some event that I cannot recall, I connected a portrait of George MacDonald in our dining room with a row of somewhat forbidding and definitely dusty books on the shelves in my bedroom. Before then I had not attached one with the other.

Although they had always held a peculiar kind of fascination for me, almost a challenge, it was a lack of other reading material rather than bravery that finally caused me to take one of the volumes down. Luckily it was *The Princess and the Goblin*. I enjoyed the tale greatly, and a natural progression took me through *The Princess and Curdie* and *At the Back of the North Wind*. Sadly, my next choice was a disastrous one for a nine-year-old: *Lilith!* After this, that particular shelf remained undisturbed for many years.

I suppose it was about ten years later that I read Greville MacDonald's biography of George MacDonald for the first time, and it was shortly thereafter that I met Glenn Sadler. This dual occurrence set me back on course, as it were. Through Glenn, I was able to sit in the Beinecke Library at Yale, surrounded by my family's letters. The joys, adventures, and many great sorrows of their lives were told in these letters in such a way as to make me a part of their experience. Thus it was an extraordinarily emotional experience for me to read again the letters that are collected in this volume.

I would like very much to salute the editor of this volume as well as the author of the letters, for no one has dedicated more of his life to the furtherance of George MacDonald's thought, beliefs, and writings than Professor Sadler.

I believe it would be appropriate to conclude with some words of

George MacDonald, and these, written May 3, 1877, seem to me to be fitting:

I write like them of the old time, but my meanings are fresh as the new flowers, while old as the Spring that leads them back to us once more.

London, September 20, 1993   CHRISTOPHER PETER MACDONALD

Foreword

When in October of 1915 the sixteen-year-old C. S. Lewis purchased an Everyman edition of George MacDonald's *Phantastes* at the train station in Leatherhead, Surrey, he had no idea what he had let himself in for. The inital impact of his reading of MacDonald is one of the most brilliantly realized passages in Lewis's spiritual autobiography *Surprised by Joy*, all the more remarkable because it succeeds in describing the indescribable, that is, something that involves a change in the very state of one's inner being. In the most celebrated statement in that passage Lewis writes: "That night my imagination was, in a certain sense, baptized."

The reading of George MacDonald climaxes the chapter Lewis titled "Check," as a reference to the chess game that he has all unknowingly been playing with God. By encountering MacDonald, Lewis finds that his "adversary" has made a decisive move toward winning the game. Two chapters and a decade and a half later, it will be "Checkmate," and Lewis will have given in and "admitted that God was God."

Since that time, and from a far more panoramic vantage point, Lewis has doubtless had a chance to reflect that at that moment when "the hills beyond the Dorking Valley were of a blue so intense as to be almost violet and the sky was green with frost," the "great Angler" was actually double-baiting his hook. Not only was he enticing Lewis into his future role as an unparalleled apologist for Christianity, but he was also luring the young Lewis into becoming the premier rediscoverer and advocate of a distinguished Victorian author otherwise in danger of being forgotten. In a model example of the doctrine of the economy of salvation, on that October late afternoon in 1915 God was arranging simultaneously for the conversion of C. S. Lewis and the literary rehabilitation of George MacDonald.

To understand the notion of "rehabilitating" MacDonald, it is important to remember some dates and facts. When Lewis picked up *Phantastes,*
MacDonald had been dead only ten years. His reputation, though waning
and certainly not at its high-Victorian peak of the sixties, seventies, and
eighties, was far from extinguished. All the leading literary journals took
extensive note of his passing. G. K. Chesterton (whom Lewis was to discover for himself three years after his reading of *Phantastes*) was among
those writing laudatory obituaries, and in the year following MacDonald's
death an appreciation by Joseph Johnson was published. But by the end
of the First War, MacDonald had been cast into the literary dustbin
reserved for those Victorians whom bright young things called "eminent"
as a term of contempt, and that included almost all the Victorians, especially if they were earnest, religious, hortatory, and wore beards. The 1924
publication of Greville MacDonald's biography of his father came too late
to restore him to prominence. MacDonald was read only by children and
by those like Lewis who never read on the principle of fashion.

The tide began to turn in 1946 when Lewis paid double homage to
MacDonald by publishing an anthology of MacDonald's writings, organized by the pattern set forth in MacDonald's own *Diary of an Old Soul,*
and by casting him, Dante-like, as a sage Virgilian guide in *The Great
Divorce* (where Lewis actually makes his first published reference to the
Leatherhead experience, though its depth could scarcely have been appre-
ciated by initial readers). By this time Lewis had himself gained such
celebrity (*Screwtape, Mere Christianity,* and the "Space Trilogy" were all
now in print) that his word alone was enough to send readers hastening
back to the forgotten Victorian. When nine years later in *Surprised by Joy*
Lewis offered the declaration about *Phantastes* cited above and credited
MacDonald with a central role in his own conversion, MacDonald was
launched on the road to literary beatification. Since then many Mac-
Donald works have been reprinted, especially the children's stories and the
fantasies *Phantastes* and *Lilith;* the latter two mark the beginning and the
end of his long writing span that stretched from the 1850s to the end of
the century. Also since then MacDonald has been selected as one of the
seven modern Christian writers (and the only fully nineteenth-century
one) to be gathered in the impressive Wade collection at Wheaton College,
Wheaton, Illinois, and celebrated in the scholarly periodical appropriately
entitled *Seven.* MacDonald has come back into literary prominence, this
time as the spiritual grandfather of the Oxford Inklings. He has found a
wholly new and enthusiastic public.

Of course, every silver lining has its cloud. As grateful as we all must be to C. S. Lewis for redeeming George MacDonald, we must also be aware that he called our attention to only one George MacDonald — MacDonald the fantasist, or as MacDonald himself would rather have called it, the writer of "faerie romances," for the modern codification of this sort of writing had not yet stamped "fantasy" on MacDonald, nor could it have, seeing that MacDonald was helping to invent the form. Still, today the all-purpose word for the kind of writing Lewis responded to in MacDonald is *fantasy*. This is the MacDonald who has been reprinted in our own time, for this is the MacDonald who mattered most for Lewis and who matters most for readers today. But it is only one of many George MacDonalds. Just as C. S. Lewis's friend Owen Barfield, in *Owen Barfield on C. S. Lewis,* was able to discern no fewer than five C. S. Lewises, so too there are at least that many George MacDonalds, some of them still waiting to be discovered. Those many MacDonalds reside in one of the most staggeringly large and varied bodies of work of any English author of any age, even allowing that Victorians in particular tended to be prolific.

The many MacDonalds include the fantasist, the children's writer, the realistic novelist, the Scottish regionalist, the Christian apologist, the preacher, the poet, the literary critic, and yet others, depending upon how we assign some of those works that mix or transcend genre. Curiously, in his own day MacDonald was often more highly valued by critics in the categories other than fantasist and children's writer, but that may be because Victorian critics (as opposed to readers) were less inclined to take fantasy and children's writings seriously. Today the situation is reversed: it is the other MacDonalds who have been overshadowed by MacDonald the fantasist and children's writer. But the important point is that there *are* so many MacDonalds and that the time has come for reexamination and reconsideration. Nothing could stimulate and aid such reexamination more than the collection of MacDonald letters here to hand.

Glenn Sadler, certainly no stranger to the world of MacDonald fantasy, having distinguished himself as an editor and interpreter of that world, has nevertheless provided us with a fuller and more varied MacDonald than we have ever had before. He has, one might say, shown us at last the MacDonald whom no one knows because he is the MacDonald who has remained forgotten even after C. S. Lewis's generous exertions on his behalf. Professor Sadler has presented us with the various other Mac-Donalds by the artful device of selecting the best and the brightest of MacDonald's letters and presenting them in the traditional chronological sequence, but with a twist. By dividing the span of MacDonald's letters into six stages and providing each stage with its own introduction and chronology of dates, Professor Sadler has done more than relieve the tedium of an endless succession of letters; he has created a collection that is close to complete and that at the same time constitutes a biography of the several George MacDonalds whom we can now recognize as having flourished under one pen. When you add to this the abundant, intelligent, yet never burdensome footnotes, the bibliography of MacDonald's works, and the discussion of secondary works about MacDonald, you have for the first time an opportunity to see George MacDonald steadily and whole.

What a fascinating and impressive story it is! What a fascinating and impressive man George MacDonald was! And how much he deserves this further rehabilitation. At a time when the literary canon is constantly being revised, often for the wrong reasons, it is more than comforting, it is exhilarating, to find, as we do in this collection, so rich a presentation of a life and mind and soul that it calls out for a reassessment of the whole writer. Would you know MacDonald the truly eminent Victorian as well as MacDonald the man who virtually invented fantasy? To get to know these and all the various MacDonalds, this is the place to start and a place to come back to again and again.

University of California, Los Angeles   G. B. TENNYSON

Preface

George MacDonald expressed the wish on more than one occasion that no biography of him should be written. However, his sons Ronald and Greville both wrote biographical accounts of their father. His second son, Ronald, wrote a short biographical sketch in 1911 of MacDonald's literary contributions, entitled "George MacDonald: A Personal Note," in which he said of his father that "there has probably never been a writer whose work was a better expression of his personal character." In 1924 Greville MacDonald wrote similarly in the foreword to his biography *George MacDonald and His Wife* that his father's "message was all in his books, and no biography could add to it." When MacDonald was sixty-nine, his friend and literary agent A. P. Watt approached him about writing an autobiography. In response, MacDonald wrote: "I will do *nothing* to bring my personality before the public in any way farther than my work in itself necessitates" (June 11, 1893; see p. 355 below).

But one cannot read George MacDonald's fiction and poetry without being aware that he does bring his own personality into his work, often quite intentionally. One discovers that some of MacDonald's best writing occurs when he allows his own convictions and visions to take over what he is writing. It is George MacDonald's special, distinctive vision of life that continues to fascinate so many of his readers. Starting with G. K. Chesterton, who dubbed MacDonald "St. Francis of Aberdeen," he has had some impressive admirers, including C. S. Lewis, J. R. R. Tolkien, and Maurice Sendak — writers and artists who have claimed that he had an influence on them. In an attempt to discover more about what it was in George MacDonald's personality that attracted readers to him, I began work on this volume of letters. It was my intention to allow MacDonald's character and philosophy of life to be revealed through his letters. As I continued to read his letters, I became impressed with MacDonald's ability to face life's adversities, and I was moved by the words of comfort and encouragement that he wrote to family members and friends. I discovered in his letters the same message of hope that I had found in his books.

For biographical reasons, the letters are arranged chronologically according to the major periods in MacDonald's life. By taking this approach, I have tried to follow the major events in his life and show how he responded to them. MacDonald did not hesitate to discuss family matters with close friends, and he shared openly his personal experiences.

I am indebted for biographical information and previously published letters to Greville MacDonald's biography, and I have reprinted many appropriate letters from it. In an effort to check the accuracy of transcriptions of these letters, I have consulted holograph manuscripts whenever possible. For the most part, I found Greville MacDonald's transcriptions to be surprisingly accurate. Where there are significant omissions or errors, however, I have made the necessary corrections. Unfortunately some original letters have not survived.

Reading through a writer's personal correspondence becomes an engrossing activity and a very personal matter. One cannot help but gain an impression of the writer's character and his values. As far as I can determine, George MacDonald represents justly in his letters the man himself. He makes no effort to conceal his true feelings or to impress his reader with his own cleverness. Unlike some of his contemporaries, MacDonald never intended his letters to be published. For readers who do not share MacDonald's Christian worldview — some of whom may think that "he is just too good to be true" — I can only say that the optimism he expresses throughout his letters represents what MacDonald himself actually believed: his sincerity is consistent throughout everything he wrote. This is not to say that he did not have — as many Victorians did — moments of dark doubt and deep despair, especially as he had to endure the loss, one by one, of his children; nor is it to say that he did not suffer the normal anxieties of old age. But he held with tenacity to his vision of life-in-death to the end.

It is, I think, George MacDonald's incurable optimism that continues to make him, both as a writer and as a man, so enduring to readers. He had the remarkable gift of self-help. The letters of encouragement that he wrote to his family and friends were the source of much of that optimism: as he bolstered the spirits of others, he helped himself. More than any other writer of the nineteenth century, George MacDonald practiced the theory of positive thinking. Although it is perhaps regrettable that his letters do not reveal more about his craft as a writer, for a living portrait of George MacDonald, the man, there is no better source than his letters.

Howglen Farm   G.E.S.
Catawissa, Pennsylvania

Acknowledgments

This book has taken far longer to complete than I had anticipated when it was begun in 1972. Because George MacDonald's manuscripts are scattered widely throughout Great Britain and the United States, locating the manuscripts for a selection of his letters was time-consuming. This volume could never have been completed without the assistance of many individuals and institutions.

For providing encouragement and assistance, I owe thanks to the following: the late Clyde S. Kilby, Professor Emeritus of English, Wheaton College, Wheaton, Illinois; Ada Nisbet, Professor Emeritus of English, University of California at Los Angeles; Francelia Butler, Professor Emeritus of English, University of Connecticut; and Hugh T. Keenan, Professor of English, George State University. I would also like to express special thanks to Professor K. J. Fielding, Edinburgh University, for guiding me during the time I held a research fellowship at Edinburgh.

While completing a doctorate on MacDonald at Aberdeen University in Scotland, I made many lasting friendships. I would like to express my thanks to those in Huntly, Aberdeenshire, who have helped me, especially Margaret Troup and Jimmy and Morag Black of Greenkirtle ("The Farm"). Belated thanks are due to the late Colonel Maurice MacDonald, who shared with me reminiscences of his grandfather and gave his approval of the project. I am also grateful to Christopher MacDonald, who kindly shared family photographs with me. Among those in England who have helped me, I would like to express my special thanks to Freda Levson, MacDonald's great-niece, for always being willing to answer my queries regarding the MacDonald family and for providing the genealogical chart of the MacDonald family, as well as many family photographs. My thanks also to Naomi Lewis, critic and author, for sharing her reading of MacDonald with me. I would also like to make special mention of the late William Raeper, who will be especially missed by members of the George MacDonald Society, and whose informative biography *George MacDonald* was indeed very helpful.

Several institutions should be acknowledged. For granting permission to publish letters taken from *George MacDonald and His Wife* (1924) by Greville MacDonald, I would like to thank the Unwin Hyman Press. For the use of collections of holograph letters, I would like to thank the following: the Trustees of the National Library of Scotland; King's College, Aberdeen University; the County Library of Aberdeen; the Brander Library, Huntly; the Bodleian Library, Oxford; the British Library; Dr. Williams's Library, London; the John Rylands University Library in Manchester; Manchester Public Library; Cambridge University Library; the University of Nottingham; Fitzwilliam Museum, Cambridge; Tennyson Research Center, Lincoln; and the University of Reading.

A number of American institutions deserve thanks for permission to publish MacDonald's letters: special thanks are due the Beinecke Rare Book and Manuscript Library, Yale University, and its staff members Vincent Giroud and his predecessor Marjorie Wynne, who have patiently assisted me for many years; the Houghton Library, Harvard University; the New York Public Library; the Huntington Library, San Marino, California; the University Research Library, University of California at Los Angeles; and the Marion Wade Collection, Wheaton College, Wheaton, Illinois.

For the loan of individual letters I would like to thank John Wellwood and also Katherine Macdonald, who kindly made the Alexander Munro letters available to me.

I would like to thank the Faculty Professional Development Committee of Bloomsburg University for an award in 1988 toward the publication of this volume.

For assisting with the preparation of the manuscript, I owe special thanks to Melissa Witte, Penn State University, and to Judy Reitmeyer, College of Business, Bloomsburg University. I would also like to thank Jennifer Hoffman at Eerdmans Publishing Company for seeing the manuscript through its final stage.

Finally, I would like to offer sincere thanks to the members of the George MacDonald Society, London, and the many readers of MacDonald, on both sides of the Atlantic, who have shared with me their thoughts on the life and writings of George MacDonald.

G. E. S.

George MacDonald's Family Tree

Compiled by Freda (Troup) Levson

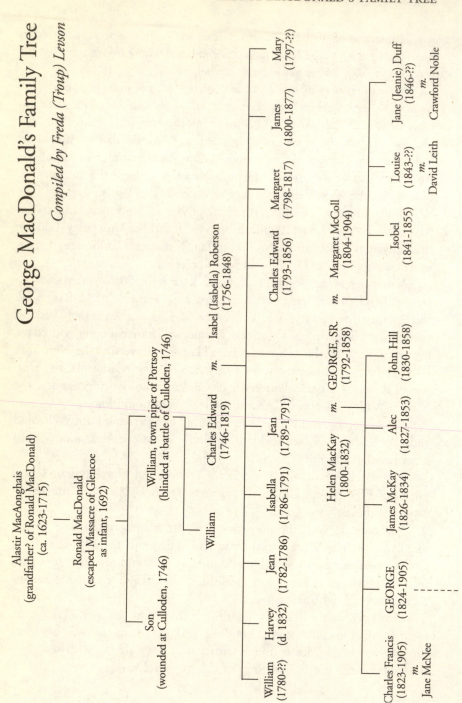

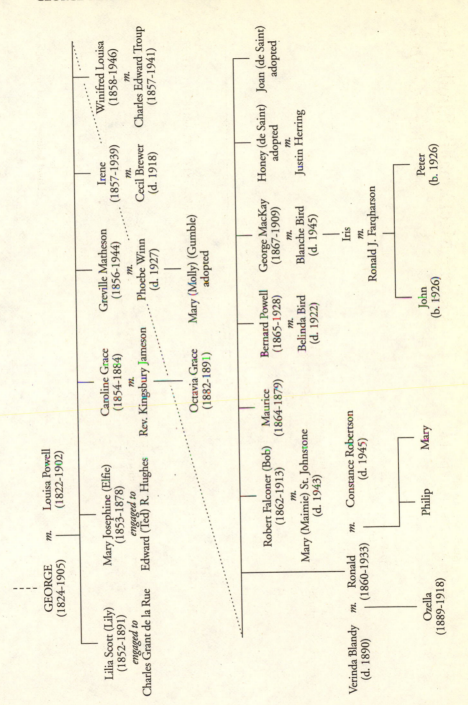

PART I

Early Years: Huntly and Aberdeen

INTRODUCTION

George MacDonald seemed almost predestined by the time and place of his birth to follow a life of religious inquiry. Born on December 10, 1824, in the small farming town of Huntly in Aberdeenshire in northeast Scotland, George MacDonald found himself drawn at an early age into religious debates and activities, which he would later write about in his autobiographical novels *Alec Forbes of Howglen* and *Robert Falconer.* Such boyhood experiences — recorded in the earliest of his letters that have survived — reflect a moral sensitivity that remained with him throughout his life.

Both as a young boy in Huntly and later as a student in the 1840s at King's College, Aberdeen, MacDonald was actively engaged in the religious controversy over faith and practice that was going on around him. We discover in his boyhood letters, in which his efforts to please his father are apparent, a significant pattern that developed throughout MacDonald's life. When writing to his father, MacDonald often found himself trying to explain his own feelings in terms of what he had been taught to believe. While a student at Aberdeen, MacDonald wrote often to his father about his religious anxieties, which had been fermenting in him since his childhood: "I hope I wish to serve God & to be delivered not only from the punishment of sin, but also from its power. . . . Pray for me that I may be enabled to serve him as I ought, and that I may not be led away by the deceitfulness of sin — or of my own wicked nature" (see p. 8 below).

The dilemma that MacDonald faced, as he tried to explain it to his father, was how to accept what he had been taught as a child and still remain true to his own convictions — how to accommodate his boyhood

I

beliefs to his frequent changes in mood. "Pray," he wrote again to his father, "that I may not be that hateful thing, a lukewarm Christian" (see p. 11 below).

MacDonald's decision in 1848, at the age of twenty-four, to enter Highbury College in London (then one of five Congregational Theological Halls) launched him on his ministerial career. But in spite of his decision to become a minister, his religious doubts continued. As he wrote to his future wife, Louisa Powell, "However ill I may bear them [his difficulties] at times, I regard my trials here as helps, not hindrances. But my difficulties are those which a heart far from God must feel, even when the hand of the Heavenly Father is leading it back to himself. It seems a wonder that he can bear with me." And perhaps with marriage in mind, MacDonald asks: "What is it that is the principal cause of everyone's unhappiness who is not a Christian? It is the want of enough to love. We are made for love — and in vain we strive to pour forth the streams of our affection by the narrow channels which the world can give" (see p. 21 below).

As a young man in his twenties, MacDonald found in romantic love a temporary relief to his religious anxieties as he contemplated entering the ministry — thus hoping to resolve his feelings of spiritual unworthiness. His youthful inability to accept the harsh doctrines of Scottish Calvinism conditioned him even further to become an individualist who would find comfort and poetic inspiration in dreams and visions. As a man and as a writer, MacDonald never totally overcame these early feelings of spiritual inadequacy. Throughout the letters he wrote to family members and friends, we will find MacDonald constantly encouraging others as he tried to hold on to his own faith.

Much has been written about MacDonald's early loss of his mother and how he may have suffered permanent psychological disturbance because of the early deaths in his family. Although MacDonald was only eight when his mother died, there is no evidence in the letters he wrote as a young boy or youth that her death caused any such abnormality in him. After the death of his own mother, MacDonald seems to have transferred readily his affections to his stepmother, Margaret McColl MacDonald, and he continued to write to her as if she were his real mother, even after his own father's death.

MacDonald wrote openly about his early feelings and religious experiences in his application letter for admission to Highbury College. In answer to the questions "How long have you entertained the desire of becoming a Minister? What first awakened this desire? And what are the motives which now induce you to offer yourself as a candidate for the Christian Ministry?" MacDonald replied:

> I can hardly say how long I have wished to be a minister — perhaps two years. The desire awoke so gradually in my mind that I cannot tell when it began. When I saw the truth myself, I wished to tell it to others. As the darkness cleared away and I saw that the evil things, things which opposed my progress — difficulties I met with in the Bible — were phantoms and no realities in themselves, I thought I could help others. . . . I think I know something of the workings of the human soul, for from childhood have I studied it in one shape or other. I will not say that the highest motives are the greatest with me — nor even that they have much influence — the glory of God, and the good of mankind. . . . I have many difficulties, such as at one time I could not have contended with such as make me fear whether I be a Christian, but I cannot wait till these are gone, before I follow this work. I will go forward looking to my God — and I trust he will help me. (See pp. 23-24 below.)

Having completed in two years his training at Highbury College, MacDonald accepted his first (and only) pastorate at Arundel in Sussex. With renewed confidence, he wrote to his father on October 16, 1850: "I have faith enough to expect good from your prayers. In all things I hope God will teach me. To be without him is to be like a little child, not learning to walk, left alone by its mother in Cheapside — and far worse than that faint emblem" (see p. 36 below).

MacDonald would continue in his letters to use images from childhood experiences as he searched for evidences to support his belief in personal immortality.

Significant Dates and Events

1824	MacDonald is born on December 10 in Huntly, Aberdeenshire.
1826	The George MacDonald family moves to The Farm, Huntly.
1832	MacDonald's mother, Helen MacKay MacDonald, dies.
1839	MacDonald's father marries Margaret McColl.
1840	MacDonald enters King's College, Aberdeen.
1842	MacDonald misses the 1842 session, presumably because of lack of funds.
1845	MacDonald receives the M.A. degree and takes a position as tutor with the Radermacher family in London for two years.
1846	MacDonald publishes anonymously his first poem, "David."
1848	MacDonald attends Highbury Theological College, London. He becomes engaged to Louisa Powell.
1850	MacDonald accepts a pastorate at Arundel, Sussex, England.

George MacDonald to His Father,   Portsoy
George MacDonald, Sr.   15 August, 1833

My dear Papa,

  I return you many thanks for the kind letter I received on Wednesday. I am happy to hear that you are well. I have been unwell for two or three days, my throat was a little sore and my head very painful but I am quite well now and have been in the sea today and like it very much. When I was down at the bathing I met a boy who was once a schoolfellow of mine at Mr. Stuarts *[sic]* school[1] and he showed me the carcass of a whale which had been cast on the shore. Mrs. Morrison told me that the men at the green got a good deal of fat of it. We drank tea at Mr. Knits on Wednesday, we were at his cottage up the town where they have a fine garden and plenty of fruit and we got as much as we could eat. Johnny[2] is very amusing, when we bid him go bathe he says *baale,*[3] he seems to be more frightened at the tub than at the sea. We are all quite well. I hope the Doctor is getting well. Would you be so good as [to] come down and stay with us till we go home. Aunt[4] makes me drink the water but I am unwilling to do it. I am sorry that my writing is so bad but my pen is very bad.

I remain
my dear Papa
your affectionate son

George Macdonald

  1. The private "Adventure School" in Huntly that MacDonald attended, described in *Alec Forbes of Howglen.*

  2. MacDonald's brother, John Hill MacDonald (1830-1858).

  3. "Bail" or "bale," meaning "no."

  4. Miss Christina MacKay, who came to take care of the boys after their mother's death in 1832.

To His Father   Portsoy, August 1, 1834

My dear Papa,

As you desired me to write to you by the first opportunity I have complied with your request. I received your kind letter just as I was coming out of a boat in which I had been sailing and thank you for it. Mrs. Mortimer intended that I should have slept in Mr. Andrews but in your letter you bade me go to Mrs. Morrisons. I have bathed every day since I came and I drink the salt water every two days.[1] I have been at Fordyce, I think it was on Wednesday. We were in a very old house with a castle attached.[2] The woman in the house took us up to a room and brought out the gin bottle. Mrs. Mortimer pretended to take some of it and got off with a very good excuse. Jane pretended to take some of it too but did not taste it. Margaret and James[3] did take some of it but when it came to me (I had whispered to Mrs. M. that I wouldn't take it) I said I can't take it so I got away and did not break any of the rules of the Temperance Society. There was a Prussian schooner in the harbor and William[4] and I went out with it yesterday morning and came back in the pilot boat. We went out in the evening in a boat that was going out to a ship that was lying anchor not very far from the shore but we did not go on board. When we were out in the foreign schooner we were far out of sight of land[5] and I did not think it very easy to get over the ship's side into the boat. I am very fond of the bathing and William will perhaps learn [sic] me to swim. You may tell Aunt to send down a shirt to me as she said she would do. Tell Charles[6] that I am sorry that I have not written to him. Tell Alex and Johnny that I will bring up some marble stones to them.[7] You will excuse my bad writing. I have not more to say at present but in the mean time I remain

> my dear Papa your
> affectionate Son

GEORGE MACDONALD

1. Greville MacDonald notes that this was "a usual prescription of the faculty as an adjunct to sea-bathing" (*George MacDonald and His Wife* [London: Unwin Hyman, 1924], p. 62).

2. Possibly the House of Troup, mentioned in a letter by Helen MacKay Powell, MacDonald's cousin, dated June 8, 1872 (see p. 191).

3. MacDonald's cousins.

4. Possibly William Matheson, brother of MacDonald's lifelong friend Greville Matheson.

5. This was due to the mist and not to the distance.

6. MacDonald's brother, Charles Francis (1823-1905).

7. MacDonald's brothers, Alexander (1827-1853) and John Hill (1830-1858). Greville MacDonald notes, "The Portsoy serpentine is very beautiful and its marbles were greatly prized by the boys" (*George MacDonald and His Wife*, p. 62).

To His Father [1836?]

My dear Father,

It is now time for me to be thinking of what I should betake myself to, and tho' I would be sorry to displease you in any way, yet I must tell you that the sea is my delight and that I wish to go to it as soon as possible, and I hope that you will not use your parental authority to prevent me, as you undoubtedly can. I feel I would be continually wishing and longing to be at sea. Though a dangerous, it is undoubtedly an honest and lawful employment, or I would scorn to be engaged in it. Whatever other things I may have intended were in my childhood days [so] that you can hardly blame me for being flighty in this respect. O let me, dear father, for I could not be happy at anything else. And I am not altogether ignorant of sea affairs, tho' I have yet a great deal to learn, for I have been studying them for some time back. If it were not for putting you to too much trouble I would beg an answer from you in writing, but I can hardly expect it, though I much wish it,

Your affectionate son

GEORGE.

I have been trying to persuade myself to give up the idea, and I was afraid you would not give your consent, but I cannot make it out, at least let me try it.

George.

To His Father   Aberdeen,
                                                                5 January, 1841

My dear Father,

I am much obliged to you for the kind letter which you sent me some time ago. I hope I wish to serve God & to be delivered not only from the punishment of sin, but also from its power. Pray for me that I may be enabled to serve him as I ought, and that I may not be led away by the deceitfulness of sin — or of my own wicked nature.

Our potatoes & meal are both almost done. Be so good as [to] send a fresh supply as soon as convenient.

I think I would be better [if I had] some of the stuff which the Doctor used to give [Alex] & me. The glands at the back of my ear have been a little swelled & painful for some time altho' nothing to signify. I am glad to hear that John Green has been applying for church membership. I have no doubt but he is a pious lad, but I am afraid he will suffer some persecution for it. How is your new clerk like to suit you? Is George Marr liking his new place? When was there any word from Mr. James Legge[?][1] I have not heard hardly anything about him this long time. Has there been any word lately from our friends in New South Wales?

I suppose you are glad that Mr Kennedy[2] was not at the Soiree at Huntly. He was at our Sabbath school one in the Old Town on that evening. I am very much attached to Mr Kennedy. I like him as well as Mr. Hill,[3] but he has not such a presence as Mr Hill. He preaches most excellent sermons, &, let the subject be what it may, he never closes without saying something, however short, to the unconverted.

I hope mother & all the rest are keeping strong. I was glad to know from her letter that you have hardly suffered any from rheumatism this winter.

Be so good as [to] find the enclosed to James —

                                                        I am
                                                        Your ever affectionate Son,

                                                        Geo. MacDonald

---

1. An elderly native of Huntly told the story — which cannot be substantiated — that MacDonald had a brief romance with Rosie Legge, sister of James Legge, who became a missionary in China and also attended Highbury College in London. Reportedly, Rosie

returned to Huntly from finishing school in London, and there was a short romance —
which ended abruptly when young George found her selling lace on Sunday.

2. Rev. John Kennedy, D.D., a strict Calvinist and advocate of Temperance, was
minister from 1836 to 1846 at Blackfriars Congregational Chapel (now Skene Street
Church), Aberdeen, where MacDonald attended as a student. He regularly gave evening
meetings for young converts at which he spoke strongly in favor of Calvinism and discipline.

3. Rev. John Hill, leader of the strict Sabbath Schools, whose followers were known
as "Missioners." Hill was minister of the Mission Kirk in Huntly. He spoke against dances
and drunkenness in the town's markets and in the pulpit.

To His Father   Aberdeen 28th Oct. 1841

My dear Father,

I ought to have written to you sooner and intended doing so last
night, but I was very sleepy when I remembered I had to do it & besides,
as it was too late for going out to the Post Office, and the mail starts at
6 o'clock, it would not have reached you sooner than it will when written
tonight.

I reached Aberdeen well, and got not one drop of rain by the way,
though my feet were rather cold. I found all our friends well, & our
lodgings very comfortable, although the lad who lodges along with us is
not so much of a gentleman as we could wish, yet I hope he will not be
any the worse in that respect for lodging with us.

We were examined yesterday forenoon on Latin & Greek. I got on
very well, and answered almost all the questions. So that there is not the
least fear of my passing. The examinations were not very difficult, but
sufficiently so. We commence operations on Monday.

I saw a most splendid procession today of the Chartists going out to
meet Fergus O'Connor. There were about two thousand of them in the
procession[,] and taking all who accompanied them, there might have
been fifteen thousands on the streets. There were several different bands
of music & banners & mottoes innumerable. There were [sic] a coach,
which happened to be coming up & three open carriages which went out
to meet O'Connor, two with four horses and one with six horses in which
was the chap himself, a pretty good looking man, but not a good figure
— tall & stout. I was down at the links for a short time while he was
addressing the people but he was just finishing when I went there. The

scene was really splendid. Especially when they were moving off the mound. They seem in general peaceably disposed, & have a grand soiree tonight.

You must have heard long before now that R. Spence[1] got nothing at the competition — indeed it could hardly have been expected. I was delighted when I heard the first bursar's name called out for [Lou?]. He is a poor lad from Orkney who was at the Grammar School[2] with me and then was a good scholar. He completed last year & got only five pounds, but wouldn't keep it because it wouldn't keep him. Mr. Cruckshank's friend has got one, but I am not sure of the amount.

I hardly recollect any more news to give you, but I hope to hear from you soon. Tell A. or I.[3] to write to me soon & I will write to them again. Give my love to Mother & Aunt. I hope by this time your business is settled. Do tell us as soon as you can all about it. I will be [at] some expense for books just now, but I do not know exactly what I will need yet. I will let you know. I am some in doubts whether or not I should study Chemistry for as there is only one prize given in Greek & one in Latin with four or five in Mathematics[,] I have not so much chance for a prize as I would like.

> Hoping to hear from you
> soon
>
> Love,
> Your ever affectionate Son,
>
> Geo. MacDonald

1. MacDonald's cousin Robert Spence.
2. The Old Aberdeen Grammar School.
3. MacDonald's brothers, Alex and Ian.

To His Father   [Fulham] London
                                                     8 November 1845

My dear Father

I got your very welcome letter yesterday. I was wondering that no one at home was writing to me. Before I tell you any thing else, I must tell you that on Friday last week, Dr. Morison sent me a letter by a messenger who waited for an answer, saying that he wished to propose me a member that evening, but did not like to do so without a line from me to say *yes*.[1] I consented but with fear & trembling as I told him I have had a good deal of distress since, but am better now — much. I think I am a Christian although one of the weakest. I do not think Christ will allow me to go to his table unworthily although I should not have come forward so soon had not the Dr. urged me. I am sure he never saw Mr. Still's recommendation, but he seems satisfied with me himself. I shall have to see one of the deacons next week. My greatest difficulty always is "How do I know that my faith is of a lasting kind such as will produce fruits?" I am ever so forgetful and unwilling to pray and read God's word — that it often seems as if my faith will produce no fruit. My error seems to be always searching for faith in place of contemplating the truths of the gospel which are such as produce faith and confidence. But I trust that if God has led me to Christ, He will keep me there. My mind is often very confused. I have made more progress — much since I began to pray more earnestly for the spirit of God to guide me. Pray that I may not be that hateful thing, a lukewarm Christian. Tell Mr. Hill, with my love, that I hope he will not forget me.

The Dr. [Dr. Morison] & family are very kind. I am quite at home with the Dr. I suppose you have heard ere now that Mrs Alex has been safely delivered of a daughter on Friday. I wrote yesterday to Alex to ask for her but have not yet heard. I shall call today — most likely. I am perfectly comfortable here. They are very kind — and then one ought to give up thinking of little things which do not quite suit one's ideas of propriety. The worst bother is ill-brought up & noisy children — especially the younger ones who scream frightfully — two girls like Bella & Louisa.[2]

I have every reason to believe that they are perfectly satisfied with me. I understand so in more ways than one. I have been the means of improving their behavior in the house a little, for which there was very much room, but I cannot expect to make them very polite or refined so long as their superiors are not so.[3] Their father has visited me in the schoolroom once this week and expresses himself pleased. My health is not very good. My bowels are troublesome. I need medicine pretty often but I expect to get over it by degrees. It results from a continued tendency to inflammation, but I shall take care. I am glad Alex is staying at home. Johnny's not being successful I think nothing of, farther than the loss if it can be called *loss* of the money — With love to mother & yourself and hoping you will write soon. I am, my very dear father, your affectionate son,

GEORGE

I ought to have written again to Uncle long ago. My time does not come to much for reading between one thing and another but I am acquiring knowledge & improving very much steadily — tho it may be slowly. I am reading just now — a recent publication: Darwin's account of a voyage around the world which though in many places is too scientific for me as yet — I think you would enjoy very much. It forms 3 vols. in Murray's Cheap Copyright editions like Borrow. I wish you would read Dr. I [Prje?] Smith's work on Geology. It would give you much pleasure and satisfaction.

Again I am your very
affectionate son

GEORGE

1. Dr. John Morison, minister of Trevor Chapel in Brompton, a friend of MacDonald's father, who took an interest in the young George and other youth. Dr. Morison wished to propose MacDonald as a candidate for membership in the chapel.

2. MacDonald's half-sisters, Isobel and Louise.

3. See MacDonald's story *The Wise Woman* or *The Lost Princess* (1875; rpt., 1992) about two spoiled little girls.

To His Father   Park Cottage
                                                                          Dec. 26, 1845

My very dear Father,

I am sorry I have not written to you, but it slipped out of my mind, or mother. I did not think so much about it after having written to my mother. There was one thing in your last letter which vexed me a little. You wished me to write to mother and write as if defending her, or at least using arguments to show that I ought to write to her. It seemed as if I had required to be put in mind of her kindness — and I was very sorry I had put off writing to her so long — but I thought you need not have written so to me, as if I loved her less than you could wish. But I do not think you meant so. I do not know if I have said what I mean, for there is such a talking about me, I scarcely know what I am writing.

I think, my dear father, that God is now with me, for whenever I grow remiss, which I am sorry to say is very often, I always grow unhappy, & find my foundation slipping from me — and I trust this is God's kindness to me. I should be unhappy to think that he did not lead me in everything, and I try to trace him in little things. He has been very kind to me in bringing me here. I believe Mr. R.[1] had been more than once very nearly engaging with others, and had written to me to agree with him if I recollect rightly, but found he had just taken another situation.

I dined at Morison's yesterday, being Christmas. Out of fifteen including three or four children — there were 8 pure Scotch, only one pure Englishman. Perhaps Uncle has met Mr. & Mrs. Christie, Mrs. C. is the daughter of Dr. Philip of the Cape of Good Hope. They have been missionaries in India.

I am sorry I am not yet able to send you any money — as my Aberdeen accounts are rather heavy & I shall not be able to settle them quite this term. I may be able to send you some next time. I can account for every halfpenny I have spent of my salary — whether well or ill. Uncle insisted I should keep an account of it, and I have done so.

I am much better than I was in Scotland, and if I get off without a bad cold this winter, which I have not yet had, I expect to be very well next summer. I am not in a humor to write more just now. I must write to Uncle soon. Give him & Aunt my love & with love to Mother & yourself.

You're my dear Father.
Your very affectionate Son,

George

Please put Alex in mind to write to me —

1. Possibly Mr. Radermacher, in whose family MacDonald served as tutor from 1845 to 1847.

To His Father   London, February 10, 1846

My dear Father,

I have had no word from home this long time so I shall not wait longer but let you know that I am not forgetting you. I have not much news to give you. Everything goes on much in the same way as before. The boys are improving, but from various circumstances, I fear I shall never be able to make them behave as I would wish.

I think God is leading me slowly on to know more of him. What I most need is a deep sense of sinfulness, and the evil of it. I think the want of this must be very much the reason why so many Christians are careless and lukewarm.

I see Bunyan holds the opinion that the righteousness of Christ is imputed by God previous to faith, which is only a sign that this righteousness has been imputed, I cannot agree at all with this view.

I must tell you[,] my dear father, that I am very sorry for my conduct to you in many instances for many years back. I shall not say forgiveness for I know you have forgiven me — but I do hope opportunities may yet be given me to show you how much I love you, and that I am sorry for my behavior. Often was I so after I had done wrong, but my pride and bad temper made me often offend. I should like much to have a letter from mother if she could find as much time to write one. Please put Alex in mind of writing to me.

Perhaps you have seen a poem of mine in the Scottish Congregational Magazine.[1] They have quite spoiled the sense of it in one place.

I am not much in a humour for writing to night, so I shall be done, hope to hear from you soon.

> With much love again mother
> Same, my dear father,
> Your very affectionate Son
>
> George MacDonald

---

1. "David" (Feb. 1846). This poem, consisting of 114 blank-verse lines, was Mac-Donald's first published poem. In it he described the grief-stricken King David after the death of his son Absalom.

To His Father London, March 13, 1846

My dear Father,

It is high time that I were answering your last welcome letter. I could not help mentioning at the Doctor's that I had not heard from you, because they asked me, but you must not think I was complaining. Far from it — even if I had a thought of complaint in my heart, which I had not, I should not have uttered it. I should not wish you ever to write to me but when you feel inclined to do so, for I know well that I am no more forgotten when you do not write than when you do.

I am glad to say that two of the boys under my charge are in some concern about religion. This has given me much pleasure, and I pray God they may be kept of him. You have no idea how ignorant they were when I came. They are twins of 12 years old — one of them some months ago asked me, when reading the New Testament[,] if Jesus Christ wasn't crucified four times — and another of them nearly two years older thought he was so twice.

I do not know, or rather I do not trouble myself much[,] about my future prospects. I certainly should like something else too, but I hope I am willing to remain here as long as God wishes. If he shows me plainly that he wishes me to give myself entirely to him & his service, I am ready to do so, trusting that he will make me fit for it — but I have formed no resolution at all on the matter. Pray that his will may be done in me.

I mean to write to Uncle and mother soon. Give them & Aunt my love — I shall not write more just now, but am, my dear dear father,

Your very affectionate Son

[George MacDonald]

To His Stepmother, Margaret McColl MacDonald London
June 15, 1846

My dearest Mother,

Will you accept of some of my work?[1] You will excuse faults, seeing it is my first attempt. I should have got them made up, but both my time and purse were very limited, and I was not sure that they would fit you. I can sew very well now — always mend my own clothes — use my thimble — a nice silver one — like a lady. I have patched my trousers two or three times — an accomplishment I have attained since I came to England, and a most useful one I find it to be! I don't know when I heard a word of little Jeanie.[2] Tell me about her when you write. . . . God is very good to me. Oh! I was so far from him two or three years ago, and I trust I am always coming nearer to him now.

[George MacDonald]

1. A pair of slippers that MacDonald made for his stepmother.
2. MacDonald's half-sister Jane, then an infant.

To His Father   London, April 11, 1847.

My dearest Father,

Rain has again kept me from going up to Brompton, for I have had a bad cough for some time & am not strong, but I hope when the warm weather comes, I shall be better. I wish to tell you what my present views are — not at all as positive — but as seems best to me just now. For several reasons which I shall try to give you, I think it better not to go to college till the commencement of the session next year. One reason is that I wish to lay in a good stock of clothes, if I can, which will make expenses much less at college. Another is that I wish my opinions & feelings & motives to *solidify* a little more. I wish to have more distinct & definite objects in view before entering on the work of the ministry, if God will accept me for a workman. Perhaps I should wish also to overcome more the difficulties of my situation, which has so little in it to give me pleasure. Certainly no liking for it induces me to stay. I am also a little unwilling to give up the continual trials of my temper which I have here[1] — not that I like them, but I cannot help regarding them as very good exercise — although I so often fail in overcoming my temper. Yet I think it is somewhat improved. I hope it is a little better. I scarcely think however that I can agree to stay another winter without they give me a fire in my room, for my illness is owing in a great measure to sitting in the cold. I have a right to it I think, from my situation. How can I read in the winter otherwise. Every body says I ought to have it. It is a strange house to live in, but

God has blessed it to me very much, & though I have not been able to study much, I feel my mind strengthening, and my views enlarging. I look forward to much increase of knowledge & power of thought in years to come, and I hope God will keep me from using his glorious gifts, without rendering him the homage, & devoting them to his service.

I should like also to spend some time with you before I commence study in earnest. My health will be better for it & it will tend to good in many ways — but this is in the dim future. 'Tis true this feeling has been gradually gaining ground on me, and for a long time nothing has appeared to me of importance compared with that. I fear any employment besides in which I could take a real interest — lest it should make me forget God. What a mercy I was not allowed to follow out Chemistry! But on the other hand I fear myself. I have so much vanity — so much pride, and have made so little progress in the life of faith. I am so continually forgetting the prize of the high calling, that it seems presumption to think of it. I have not prayed much about it, for animal spirits are seldom good. What should I be now without religion? With nothing here to make me happy besides, with health bad enough to make me generally feel miserable, though nothing is seriously the matter with me. Yet I am able I trust to thank God for all these, for thus I hope he has led me to find the joy of being — the *real existence*. Although I have not yet experienced much real continuous joy — from sin, difficulties, anxiety, & forgetfulness, I seem to see a glorious light before me, into the fullness of which glory I trust he will lead me. I did not wish you to understand me as having finally made up my mind as to the ministry — it has seemed so far in the distance, as if it was scarcely time to think of it yet. I trust however God has been leading me in his own mercy — incomprehensible; and I feel as if I could be of use in his vineyard, from the difficult paths in which I have been led. I love my bible more. I am always finding out something new in it. I seem to have had everything to learn over again from the beginning. All my teaching in youth seems useless to me. I must get it all from the bible again and yet how often am I impatient with it as if it were a task and anxious to get to something else. I have of late seen more of the necessity of studying Christ's character, and I am in the habit of reading the gospels every day. That seems the only thing that helps me to overcome my temper, & be patient. This seems to give a ground work for the exhortations of the Epistles to build upon. If the gospel of Jesus be not true, I can only pray my maker to annihilate me, for nothing else is worth living for — and if that be true, everything in the universe is glorious, except sin. I have many difficulties yet, but I trust he who made my intellect & affections will deliver me from them all & make me what he my owner would have me to be. Religion must pervade everything — absorb everything into itself. To the perfectly holy mind, everything is religion. It seems to glorify everything — (Yet how cold is my heart while I write). One of my greatest difficulties in consenting to think of religion was that I thought I should have to give up my beautiful thoughts & my love for the things God has made. But I find that the happiness springing from all things not in themselves sinful is much increased by religion. God is the God of the Beautiful, Religion the Love of the Beautiful, & Heaven the House of the Beautiful — nature is tenfold brighter in the sun of righteousness, and my love of nature is more intense since I became a Christian, if indeed I am one. God has not given me such thoughts, & forbidden me to enjoy them. Will he not *in them* enable me to raise the voice of praise "To him that maketh the mountains of brine. Softly sink in the pale moonshine!" But everything else is insignificant — even God's most beautiful works — when we look at the only injured dying for the only injuring. It *does* often seem to me too glorious to be true. And yet I have had little sorrow for sin — very little — & but very feeble views of the hatefulness of sin. But these seem to me very important & principal parts of *sanctification* — which God's spirit will I trust go on to teach me. I am told to believe in my Redeemer, who hath already paid the ransom, whether I understand it properly or not. He is exalted to give *repentance* & the remission of sins. I look upon Repentance as a work including everything else in religion. The first part of Repentance is turning to God by prayer for direction. The last act is the last struggle against an evil thought — the last effort to trust in Him, the last feeling of sorrow for wrong doing & perhaps the last thought of gratitude for his unspeakable goodness, which *last* thought will *never never* come.

I must go on to the rest of your letter else I shall be weary before I have finished mine.

As to expense, having made no inquiries I can say nothing. The time I think is three years — but I am in no particular haste to be out as a preacher, even if I do go — for I am very much of your opinion with regard to young preachers. Is it not better for the character to be *consolidated* first with fixed principles of acting in everything? But more of this afterwards. If I do go, I should like to go to Homerton to Dr. Pye Smith, certainly not to Highbury. My ultimate wishes *are not* yet. Perhaps the best thing for me would be a quiet country charge — small enough to enable me to attend thoroughly to all the pastoral duties, & intelligent enough to urge me to use my intellect & holy enough to make us advance each other in holiness. Ambition points to the Metropolis — but is not ambition a terrible thing for a motive to the ministry. God keep me. I am like a straw in a whirlwind. Pray for me, for I trust your prayers for my conversion have been heard, and our Heavenly Father who loves to hear prayer, will hear you, when perhaps I may be unable to pray myself for things of which I may have forgotten my need. I am in great danger — and my fear is of being insensible to it.

To answer another question I have smoked a good deal since I came to London, tho' not much lately. When I am well it is a great enjoyment to me. Mr. R.[2] is a smoker. He gave me a beautiful pipe. But I should not have much right to claim much love for you, if I would not give it up at your request. I was almost sorry it was not a greater sacrifice. And yet I would not have you think it no sacrifice. So I promise you never in this world to smoke again. That is settled now. I am equally bound by a promise as to snuff. So no more tobacco for me. Joy go with it.

I cannot begin [?] to Campbell immediately, as I have no books on hand — but the next I take shall be his — probably this week. I am a very slow reader, and I think a careful one — at least in some respects.

I fear I have said much in this letter that may lead you to think me farther advanced than I am. It is difficult often to know in one's mind what is mere opinion, and what is *spirit & life* — fixed, actuating principle.

Now I think I have complied with your request to write long & soon. Tho' perhaps neither *very* long nor *very* soon. Give my love to dear mother & Uncle & Aunt. Kiss Bella & Louisa for me. They will understand it. I will write to dear Alex soon.

Give my love to Mr. Hill[3] — how I do love him — I am sorry I have not written to him. Give my love to Agnes too. His family is little now — May God be with him & you all —

I am, my dearest Father
Ever your affectionate Son

George

My heart almost failed me at the thought of being here so long yet, but I think its [sic] the better way. Please let me have your opinion soon.

I had a most welcome letter from Mr. Hill the other day. Will you with my love, tell him my present wishes.

Please give Uncle the enclosed note, which I had yesterday from Dr. Adams.

Will you tell mother, with my love, that I shall write to her tomorrow. Pray for the Holy Spirit for me, that is what I need. I have many doubts yet of my own condition, & I fear too good grounds for doubting. But I hope my Heavenly Father will lead me into *all* truth. All the knowledge of this world does seem so incomplete — so spiritless without religion — and I think few minds are more capable of deriving delight from the knowledge of this world's truth than mine. But when the light of religion is thrown upon it, it is as if it were a soul to the knowledge which was dead before.

I should have much to say to you if I were with you, and many a long conversation I trust we may have before *very* long. May I never cause you a thought of pain, as I have so often done in years that are past. May God care for us all & watch over us. Give my love to Johnny. I shall write him a little note tomorrow too. I suppose Alex is travelling just now. Give my love to Grandmama too. I must write to dear Uncle soon. I am

> My dearest Father,
> Your affectionate son
>
> GEORGE

1. Referring to difficulties MacDonald was experiencing as a tutor.
2. Probably Mr. Radermacher.
3. John Hill, minister of the Mission Kirk in Huntly, who preached against dances and drunkenness.

To James MacDonald, Huntly[1]

London,
May 22, 1847

My very dear Uncle,

I called on Dr. Adams, but had again the misfortune to find that he was out. I do not think I am right to use the word misfortune, for the conviction is, I think, growing upon me that the smallest events are ordered for us, while yet in perfect consistency with the ordinary course of cause and effect in the world. I am strongly inclined to think that whatever has

a moral effect of any kind on our minds, God manages for us — and even
much more than this. How far the events of those who do not at all seek
to serve Him are controlled by Him, in regard to these individuals personally, is a question about which I have no opinion at all — at least not
a settled one. Perhaps it would be presumption to form one on such a
subject. . . .

> Your very affectionate
> nephew

GEORGE

1. Greville MacDonald notes that James MacDonald "looked askance at his nephew's
emancipation, and now opposed the wish of many that Huntly should hear my father
preach, his avowed objection being his beard. But he gave way at last" (*George MacDonald
and His Wife*, p. 242).

To Miss Louisa Powell[1]   Fulham
                                                                [1848?]

. . . The difficulties with which I told you I was surrounded are not
the results of my situation.[2] However ill I may bear them at times, I regard
my trials here as helps, not hindrances. But my difficulties are those which
a heart far from God must feel, even when the hand of the Heavenly
Father is leading it back to himself. It seems a wonder that he can bear
with me.

What is it that is the principal cause of everyone's unhappiness who
is not a Christian? It is the want of enough to love. We are made for love
— and in vain we strive to pour forth the streams of our affection by the
narrow channels which the world can give — and well is it if, stagnated
in our hearts, they turn not to bitterness. The religion of Jesus Christ is
intended to bring us back to our real natural condition: for all the world
is in an unnatural state. This will give us that to love which alone can
satisfy our loving — which alone, as we climb each successive height, can
show us another yet higher and farther off — so that, as our powers of
loving expand[,] the object of loving grows in all those glories which excite
our love and yet make it long for more.

1. MacDonald's future fiancée.

2. MacDonald was experiencing difficulties as a tutor. He relinquished his position as tutor in the spring of 1848 and spent the summer in Huntly.

George MacDonald's Testimonial[1]   [Huntly, August 8, 1848]
                                                        10/1

HIGHBURY COLLEGE.
QUERIES TO CANDIDATES.

The reply to the first must be extended, as circumstances require. — The others may be answered in a concise form and in order. All the answers to be written without any assistance.

QI. As it is indispensably necessary, that every minister of the gospel of Christ should be himself a real Christian, you are desired to state the grounds on which you believe this to be your character, together with any memorable circumstances connected with your first religious convictions, and the period of their commencement.

AI. I have been familiar with the doctrines of the gospel from childhood. I always knew and felt that I ought to be a Christian, and repeatedly began to pray, but as often grew weary and gave it up. The truths of Christianity had no *life* in my soul. I feel some reluctance to mention the circumstances which at last, about five years ago, induced me to try to find God. Previous to this I had acquired considerable distaste for the truths of the Bible, and believe had it lasted till now, I should have nearly if not altogether reached infidelity. And for a long time I did not seem to make any progress, though my more intimate friends perceived a change in me. By and by I became more in earnest especially when I thought of the possibility of becoming a member of a Christian Church, which seems far too good a thing for me, and indeed was so at the time. But I could feel little or no abiding joy in religion — I looked to myself and not to the atonement. All I had been taught in my youth I required to learn over again. In my distress I could only cry to God to help me, and often in the midst of it felt assured he heard me. I set myself in some measure to do what was right. I began to see some of the beauty of religion, some of the grandeur of the Truth. I read my bible, and continued amidst much that was evil in thought and behaviour to cry to God. My unhappiness compelled me to it. The Truth has been slowly dawning upon me. I have seen I trust that Jesus is my Saviour — though this has had but little of the effect it ought to have upon me. I know I should never be happy till my whole soul is *filled* with love to him, which is only a reasonable thing. I hope I am a Christian partly because I see something of the glory of the Truth, and partly because in some degree I try to do the will of my Lord and Master. I wish to be delivered from myself. I wish to be made holy. My hope is in God.

QII. By what church were you first received into Christian fellowship, and at what time? Of what church are you now a member? and when were you admitted to its communion?

AII. I was received into fellowship by Dr. Morison's church at Brompton,[2] in December 1845 — at least it was that month when I first sat down at the Lord's table. I am now a member of the church of Huntly, my native place, and was received, on the testimony of Dr. Morison, in the month of April this year.

QIII. Have you been accustomed to engage in social religious services, — in prayer meetings, in instructing the young, in addressing the poor, or in any special plans for spiritual usefulness?

AIII. I have been in a limited degree engaged in all the services mentioned.

QIV. How long have you entertained the desire of becoming a Minister? What first awakened this desire? And what are the motives which now induce you to offer yourself as a candidate for the Christian Ministry?

AIV. I can hardly say how long I have wished to be a minister — perhaps nearly two years. The desire awoke so gradually in my mind that I cannot tell when it began. When I saw the truth myself, I wished to tell it to others. As the darkness cleared away and I saw that the evil things, things which opposed my progress — the difficulties I met with in the bible — were phantoms and no realities in themselves, I thought I could help others. In the deepness of my distress, I sometimes thought that God was leading me thus that I might be of use afterwards to others. I think I know something of the workings of the human soul, for from childhood have I studied it in one shape or other. I will not say that the highest motives are the greatest with me — nor even that they have much influence — the glory of God, and the good of mankind. But I believe them to be the highest, and I trust that God will give me more of these as I advance in the Christian life. I know that much that is evil mingles with my motives for desiring the ministry — ambition and perhaps more of vanity intrude; but I regard them as evils, and look to be delivered from them. I desire the ministry because I think it the greatest and the best of employments. I look forward to eternity & find nothing on earth but the work of the ministry worth following with heart and soul. I cannot be or at least ought not to be enthusiastic in anything else. It combines all wisdom and knowledge — all that is beautiful and true into one glorious whole. I think, after all disadvantages, there are most means in the ministry for personal advancement in holiness; and this seems to have been one strong reason with me for desiring the work. I have many difficulties, such as at one time I could not have contended with, such as make me fear whether I be a Christian — but I cannot wait till these are gone, before I follow this work. I will go forward looking to my God — and I trust he will help me. I desire that an entrance may be ministered unto me abundantly, and therefore I would wish to be a minister.

QV. What are your views of the principal and distinguishing doctrines of the Gospel?

AV. I believe in the degraded and worthless condition of man as regards that which is good and holy — I believe in the perfect and full atonement of Jesus Christ — that he has, as it were, saved all men already, if by unbelief they did not put themselves out of this salvation. That whosoever will may know of the doctrine — for God will bring him through all difficulties — by the help of his blessed Spirit.

QVI. What are your opinions respecting Infant Baptism, and Church Government?

AVI. I am inclined to think Infant Baptism a good and right thing; but do not think it proved that the apostles did or did not baptize infants. I think though churches ought now to be governed on the general principles adhered to by the apostles, and the Christians of their time as directed by them, yet certain deviations in mode are admissible for change of circumstances. I believe that congregational independence comes nearest to the former; and that in no other church is the latter attainable in an equal degree. I have studied the subjects to such a limited degree that a more fixed or particular opinion would be valueless.

QVII. What advantages of education did you enjoy in youth? And what course of study have you subsequently pursued?

AVII. I have passed through the usual classes at King's College, Old Aberdeen. My studies since have been desultory; chiefly metaphysical.

QVIII. Have you a predilection for study? and are you desirous of pursuing with diligence and perseverance the literary and theological studies prescribed by this Institution?

AVIII. I like study for the sake of the things studied — not otherwise. I hope to be enabled to do my duty as regards the studies prescribed at the Highbury College, should I be happy enough to be accepted.

QIX. What is your age? What has been your occupation?

AIX. I am in my twenty fourth year. Since I left college, I have been chiefly employed as tutor in a family in the neighborhood of London. The rest of the time has been spent at my father's house.

QX. What has been the general state of your health? Have you reason to think that it will allow of vigorous and regular application to study?

AX. My health has not been *vigorous* — but I think will allow me to study so that my progress will be quite satisfactory to my tutors. I have every reason to think so, for I have no decided complaint.

QXI. Have you any pecuniary resources for meeting those expenses for which the Institution does not provide, — apparel, books, &c.?*

AXI. I have.

QXII. Have you applied for admission to any other College?

AXII. I have not.

I hope to be able afterwards to repay the college its expenses on my account; and am willing to enter into an obligation to do so, especially should I change my opinions so far as to make it a matter of regret that I had been educated there. I have no fear of this however, farther than the danger I am in of falling away from the common faith.

George MacDonald

*Each student contributes one pound when fully received, for the improvement of the Library.

1. Unpublished testimonial, written by MacDonald as part of his application to Highbury College, London.
2. See Greville MacDonald, *George MacDonald and His Wife,* p. 91: "The Revd. John Morison etc."

To Louisa Powell   Highbury College,
                                                              My Study,
                                                   October 23rd, 1848

. . . I meant to write a much longer letter to my Louisa and many beautiful and wise things (to me) I wanted to say, but now the impulse has left me. May our Father in Heaven be with you and bless you, and make you better of your present suffering.

Is love a beautiful thing, dearest? You and I love: but who created love? Let us ask him to purify our love to make it stronger and more real and more self-denying. I want to love you for ever — so that, though there is not marrying or giving in marriage in heaven, we may see each other there as the best beloved. Oh Louisa, is it not true that our life here is a growing unto life, and our death is being born — our true birth? If there is anything beautiful in this our dreamy life, shall it not shine forth in glory in the bright waking consciousness of heaven? And in our life together, my dear dear Louisa, if it please God that we should pass any part of our life together here, shall it not still shine when the cloud is over my head? I may see the light shining from your face, and when darkness is around you, you may see the light on mine, and thus we shall take courage. But we can only expect to have this light within us and on our faces — we can only expect to be a blessing to each other — by doing that which is right. . . .

To Louisa Powell   [Highbury College, London]
                                                         Friday morning
                                                                [1848]

My dear Louisa,

I am indeed made glad by your letter, for to tell you the truth it is much more than I expected for I thought the severe pain you have been suffering would make you incapable of thinking. I doubt not you see reason to thank God for it already if it has only been the means of helping you to think. I am not yet going to write you a long letter for indeed I am not very happy myself having been struggling for some time with wrong and painful thoughts, which seem to take from me all right to look to Jesus. But I hope to be delivered from them and triumph over them.

Pray for humility for me dear Louisa and the feeling that my salvation is entirely owing to Christ Jesus.

I wish much to write about your letter which has so much in it to make me glad — but I cannot just now. Do not think I am making more of it than I have grounds for thinking. Is it not a cause for great thankfulness if in the least degree you see more of the desirableness of God's favor, and have a little more hope of attaining it. When this hope fails you through the returning coldness of your heart, go to God in prayer to bring it back again. Pray or try to pray in spite of the deadness of your feelings.

I enclose you a little bit I had written for you, but forgot to put in my last note.

I believe you are only coming thru the same difficulties and trials of thought which I have felt & still feel, and could you see some of my letters written some time ago, you would recognize your own feelings in many parts.[1] I have one before me now which perhaps I may show you.

Will you send me Charlotte's[2] address as soon as you can, and tell me when you think of returning home. The bell has rung for prayers, and I must stop.

Wishing you much more happiness than you see even in the far distance — I am my dear Louisa,

> Your truly affectionate
> friend,
> George

1. MacDonald often wrote to his future wife of his doubts and tried to encourage her and relieve her sense of unworthiness.
2. Louisa's sister Charlotte.

To Louisa Powell   May 12, 1849.

. . . You tell me about the sea and the sky and the shore so beautifully, so lovingly, so truthfully, that I love you more for it. . . . Tell me again about everything round about you; every expression the beautiful face of Nature puts on. Tell me, too, about the world within your own soul — that living world — without which the world without would be but a lifelessness. The beautiful things round about you are the expression of

God's face, or, as in Faust, the garment whereby we see the deity. Is God's sun more beautiful than God himself? Has he not left it to us as a symbol of his own life-giving light? But I cannot now explain all that I mean. . . .

To Louisa Powell[1]   Highbury [London]
                                                        May 15, 1849

I have just read your letter, dearest. My hands were cold, and when I opened the bit with the flowers they felt warm. But I have put them in my dear Milton, instead of water; and they shall die in their beauty. What a pretty little white thing this is! I shall send you in return a rose [from] a little tree of James Matheson's which Mrs. Grover has put in my room. I hope you will have the letter today which I posted this morning. This one you will have tomorrow at least. Do write in the book whenever you are alone, and not disinclined to write. I have had a letter from you every day as yet. I hope very day will have that bright bit in it till you come back. I saved the one today till I came out of Dr. Henderson's class that I might enjoy it at peace. Only a week today since you went. Well, I would not have you back one hour sooner, if my heart were like to break with its longing. You have beautiful things around you, and beautiful things are creeping into your soul, and making a home for themselves there — and my wife is growing more beautiful for me. Does not He deserve thanksgiving who made man male and female? If you have any joy in me, my own, will you not try to give God some thanks for it. Write to me about the sea & the sky, and all those never-ceasing beauties, ever changing yet still the same great truths. The *sense* of which makes a man feel great too. These truths ever the same yet ever presenting new aspects of beauty, different to different minds, different to the same mind at different times — yet ever in essence one and the same. I am glad you are able to walk so much, but yet you do not tell me how your toe really is. I hope it improves. I am indeed glad to hear you are so wild. I am not much afraid of the conceit. I have just copied Greville's poem for you to copy for me. *Your* poet never wrote anything to equal *that*.

Being somewhat stupid, and my thoughts disappointing me, I have taken myself to trying to translate a little poem of Goethe's entitled

Nähe Der Geliebten.

I think of thee when of the sun the shimmer
From the sea streams;
I think of thee when of the Moon the glimmer
From deep wells beams.

I see thee, when upon the far Way's Ridge
The Dust-cloud wakes;
In the deep Night, when on the narrow Bridge
The Wanderer quakes.

I hear thee there, when with a rushing low
Falleth the Wave,
In the still Thicket loitering oft I go
Quiet as the grave.

I am with thee, tho' thou art so far,
Yet thou art near!
The Sun doth sink, soon lighteth me each Star —
Oh! wert thou here!

This (the German of it I mean) is rather a favorite of mine. If you like I will send you the German to compare.

What a strange picture of Turner's I saw yesterday at the Exhibition. A Rainbow over a stormy sea, ships, far & near, boats, & a buoy. I could make nothing of it at first. Only by degrees I awoke to the Truth and wonder of it. I lost much enjoyment, however, by going without my optical assistance.[2]

Now my Louisa I meant to write you a new letter, but I cannot this time. Perhaps I may write again tonight. I do hope tomorrow will bring me one from you. Put a kiss in it for me dearest and tell me where it is.

I must go out for Greville[3] and [I] were going to see Helen tonight but I have since thought that she will very likely be at the Limes being Tuesday — so I shall go down early & save him the trouble of dressing. I don't mean to stay very long though, but come home to read & perhaps write again to you. I dare say I am more disappointed in stopping before my sheet is full than you will be. Give my kind regards to Josephine & Hannah.[4]

I have to write a note to Alex[5] to tell him the nonsense of my application so I must stop now. I wonder how many times I shall tell you that I am yours truly and lovingly — how different *truly* looks & means when joined with the other word.

Ever dearest your
George

1. Apparently MacDonald wrote a series of intimate betrothal letters, which have been lost or destroyed; of the four mentioned by Greville MacDonald, this is the third.

2. Greville MacDonald notes that his father "was partially short-sighted" (*George MacDonald and His Wife*, p. 123).

3. Greville Matheson, MacDonald's lifelong friend. See *George MacDonald and His Wife*, p. 120.

4. Josephine and Hannah Rutter, close friends of Louisa Powell who accompanied her on her visit to Hastings.

5. Probably Louisa's brother Alexander Powell, who married MacDonald's cousin Helen MacKay.

To His Father

Cork,
July 25, 1849.

My very dear Father,

I was in Youghal when your letter reached me, and have scarcely had time to reply. But since I went down last week with Mr. Peterson & his family to visit some friends. In consequences of this unexpected illness of Mrs. Peterson's mother, they returned next day. Rev Watsonberry on a visit to the Cork people, I remained to preach at Youghal, for their minister has left them, & it is doubtful if he will return to his charge. Revd Watsonberry still is in the neighbourhood. I mean to go down again to Youghal on Saturday to preach on the Sunday. I am glad of the relief, for I find it quite enough as I am presently situated to prepare one sermon a week which is all I have had to do yet from the few I brought with me. My conscience has never been more at ease with regard to my studies. I am very glad I came here, to let me try myself a little; and though I have not so much confidence in my capabilities as perhaps you have, yet I get on pretty well, tho' I am very doubtful how I shall ever be able to write more than one sermon a week. When I say good I mean in some degree satisfactory to myself. I enjoyed my visit to Youghal very much. The Blackwater is a very fine river, & the scenery superior to that on the Sea. Yesterday morning before my return I went some six miles east from Youghal to see the devotions of the poor Catholics at one of the round towers of Ireland and by two holy wells, and a holy stone, said to be floated from Rome, under which they creep for rheumatism, etc. They were kneeling on the graves and by the wells and by the stone, counting their beads and washing themselves. Some of them very respectable looking country people. I have caught cold however & am not well today & yet must go some miles down the river to dinner which is a plague. They want me to go to Killarney before I leave, & indeed I should be sorry to leave without seeing those lakes; but, though I think this more valuable than many a book that you would quite approve of my laying out the money for, I don't know what you will say to it. You are a lover of nature, too — and yet I think perhaps it is more to me than to you — I don't know, though. I hardly know how I can avoid it however — as Mr. Peterson wishes to go with me. It would not a great expense, but I will hear from you before. I am in no want of money for I had my expenses paid, & some thing more which is hardly yet done, and I had five pounds given me since I came which is not yet touched. My travelling expenses were more than you expected. Indeed with which you sent me I could not have done it, especially as I required some things before coming. You cannot know living at home, how money is needed, and though I confess not to have been so careful many times as I ought, as I have confessed, yet I would not like you to be the judge of the amount of money required *on every occasion*. You will not misunderstand what I say I hope. I hope to be very little more expense to you — I have more chance of preaching this winter & if my Aberdeen accounts were settled I should feel greatly comfortable.

I have not time to write much more. I am sorry to hear that mother has been worse but hope she is still improving. Give her my love. Charles & Alex want me to go to Manchester on my return, which I think I could manage for being little more than return by Bristol — indeed I am not sure but it is less. I hope you will write to me soon. You do not say whether you had a letter from me a few weeks ago, a pretty long one for me. I mean to try to write to you again next week, for indeed my conduct in this is not worthy of blame. I hope you are pretty well, & believe me my dear father

Your very affectionate son

GEORGE

[By the way, the Queen was here last Friday. I didn't see her — for I am no worshipper of royalty. . . . I believe there was no great enthusiasm amongst the lower classes — how could there be! — but she was received with every possible demonstration of loyalty — a great deal more show than I was pleased with, considering the state of the country. . . .][1]

1. This letter appears in Greville MacDonald's biography (p. 128). The section enclosed in brackets is not in the manuscript letter but is added in the biography. A page may be missing from the manuscript.

To His Father
                                                                    Highbury,
                                                                Feb. 23, 1850.

I intended going down to Stebbing today, & supplying for a month according to their request, having made up my mind to accept an invitation if they should see fit to give me one. Yesterday, however, a note came from one of the deacons at Stebbing, telling me (to be brief) that I had better not go, as I was not acceptable to many of the people. I think they were rather too hasty in inviting me, without knowing enough of the feeling of the people. The more intellectual part, I believe, would have liked me to go — indeed, I think this is the feeling about me generally in other places — [but] many say they can't understand me.[1] I tried to be as simple as possible at Stebbing — but I fear many people think they understand phrases they are used to & not much more. They are a nice, kind-hearted country people at Stebbing, but I cannot say I am disappointed at not going — rather the contrary — believing I shall have some place more suited for me — tho' it seemed my duty to go. But God takes care of me — though I don't deserve it. Perhaps my manner is too quiet to please dissenters commonly, however I must not do violence to the nature God has given me, & put anything on — what is natural will come, as I am more used to preaching. I must say that I think, if people will try, I can make them understand me — if they won't, I have no desire to be understood. I can't do their part of the work. . . .

1. MacDonald often had the problem of being "too intellectual" for some congregations, especially "country people" like those at Stebbing and later at Arundel.

George MacDonald, Sr., to His Son George Huntly,
29th April, 1850.

. . . As to ministers' stipends in general, they are in most cases but too small. I have always preached up this doctrine, and I am safe to say that my practice in support of a better paid ministry has been quite consistent with my profession. . . . Should you prove acceptable and receive a call [to Whitehaven], I trust you will, as in the sight of God, seek to discharge the duties of the Office with the main design of glorifying God by doing good to souls. . . . You may find yourself more comfortable than in a place of greater gentility, where much of the conceit of this world and the pride of life frequently prevail, making a minister's position anything but comfortable.

I consider the salary could not well be less than what you mention. . . . It requires much prudence on the part of any minister, whether old or young, when necessity compels him to bring his own necessities before the church. Not a few who would hug to their bosom the poor starveling, would dash him from them to be trampled under foot when the necessity of an increased stipend was needed! . . . I hope you will by and by be in circumstance to pay off your small debts, and make conscience of never venturing on taking a wife before then. If you begin thinking lightly of such a case, depend upon it the carelessness will increase until none but yourself and such as are in similar circumstances can paint the agony it will entail. . . .

George MacDonald, Sr., to His Son George Huntly,
24th May, 1850.

My dear George,

Almost all the family have gone to meeting save myself, and I am just away from having worship with the farm servants. The children are off to help each other to bed, the voice of the mill has ceased — the falling water alone with its continual buzz is the only thing that falls upon the ear, where I am sitting. The evening is calm, warm and beautiful. The midges sport in thousands above the water, and nature, long detained from its summer garb, is now getting into lovely verdure. What a change in the course of one short week! — plenty of grass now for the starving cattle,

and the corn crops are advancing as if within the tropics. But our seasons
are changeable, as you may well remember, and how long such a state of
things may remain, it is impossible to say. . . . We have ground for confidence in our God, the author of all blessings, that He who spared not
His only son, but delivered him up to the death for us all, will with Him
also freely give us all things. . . . Charles wishes you to go to Manchester,
and says that Dr. Halley[1] seemed anxious to see you. But perhaps Charles[2]
only thought so, because he might so wish it. . . .

1. Minister of Nevington Chapel, Manchester, a chapel at which MacDonald was
asked to preach.
2. MacDonald's older brother, who was trying to help him get a minister's position
in Manchester.

George MacDonald, Sr., to His Son George   Huntly, 31st May, 1850.

. . . Your long letter yesterday gave me something of variety to think
about which pleased me, notwithstanding that part of it was rather too
philosophical for the case of my mind; but in so far as I am able to see,
the views of both of us are very much alike. . . . Like you, I cannot by
any means give in to the extreme points either of Calvinism or Armini-
anism, nor can I bear to see that which is evidently gospel mystery torn
to pieces by those who believe there is no mystery in the scriptures and
therefore attempt to explain away what it is evidently for the honor of
God to conceal. I see so much of mystery in nature, and so much of it in
myself, that it would be a proof to my mind that the scriptures were not
from God were there nothing in them beyond the grasp of my own mind.
As to the responsibility of man and his power of choice, I think there can
be no doubt.

As to the "new faith" folks, I believe they hold many important things
in common with ourselves. . . . They have without the least compunction
split in pieces many churches and in various places kept possession of the
places of worship. . . . Is it to be endured that for the sake of a few
speculative minds a whole community of common sense but pious Christians shall become agitated as the billowy ocean, and the pulpit and the
house of God made the place and the season for a sort of debating society?

I consider the peace of a Christian Church too important a matter to run the risk of the disunions and hatred which have been created in too many quarters around us.

Let me hear from you before leaving the College, and I shall do my best if need be. . . .[1]

1. MacDonald frequently needed financial assistance while he was at Highbury. His father helped him as much as he was able.

To His Father

Arundel
[October 4, 1850]

In great haste and half-dressed I am writing, my dear father, to tell you that the Church at the meeting last night [determined] that I should be their minister. . . .[1] They give me £150. . . . I expect to find the work of preaching grow easier and easier, but will be oppressed at first, I fear. That will teach me more faith. Mr. Godwin told me that the accounts he had heard lately of my acceptableness were very gratifying to him. This is something from him, as my sermons have seldom been other than censured by him as unsuitable for the people. I will send you some of my poetry and a sermon or two soon; for I have not time to spend on the composition of sermons, which I preach in a very different style from that in which I write them. . . .

1. This was MacDonald's first and only official pastorate.

To His Father

October 16, 1850

My dear Father,

I am sorry I have been so much longer than I said without answering your very fine letter, but I had more to do since in the way of visiting than I expected. I don't think I shall be able to answer all your questions yet but will know more about the plan by and by. I accepted the invitation in words, when I was visited by Mr. Hounsom with the formal document, signed by all the church except five, who had not heard me, and whom they thought it better not to ask to sign it. I wrote after that a letter to the church to the same purpose which you can see if you wish. I preach for the first time as their Pastor next Sunday. I don't know where I shall be stopping yet, but Arundel, Sussex is quite enough. Your last letter gives me much pleasure. I have faith enough to expect good from your prayers. In all things I hope God will teach me. To be without him is to be like a little child, not learning to walk, left alone by its mother in Cheapside — and far worse than that faint emblem.

As you see I have no intention of coming to see you now; but we hope to be married in the spring — to which Mr. Powell is quite favorable, and if you would receive us, we should like, if we could, to visit you then — perhaps in April — I should of course have much pleasure in letting you and Louisa know and speak to each other — I mean you and them particularly — and should like her to see the sky and the hills which first began to mould my spirit.

You ask whether the church is of long standing. I cannot say how long — but there is a very old lady still alive, though in her dotage, who was principally the means of forming the church. There are fifty seven signatures to the *Call* — I think the church has not been much more than three months without a minister — I should think four months — eighteen days of which I have preached to them. The last was there five or six years. The proximate cause of his removal was a disturbance raised by some — self-seeking person, I suspect — who would have something else in the place of wine at the sacrament — but I do not think that would have ended so if he had acted prudently; and had been diligent amongst his people — but he lectured on science three days a week at Brighton, and forgot his flock too much. This I need not say is between ourselves. I am happy to add that the troublesome party has since left the church — and I have not the slightest fear of arrogance from that quarter. And for the rest, I hope to do my duty at least so well as to make my church love me too much to annoy me. They seem a people that would make much of their minister. I think I told you the salary is £150 of which about £63 is from an endowment in the funds. I think they could do more. The congregation is small, but increased while I was there — and if the chapel — a very nice one — was filled, I shall expect an addition — They allow 8 weeks holiday for which however they only raise to £6 to meet expenses — It ought to be double that — but I can take nearly a month, & be absent only three Sundays for which this would pay the supplies and I might manage something more by exchange. The last minister is a young man and is now one of the masters in the large dissenting boarding school at Brighton. The people are a simple people — not particularly well informed — mostly trades people — and in middling circumstances — They chiefly reside in the town which has between two & three thousand inhabitants. There are none I could call society for me — but with my books now & the beautiful earth, & added to these soon I hope my wife — and above all that God to care for me — in whom I and all things are, I do not much fear the want of congenial society.

Louisa is at this moment being beside me copying my ode on Light for you. Though she has caught cold & is hardly well enough to do it — I hope she will be able to finish the unit with this. It was not intended to stop where it does but I was interrupted by going to Whitehaven & I fear it must. I send you a sermon such as it is. It will require some ingenuity in you to follow it. There are little figures to tell you how to follow the pages — but as I told you, I have no time to dress up my sermons yet. When I find I can write with perfect comfort, then I shall gradually be more great — but I don't wish to preach at all as I write — I am informing though in this. Uncle William's story has give[n] us some amusement.[1] I am glad he takes any interest in me. Pray remember me very kindly to him. I saw John Hill on Monday, and am happy to hear from him that dear Mother is looking so well. I am glad to hear from you that Aunt looks cheerful now & then. I wrote to Aunt which I hope she received. She must not think of answering it — though I should be very glad to have a note from her — were it not that it would be perhaps too painful for her.

I think I have answered all your questions now — Address to Arundel when you write — please. It will be a pleasant feeling that I have a flock of my own to care for & minister to — I am glad you like Troup[2] so much, and think you do right in all wishing & exchange with the Arundel people — I only envy him just now because he is nearer you and the rest of my family — My time is about up to save this post — will you give my love to dear Mother, and kisses to the bairnies[3] — and believe me, my very dear father

Your affectionate Son

George

1. The story is told by Greville MacDonald that "a couple of years" before MacDonald's mother died, when he was about six years old, "George was strutting about in his first pair of trousers before his Uncle William, when the latter vowed he now needed only a watch and a wife to make a man of him. 'I can do well enough wanting the watch,' promptly answered the little fellow, 'but — but, I would like that I had a wee Wifie!" (*George MacDonald and His Wife*, p. 53). This account is taken from a letter from George Mac-Donald, Sr., to his son George dated October 7, 1850.

2. Robert Troup, MacDonald's childhood friend, who was a copastor at the Mission Kirk in Huntly and a popular preacher. He later married MacDonald's cousin, Margaret MacDonald.

3. Scottish for children.

To His Father

Arundel,
October 29th, 1850.

I only write you a short note just now, looking for a longer letter from you soon according to your promise. I will do as you wish and ask Mr. Giles[?] to come to my ordination. I hope to be able to see Aunt before very long, but I do not feel willing to leave yet for some time — and if Mr. Giles would come and preach for me, it would be a relief to me, so I wish when I do go, to be absent a Sunday. My congregation I think increases, and the week meetings on the whole are better. We have a prayer meeting every Monday and a lecture on Thursday, for which I do not make much preparation — but gather up the gleanings of the Sunday. I mean on those same evenings to have bible classes one for young men and the other for young women. I shall have plenty to do — what with preparing for the pulpit, which is the hardest part, and more general study. I hope to be able also to visit a good deal, particularly amongst the poor and unwell. "Inasmuch as ye did it"[1] encourages me to this.

I expect the ordination will take place towards the end of Nov. I don't like it —

Perhaps it would be as well to send me back the sermons when I think of it, for I used up the most I had to light my fire lately, thinking it the best use to make of them. I will send you some more some time soon — but it is not air — there are no such things as *written sermons*. It is a contradiction in terms — a sermon ought never to be printed — or read — I am delighted at the thought of your coming to see us — and am glad you are trying homeopathy for I am favorably inclined towards it myself. I am glad too you feel better whether you attribute it to that or not.

I can't tell you the [number] of the [congregation] as you ask. It is not large but improves I think. I am not too sanguine, however. I hope I am as yet with Mr. Hounsom where I was staying before. I shall not be in lodgings for a week at least. It will depend on Mr. Powell whether I take a house at once — there happens to be a desirable one vacant now — and houses being very scarce in Arundel — he is coming down to me Saturday to stay till Monday. The people seem to like me. I hope to be useful amongst them with God's self. Love to dear Mother —

I am, my very dear Father,
Your loving son,

George

1. Referring to Matthew 25:40: "Inasmuch as you did it to one of the least of these my brethren, you did it to me."

Miss Louisa Powell to George MacDonald   The Limes,
November 7th, 1850

. . . How dear of you to write; but you must not do it if it is at all likely to hurt you one bit. Mrs. New[1] or somebody would send me a report. God keep you and both of us in willingness for His goodwill. . . . Papa has been so very kind to me. I know he loves you. He says he will find a corner somewhere when you are quite better enough to come.[2] Good night, my best and dearest. . . . I should like to be an angel or fairy just to see how you are sleeping. But He is keeping you and I will praise Him. . . .

November 8th, 1850

. . . I suppose you feel weak after the leeches, but I hope they will have had a desired effect by this time. Do not think that you must write to me; I should not be frightened if you think it better to let someone else. Alex will write for you while he is with you. . . . I hope, dearest, you will try and keep your thoughts and mind very peaceful. You have all the love you could wish, but till you are a little stronger, only think of it as a very commonplace sort of thing, and only just exactly what you have a right to. Think no more of me than as a good little girl that will be quite pleased when God makes you better enough to come. . . . I must tell you that I feel quite well today. I walked down to Hackney before breakfast with your letter. . . . Dear Papa sent me his love last night and said that he loved me very much, and that he loved you very much. This was precious to me.

1. MacDonald's landlady.
2. The house was then very full of guests.

To His Father   The Limes,
                                                November 15, 1850

My dear Father,

Louisa has told you of my visit to Dr. Williams,[1] and of his prescription, and orders not to preach for six weeks or two months. I have very little fear that my complaint is slight and will soon leave me with proper care — But I believe the lungs are in some measure affected. And I am not surprised at learning this — don't think it is much though. It is somewhat discouraging to be thus laid aside at the beginning — but the design of God in doing so will perhaps appear soon — or if not now — we shall know afterwards — if never — it is well not withstanding — There is a reason, and I at least shall be the better for it.

I find Louisa has forgot to tell you that Dr. Williams amongst other things has ordered me cod-liver oil twice a day — a dessert spoonful — in other stuff. Quantity to increase.

Now the question is what am I to do with myself — I must not stop here much longer — and I fear I must not go to Manchester — for the South is so much preferable for my health at this particular time — and then — this is my greater one of my chief causes of uneasiness that I have no money — All my spare money I laid out on books — very necessary to do when going to a country place like Arundel, where I can have no society, and no books of any kind, except what I have of my own. I could have gone on till the quarter if well but had no provision for this. I shall have to pay all the supplies — I mean I expect it will come out of my income. I expect the people will wait for me though — £2 a week [to pay substitutes] out of £150 a year won't leave much but this won't last long — Perhaps Alex will be able to lend me a little or Charles.[2] I shall see. How would it do to go & stay with Aunt[3] at Newport a-while — I mean pay her for it?

There is another invalid in the house now — a sister of the late Mrs. Powell — Mrs. Burnham of Wellingboro. She has had nearly the whole of her right breast removed for cancer. The operation was performed last Wednesday. She is going on pretty well.

I don't think there is any cause for uneasiness about me as to the result of my complaint — Mrs. Powell went with me to Dr. Williams, and was much pleased with his opinion of me. Love to Mother & yourself from your Son, I feel better today —

George

1. Greville MacDonald notes that this was the "Father of the late Dr. Theodore Williams, the earliest advocate in Britain of outdoor life and mountain air for the tuberculosis" (*George MacDonald and His Wife*, p. 145).

2. Alex and Charles, MacDonald's brothers.

3. Macdonald's paternal aunt, Mary Spence, with whom he spent his days of convalescence at Newport, Isle of Wight.

To His Father   Newport, December 17, 1850

My dear Father,

It is very kind of you to write to me so often. I had your letter last night. I hope I shall write quite often enough to keep you from feeling uneasy. I don't think I can give you any news as to the state of my health. I feel very doubtful whether I shall preach much longer. I feel if I were to begin again now, it would bring back the attack. I am pretty sure, I am not nervous about myself — I have never been frightened about myself. I know you have often thought I fancied I could not work and often it may have been so but not always and it is but lately that I said I was sure something would show it was no fault of mine but that something was wrong. It was in the very midst of forcing myself to do what I did not *feel* as if I were able for that my attack came — However it may partly be fancy. All I know is that when I have work to do, I will try to do it with God's help & then if I fail, it is not my fault. But I am not unhappy about it. Though I do not seem to get on very fast. Perhaps such attacks might come & go, & one yet warstle on for some years — But I have no idol of chance,[1] as many called Christians seem to have. All will be well with me. I know you would give me the best you could — my heart's desire if you could — And I know God is better than you — and it was Christ himself that taught us to call him Father. If I were to die tomorrow, I would thank God for what I have had, for he has blessed me very abundantly! I could say "I have lived."

Your loving Son

George MacDonald

1. Greville MacDonald notes that this phrase "recalls a word of Sir Philip Sydney that my father would quote in later years: 'Since a man is bound no farther to himself than to do wisely, chance is only to trouble them that stand upon chance.' The axiom of my father's, already quoted, is even more notable: '*The roots of the seen remain unseen*'" (*George MacDonald and His Wife*, p. 147, quoting from George MacDonald's *Castle Warlock* [London: Sampson Low, Marston, Searle & Rivington, 1882], vol. 1, p. 124).

To Miss Louisa Powell   Niton,
December 27th, 1850

I had your sweet letter to-day, when I posted my one to you. . . . Caleb Morris[1] is one of the few who stand so high that they can see a good many things at once. Most people are always peeping through pin-holes in bits of paper; and often very ready to tell the man on the hill top with his eyes wide open what wonderful things they see. . . . I think I should like Caleb Morris to marry us better than anyone except Mr. Scott.[2] . . . I am surprised to find so many of my notions in Dr. Arnold's letters[3] — only much enlarged and verified beyond my shelled-chicken-peepings. . . . I wish the Church were better. I think I should almost go into it. Don't fancy I am changing. Indeed I am not saying more than I

have always said, that my great objection to it was the kind of ministers
the system admitted. If Dr. Arnold's plan could be carried out — which
it never could till all men, or nearly all, are not mere Christians (that
sounds very dreadful, does it not?) but thoroughly earnest men — I should
have very little objection left.

Saturday night. I had your letter to-day and the poor flattened rose —
crossing your violets on the way. I was out nearly an hour and a half and
enjoyed it, this bright beautiful day. I walked down nearer the sea, but yet
a long way above it. I could see the blowing of the irregular tiny waves
over the level sand, of which a little was bare, and a man or boy, I don't
know which, was walking on it, with such a clear black shadow. The sun
flashed on the sea, and a sloop-rigged boat left a snail track behind it. The
horizon was a luminous mist, I enjoyed it more than yesterday.

Sunday morning. I lay simmering in bed, till half-past ten this morning,
without mental energy enough to look at my watch. I have been out before
the door and it is very mild, and the sea sounds on — the first time I have
noticed its low monotonous tune. I have had your dear little letter this
morning. Thank you for all your dear love. . . . I shall write a little of my
poem[4] this evening. I fear it will disappoint me as usual. . . . It is little
more than a week now till I see you once more. I am sure I shall never be
well until I have you with me always. . . .

1. A free-thinking minister.

2. A. J. Scott, who held the chair of English language and literature at University
College, London, in November 1848, was a major influence on MacDonald's thinking.
Scott was charged with heresy before the Presbytery of Paisley and lost his license to preach.
He would not subscribe wholly to the Westminster Confession of Faith, refusing to accept
that "only the elect" will be saved. See MacDonald's letter to Mrs. A. J. Scott dated May
27, 1851, pp. 52-53. The Scotts became lifelong friends of MacDonald and his family. See
also *George MacDonald and His Wife,* p. 194.

3. Referring to *The Life and Correspondence of Thomas Arnold* (1844), in which
MacDonald apparently found striking similarities to his own ideas.

4. The poem *Within and Without* (1855).

PART II

Marriage and Fatherhood

INTRODUCTION

George MacDonald and Louisa Powell were married on March 8, 1851, at a chapel in Hackney known as "The Old Gravel Pits," where the Powell children had been baptized. As a wedding present, MacDonald gave his bride a love poem, "Love Me, Beloved," from the religious poetic drama *Within and Without* (1855), in which he tried to link his spiritual love for God to his love for his wife. From the religious content of this metaphysical drama and from the letters MacDonald wrote to his future wife, it is apparent that he was still trying to cope with feelings of spiritual inadequacy:

> Pray God, beloved, for thee and me
> That our souls may be wedded eternally.

With renewed confidence, however, MacDonald wrote a month later (April 15, 1851) to his father about his new-found marital contentment, commenting on his new pastorate: "I am far happier, much more at peace, and I hope learning now rapidly the best knowledge." He continued in the same letter to link the joy of his present state with his developing thoughts on doctrine, though he also betrayed his concerns:

> I firmly believe people have hitherto been a great deal too much taken up about doctrine and far too little about practice. The word doctrine, as used in the Bible[,] means *teaching of duty* not *theory* — I preached a sermon about this. We are far too anxious to be definite, & have finished, well-polished, sharp-edged systems

45

— forgetting that the more perfect a theory about the infinite,
the surer it is to be wrong, the more impossible it is to be right.
I am neither Arminian nor Calvinist — to no system could I
subscribe. (See p. 51 below.)

The first few years of George and Louisa MacDonald's marriage were
indeed difficult. There was no time for a honeymoon, and getting used
to life in Arundel meant certain adjustments. For one thing, within a year
their first child, a daughter christened Lilia Scott, was born, and in the
same month MacDonald had to cope with "some members of the church,"
as he wrote to his father (July 27, 1852), "who are very unteachable" (see
p. 54 below). He had hoped that his resignation would not be required,
but a year later, in May 1853, he finally was forced to resign. To make
matters worse, his brother Alec had died the month before in April. On
July 23, 1853, Louisa gave birth to their second child, Mary Josephine.
These early years of their marriage seemed to MacDonald and his wife to
form a pattern of births and deaths. Desperately MacDonald tried to
establish himself in a career that would provide for his ever-growing family.
As he and his wife struggled, MacDonald continued his intellectual search
for evidences of divine goodness. In spite of the difficulties he faced,
MacDonald tried to hold to his belief that "God is our loving true
self-forgetting friend" (see p. 59 below).

The years 1851 to 1863 (the year MacDonald published his first novel,
David Elginbrod) were filled for him with external and inner conflicts —
the struggling minister turned writer trying to provide for his family as he
searched within himself for answers to the adversities of life. But for all
the difficulties he had to face, MacDonald was comforted by the emotional
security of his marriage and continued to teach that "death is only the
outward form of birth" (see p. 99 below). This idea he would try to explain
symbolically in his adult faerie romance *Phantastes*, published in 1858, the
year in which both his father and his brother John Hill died.

Finally there came a brief rest for the MacDonalds. Lady Byron became
MacDonald's patron, and in the winter of 1856 the MacDonalds took a
trip to Algiers that must have seemed like a honeymoon to them. With
great anticipation, MacDonald and his wife wrote from Marseilles in a
shared letter to the wife of MacDonald's lifelong friend Professor A. J.
Scott: "We are looking towards that place as a promised land of rest and
warmth" (see p. 115 below).

The MacDonalds were indeed fortunate to have friends like the Scotts and Lady Byron, who often helped them when they needed it most. In exchange for such financial help, MacDonald would frequently write letters of personal encouragement and hope to his friends, often dedicating poems to them. As he himself suffered, MacDonald gained strength from his encouragement of others. On October 15, 1858, after his father's death, he wrote with affection to his stepmother:

> May God help you, dearest Mother, to go nearer to Him — that is the only thing that can comfort you for the loss of my father. There is no gift so good, but its chief goodness is that God gives it, and what he gives is not to be taken away again. Whatever good things we can fancy for ourselves, God has better than that in store for us. Even your sorrow is turned into joy, if you can say to God, "I am willing to be sorrowful, since it is thy will. . . ." (See pp. 129-30 below.)

For the next several years, MacDonald would find much in his life that would test his incredible belief in divine goodness.

Significant Dates and Events

1851   George MacDonald marries Louisa Powell on March 8. MacDonald privately publishes a translation of "Twelve of the Spiritual Songs of Novalis" for his friends.

1852   Lilia Scott is born on January 4.

1853   MacDonald resigns his pastorate. MacDonald's brother Alexander dies in April. Mary Josephine is born on July 23. MacDonald moves to Manchester.

1854   Caroline Grace is born on September 16.

1855   MacDonald publishes his poetic drama *Within and Without.* MacDonald's half-sister Bella dies on August 24.

1856   Greville Matheson is born on January 20. Lady Byron becomes MacDonald's patron. He spends the winter in Algiers with his wife and his daughter Mary Josephine.

1857   Irene is born on August 31. MacDonald publishes his *Poems.* The family moves to Hastings, England.

1858   MacDonald's brother, John Hill MacDonald, dies. MacDonald's father dies. MacDonald publishes *Phantastes.* Winifred Louisa is born on November 6. MacDonald publishes *Hymns and Sacred Songs* (Manchester).

1859   The MacDonalds move to Tudor Lodge, Regent's Park, London. MacDonald accepts professorship of English literature at Bedford College, London.

1860   Ronald is born on October 27.

1862   Robert Falconer is born on July 15. MacDonald meets Charles Dodgson [Lewis Carroll].

To His Father Upper Clapton
January 9, 1851

I have just come from consulting Dr. Williams. He seems so far satisfied with me — but not pleased that I did not take the oil constantly — which now I will do, sick or not — but he says that will go off.[1] He allows me to preach if I begin gently. . . . Many thanks to you, my very dear father, for writing so often and so kindly. I hope to be married in March. Mr. Powell quite intends it. I fear we shall not be able to come to Scotland. Dr. Williams does not approve of it. But we will hope to see you in the South.

1. Taking the cod liver oil was a constant trouble to MacDonald. The following from his father is amusing enough: "When you told me of having bought two gallons of Oil I thought I saw you scouring the country with an oil pig carried by a string tied round the neck — a strange piece of clerical luggage. I brought also to my recollection the *true* story of the late F_____ E_____, minister of C_____. He went drunk to the pulpit one Sabbath, and after the people had finished the first psalm-singing, he got up out of *a sleep* he was indulging in and bawled out to the congregation 'Roar on boys, there's mair in the black pig in the foot of the press.' I hope then that the oil pig will do you more good than the black one did to F_____!" MacDonald's father told him this amusing anecdote because he took so much oil one would think he was drunk with it. See *George MacDonald and His Wife*, p. 149.

To His Father [Arundel, January 16, 1851]

Most preaching seems to me greatly beside the mark. That only can I prize which tends to make men better — and most of it "does na play bouf upo' me" [does not even bark at me]. . . . I finished my poem [*Within and Without*] at the Island, but it must wait your perusal when you come to see us, for I cannot copy out more than 2,000 lines. Will you come and see us in the summer? . . . Mr. Powell is to bring Louisa down to see me some Saturday soon and stay till Monday.

To His Father   Arundel
                                                      April 15th, 1851

My dear Father,

Will you excuse my writing to you on these scraps of paper, as I have none at hand, and am not willing to call Louisa from the garden where she is sowing some flower seeds. I ought to have written to you last week especially as I had such a long letter from you; and I should have done so, had you not had one from me about the same time I received yours. Cold blustery winds prevailing for the past ten days, and I have not been so free of cough or so well — but I think nothing of it, as I quite expect the warm weather when it comes will make me better. Louisa has been very well, I am happy to say. I am far happier, much more at peace, and I hope learning now rapidly the best knowledge. I hope our Lord is training me more & more to find my completeness in him — I cannot yet say much about my congregation [which] continues small, but I think — if any differences they improve. It would be very foolish to judge yet, seeing I have been so interrupted in my labors. My greatest desire is, if I have my health again, to go out itinerating. As I expect to be on very good terms with the church people here, I hope for better congregations in the evening when there is no service in the parish church. Amongst our visitors this week before last was the vicar — I mean at our house — not the chapel. Next Friday (being Good Friday) I preach to the children of our Sunday School & there is a tea-meeting in the evening — at which I hope to have the company of Mr. Morris [Caleb Morris] of whom you have heard me speak when at college. He resides in the same house with us — the Miss Leslie's. I have been with him at Highbury since — and now he is settled at Worthing, a town of some importance, ten or twelve miles from here.

[Written by Louisa MacDonald:] George is gone down stairs to speak to a woman whose baby wants baptizing next Sunday so I have been rude enough to take up his pen to tell you that he is pretty well though his cough he mentioned is troublesome & keeps him in doors while these cold winds blow, but this does not prevent his giving us some very good sermons. I should like you to hear him preach very much.

[MacDonald resumes:] I forgot if I told you that when the census was taken there were only 117 in my chapel in the evening which is my best congregation. The chapel, tho' not built of flint is framed with it, and looks very pretty for a country chapel.

About Mr. Troup's [late] measures, I certainly don't think he has acted prudently nor courteously to his people. I certainly, since you ask me, do not think a minister has any right whatever to give his pulpit for any one against the wish of his people. His pulpit is only a tool for doing good. And certain I am that no good will be done against the will of the people. But while I think he has in the abstract [been] wrong, of course I feel there is room for *me* to doubt whether he has been aware to the full of the feelings of his congregation. And I venture to guess that his motives for acting as he has done may be misunderstood. From what I know of him, I don't think he would act in any way that would knowingly *"insult"* the people but it is possible — mind I don't know — I am only conjecturing — that he believes his friends in Huntly make more of the matter than it is worth, is trying to get them over it by degrees in this way — a mistaken one certainly. Please not to say so, as it might make them think Mr. Troup is of the *new faith*[1] — and I have no authority for saying what I do. I certainly believe far too much has been made of the matter, and while the new party have not acted properly I think — I am not sure that all the blame is theirs — in the directions that have followed. It is a question more of philosophy than of religion — and many of their most earnest advocates on the other sides have been extremely unfitted for that or any controversy — this especially, which involves the most abstruse & delicate questions. I firmly believe people have hitherto been a great deal too much taken up about doctrine and far too little about practice. The word doctrine, as used in the Bible[,] means *teaching of duty* not *theory* — I preached a sermon about this. We are far too anxious to be definite, & have finished, well-polished, sharp-edged systems — forgetting that the more perfect a theory about the infinite, the surer it is to be wrong, the more impossible it is to be right. I am neither Arminian nor Calvinist — to no system could I subscribe.

Have you heard — of course you have, that John is wishing to leave Dr. Munro.[2] We hope to have him here for a little while when he does. I am anxious to see him and speak with him.

I do hope & so does Louisa that you will come. Pray do — we shall be only too delighted to see you. Don't get off the humor of coming. Listen to Mother. She is a wise woman, and I am sure you think so. Please do come. You could come while the Exhibition was open — and our friends in London would be very happy to go with you any where there after you left. Louisa joins me in love to you & mother and the little sisters. She sends the bairns[3] some primroses, of which our woods are full. I am glad to hear the free church improves in doctrine. It will be long before the hard lifeless Calvinism is out of it — long before believers among them will be content not to be the *peculiar converts* of Him who loves all men —

> I am my very dear Father
> Your loving Son
> George

1. Both MacDonald and Robert Troup had attended Blackfriars Street Church, Aberdeen, as students. Twenty-two-year-old John Kennedy was the son of an independent minister and was the new pastor at Blackfriars Street Church. His "new views," which MacDonald and Troup and others followed, involved a concern for the poor and Sunday school teaching. Kennedy also spoke out for the emancipation of the black slaves and was in favor of the Foreign Bible Society. Such views were considered as "social gospels" and disliked by those who followed strict Calvinism, which insisted that only the elect would be saved and therefore that evangelism was of no importance.

2. MacDonald's brother John Hill wanted to leave the boring life of a schoolmaster — MacDonald's brothers John and Alec both had come for his ordination.

3. Children.

To Mrs. A. J. Scott   Arundel, Sussex, May 27, 1851

My dear Madam,

In the hope that you have not forgotten the expression of a wish that I should write to you, I venture now to address you. This I have long contemplated doing, and regret that I have not sooner availed myself of the opportunity of knowing you, and through you Mr. Scott, better. Though I have never had the pleasure of an interview with you, I write without fear or constraint; believing that a soul that responds so mightily to the expression of Mr. Scott's inner life, cannot be much out of harmony with yours. Allow me to beg your acceptance of the enclosed little poems, which I wrote some months ago, in considerable depression of spirits, and a low state of bodily health as well. I scarcely think any apology is necessary for offering you in this form some of the inner thoughts of my heart, believing that the only thing that could render such an offering unsuitable, would be a want of sympathy in the one to whom it is made, and this, as I have already said, I feel certain cannot be the case with you. I shall be thankful to know something of Mr. Scott's health and engagements;

and anything about him that you may kindly think proper to tell me. One lately his pupil, and now my wife, will be equally interested with myself and rejoices to hear good news either of Mr. Scott or yourself. Should you ever be in the neighbourhood of Arundel, it would give us intense pleasure to see you. Mrs. MacDonald desires to be respectfully remembered to you; and she and I would wish with all reverence to offer our loving thoughts to Mr. Scott.

I hope you do not find the climate of Manchester disadvantageous. May you everywhere and always have peace and confidence.

> Believe me,
> My dear madam,
> Most sincerely yours,
>
> GEORGE MACDONALD

An Address Read by MacDonald to His Congregation [July 5th, 1852] at Arundel, Shortly Before His Forced Resignation

It having been represented to me that a small party in the church has for some time been exceedingly dissatisfied with my preaching, it has become my duty to bring the matter before the assembled church. My first impulse was at once to resign, as the most agreeable mode for me to be delivered from the annoyance. On mentioning this to some of my friends in the church, the proposal was met with no opposition, although it drew forth expressions of sorrow, and the declaration of benefit derived from my labors. But from the advice of two of my friends engaged in the same work, and from the awakened perception in my own mind that, as I came at the invitation of the whole church, it would be unfair to the other members of the church to resign unconditionally on account of the dissatisfaction of a few, I resolved to put it in the following form: Will you, the Church, let me know whether you sympathize or not with the dissatisfaction of the few? Such a communication from you will let me know how to act: I put it thus from the feeling that this is my duty. With my own personal feelings I have nothing to do in this assembly. I retire and await your decision.[1]

1. See Greville MacDonald, *George MacDonald and His Wife*, pp. 181-82, regarding the reply of the Congregation:

> It is by no means our wish that the Revd. G. MacDonald should relinquish the office of Pastor of this Church; such a course would cause much regret. But if on reflection he continues to hold and express such an opinion it is evident that it will cause serious difficulties in the Church.

These propositions were agreed to by about 20 members.

To His Father   Arundel
                                                                July 27th, 1852

My very dear Father,

It is now a very long time since I have written to you or heard from you. I am not very sure, but I think I must have heard from you last. Why did you not write and scold me? But I suppose you have been so satisfied with the society of your two younger sons that you could do better for a while without hearing from one of the elder. I have been very much occupied with one thing and another — particularly with some annoyance given me by some members of the church who are very unteachable. I thought it not unlikely at the time that I should have to leave — but it has brought out on the other hand expressions of attachment and benefit, which have more than comforted me for the opposition of a few. However, if God put the means at any time in my power, I mean to take another mode of helping men; and no longer stand in this position and persecutions. By and by we shall be free in another world. Let us do our work in this, ever making it our one business to be subject to the Son of Man — the children of God — led home to him by following Christ.

Little Lily grows nicely — is a little fretful with her teeth, but does not fall off in firmness of flesh — *fat* you cannot call her — her largeness seems all of firm muscle — and a great child she is. I was absent more than last week, but when I returned, she had not forgotten me.[1] Jane[2] has been very poorly — I am anxious now to hear how she is — Charles[3] has not answered my last letter in which at his request I suggested a choice of names for his little child.

I suppose you are enjoying John's[4] society very much. He is a most superior youth. I think he is decidedly the first of the family in talent and a great one amongst his generation, as the time will show. I hope he will take no steps *whatever* about going to a dissenting college without letting me know. I wish to hear from him. I wrote to him last. I hope he and his colleague Mr. Cecil will come and see me at Christmas.[5] I half expect a visit from Caleb Morris by and by. I have a great affection for that man. I spent the greater part of two days in his society last week. He is almost the only minister of standing whom I respect intellectually, morally and spiritually. People think he has gone down, because he has taken to teaching in his own house instead of preaching on Sundays. He thinks he has risen, and I agree with him. O for a few that really wanted to learn, to be earnest divine men — partakers of the divine nature — in one word *Christians* — what a hidden meaning — hidden to most that use it — lies in that word.

Give my dear love to mother & the children. I hope you are pretty well — & able to write some very soon. Love to Alec & John & much love to yourself from

Your son George —

Louisa sends her love to you. I wish I could bring her to see you. Have you quite forgot your almost promise of visiting us this year.

1. MacDonald's daughter Lily was about six months old at this time.
2. MacDonald's older brother Charles' wife.
3. MacDonald's brother.
4. MacDonald's younger brother John Hill.
5. Greville notes that "this intention was carried out. Mr. Cecil writes to my mother in the following March of 'the agonizing regret' with which he thinks of Arundel, 'yet with a warmth that would thaw me were I in Nova Zembla!'" (*George MacDonald and His Wife*, p. 181). Henry Cecil was a good friend of John Hill MacDonald at Sheffield Academy and later of George MacDonald. For Cecil's account of MacDonald's experience at Arundel, see *George MacDonald and His Wife*, p. 173.

To His Half-Sister Bella

[Arundel]
[January 19, 1853]

My very dear Bella,

I fear you will think that I am not pleased to have your very nice present, since I have been too long in answering, or rather in thanking you for it. But indeed it was very kind of my dear little sister to think of me, & work me such a nice purse. I have it in my pocket now. If there were more money in it, I should like to send you something, but I cannot, for our Heavenly Father has given me everything almost that I could wish except money; and, more than that, I am sure he will give you and me every thing that a loving heart can wish to have, with his own love for the best thing. I will copy for you a little poem I wrote some years ago for a sister of your sister Louisa, and perhaps you will like that as well as anything else I could send you.

How much I should like to spend a winter at home again, a snowy winter, with great heaps and wreaths of snow; and sometimes the wind storm howling in the chimneys and against the windows & down at the kitchen door. And how much I should love to spend one long summer day in June, lying on the grass before the house, and looking up into the deep sky with large white clouds in it. And when I lifted my head I should see the dear old hills all round about; and the shining of the Bogie, whose rush I should hear far off and soft, making a noise hardly louder than a lot of midgets. It would be delightful if I could go to sleep here some night, and waken there with Louisa & my little Lil, all at home. And then the warm evenings, with long grass in the field where the well is, and the corn craik crying craik — craik — somewhere in it, though nobody knows where. Everything looks so different here. Behind the town there are a number of hills, or rather braes, very low hills, but with sweet short grass, on which such numbers of fallow deer are feeding. Here and there are plantations of very fine trees, very large some of them; and down in one of the hollows rises and runs a very clear stream of water, most wonderfully clear. Clearer than the Bogie, and so nice to drink in the hot days. But all in front of the town is very flat, and covered with very green grass, even now as green as in spring, for we have had such enormous quantities of rain, and hardly any cold weather. It is so flat you might fancy it was rolled out flat. There are a number of wide ditches with water all through it; and from one bedroom window we can *almost* — see the sea (looking over this flat country) about three or four miles away. We have a river that runs through the town, up which vessels come of a good size, bringing things and taking away things; but it is a very quiet little town — not so much bustle as Huntly. The sea waves do not break on a high rough rocky shore, as where you have seen the sea-side, but on a beach of sand and little stones without any rocks, and you could walk into the sea a long way some-times without getting into deep enough water to drown you; it grows deep so gradually. The fields grow much richer crops than with you, and there are many more trees growing about the fields; but it is not such a beautiful country to my mind, nearly, as the one I left. . . .

I am your loving brother
George —

To His Father   Arundel,
                                                              April 5, 1853.

My very dear father,

I thank you gratefully for your last precious letter, which I shall not lose sight of as long as I live. It was very kind of you to write so much and so freely about my beloved brother, who is dearer to us all now than ever before. Of him we need never say he was; for what he was he is now — only expanded, enlarged and glorified. He needed no change, only development. Memory and anticipation are very closely allied. Around him they will both gather without very clear separation perhaps. He died in his earthly home and went to his heavenly.

Louisa will write to my mother herself. She is very grateful to her for sending the beautiful hair to her.[1] He is more to be envied maybe than if it had been his wedding-cards.[2] But for them that love God, no one is to be envied more than another; for all are clasped to the bosom of love and fed daily from the heart of the Father, whether here or in the other world — all one.

I too am thankful to dearest mother, not for the love and care she showed him, for of that it would be irreverent almost to speak — but that she would not let them hide this beautiful face with the hideous dress of that death which the vulgar mind delights in making as frightful as the power of ugliness can.[3] Let the body go beautiful to the grave — entire as the seed of a new body, which keeps the beauty of the old, and only parts with the weakness and imperfection. Surely God that clothes the fields now with the wild flowers risen fresh from their winter-graves, will keep Alec's beauty in His remembrance and not let a manifestation of Himself, as every human form is, so full of the true, simple, noble and pure, be forgotten.

1. MacDonald's stepmother had sent a lock of Alec's hair as a remembrance.

2. Possibly referring to the fact that Alec had been unable to marry the woman of his choice, Hannah Robertson, daughter of an eminent surgeon.

3. MacDonald's sonnet "A.M.D." was written for his brother Alexander, who died in April 1853. (See MacDonald's *Poetical Works* [London: Chatto & Windus, Piccadilly, 1893], vol. 1, p. 261).

A.M.D.

Methinks I see thee, lying straight and low,
Silent and darkling, in thy earthy bed,
The mighty strength in which I trusted, fled,
The long arms lying careless of kiss or blow;
On thy tall form I see the night robe flow
Down from the pale, composed face — the head
Crowned with its own dark curls: though thou wast dead,
They dressed thee as for sleep, and left thee so!
My heart, with cares and questionings oppressed,
Not oft since thou didst leave us turns to thee;
But wait, my brother, till I too am dead,
And thou shalt find that heart more true, more free,
More ready in thy love to take its rest,
Than when we lay together in one bed.

To His Father   Arundel, April 29, 1853

My very dear Father,

I had made something like a resolution in my own mind to write to you every week. I did not do so last week, but Louisa did help me to keep this resolution by not heeding the shortness of my letters, for then I can write freely & happily. I hope you are much better and stronger and my Dear Mother too. How delighted I should be to see you both. It seems nearer now than it was before. You would think of Alec — for they say we are like. Perhaps you would see this likeness more after the absence of both of us for a time. But my way of thinking and feeling would not help to make you more sad. I grow younger and happier. I see an outlet now from miseries of the mind, unknown to any which form portions of my earliest recollections, and have grown with my growth — but which by & by I shall quite outgrow. Swedenborg says the angels are always growing younger. In this saying, which is *logically* absurd, there is a very deep meaning. Oh I know a little now, & only a little, what Christ's deep sayings mean, about becoming like a child, about leaving all for him, about service & truth & love. God is our loving true self-forgetting friend. All delight, all hope & beauty are in God. God is — therefore *to be* is blessed. My dear & honored father — if I might say so to you — will you think me presumptuous if I say — leave the Epistles & ponder *The Gospel* — The story about Christ. Infinitely are the Epistles mistaken because the Gospels are not understood. Because Christ is not understood & felt in the heart — because the readers of the Epistles too often possess nothing of that sympathy with Christ's thoughts & feelings & desires which moved and glorified the writing of the Epistles. They cannot receive from them the true impression. The Epistles are very different from the Apostles' preaching. The Gospels form the sum & substance of the apostles' teaching, & preaching. The Epistles are mostly written for a peculiar end and aim & are not intended as expositions of the central truth in general forms. Hear the words of Christ — Always say — Understand & so thus — This is the true Faith — & God and Everlasting life. You will not be displeased with this little sermon. Of course, I speak in it generally.

God has provided for us very lovingly. Our salary is reduced — but not so much as we feared, and our sister's[1] boarding with us has helped much to take us through. I fear no want, the rational mode to me is just what Christ says. "Leave meat & drink to God — seek the Kingdom of God & his righteousness" — Ah there is a grand word to come of Truth & Love & Blessedness & God. My dear love to Mother,

> I am, my dearest Father,
> Your loving Son
>
> George

1. Louisa's sister Carrie.

To His Father   Arundel,
                                                        May 20, 1853.

. . . I am always finding out meaning which I did not see before, and which I now cannot see perfectly — for, of course, till my heart is like [Christ's] great heart, I cannot fully know what he meant. The great thing for understanding what he said is to have a living sense of the reality that a young man of poor birth appeared unexpectedly in the country of Judea and uttered most unwelcome truths, setting at nought all the respectabilities of the time, and calling bad, bad, and good, good, in the face of all religious perversions and false honourings. The first thing is to know Jesus as a man, and any theory about him that makes less of him as a man — with the foolish notion of exalting his divinity — I refuse at once. Far rather would I be such a Unitarian as Dr. Channing than such a Christian as by far the greater number of those, that talk about his Divinity, are. The former truly believes in Christ — believes in him far more than the so-called orthodox. You will find some thoughts of mine on this matter (though the Editor begged leave to omit the most important portion) in the *Christian Spectator* for May. . . . They are in an article headed "Browning's Christmas Eve."[1] The life, thoughts, deeds, aims, beliefs of Jesus have to be fresh expounded every age, for all the depth of Eternity lies in them, and they have to be seen into more profoundly every new era of the world's spiritual history. . . .

You must not be surprised if you hear that I am not what is called *getting on*. Time will show what use the Father will make of me. I desire to be His — entirely — so sure am I that therein lies all things. If less than this were my hope, I should die.

I expect to find a few whom I can help in Manchester. The few young who are here and not [adversely] influenced by their parents, the simple, honest and poor, are much attached to me — at least most of them — and that means but a very few. If I were in a large town I do not think I should yield to them and leave — but it is better for me to be driven away than to break up such ties as may be supposed to exist between a true pastor and true people for the sake of getting a larger salary. . . .

1. *Christian Spectator*, May 1853, p. 261. The article is signed "G.M.D." Reprinted in *A Dish of Orts. Chiefly Papers on the Imagination and on Shakespeare*, enl. ed. (London: Sampson Low Marston & Co., 1893), pp. 195-217.

To His Father

Worthing,
June 3, 1853.

. . . Mr. Godwin[1] says I want a place with a number of young men. He says they can't understand me in Arundel; but I know that some of all classes do understand me, and I am happy not to be understood by those that do not understand. . . . Some say I talk foolishness, others go away with their hearts burning within them. May God fashion me after *His* liking. . . .

Whether I shall go at once to Manchester and preach wherever I have an opportunity, remains not yet decided. I should be glad to rest, and preach nowhere for a month. . . .

I can hardly say I have any fear, and but very little anxiety about the future.[2] Does not Jesus say, Consider the lilies? We have only to do our work. If we could be forgotten, all Nature would go to wrack. . . . Jesus lived a grand, simple life in poverty and love. . . . His spirit is working in the earth — and in my heart too, I trust. But no man can speak the truth in a time of insincerity — like this and like most times — and tell people to their face that they cannot serve God and Mammon, without making foes. . . .

How strange the dear old fields will look to me with the iron nerves run through it, which makes the dear, rugged North one body with the warm, rich, more indolent South![3] When I think of that noble brother of mine for whom the evening and the rest came so early in the day, it is oftenest as running with him through the long grass of that same field on a warm summer night, trying to catch the cornscraich, till recalled by you and reprimanded for trampling down the grass. And the well, too! from which on hot noon-days I so often fetched you a jug of cold water when you came into the house hot and thirsty. . . . On the next page to fill up I write a little hymn which I made for a dear friend of Louisa's and mine [Josephine Rutter] after her recovery from a very severe illness. . . .

1. Professor John Godwin, who taught systematic theology and New Testament exegesis at Highbury College, London. He was engaged to Louisa's sister Charlotte.

2. "There are those who say that care for the morrow is what distinguishes the man from the beast; certainly it is one of the many things that distinguish the slave of Nature from the Child of God" (George MacDonald, *Castle Warlock,* vol. 2, p. 132; cited by Greville MacDonald, *George MacDonald and His Wife,* p. 186).

3. The railway that had just opened cut through The Farm. See Greville MacDonald, *George MacDonald and His Wife,* p. 186.

To His Wife   [The Limes, July 1853.]

. . . It is all over now and they are gone.[1] Everything has gone very
well — no drawback. We are going to the Forest where we went last time
to tea. Lily[2] has been very good. . . . She looked so sweet in her pretty
white dress and bonnet they got for her. . . . She had a little champagne,
a little raspberry ice and some grapes. . . .

. . . I have been very idle with the girls all the morning; but we have
been very happy for the day after the wedding. We romped a good deal
at the Forest. I laughed very much, and was merry, and seemed to have
clearer brains for it. I am sure it is good. I understand the Bible better for
it, I think. It seemed to me there was one, more lady-like than anyone
there, wanting. Is it my imagination that makes you seem so? . . . Or is
it a fact? I think perhaps you would be even more pleased with the former
supposition than the latter. Carrie[3] and I found a dead bird yesterday and
we went out this morning and got a spade and went and buried it under
a tree, and Carrie put roses over it before the earth. And when we had
buried it, we found another lying close to the grave, which we buried
too. . . . Mr. Godwin and I were very good friends. I wish he would say
nothing more — we should get on so nicely — for I cannot help and do
not wish to help loving him. . . .

1. Referring to the wedding of Louisa's sister Charlotte to Professor John Godwin.
Louisa had had to remain in Arundel because of the impending birth of her second child,
Mary Josephine, who was born on July 23.
2. MacDonald's first child, about one and a half years of age at this time.
3. Louisa's sister.

To His Wife   Manchester, Sep. 7, 1853.

My dearest Love,

Here is a little hymn I made for you last night, to keep away other
thoughts, and because I could not sleep. . . . I did not know dearest that
my letters seemed to show me out of spirits. Indeed I should have quite
denied it all yesterday, but then I was not very well — nor today. But I
have been to Harrison today who has carefully examined my chest, and

says he can discover no disease — there is only some degree of weakness of action all over. My heart is all right except an increased action what he thought was only from my deep respirations while he was examining me. With care of my general health & diet & proper exercise & not too much mental work I shall do very well. He has prescribed phosphoric acid for a fortnight — three drops a day — after which I must go to him again. I have likewise been to see Mr. Scott this morning, who was busy, & therefore after talking a little, asked me, if it would not be too bad to bring me up the hill twice in a day, to go back to tea this evening which I was happy to say I would do. It is getting near time for me to go. He was very kind and said he was always glad to see me, though he was busy, I will go and dress and then finish this. . . . Charles[1] is very kind and seems to become more tender. He is very encouraging and good too about my position — and seems uneasy and troubled if I am not so well. I suppose Charles Edward[2] & Alec's death have made him so. This evening Greville[3] will be with you. I am sure he will if he can.

Thank you dear love for your much precious love — the most precious thing I have — for I will not divide between the love of God directly to me and that which flows through you. Your love makes me strong. In answer to a question you asked — Charles does not wish me to wait for a *call* — but we must wait till we see more clearly what can be done. We cannot tell yet. He would like me to preach in a room, but some little nucleus seems requisite first, and there is very great difficulty in finding a suitable place, without at least more expense than it would be right to incur. I shall be glad to have the furniture at Lime Street. Thank you for the dear story about Lily & your true beautiful meaning to it. Don't neglect bathing & bandaging your poor foot. My love to Annie[4] & my dear beloved wife. I am darling your husband.

A Mother's Hymn.[5]

My child is lying on my knees;
    The signs of Heaven she reads:
My face is all the Heaven she sees,
    Is all the Heaven she needs.

And she is well, yea bathed in bliss,
    If Heaven lies in my face;
Behind it all its tenderness
    And truthfulness and grace.

I mean her well so earnestly;
    · Without a questioning,
'Twere little to let life go by
    To her a truth to bring.

I also am a child, and I
    Am ignorant and weak;
I gaze upon the starry sky
    And then I must not speak.

For all behind the starry sky,
    Behind the world so broad,
Behind men's hearts and souls doth lie
    The Infinite of God.

If I, so often full of doubt,
    So true to her can be,
Thou who dost see all round about,
    Art very true to me.

If I am low and sinful, bring
    More love where need is rife;
Thou knowest what an awful thing
    It is to be a Life.

Hast thou not wisdom to enwrap
    My waywardness around,
And hold me quietly on the lap
    Of love without a bound?

And so I sit in thy wide space
    My child upon my knee:
She looketh up into my face,
    As I look up to Thee.

L. P. McD. G. McD.
September 7, 1853

1. MacDonald's older brother Charles.
2. MacDonald's uncle, who was unsuccessful in business ventures and getting deeper into debt.
3. Greville Matheson, MacDonald's close friend from his days at Highbury College.

4. Louisa's sister Angela.

5. A slightly revised version of this poem is reprinted in *Within and Without* (London: Longmans, Brown & Green & Longmans, 1855), Part IV, Scene 4.

To His Wife   Manchester, Sept. 26, 1853.

I fear my dearest this will be a very shabby letter to you. You may see I fear it by the outcome. I have begun to put my lines apart. I have no news to give you today. I have seen no one and have spent rather a sad morning in my own company. Purely physical sadness — if such a thing could be: as if all our ailments were not mental! But I mean it was the sadness, which, if I had been a woman, would have been relieved by tears, and, as I am a man, was bettered by a long walk through wind and sunshine, and green fields and cows. I came home better. I could know that all around me was peace, that it was well with all the world and with me; that God was at the heart of things; and yet I was one Unrest in the midst of the Rest. Well, it is God's business, and he will mend it. Oh, the great Fact of God shooting up into great heights of space, grand indisputable Reality! God and I — I a creek into which ebbs and flows the infinite Sea! Worth waiting centuries and ages for the working out of that truth and bringing it to its full reality and consciousness — when we shall feel that it is so. It is worth all suffering — yes that suffering that springs from vacancy, abortiveness & futility — to be at length one with God; when my being shall be completed by having all the veils between it and the full consciousness of the Divine rent asunder — when it will be flooded with the central brightness. Here is a little sermon for you, dearest. Not untrue because a sermon — nor even untrue, because I feel I might feel it much more than I do: for surely it is my hope and the deep ground of all my looks into the future which shall become the present. . . .

I am very pleased with your account of how Lily received Mary Anne [the nurse]. I love that deep, quiet way — I would rather have the blood eloquent on her face than the words on her tongue. . . . It is a very good thing for us to be parted sometimes. It makes us think, both more truly about each other, and, [because] less interrupted, about our God. . . . We must seek Him. We may, however, say to ourselves — "One day these souls of ours will blossom into the full sunshine;" when all that is desirable

in the commonness of daily love, and all we long for of wonder and mystery
and the look of Christmas-time will be joined in one, and we shall walk
as in a wondrous dream yet with more sense of reality than our most
waking joy now gives us. How is my Lily? and my sweet Blackbird?[1] She
laughs as the Blackbird sings.

[George MacDonald]

1. MacDonald's second daughter, Mary Josephine, born July 23, 1853.

To His Wife   Manchester Sep. 27, 1853.

My dearest,

Annie's letter enclosed to me in yours of this morning, opened the
eyes of my memory to a great mistake under which I have been laboring.
I have scarcely a doubt that I owe Mr. Cooper £6 more. Indeed I may say
I am *sure* I do, and I likewise understand I think after much thought how
I have made the mistake. What a good thing it has been for me that I did
so — for I have had the burden of only £6 lying on me instead of £12 and
I did not come to know it till I was able to pay it, as very nearly so. I
hope this will not trouble my sweet wifie. It has done me good — real
good, I think, for even in poverty like ours, one is so much more ready
to trust in what one self has than in what God has ready to give when
needed. I am glad you went to Mr. Morris's last Sunday and more glad
still to find your growing strength of mind that justifies you in even
displeasing your dear father, when an elevating of the souls towards your
heavenly father is the object of your hope. . . . Dearest we shall be all right
soon I hope — perhaps not *very* soon — but not *very* long we will hope
in the father — I know of nothing definite yet, or even approaching
definiteness, but my hope keeps up, and my time or trial has not been
lost. I think I have made a little advance in faith — and you have too
Dearest.

I am
all your own
Dearest Louisa
George MacDonald

To His Father Manchester, October 17, 1853.

My very dear Father,

I lay aside a paper I am engaged on for the C.S. [*Christian Spectator*] and which I must post tonight, to write to you, for I am not pleased with myself for not writing to you before now, although I have comforted myself with the thought that I wrote last not that in any way releases me from the obligation. I brought Louisa and the children here the other week on their way to Liverpool. They staid [stayed] here a few days — & now they are with Alec & Helen[1] there. I am with Charles as before. I have made application for the post of librarian & Clerk at Owen's College, & Mr. Scott is doing what he can for me — but it is of course quite uncertain whether I shall succeed. A good many are applying I have reason to think. The chief difficulty would be my inexperience in Book-keeping but I have been studying that and Charles says I could do it quite well. The salary is only £100 — but I should not have very numerous duties, and should have time to increase my income by other means. Do not think I intend giving up preaching — but I shall be very happy not to be dependent on it — if so it pleases God. Preaching I think is in part my mission in this world and I shall try to fulfil it. But I wish to raise a church for myself or rather to gather around me those who feel I can teach them to their profit. Say nothing of my application as I may be disappointed and it is as well not talked of.

A London publisher is about to publish my poems[2] — taking all the risk, and promising me half the profits, if there are any. This too will be as well unmentioned till it is fairly a-going. He expects to bring the book out about Christmas. The editor of the C.S. [*Christian Spectator*] introduced me to him. You would laugh to see me studying book-keeping of a morning and correcting poems of an evening. I preached at Stalybridge last Sunday. I have no more preaching engagements on hand. There are half-a-dozen vacant churches in Manchester apparently, but I have been introduced to none of them & indeed I would rather not — for various reasons — though of course I would not refuse if asked & preach. My youngest child has had a dreadful cough, but she is getting better. Charles and Jane[3] are most kind to me & make me feel quite at home and not as a dependent, tho' I am at present — yet from them I do not feel it painful. However, I hope it will soon be over now — My love to mother & the children & much love to yourself my dearest father from your son George.

1. Alexander and Helen MacKay Powell. Louisa's brother Alexander married Mac-Donald's cousin Helen MacKay.

2. MacDonald hoped that his long poem, *Within and Without,* would finally be published by a London publisher, Freeman, but this did not happen.

3. MacDonald's brother and his wife.

To His Father   Liverpool, November 16, 1853.

My very dear father,

I am sorry that you should feel any uneasiness about me and my position. It is in a time like this especially, unavoidable that the friends of any public man who cannot go with his side, should be more or less anxious about him. It is too quite impossible for me to explain to you thoroughly the position in which I find myself — but your faith in God, and the faith of individual good men in me should quiet your fears. As to the congregational meetings and my absence from them, perhaps if you saw a little behind the scenes, you would care less for both. I will not go where I have not the slightest interest in going, and where my contempt would be excised to a degree very injurious to myself. Of course I do not deny individual goodness when I disclaim all favor for their public assemblies. Nor even if they be productive of good, am I bound to do good in a way against my liking, when I can do it in the way natural to me, and of course appearing to me better. I have no love for *any* sect of Christians as such — as little for independents as any, nor has what I have seen of them tended to produce other feelings. One thing is good about them — which is continually being violated — that is the independence — and independent I mean to be, in the real sense of the word — at least while things are as they are. Some of the best even amongst them will not go to these great show meetings. For their opinion of me, I do not care; nor can they hurt me; for there is a numerous daily increasing party, to whom the charge of heterodoxy is as great a recommendation from the hope of finding something genuine, as orthodoxy is to the other, in the hope of finding the tradition of the elders sustained and enforced. For popular rumor surely you need not care — as if it *could* be true, and were not the greatest liar under the sun! And from all its lies God can keep his own. Let us beware of worshipping this idol of the populace in any sense, even by fearing before it — and so seeking the praise of men and not the praise of God. Nor is the character of many of the leading ministers such that they ought not to be classed under the term *populace*. For my part I do not at all expect to become minister of any existing Church, but I hope to gather a few around me soon — and the love I have from the few richly repays me for the abuse of some & the neglect of the many. But do not think that therefore I believe that all that went before us have been mistaken. I wish I could talk to you about it instead of writing — it is such a wide subject, and fitter for a long essay than a letter. But does not all history teach us that the forms in which truth has be[e]n taught, after being held heartily for a time, have by degrees come to be held merely traditionally and have died out and other forms arisen. Which new forms have always been abused at first. There never was Reformation but it came in a way people did not expect and was cried down and refused by the greater part of the generation amongst whom it began. There are some in every age who can see the essential truth through the form, and hold by that, and who are not alarmed at a change, but others, and they the most by far[,] cannot see this, & think all is rejected by one who rejects the form of a truth which they count essential, while he sees that it teaches error as well as truth, and is less fitted for men now than it was at another period of history & stage of mental development. But I cannot[,] as I have said, enter into this. But why be troubled because your son is not like other people? Perhaps it is *impossible* for him to be the same. Does not the Spirit of God lead men and generations continually on to new truths[?] And to be even actually more correct in creed with less love of God, & less desire for truth surely is *infinitely* less worthy — nay — beside the latter it is contemptible. But if you believe in the Spirit of God — Why fear? Paul, I think, could trust in God in these things and cared very little about orthodoxy, as it is now understood — "If in anything ye be otherwise minded, God shall reveal even this unto you"[1] — are the words of his about the highest Christian condition. And Jesus said, If any man is willing to do the will of the Father he shall know of the doctrine.[2] Now real earnestness is scarcely to be attained in a high degree without doubts & inward questionings & certainly divine teachings — and if you add to this the presumption that God must have more to reveal to every age, you will not be sorry that your son cannot go with the many, who, even allowing them a greater degree of real Christianity than my experience can accord to what seems to me their babyhood, are deficient in their habit of thought and content to take for granted — where a little attention might awake doubts innumerable. And if there is to be advance, it must begin with a few, and it is *possible* (I cannot say more, nor does modesty forbid my saying this) I may be one of the few. But increase of truth will always in greater or less degree look like error at first. But to suffer in this cause is only to be like the Master; and even to be a martyr to a newer development of truth (which certainly I do not expect to be required of me in any extreme form in the present state of thought in the country) is infinitely nobler and more desirable than *success* in the common use of the word. Low Christians have always been more trouble to the higher than *what they call the world.* Paul's great annoyances came from them. And they are to be borne, but not for the sake of a false unity and personal comfort to be yielded to, & the errors of unchildlike & worldly — (carnal) pandered to & increased. And as far as England is concerned the Spirit of the Child seems most deficient in our churches — there is more of it in what the churches call the world, perhaps. Not therefore that there is less religion in the world. I believe there is much more than ever, but it is not so much in the churches, or religious communities (as such at least) in proportion, as it was at one time. In every sect there are those before others. In church & chapel there are those with whom I can hold close communion, but I must wait awhile before this communion is possible to the degree I should desire it. Your Huntly young men would not refuse me, however the betitled and pompous doctors of the law would let me down & better men than I with the term indefinite and indefinable of *German* and *new view.* If this seems like glorying, I will venture to take Paul's defense, of being compelled thereto — for if it be alleged against me that some condemn me, what have I to say but that others, and they to my mind far more estimable, justify and receive me. Your own Troup[3] would be cast out by many. But I will not write more about it, sure that one day either in this world of the next, it matters little to me, my father and I will hold sweet sympathetic communion with each other about God and Jesus and truth.

I preached last Sunday & will preach next & on the 6th Dec. in R. Spencer's[4] old chapel here. A few young men in Manchester are in the meantime wishing to meet together in some room, and have me for their minister. But it has not come to anything definite yet. But that is what I have wished from the first; and if they give what they can to support me, I will be content and try to make it up if necessary in other ways. But it does not seem very improbable that if I had a beginning once, I should by & by have a tolerable congregation, but may God keep me from trying to attract people.

Our friends here are very kind. By the way whoever said to you there about Mr. Powell's seeming inhospitality was mistaken for he is the most hospitable man in the world. True he had not been so cordial to me of late, but there are plenty of reasons in my present condition of things & in my peculiarities for that. Louisa and Helen both send their love to you — one to her father the other to her Uncle. When we are once more in our own house which we hope will be soon, we shall be applying for meal. I go to Manchester next week till required here again. Have you heard from John yet? I have a long letter (my first I am sorry to say) lying not yet finished for him. My dear love to Mother & the bairnies.[5] Your next letter will probably find me in Manchester. I am my dearest father, Your loving Son

George MacDonald

1. Philippians 3:15.
2. John 7:17.
3. Robert Troup, co-pastor of the Mission Kirk in Huntly.
4. Rev. Robert Spencer, who had recently left a chapel in Liverpool.
5. Children.

To His Wife   Tuesday Evening
                                                    November 29, 1853

My dearest true Love,

Thanks for your dear letter this morning, and for your stronghearted-ness. But I do not think of this matter despairingly as you seem to think. It is not over by any means. When I told you Francis was so satisfied with it, I meant, as I understood it, and correctly, that he expected it would all go right for me and therefore for him. Charles put the question to Dr. Davidson whether it would be necessary to require of their minister that he believed in the vicarious atonement — He said certainly not. Charles means to make the young men go with him to consult Dr. Davidson and Mr. Scott. They have not taken J. W. Kingsley into their Counsels, for he seems desirous of making a great stir, and getting some so called great man to undertake it, or at least to get some rich man in Manchester on our side. If it should be so, and even then they were to choose me, I should enter on it with much less pleasure, and should be very happy when I had driven away the out man, as I dare say would be the result without my setting myself to do it. Oh the trust in man! In riches! God taketh no pleasure in the legs of a man! And what would they take him for but to be *legs* for their stool to stand on — If we have the right thing we shall in the end succeed. Even to a measure of outward success. Those that hold on will conquer. I went to call on Mr. Scott at the college but he had not been down today. . . .

. . . The change of feeling on many points of common belief spreads much among the ministers, although of course most can only follow in the wake of the few. Cant is giving way to real thought and action — a true revival springing up in other quarters besides Arundel. But our great danger lies in acting or feeling as a party. I wish to be in a condition in which I can do my work for the Truth's sake, without any reference to others who oppose my teaching. We ought never to wish to overcome because WE are the fighters, never feel THAT IS MY TRUTH. Every higher stage of Truth brings with it its own temptation like that in the Wilderness, and if one overcomes not in that, he overcomes not at all. The struggle may be hard. I would I could be sure of the struggle, and then I should of the victory. . . . Oh, dearest, whatever you may feel about our homeless condition at present, I hope it has helped to teach your husband some things. . . . We may wait a little for a home here, for all the Universe is ours — and all time and the very thoughts of God himself. . . .

To His Wife   Manchester
                                               Tuesday, December 6, 1853

My dearest,

I got here in tolerable comfort last night, much to Jane's surprise and Charles's when he returned from Dr. Davidson's where he was calling and staid till late. He says everything goes on *very* favorably. He & Hampson went to call on Dr. Davidson last Friday I think — on Saturday. "What basis shall we have Doctor?" "As broad a one as you can." "What should we require?" "Oh, if a man believes in the Divinity of Christ and in the atonement — " "The atonement, Doctor!" "Yes — I don't mean Maurice's theory, nor Pye Smith's, nor Bushnell's — but that a man acknowledge Christ as the source of Life." Everything that Charles and I think and wish about externals too — The doctor is entirely cordial in agreeing with — more than that. He preached the other day & Francis himself does not wish to go farther than Dr. Davidson. . . . But I should be tired writing all the things Charles told me the doctor said.[1] He told them it was no use trying to get a London man — they must have a young man that could sympathize with them. He told Charles afterwards that he meant me but delicacy prevented his mentioning me then. Charles went to see him alone last night, and is delighted with him, and evidently in good spirits and expectations about the whole thing. He has done everything now that he can honorably do, and has left the thing in such a train that with Francis and Dr. Davidson there is great probability of my being in work very soon. But if not I will try our own plan. He has got Dr. Davidson to ask them all to tea, without him, for he has now formally withdrawn. So as not to interfere with their choice. They go on Saturday. I think it better & so does Charles that I should not see the doctor. Anything else I remember I will tell you when I come. I went to call on Mr. Scott today at S. Coneyo. He is very pleased to hear of Dr. Davidson's liberality. Dearest, I think I shall not come down till after Mr. Scott's lecture on Thursday. It would almost be wrong of me to lose it. Will you take my thin boots — and my hairbrush to the Hendersons and I will come there at once. I will try to write tomorrow though can't tell you positively. I think this will be best though. Now I must write a little note to Mr. Morris for his recommendation again. . . . Now dearest I must stop. It has been so dreadfully foggy it was no use to go & look for a *little* house. Charles quite agrees with our plan, but hopes we may have more to begin with than £100 — but we will not make our castles on a greater scale yet. I am, my dear sweet wife

Your own
[George]

1. MacDonald's brother Charles had been trying to get MacDonald a pastorate in Manchester but was having great difficulties. MacDonald's so-called heresy charges made it difficult for him to get another appointment in a chapel.

To His Father   Ashleigh, Anfield, Liverpool
                                                        December 21, 1853

. . . I am sorry to say — sorry because it will disappoint you — that my publishers [his name was Freeman] having accepted my poems on the testimony of others, now, on reading them himself, wishes to be clear of the engagement, which he certainly shall be. I am thankful to God for the pleasure the expected publication gave me, and so helped to keep my spirits up. Now I am able to let it go.

We are with Alex and Helen [Powell] now, but we long much for a home of our own. Much rather will we live in poverty than be longer dependent. . . . It is a blessed thing for me that my wife does not pull one way and I another. Our children are well and consequently happy. We are going through the hard time now, without which never man was worth much in the world — I mean for its salvation. May He keep me from being a time-server. . . .

To His Wife   Manchester
                                                       [December 30, 1853]

. . . It is rather a sad time for us to begin housekeeping, for everything is very dear — coals themselves 20s. a ton, and war threatening.[1] But it is all the same to God whether we begin with £10 or a thousand. . . . I am very rich in my wife and children, but wish I could support them. . . .

1. The approaching Crimean War, which began in 1854.

To His Wife   January 4, 1854

. . . Thomas Pass has called to see me. . . . I am delighted with the man. He is a carpenter by trade, a young handsome man. I made him tell me something of his history. He was so fond of Alec.[1] He is a reader of Carlyle, and all good books, with a most open noble human heart. You will be very pleased with him. He says it is not true that the workmen are such infidels, but they have no confidence in the ministers.

. . . I am waiting for some account of my darling Lily's stormy birthday. Not for many years has there been such a day here. . . . Surely, dearest, she comes up to all we could desire. I wonder whether you were allowed to give her the Clapton presents. I think it is not very delicate not to give them to you at once; but never mind. Some are very fond of power in the most paltry shapes. But perhaps there may have been some good reason for it. . . .

1. MacDonald's brother Alexander, who died in April 1853.

To His Father   Manchester
                                                        February 6, 1854

. . . I think if you saw everything in us you would not judge, even if you should think us mistaken, that we had acted presumptuously. . . . All I meant to say was, that though you have good and just cause to be anxious about our proceedings, I think that you would be relieved, if you could see simply how we thought and acted. And all that has happened since has been of a kind to make us never think of regretting the step we took in coming here to lodgings. . . . Pray to God to make me more humble and wise and earnest, and not self-seeking. Would you be so kind as to send us some meal now?

To Miss Ker[1]   [1854]

My dear kind friend,

I take this to finish it for my wife, for she has other writing to do before posttime tonight. We do not know what your arrangements about Alderly are, but we seem to know you so truly, that you will not think we are careless of your great kindness because we have yielded to the pressing entreaties of our friends here, to remain another week. But indeed we refused for some time lest it should seem that we undervalued the place of refuge you had given us. We hope to go to Alderly, if still quite convenient to you, on Monday or Tuesday. I will write to Miss Hammersley and let her know.

Might I trouble you to send me Mrs. Scott's address, as I am not sure that I have it correctly.

With earnest memories of
Mr Scott,
I am,
My dear Miss Ker,
Yours most truly,
GEORGE MACDONALD

1. Miss Ker, sister of Mrs. A. J. Scott, had offered the MacDonalds a farmhouse at Alderly for MacDonald's convalescence.

To Mrs. A. J. Scott[1]   Liverpool,
                                                        February 23, 1854

My dear Mrs. Scott,

I am ashamed of not having answered your welcome note before now, but you who are on a visit yourself will be more liberal in making excuse for me than I can be for myself. It was very kind of you to think of us when surrounded with so many old friends to occupy your thoughts and heart. But the Heart is like Him that made it, and every new love brings its own room and thoughts along with it, from Him that gives it. Now if you were a benefactress of the common kind, our prolonged stay here would be cause of uneasiness to us, lest such a *common* mind should attribute it to want of appreciation of her kindness, and think we undervalued the truly large gift of so many days in a free house and a free lovely country in Spring time. But as you are one of the glad beautiful thoughts that move through our hearts, and never pass through them without giving pleasure and strength, we ought not to fear, but leave our defence to yourself. We are still with our friend Miss Rawlins, whose health, we have the pleasure to believe, is better for our being with her. She is most sweet and kind — indeed most munificent, as we shall be able to tell you when we meet again. I wrote to dear Miss Ker, and then fixed on Tuesday or

Wednesday last for going to Alderly, but being again prevailed on to stay, I think it will be Tuesday next before we go there. I have not yet called on Mr. Ker, but I hope to do so before I leave. I trust you enjoy your visit, and get stronger and clearer by means of the revival of its joys. My wife sends her warm love to you.

Believe me,
my dear Mrs. Scott,
Most affectionately yours

GEORGE MACDONALD

1. MacDonald met Alexander John Scott (1768-1866) at Manchester, where he was the first Principal of Owens College.

To His Father

Alderly Cross, Alderly,
Cheshire,
March 17, 1854.

If you could have a panoramic vision of our changes of abode for the last six months, you would see that the last two residences, although both by far the most comfortable we have occupied, are very interestingly contrasted. We have left the town-residence of a rich manufacturer, with a carriage at our command almost, and are now since yesterday morning, resident in a large, low, stone-floored, four-doored room in a farm house in the rich dairy country of Cheshire. We have this large room, called the house-place, and two large bedrooms over it. The room is not much more than seven feet in height with two large beams crossing the ceiling; and the old bookshelves and cupboards are fitted with excellent books in English, German and Italian. Over the fire is the only specimen of the kitchen crane I have seen since I left Scotland — only more complicated and perhaps more convenient than those at home. The country round is very beautiful. . . .

Do not give yourselves any annoyance about accommodating us, else we shall hesitate about going. . . . I assure you my wife is a better one to do without than I am; and I think I am very fair. . . . But I know well what real comforts there are in my [old] home. . . . One thing[,] however, we must have — that is, a promise that you and mother will not leave your room. And for fare, Lou is more Scotch than I am, and devours pottage [porridge] and cakes like any native — so does Lily. So you see we are not dainty. . . .

My book, *Within and Without,* is in the hands of an Edinburgh publisher,[1] and I think he will publish it. He is strongly urged to do so by a sister of Sydney Smith into whose hands he put it for her opinion. . . .

1. MacDonald had difficulty getting his first major work of poetry published. Freeman and Macmillan both turned it down, but it was finally accepted by G. Longmans and published in May of 1855.

To Miss Ker   Alderly Cross
                                                        March 20th, 1854

[written by Louisa MacDonald]

My dear Miss Ker,

I feel almost that I ought to condemn myself as ungrateful when I think how many days we have been enjoying your kindness & I have not written to tell you how very comfortable & happy we are. My husband and I were agreeing that this is decidedly the most romantic piece of our married life. We are *so* enjoying ourselves, everything is just to our mind. We use your things with great delight and respect I should say most truly had not my little naughty baby today committed a misdemeanor, which has troubled both her Papa and me very much, for I feel convinced that it will be a sorrow to you, it is the breakage of a tumbler the shape of which I am sure speaks it is an *old* favorite. Do you know which I mean[?] . . . I cannot tell you how grieved I am.

The day we came was most sunny and the air so mild and lovely. I am sure it was the very best thing that could have come to my husband. He does so enjoy the country, the quiet and these delightful old rooms. The last two days have been very cold & he has not been out so much as he suffers in his chest.

[written by George MacDonald]

I have sent my wife to put on her bonnet, as I want her to go out
with us — for we have visitors today. So I will finish this note. You have
given us a great gift[,] dear Miss Ker, in sending us to this lovely place
and interesting dwelling. I am happier for it, and expect to be much better
when the weather becomes warmer. We intend going to Scotland for a
little while, as I am not allowed to preach for some time. But I dare say
Mrs MacDonald has told you all this. Please remember us with much love
and respect to Mrs Scott & believe us my dear Miss Ker your grateful
friends

George and Louisa
MacDonald

To His Father   [June 1854]
3 Camp Terrace
Lower Broughton

. . . My best thanks for your letters and for the cask of provisions. . . .
Give our love to dear Mother and thanks for the beef, which if it be only
nearly as good as the last she sent us, we shall excessively devour. It is very
kind of her to send it.

You send us good news, too, of John.[1] I wish he were near us now.
Alec and he would be such a comfort to us. Charles is a true friend —
but how strong we should be if we were all together! But we are all together
in God; and that is enough. . . .

You seem amused and somewhat indignant at my wearing my beard.
Don't fancy it a foot long though, in place of an inch; and believe that I
feel nearer to nature by doing so. Having been an advocate for it from my
boyhood, I hope ere I die, when my hair is as grey or white as this paper,
and when no one for whose opinion I care a rush will dare to call me
affected, to wear it all just as God meant it to be, and as men wore it
before some fops began to imitate women. . . .

1. Greville MacDonald notes that "they were all anxious about my Uncle John. He
was still in Russia, and on account of the war would have considerable difficulty in

returning" (*George MacDonald and His Wife*, p. 212). John was restless and traveled a good deal in an effort to discover what he really wanted to do. He had gone to Moscow for adventure.

To His Father   3 Camp Terrace
                                                                 June 26, 1854

. . . Louisa and I send our best thanks for your very kind gift. Indeed it goes into my heart to think you should be sending us this when I fear you are ill able to do without it. It is a precious gift to me, as coming from you especially, whom, but that I think God has chosen me for other work, I ought to be helping now. The only reward I wish you to have for it, is to know certainly at some time that in thus helping your son and his family, you have been helping one whom the Father has been teaching through suffering to help the rest of his children.

Meantime I was never so happy all my life. . . . Next Sunday evening I begin the realization of a long cherished wish — to have a place of my own to preach in where I should be unshackled in my teaching. This I now possess. May God be with me. No one can turn me out of this. It will be taken and the agreement signed in my name. If anyone does not like what I say, he can go away and welcome; but not all can turn away. I call them together — not they me. A few friends contribute the rent of the place, and a box will be at the door for contributions of free will for me. We will have no odious ungodly seat-rents and distinctions between poor and rich. But you know comparatively little of this in your place. I shall have new & deeper spiritual dangers. . . .

To His Father   3 Camp Terrace
                                                                 July 19, 1854

Thank you for your kind letter containing the good news about John's safety. I suppose he could not now leave Russia if he would except by stealth. . . . I have preached three Sundays now, and am quite satisfied as far as I have gone. I want no hasty success. I want to do God's work and be God's servant. Who ever did this fully without more or less failing? — according to the world's idea of failure and success. The world's judgments are simply those of Peter when he opposed Jesus, and said "This be far from thee, Lord."[1] No man ever failed, according to this judgment, as Jesus himself failed.

My principal temptation to desire success is that you should one day have the pleasure of seeing your son honored before you die. In a small (and I may without ostentation, and quietly to you, say) select circle, you would find this the case already. Popularity I can hardly expect, for reasons which my friends could tell you better than I.

I am so pleased you like my writings [in *The Christian Spectator*]. Much of my taste for literature has come from you. It is not therefore wonderful that you should like my little sketches. You will find one in next month's, I believe — "The Broken Swords."[2]

I don't know if I told you I am making 9s. a week — that is by three lessons a week — during the College vacation. . . .

Now, could you not come and see us this summer or autumn? — for I do not see how I can go Northwards — for lack of money and time too. We could receive you very well now — for we are quite settled. We expect another little child in September. Do not let this make you uneasy about us. In the story about the schoolmaster you have just what I think about it. God cannot forget his children.

1. Matthew 16:22.

2. A fairytale published October 1854 in the *Monthly Christian Spectator*, reprinted in *Adela Cathcart* (1864). See *The Gifts of the Child Christ: Fairy Tales and Stories for the Childlike*, ed. Glenn Edward Sadler (Grand Rapids: William B. Eerdmans, 1973), vol. 2, pp. 153-74.

To His Father   Sunday Afternoon
                                                              September, 1854

My very Dear Father,

Thank you for your letter received this morning. I wrote yesterday to announce the arrival of my third daughter.[1] Louisa & she are doing very well indeed — could hardly be better. Perhaps more outward prosperity will come along with this one. I am far happier than I was before, notwithstanding internal adversities, and hope to surmount a portion of these goals.

I shall be very glad to have John's books, old schoolbooks or college books rather as well, for he had all mine & they would be useful to me now, especially as my library is much smaller than convenient for a would-be literary man. An old Latin Dictionary even would be an acquisition to some. . . . He did not say to me that he had left Goethe for me, but I believe he said so to Charles — at any rate, I know he would let me have it, as it would be very valuable to me, & I don't think anyone there can use it. There was a book he offered to lend me a sort of compendium of natural Science, which he had in a prize — very handsome book — that I should like to have. . . .

. . . I am quite pleased to hear the nature of the complaint made against the broken swords.[2] I am satisfied I am right, but it shows a real interest in my story to wish the hero prosperous in a world of sense — and from Dr. McColl[3] too. I am so pleased because it shows he, an officer, and a man of honor, is quite satisfied that he had wrought out his restoration to military society and honor. Not that I doubted his right to this from *my* point of view. My object was principally to show that the most external manifestations of manhood are dependent on a right condition of heart, at least, it was only after, and by means of the most painful self-denial in the case of the girl that the youth regained his moral & physical equilibrium.

I quite agree with you that there are far worse things than any amount of war and bloodshed; but I am not politician enough to be able to apply my principles to the settling of the question of this war. It seems base to help the Turks instead of the Poles or Hungarians — one of whom is worth 100000000 of the other. But I am ignorant in these things.

Mr. Scott thinks a great good from the war will be the uniting by Sympra, they the highest & lowest ranks in this country. . . .

1. Caroline Grace, born September 16, 1854.
2. MacDonald's short story of that title.
3. Dr. Duncan McColl, an uncle of MacDonald's stepmother, to whom he dedicated *The Portent* (1864).

To His Wife

. . . I was preaching last Sunday about forgiveness, and I felt that not to forgive was just to send one to the hell of our little universe. Not to be forgiven and taken in by any human heart is the worst mishap that can befall. May I be taught a lesson hard to learn. You do not need it so deeply as I do — you only break out in thunder and lightning! I have a cold smile deep in my heart like a moth-eaten hole, when I feel really wronged. . . .

[Feb. 5, 1855]

My poor child, what is to be done with you and all your sad household? I wish I were there to be nurse in general, and to you in particular, and Carrie[1] too when I might. . . .

Well, you will be glad to hear that at last I have found a publisher — the *great* house of Longmans.[2] But we *may* quarrel yet, so say nothing about it, except to Carrie, with my dear love, if she is able to hear it, and say she must get well and read her brother's first book. . . . Mr. Scott thinks me very fortunate. Carlyle's first teller for the *French Revolution* was that he should pay £20 or something and have none of the profits. He finally agreed as I have done or rather will do. . . .

1. Caroline Powell (1832-1876), Louisa's youngest sister, who was ill, thus making it necessary for Louisa to nurse her as well as the children.
2. The publishers who did finally publish *Within and Without* (May 1855).

To His Father

Manchester,
February 8, 1855

. . . I send back by this post to Messrs. Longmans of London the signed agreement between them and me for the publication of one of my poems. I have now got the right publishers and it is a very advantageous agreement for an unknown author. . . . Next week I commence two courses of lectures — one for ladies in the morning, the others for anybody in the evening — both at my house. I hope they will bring me in enough to leave a possibility of visiting you in the summer. I can hardly go another year without seeing you. . . .

Will you allow me to tell you one thing founded on the deepest conviction — that in Scotland especially, and indeed in all dissenting modes of teaching in England, a thousand times too much is said about faith. . . . I would never speak about faith, but speak about the Lord himself — not theologically, as to the why and wherefore of his death — but as he showed himself in his life on earth, full of grace, love, beauty, tenderness and truth. Then the needy heart cannot help hoping and trusting in him, and having faith, without ever thinking about faith. How a human heart with human feelings and necessities is ever to put confidence in the theological phantom which is commonly called Christ in our pulpits, I do not know. It is commonly a miserable representation of him who spent thirty-three years on our Earth, living himself into the hearts and souls of men, and thus manifesting God to them. Can anyone fear the wrath of God, who really believes that he is one with that only Savior? If your suffering friend[1] could but see in her fear how full of love God's heart is to her, by seeing his real nature expressed in the most tender-hearted helpful man that ever lived, while he would not yield one hair's breadth from the will of God, surely fear would go, and love would come.

I am pleased to hear the news about Margaret and Mr. Troup.[2] They will make a very suitable couple, I think. Maggy has always been a favorite of mine; and for Troup I have a real esteem as you know. . . .

I hope we shall have peace now — but who can tell? Any more word from John? . . .

1. Possibly a reference to MacDonald's half-sister, Bella, who at age fourteen was stricken with a lung disease. Louisa had hoped that Bella could attend the Ladies' College in Manchester, but that was impossible.

2. Margaret MacDonald, daughter of George MacDonald's cousin James, and Robert Troup, who were engaged to be married.

To a Poet[1]   Camp Terrance, Saturday Evening
                                                        March 31, 1855

My dear Sir,

    I should be sorry to meet you again before having acknowledged the honour you have done me in sending me your book, and having expressed the pleasure which the slight acquaintance I have already been able to make with it has afforded me. Indeed, my dear Sir, whatever form the expression of our thoughts may assume, we must mean the same thing at heart. It would be absurd, from the glances which I have cast on your pages, even if it would not be unbecoming and presumptuous on a full examination of them, to give an intellectual judgment upon them. But the heart judges rapidly; and I think possesses the right to speak its judgments. Allow me to say that I truly honour you for the spirit of truth and religion which you reveal in your book; and if you really are like the image of yourself which it has called up in the phantasm world within me, I hope I am capable of nothing less than loving you deeply. You love God — that is everything. Some of your verses have given me much delight, and I have little fear that a further reading will do other than increase that pleasure.

    Mr. Scott — Professor Scott I mean — called on us yesterday, after I received your kind present. I mentioned you to him; and he expressed himself with regret as to not having made your acquaintance, as he intended doing after knowing your book. His many engagements and poor health prevented him.

Believe me,
My dear Sir,

Most truly yours,

GEORGE MACDONALD

1. Possibly Henry Sutton, a minor poet, whose sister Julie Sutton translated MacDonald's *David Elginbrod* into German. See the letter to Sutton dated June 28, 1868, p. 163.

To His Father   Manchester,
                                                     June 3, 1855.

My very dear Father,

I spent last week mostly in London, else I should have written to you
before now, as indeed I ought to have done before leaving for London.
Thank you for letting me know about dear Bella. The weather is warmer
now — perhaps that may have had some good effect since you wrote, but
I fear there will be no permanent benefit. Do you fear a rapid decline?
Should she not get better, will she likely remain with you till the end of
the month? These are sad questions to put, but you know why I put them.
How does dear mother bear it? It must be a dreadful trial to her. Life
grows so sad sometimes — "but there is the one who makes the joy the
last in every song" and no trial is too sad which makes us look more to
the eternal love — the great sea on which all other loves are but the surface
waves. None of us will live very long here, and then we shall go into the
great unknown wondrous world, which so many of our dear friends know
already, and where they are quietly awaiting our arrival.

Is Bella able to be removed to the seaside — or rather I suppose the
hills would be the place for her.

I cannot say much about my book yet for not having been reviewed,
the sale I suspect is as yet but small. However privately it gives me as much
satisfaction as I should be justified in expecting — Charles has just been
in and tells me no better news of Bella. Of course if she continues on, we
should not think of visiting you this summer. I should come alone, and
you and mother would perhaps come and see us soon.

I am tired and have to write another note, and preach this evening,
so I will not fill my sheet — but with much love to mother & yourself
and Bella, I remain,

                                        My very dear father,
                                        Your loving Son
                                        George

To His Wife   South St. Andrew's Street,
                                                      Edinburgh,
                                        Monday night 11 o'clock,
                                               [July 2nd, 1855]

Dearest own wife,

I am seated with a pint of Edinburgh ale before me at the old fashioned
mahogany table of the commercial room of a second rate but respectable
hotel. It has been a long day since I saw the last of your eyes at the station.
The rain cleared off when half our journey was over. The carriage had
stopped, and I lay down and slept and woke & the sun shone. The journey
is huddled all together in my brain. I hardly remember anything, but that
I wish you had seen a sweet-looking Scotch woman with whom I fell in
love — a country woman between 40 and 50 — oh, so sweet and simple!
George Smith[1] is with me still; and has been such a help to me. We came
here, having left our luggage at the station from which we start (in different
directions) in the morning, had tea & a steak, washed and went out about
half past eight and have been wandering about till 11 almost — chiefly
through the old town — which has *all* the attraction for me. We went on
to Calton Hill and from there into the old Canongate at the end of which
stands Holyrood House,[2] the outside of which I contemplated for some
time, especially the storm-windows, as they call them in Scotland —
projecting windows on the roof — thinking of the beautiful women, and
grand men who may have met by means of them at night. Was this naughty
of me? I could hardly help it. I don't care about Queen Mary though. She
was too naughty to love — and Holyrood House is hardly as interesting
to me as to most Scotchmen for *her* sake. But the Canongate and the
Cowgate! oh such houses! oh filth! and misery! and smells! and winding
common stairs! and *grated* unglazed windows on the landings! and squalid
figures looking down from two, three, four, five, six, seven stories! (Some
houses we counted ten stories at the back, and then are others of two, or
three, or four more!) Such curious houses they are, with crowded gables
to the streets, and every few paces a narrow court running through between
to more and more mysteries of stairs and lofts [—] crowded, abominable
dwellings. Some of the dark *closes* & entries look most infernal, and in the
dim light you could see something swarming, children or grown people
perhaps, almost falling away from the outlined definiteness of the human.
It was more like some of the older parts of Aberdeen than anything else
I had seen, but worse, much worse. Dearest, you must come here with
me, you would be so interested. It is like no other place. To think of it

after our orderly *clean* commonplace well-behaved Manchester, it is hardly
credible! And yet I saw nothing wrong though much that would be wrong
when I could not see it. You know Edinburgh is built very much up and
down hill; and so in some parts narrow closes, some so narrow that your
little arms could touch both sides, run from top to bottom of the hill
through these great, tall houses. Glancing down one of these I was arrested.
It was very narrow, and went down, as if to Erebus, and suggested bad
and dangerous places, down into the unseen and unknown depths. But
across the upper part was barred the liquid hues of the sunset, against
which stood the far off hill with some church tower or something of the
sort in relief against the infinite clearness. It is twelve — and I am going
to bed. Dearest, I hope you will not be frightened to-night. God, the Sky
God — the Green Earth God be with you; *our own God,* as David says. I
don't go till 10½ [10:30] to-morrow morning. Kisses to my brood. . . .

1. The publisher who published *Phantastes* in 1858.
2. Famous scenes on the Royal Mile in Edinburgh.

To His Wife   [July 4th, 1855]

I am seated alone, a few miles on my way to Huntly. I have passed
in the distance the stone crown which tops the square tower of my old
college, and the pagoda-looking towers of the old cathedral — and beyond
lies the sea. . . . When I get nearer home I shall want to be looking out,
and not to write. It would be pleasant to point out to you the old places
where your husband wandered and grew, and partly became the man you
love now, notwithstanding his faults — which I hope will always be growing less. . . .

I shall feel something like the Ancient Mariner. "Is this the kirk? Is
this the mill! Is this my own countree?"[1] A girls' school is crowding into
the carriages — not mine; and a country girl has flashed a look of you on
me, darling, and it makes my two weary eyes rather dim when I write
about it to you. We are passing through a bleak country now. Now we are
at the town of Inverury, 20 miles from home by the old road — how far
by this I don't know. The country folks stare rather at me, and the louts
laugh — my red cap[2] and hairy face afford them amusement. It is a

beautiful bright morning with a pale blue sky, and white clouds sleeping in light, and a triumphant God-like sun. . . . I seem to see better in this clear air and plentifulness of light than I have seen for a long time. I hardly wish to put my spectacles on. . . .

1. MacDonald misquotes Coleridge here. The lines from *The Rime of the Ancient Mariner* actually read:

> Is this the hill? is this the kirk?
> Is this mine own countree? (ll. 466-67)

2. Greville MacDonald describes it as "a tasselled red smoking-cap he travelled in" (*George MacDonald and His Wife*, p. 230).

To His Wife

The Farm, Huntly
[July 4th, 1855]

Dearest, I am sitting on grass with water bubbling on both sides of me. We have all met and I am loved to my heart's content. My father is not much changed, only stouter, and fuller in the face. My mother is very dear. . . . My sisters met me at the station, and now as I sit here they are ministering to me with wild roses and wild peppermint beloved, like two fairies. They are sweet dear things. Bella and I both cried. She is so thin, I should not have known her. Mother was very pleased about the cakes, but Bella has not tasted them yet. When I put your letter in my pocket my father quoted that line about not reading dear words with others near.[1] Uncle and Aunt and cousins are all so loving. . . .

1. "Julian (feebly), 'A letter from my Lilia! Bury it with me — I'll read it in my chamber, by and by; dear words should not be read with others nigh'" (*Within and Without*, Part IV, close of scene 25; cited in *George MacDonald and His Wife*, p. 230).

To His Wife   Huntly
                                                        July 5, 1855

. . . I have brought out a table and chair from the house and am sitting
under the overhanging boughs of a small tree which was just planted when
I visited home last. It is evening, and the birds are singing, and this
afternoon I have been walking through one of the fields with my father,
so full of the flowers of which I send you some; and down in the nursery
lies my poor thin sister,[1] very quiet — or rather sits, for she sits in bed
with her knees up and her head leaning upon them — so thin is she! . . .
She lies like a seed waiting for the Summer to which this Summer is but
a Winter. My father is so kind and liberal — more so even than I had
expected: he has no objection at all to my moustache, though he would
like it off to make me more acceptable; but he does not seem to care
much. . . . He enjoys Browning so. I have been reading several, amongst
them — *The Spanish Monk.* He seems so to enter into the dramatic, and
sees no reason why I should not read it to anybody.

Dear love, I can hardly bear your not being here. . . . It comes so often
when I see beautiful things. There is not much beauty here, but much to
my heart: and there would be to yours, and you would love my home,
with its rough stones nearly covered with ivy. Here comes Louie[2] hauling
a great mat from the lobby, which she has now put under my feet, lest
the grass should be damp.

How do you sleep, dearest? Have you been frightened at night? Why
have I not a letter from you? Here are some flowers we picked from the
field. The forget-me-nots are from Louie and Jeannie[3] to you, and the
roses are from the same for Lily, with love to you both. . . . I must write
a story here. I am looking for one somewhere in my brain. I will pray to
God to let you come if it pleases Him; and then perhaps you will. . . .
How you and my mother would love each other! Get as much of the table[4]
done as you can without hurting yourself — and then perhaps we can
somehow get you here.

I think Bella is a trifle better today, but she has not been up since I
came. She does not suffer much. It is touching the interest with which
she shows me little trifles of gifts and thinks so much of them, the darling!
— do send the handkerchief.

1. MacDonald's half-sister Bella, who was very ill.
2. MacDonald's half-sister Louise.

3. MacDonald's half-sister Jane.
4. A table Louisa was painting for her brother, Alexander Powell. See p. 96 n.3 below.

To His Wife Friday afternoon, Huntly,
[July 8th, 1855]

I wish you were here. My father and mother are so kind. . . . My beard is safe, I think! I talk Scotch to all the people, and one old schoolfellow tells me that will get me over the effect of my beard and moustache! . . . O, I want you so much. It is so often on my lips, dear wife. . . . What money have you? I am going to write something for *The Spectator,* and ask him to advance something on it. Charles owes you about 25s. Shall I write to him to take it to you? O that fine old man, my father! He *is* the man to tell anything to. So open and wise and humble and kind — God bless him! My father will be 63 on the 3rd of Dec. I asked him to-day. It has been so hot to-day, and Bella has been sitting out in the shade, but there is very little hope of her. She is very patient, the dear child. O how you would luxuriate in the sun! I am sitting now with a jug of milk by me, drinking away. . . .

Saturday night.

"Thou mightest have left us in darkness, but that would have been unworthy of God." This is a sentence in my father's prayer this evening, which will just be a little window into his thoughts. . . . Could you go to Cornish's opposite the infirmary and get a fairy tale book of Grimm's — 3s. 6d. I think. It is in red boards with woodcuts — I think it would amuse Bella. My uncle offered me a guinea for my moustache tonight, seriously though funnily. If he knew how bitterly hurt his own son was at his compelling him to shave, he would not have risked it. If fathers knew how liberality makes their sons love them, they would exercise it oftener. But my noble old father told me that for his part I might let it grow till I stuffed it in my trousers!

To His Wife   Huntly
                                                                July 10 [1855]

My days pass so quietly — I hardly go anywhere but saunter about the house with Shakespeare in my hand or pocket. If you had been here after I wrote to you last night, you might have seen me in less than an hour on the far horizon — the top of a hill [Clashmach] nearly 1,000 feet high 2½ miles off. You would have seen my white mare and myself clear against the sky. . . . She is a dear old mare. I love her, and cannot believe that she returns to the elements when she dies. She will perhaps be our mare in a new world — though this thought is too covetous to enter the new heavens and the new earth perhaps. However, if only she lives I don't care so much about having her.[1]

                                                                       July 10

Dearest, my mother has got such a nice servant that she longs for us to have to take care of the children. She was three years with her and she was so kind to them and good-tempered, and cares for her master's interest — a good-principled girl — and she would come with me.

We have had a letter from John to-day from Moscow, but by this time he is at Leipzig, where he expects to find a situation, and if he fails he will sail with a friend for America. There is no word of his coming home. . . .

I have been in my old room for the first time now, this minute — and have seen dear Alec's hat which my sisters take care of. You would like my little sisters. Louie sends her love to you and Lily and all of them.

. . . I hope poor baby is better by this time, and that you have been sleeping better. I wish I could get you here. Perhaps still. I will stay over the wedding,[2] which is to be in a fortnight — perhaps I will not stay longer except you come. . . . You are a dear, good, sweet wife, soul and body. Now I must stop. I have just been out to drive away a cat — for they kill the little birds. . . .

                                                                     [Huntly]
                                                                11 July, 1855

. . . I had such a nice ride last night, and met a countryman who had heard me preach (and who had been at school with me, I am since reminded). His face was radiant through a profusion of dirt caused by a hot day's work in the peat moss. He went back with me and accompanied me through a great part of my ride, talked about the different birds and flowers, and showed me a nest of the rose-linnet. . . . Do put things in train so that you could come as you say for the last week of my stay, if I can manage it. I have not quite lost hope yet, but it is very indefinite.

Thank you, my wife, for being so kind to my sister. My little sisters have come in. The youngest has a half-grown yellow-hammer perched on her shoulder, which she found a fortnight ago, and which is now very tame. It is now biting her tongue and now being fed with meal and water. I eat cakes made with cream every day. I have not tasted water since I came, but milk and bitter beer — not so strong as ours.

O dearest, I must have you here for a week, but, but — I don't know. You would be very pleased with my cousin Margaret who is going to be married. She is so sweet and loving and quiet. . . .

1. Greville MacDonald notes that this mare "must have been a great age when she died. Her hide was dressed, dyed green and sent to my father. To myself was later deputed the honor of covering with it the study-sofa, upon which her old lover would spend an hour or more every day, resting or sleeping" (*George MacDonald and His Wife*, p. 235).

2. The wedding of Margaret MacDonald, daughter of George MacDonald's cousin James, and Robert Troup.

To His Wife   Huntly,
                                                                                   July 13, 1855

. . . I have just had your letter and the book. . . . How much you have been doing and how tired you must be! You will have some rest, will you not now, in Liverpool? . . . I shall not stay very long after the wedding, except I find I can propose your coming once more. . . .

New true friends are better than old false ones, but it needs time to test them. Only I think the friendship of the Scotch has more foundation than much of the other countries. . . . I don't speak of individuals, you know. How could I, with your great big heart, which is big enough for me to lie down in and go to sleep, so warm and safe. . . .

To His Wife   [Huntly, July 14, 1855]

. . . Surely our hard time will wear over by degrees. It will, if it please God: that is, if we are ready to stand the harder trial of comfort — not to say prosperity. I wish I could get a situation in Somerset House that would leave me time. I would gladly go to London, and write and preach. Would you not like it? To leave Mr. Scott would be the chief difficulty to me. I shall feel it rather painful to leave my father and mother again, but it will be with the hope of seeing them again with you next year. I am glad you have enjoyed your papa's visit. Never mind, that he makes more of Flora. I know something of what my wife is worth. You have a harder trial than the others, dear, both from your husband being what he is, and poor besides — but perhaps that may be made up to you some day. . . . May the wonderful Father draw out the end as He pleases. Oh, God is so true and good and strong and beautiful! The God of mountain lands, and snowdrops, of woman's beauty and man's strength — the God and Father of our Lord Jesus Christ. I wish you saw the sky away to the North. It is so lovely — orange on the horizon, fading up through yellow and pale green into blue. This is at 11 o'clock at night. There is a slight frost. . . .

To His Wife   Huntly,
                                                   [July 15, 1855]

How careful my dear father is of everyone. I have just heard him calling in at the kitchen window to the servant to go and open the children's window, for it had been shut for the rain (which poured so richly this morning) and it would be very hot. He shuts my windows himself lest I should hurt myself. . . .

. . . I think there is scarcely one other manly, straightforward man to equal my father. But he takes very little hand in outside things. I have more and more cause to rejoice that I am not connected with any so-called church under the sun. . . .

To His Wife   Huntly,
                                                            [July 17, 1855]

. . . The servant Elsie Gordon is engaged for £7, and she will be ready
in a fortnight. My mother says she will do anything she is wished to do.
She can wash well and make the children's clothes, do a room very well,
cook plain Scotch dishes, bake cakes, etc., gets up very well in the morning,
is exceedingly good-tempered and very kind to the children. . . .

. . . The chief difficulty in getting you here is the money. I shall have
to get some from my father to bring me back, for I have just 2s. 6d., and
I should hardly have the face to propose your coming except we could pay
for that. But if Mr. Troup asks me to preach in his absence, then perhaps
I could manage it. Perhaps I may be able for a story in a day or two. Once
begun I could soon finish it. . . . Cannot you send me an idea to work
into a tale? . . .

To His Wife   [Huntly,
                                                            July 17, 1855]

. . . Do not think, dearest wife, that it is for your fault that you are
not permitted to come. Perhaps it is only to make me love you more by
being away from you, for you know what I think about that. . . . But it
will not do in the present state of our pockets. . . . My father is so often
talking about the book and me. He at least receives his son with honor. I
am afraid I have troubled him very much to-night by telling him how
ill-off we are. . . .

                                                                [Huntly,
                                                            July 20, 1855]

I have been out since twelve o'clock, have had 18 miles on horseback,
and some delightful feelings floating into me from the face of the blue
hills, and the profusion of wild roses on some parts of the road. The heather
is just beginning to break out in purple on the hillsides. Another week of
warm sunshine will empurple some from base to summit. How much
more I understand nature than I did! . . .

Louisa MacDonald to Her Husband

[Liverpool,]
Friday, July 20 [1855]

. . . I have been out a little with Papa. I do not think he will say anything about our pockets. Everything is too bright and glowing and rich and plentiful here to think of such words as "no money" or *getting on*. Indeed Manchester is altogether too disagreeable a place to mention. He is very kind to me, quite tender and sweet, and most in speaking about you and very loving to the children. So I must not mind if he shrinks from talking about our circumstances — as children do from the uncongenial subject of death. I have been in with Baby and Lily to Helen,[1] and your Lily was so naughty. I intend to go back to Manchester next Wednesday or Thursday. . . . I am as pleased as you can be at the prospect of Elsie. What a pretty name! Do not take your father's money, dear. I have 12 s., which must take me home. And then we must go upon tick[2] till I get the table done.[3] You good husband to write so much to me. . . .

1. The baby was Caroline Grace; Lily was the MacDonalds' oldest daughter, Lilia. They were visiting Helen MacKay Powell.
2. Credit.
3. Greville MacDonald recounts the history of this table, which his mother had painted: "As a matter of fact, though duly sent to my uncle, Alexander Powell, it was first unpacked by myself just fifty years later. [It] was a wonderful work of ingenuity and beauty. But on exposure the paint crumbled off in a very few days. Only the bare slate remains, and it serves now for a garden table" (*George MacDonald and His Wife*, p. 231).

To His Wife

[July 25, 1855, the day after the marriage of Robert Troup and Margaret MacDonald.]

. . . I *cannot* bear to force my departure. They are very sad sometimes, and I am sure I am a comfort to them. . . . That dear child Bella has been saving up her money for some time, as she always does to give presents — she had nearly a pound — and to-day she gave me two sets of flannels for the winter, which I should think took all she had. Her little body will be cold before I wear them. I *am* going to preach next Sunday evening. I cannot *write* more just now. . . .

[Huntly, July 27, 1855],
Sunday afternoon

. . . I have a little cold, but I don't think it will interfere much with my preaching this evening. I am regarded with some jealousy here I think, but I don't care much for that, as my nearest friends have faith in me. I think my father and mother will both go to-night, though it pours with rain. . . . They are very sad about Bella. My father says that she suffers very much after they have gone to bed, and all is still and dark; and that seemed to distress him so much. It will be our turn sometime most likely to go through this. I will be more gentle with Lily and Mary, I think, when I return. We must try all we can for their sakes as well as our own to be good, for it will never do to *look* better than we are. My love to my bairnies. And my love to their dear . . . mother from her own Husband.

To His Wife   [Huntly, July 28, 1855]
6 o'clock Monday morning

I preached yesterday about the little child. After, one old woman said she thought I went rather too far on that side of God's character. Another said to my father: "When I saw him wi' the moustaches I thought he looked grey and rough-like; but, or he had been speakin' lang, I just thought it was like Christ himsel' speakin' to me."

Since writing the above my Uncle has called me aside and given me from Mr. Troup £1 1s. to get something in remembrance of the marriage, and £1 1s. besides from himself in acknowledgement of last night's sermon. My father has some money ready to send us home. Thank you . . . for the *Scotsman*. It is very gratifying. It is thought a good deal of here, but because of its latitudinarian opinions, has ceased to be read in this neighborhood. I hear some unfavourable notice had reached Huntly before, in what paper I don't know, and probably made the first impression. . . .

Thank you . . . for your letter to-day, such a nice long one. Thank you for your precious love. . . . I never wanted you like this before. But I have been planning how and where to take you for a night — now and then perhaps — after I return, before the work begins again. It will be delightful to be able to leave the children [with Elsie] without fear. My father will send me home, though it is very little he can do. I have just 2s. 6d. I spend nothing here. I had 4s. when I arrived and I have spent 1s. for stamps, which I need not do except I liked. But one doesn't like to be going to the office for stamps always. . . .

My father has just come in (I am writing in my bedroom) and offered me £3 to send to you. I have not taken it yet, for I daresay you will not want any before you can answer this and tell me how much you need till I see you again. . . .

If I am asked to preach again next Sunday I will preach about the young man who was told to leave all he had — for the people are getting much more up in the way of living than when I left, and will need to be reminded; not that there is any harm in the thing itself. I think you could follow Him up and down, dear sweet-eyed wife.

To His Wife   [Huntly,
                                                August 6, 1855]

. . . Since dinner I have had a saunter up towards the hilly regions, and have looked down on all the Huntly valley beneath me. What a multitude of harebells there are this season! I brought home two or three white ones this afternoon to Bella. I never saw any before. But poor Bella had a bad night again, and seems to me looking worse than I have seen her before. . . . I think I shall leave in the beginning of next week — and I hope to be a better husband to you and father to my children. . . . I shall be altogether yours some day. You know what I mean. I am not all Christ's yet.

                                                Monday night.

Just a few words, dearest, for the last time from here. I have been with my father to see Alec's grave, five miles away. He lies beside my mother and my two brothers. I thought — oh, there is room for me between him and the wall. But I must be where you are, my own — only I should like if we could both be in that quiet country churchyard. My father was a good deal overcome, for it is not only the dead but the dying he has to think of. Mrs. Wilson gave me £4 to-day "for the children." My father gave me £4 too to bring us [himself and Elsie] home. I shall not want quite £3 and have £2 besides; so I shall come home with more by far than I could have made by staying. My father is so dear and kind. My mother is working away ironing my shirts now. You will love her . . . next year, I hope.[1] I think more of home, a great deal more, than ever I did. Thank you for your two letters received yesterday. I have been troubled about your talking so before those who cannot understand you as I can. Do not let your horns out of your shell, darling, except to your own friends — for you have two or three yet, though you may not believe it! You are true except in trust. But . . . I know the darkness and trouble you are in, and you are safe with me.[2]

1. Louisa MacDonald very much wanted to meet her husband's parents, but it had not yet been possible to bring her to Huntly.
2. Louisa had apparently let her parents, the Powells, know of her difficult financial situation. Mr. Powell was not always very sympathetic toward her husband's career.

To His Father   [Edinburgh,
August, 1855][1]

. . . Give my love to them all — especially Bella. I fear I shall have no better news of her. But, dear father and mother, death is only the outward form of birth. Surely it is no terrible thing that she should go to Alec. And we can't be very long behind her. There is room for us all between Alec and the wall in the churchyard. I hope it will not hurt you more to write thus. Surely if we are sure of God, we are sure of everything: He never gave a good gift like a child to take it back again. . . .

1. Written during MacDonald's return to Manchester.

To His Father   [August 1855]

My very dear Father,

I have long meant to write you some notices of my book. . . . I will
send you the *Brighton Herald* and the *Morning Post*'s opinion — also a
letter most gratifying from Mr. Maurice.[1] . . . John is with us — very
tired.[2] He is waiting to see if he can get a situation . . . you will be glad
to hear that I have as much teaching already as I think will bring me in
£3 a week. We hope for an Owens College student to board with us —
maybe, more than one. My lectures will bring me something — altogether
we have good hopes for the winter. I am better, though I still cough. How
is dear little Bella? Give her my love.

I have heard several things about my book since I returned — the
principal of which is the interest Lady Byron, the widow of the poet, has
taken in it. It seems to have taken a powerful hold on her.

I hope you will be happy in John's visit soon. It seems a really painful
effort to him to write. . . .

1. F. D. Maurice, a friend of A. J. Scott, who had been expelled from King's College,
London, for the publication of his *Theological Essays*.
2. MacDonald's brother, John Hill MacDonald, who had recently returned from
Germany. See *George MacDonald and His Wife*, p. 249.

To His Father   [August 1855]

. . . My objection[1] is simply that I do not think one-third — perhaps
one-tenth [—] of it is prayer at all. If your experience leads you to *believe*
that there is more praise or *speaking* to God in these prayers than a dreary
recurrence of vain repetitions in the form and in the name of prayer, my
experience does not. There may be times when such assemblies are very
suitable; but my impression is that there would be perhaps more real prayer
if there were less public praying. But more knowledge *may* lead to a
modification of my opinion.

I am glad to tell you that I was unanimously invited last Sunday by
a company of 70 seat-holders to preach to them. I agreed to do so for a
year to see how it will do. I was never treated with so much respect. They

say: "Speak out; tell us what you think; no one will interfere with you; that desk is yours." And all that the chapel raises, which will not probably exceed £100 and may be less, will be mine. . . . Indeed they give me all the liberty I could wish; nor have I ever seen such promise of generous faith in a spiritual teacher before. . . . I mean to have a week-evening for religious help to my friends here, either at the Schoolroom or in this house. I am gradually becoming known in Manchester, but I have not much to do that brings in money. Only when one thing is taken away, another comes — from God I think and hope. . . .

1. Refers to MacDonald's father's previous letter in which he requests that MacDonald "define his objections to public prayer" (*George MacDonald and His Wife*, p. 250).

•

To His Father [August 1855]

. . . Mr. Scott called on Friday, and before he left, told Louisa that, not thinking either of us very worldly wise, he must enquire into our circumstances, etc., for though he was not rich himself he knew many who were, and who at a word from him, would be glad to render us assistance. He is indeed a true friend. Is it not a great thing to me to have the man whose intellect and wisdom I most respect in the world for my friend, he not being ashamed to acknowledge the relation? He said he heard of my book from many quarters while in London, and that it has got into the best literary circle. . . .

I think you would like to know this translation by young Cecil of the three German verses in *Within and Without*:

"When thy present voice I hear
In the leafy murmurs near,
When I feel Thee far and wide,
Father, who hath bliss beside?

"Now the loving sun outshines —
Me with Thee and all entwines;
To the flowers hastes the bee —
To Thy love my soul doth flee.

"Till Thy love to me be less,
Life is no more weariness;
So I see and hear but Thee —
That alone sufficeth me."[1]

1. Henry Cecil, who was a fellow-master with John MacDonald (George MacDonald's brother) at the Sheffield Academy, later became a close friend of George MacDonald's. Greville MacDonald notes that Cecil had "an unbounded admiration for my father's poetry" (*George MacDonald and His Wife*, p. 173).

To His Stepmother   [August 26, 1855]

My Dearest Mother,

. . . Bella has only gone nearer to One who loves her more dearly and tenderly than you do. Or if you even think that she has gone to Alec, who has been waiting for her, it seems no such dreadful thing. God will let him take care of her till you go. I feel that if I had been in the spirit world before she came, I should have taken her to my heart so warmly that my little sister would soon have felt at home in the new place. We must weep often in this world, but there are very different kinds of tears. Bella will be kept quite safe for you there, and you will never be separated from her in heart. Schiller says — "Death cannot be an evil because it is universal." God would not let it be the law of His Universe if it were what it looks to us. And dear Mother, who could wish an easier, quieter, simpler death than my dear sister's? I should like to wither away out of the world like the flowers that they may come again. . . .

To His Father   September 27, 1855

. . . I thank you for your anxiety about the so far success of my book. True love *must* be uneasy. I hope I know enough of my own failings and ignorance to keep me from becoming conceited, and perhaps I don't think the success so great as you do. Certainly there is always danger, and perhaps a usually modest man may at moments be over favorable in his judgments of himself. I think I have more consciousness of weakness than of strength. But our safety is in God's keeping, not in our own. May He take care of me, and do what He will with me.

It is a great pleasure both to Louisa and me to have John near us — we see him often. I go and see him and he comes and sees us. . . . He has very keen feelings, and if he came to see you now, he could not have borne the thought of leaving again; and he could have stayed but a very little while. He is subject to melancholy, but I hope I may be of some use to him. I love him very dearly. . . .

To His Father
Sunday evening,
December 30, 1855

My very dear Father,
. . . I am much, much better. . . . Louisa is wonderfully well now. . . . Phoebe, her sister, is to be married to a Liverpool gentleman [Joseph King, M.R.C.S.] on the 18th of February, when we shall all, I hope, be at Clapton. . . . After the wedding we talk of going to Devonshire for two or three months. Mr. Powell has expressed himself very ready to help us, and had already paid the last quarter's rent for us. We seemed likely to be better off than we had ever been before — and now I think, in some way or other, we are meant to be much better off yet. I think we shall be able to clear off all our debts — £25, I think — however, without troubling my father-in-law. . . .

The interesting fact I wanted to tell you about my poem [*Within and Without*] is this. I had doubted whether I had not offended against probability in making an Italian the subject of such emotions as I have represented in Julian.[1] I had therefore given him a German mother. But just before my illness, I made the acquaintance of an Italian nobleman, Count [Aurelio] Saffi, who having been one of the Triumvirs in Rome, along with Mazzini, is now a refugee in this country, supporting himself by giving lessons in Oxford. He is a literary man and was giving some lectures at the Royal Institution here, residing for the time at Mr. Scott's house. He was much struck with the book, he told me, considering it the best expression of the religious feelings of the age. This, though himself a Roman Catholic. Indeed we soon formed a warm friendship for each other.

He came to see me before he left, while I was yet unable to sit up in bed. Mr. Scott says to hear Saffi speak of anything mean or base would be almost a new sensation. He seems to speak from such a height above it.

1. This reflects an English prejudice against Italians. Note that Wilkie Collins makes an Italian the villain of *The Woman in White* (1860). MacDonald had more positive feelings for characters of German origin. He tried to balance the emotional character of Julian in his poem by giving him a German mother.

To Mrs. A. J. Scott   [1856]

My dear Mrs. Scott,

Accept my thanks for your kind attention in sending Saffi's note. Perhaps some day when I am less tired than usual, I may write and tell him myself how I am. I hope your cold will soon be done, and that you will be able to come and see me — selfish — is it not? I suffer a good deal from cough and difficulty in breathing, nor has the thaw made me feel better yet. But tomorrow, the lights of life may burn a little brighter perhaps.

My wife has suffered dreadfully from face-ache — We have been like an aged couple of eighty — or thereabouts, waited on by our oldest daughter. Louisa sends her dear love and thanks. I am reckoning of coming to you by and by. My love please to Miss Ker and Susie and Johnnie —[1]

I am
My dear Mrs. Scott
Yours very affectionately
GEORGE MACDONALD

I am tortured to work more.

1. Susie and Johnnie were the Scotts' children.

To His Father
Manchester,
2nd January, 1856

. . . On New Year's Day two gentlemen called on me, who along with a third — none of them much known to me — had made up a purse of £30 for me, which they offered in the most delicate and kind way. One of the three is an Independent, another a Churchman, and the third a Unitarian.

This morning's post brought me a bank-order for £5 from Miss Ross, as unexpected as welcome, and I have written to thank her for her great kindness.

Then this afternoon some of my Bolton people called on me, bringing me my quarter's salary in advance. They had paid me up to Christmas just before I was taken ill. This will leave something considerable over after paying all our present debts. . . .

To Miss Ross
Manchester,
January 2, 1856

. . . Please to receive my warm thanks. . . . And if we have not learned by this time "to cast all on Him who careth for us," I think we are getting to learn it. Indeed, I have so much hope along with a little faith, that I have not been troubled — scarcely at all. I can see more and more that nothing will do for anybody but an *absolute enthusiastic* confidence in God. . . . You once told me of some of your early experiences; and now that you have plenty, you have not forgotten your former needs. May God bless you for your kindness. . . .

To Mrs. A. J. Scott   3 Camp Terrace
                                                    Monday [Jan. 1856]

My dear Mrs. Scott,

Thank you for your kind note received this morning. I cannot now leave comfortably till our anxiety is over,[1] which I hope will be before very long. I should like much to be at the children's party, but I do not think I shall be free before then. I shall not fail to let you know as soon as I can come. Louisa is pretty well, but suffering a good deal — You will understand the pardon. I am keeping better, though my cold is a little worse.

I wanted much to tell you of the kindness we have experienced, and meant to *call* on you before now. But I have not been able from one thing and another to manage it. On the first & second of January we had £56 given to us. Mr. Scott made us very glad with his kindness the other day. We both love you both very much.

Louisa sends her love to you.

                                    I am
                                    My dear Mrs. Scott,
                                    Very affectionately yours,
                                    George MacDonald

    1. Referring to the impending birth of Greville MacDonald.

To Mrs. A. J. Scott   Monday
                                                    [January 21, 1856]

My dear Mrs. Scott,

Our boy has come at last.[1] A little before ten last night — Sunday (two have come on Saturday and two on Sunday) he arrived. I will come and tell you about it, if all is well on Wednesday, and stay if you can have me. He is a great child, for the rest you must judge for yourself. Louisa is doing very well. She is *very* brave.

                                    I am,
                                    My dear kind friend,
                                    Very affectionately yours,

                                    GEORGE MACDONALD

    1. Greville MacDonald (1856-1944).

To His Father   Monday evening,
                                                    January 21, 1856

My Dearest Father,

   I am too tired with writing notes to do more than tell you that I have
a son at last. Before ten last night he arrived. Louisa behaved so
courageously. He is a great boy — might be three months old, they say!
He has a baby's accomplishments of feeding and sleeping perfectly. . . .

To His Wife   [Cheetham Hill,]
                                                    January 24, 1856

Dearest, sweet Wife,

   I think I am a little better to-day. I need hardly tell you I enjoy myself.
They are all so kind. I was left quite alone, and spent the time meditating
in spite of stupidity — and in reading Hoffmann's *Golden Pot* again. It is
delightful. . . .[1] I never saw Mr. Scott so happy, so merry or so loving as
last night. He talked a great deal yesterday about Art, and I have some
new thoughts about it from him. . . . It was a divine day and I saw things
as I had not seen them before. May our Father teach us — for no one,
not even Mr. Scott, can teach us but Him. Indeed we have secrets of our
own with Him and no one else. Think of and to Him while you lie there.
Tell me about little Greville. Is his hoarseness gone? . . . My love to Annie[2]
please. To-morrow we will come.

   1. MacDonald's reading of E. T. A. Hoffmann's famous fairytale had a profound
influence on him, inspiring him later to write *Phantastes*.
   2. Louisa's sister Angela.

To His Father   Mr. Scott's House,
                                               February 18th, Monday.

We have been in great confusion and haste for some days getting our
house in order to be left for an indefinite time. Now it is abandoned to
the care of a man and his wife who are glad to live there rent free, and we
are with our friends, the Scotts. To-morrow we leave for London. Phoebe[1]
is to be married on Wednesday. We shall rest in London a while before
we proceed further. . . . Louisa is surprisingly well, and little Greville is a
great thriving boy. . . . It is only a month to-day since he was born, and
Louisa has done a good deal of work. . . . The same friends whom I
mentioned to you before sent me £20 (additional to the other £30) the
other day. Mr. Scott tells me a friend in Wales has sent me £20 through
him besides; and he says whenever I want money he can get it for me.
Mr. Powell has been very kind too, and promises to help us. . . .

1. Louisa's sister.

To Mrs. A. J. Scott   The Limes
                                                  Upper Clapton
                                                February 19, 1856

My dear dear friend,
I mean this only for a note of our safe and comfortable arrival. Baby
was most good and untroublesome. I seem no worse, and have been out
today. Louisa is not so well, but I hope it is only the reaction after the
excitement of seeing all her sisters, and the fatigue of the journey. She will
write to you after the wedding which takes place tomorrow. She sends her
love to you now, and to Aunt Grace[1] and Susie and Johnny. No words
could convey my message to Mr. Scott, so it must remain unsaid.
I will not attempt either to thank you, but I hope to be ever grateful
and your friend

                                          GEORGE MACDONALD

1. Louisa's sister Caroline, the namesake of MacDonald's daughter Caroline Grace
(1854-1884).

To His Father Upper Clapton
February 27th, 1856

We bore the journey here very well indeed, but after the wedding was over, we got very tired. I have not much strength, and Louisa too is far from strong. I have been to see Dr. Wilkinson,[1] who is a personal friend and a homeopath. He agrees with Dr. Harrison that there is no mischief in my lungs, and says that after this I may be better than ever — but that I must have entire rest for six months at least. We expect to go to Devonshire for a couple of months at least. After that perhaps we may think of coming to see if you will have us.[2]

We are in no anxiety for a few months at least. I am ashamed to have written that last sentence — as if we should feel safe only as long as we had means laid up in store! . . .

1. Greville MacDonald notes: "Garth Wilkinson, M.R.C.S., a homeopath, was the well-known Swedenborgian who first re-introduced William Blake's poetry to the world — often spoiled by his own emendations. He proved very kind and most useful, introducing my parents to many who became life-long friends; more particularly to Miss Anna Leigh-Smith" (*George MacDonald and His Wife*, p. 260).

2. Greville MacDonald notes that this hope was at last realized (*George MacDonald and His Wife*, p. 261).

To His Father [First week in March 1856]

. . . To-day I feel somewhat alive again, especially as a stiff breeze has been giving a rapid motion to the surface of the river, and the white sea birds have been darting about, in and out of the water. . . . Louisa will write soon when she gets [from her brush] a picture of the place to send you. . . . We have a strong, cold east wind, so that at Dartmouth on the opposite side they are glad to shut their shop shutters — while we under the eastward hill scarcely feel it. . . . My spirits are not very bad now. Nor can I pity myself very much when they are, for I have hope that no dejection can touch. At the same time I shall never be in good spirits till I can employ myself in something that seems worth doing. I cannot even write verses for any length of time — at least I have done nothing to speak of in that way for a long time, but I hope soon to be able again though the doctors do forbid it. . . .

To Henry Sutton   Waters-Meet
                                              Lynmouth, North Devon, June 5, 1856

My dear Sutton,

I am sorry and ashamed that I have been so long in fulfilling my promise of writing to you.[1] But I was worse after reaching South Devon, as I daresay you have heard, and the little time in the day during which I was able for anything, I usually spent in work of some kind, which contributed somewhat to my peace of mind, though perhaps a promise fulfilled might have done more. We enjoyed our stay at Kingswear, opposite Dartmouth very much indeed, and the twelve weeks we were there (ending on Tuesday, when we came here) passed very rapidly. The enjoyment of the latter part of our visit was greatly increased by our changing our lodgings, which brought us into daily communication with the family of the clergyman of the place, a warm hearted, simple-minded man. Indeed we have left very kind loving friends there.

I cannot say anything very strong about my improvement. I am certainly better, but the prevalence of the east wind all the time of my stay in this quarter has doubtless retarded my recovery. Indeed I am not very sanguine about that, which is perhaps a good sign in the opinion of some people. This is one of the loveliest places I have ever seen. Most picturesque and (in the proper sense of the word, I think) romantic. I send you a picture of the goal of our first drive yesterday. We shall go some where this afternoon. I hope you & Mrs. Sutton & Rose are well — and not too much oppressed with the ordeal of Manchester. However as corn grows by very corruption of the soil, so our holy ideal will be perfected by much that is nauseous & oppressive in its immediate neighbourhood. I do not think you are so much of a Manchester man, as not to bear this abuse of it patiently. You know that I love many of the people of Manchester, but the place, except for their sakes[,] I do dislike. Is there any thing doing about Mrs. Moore's business? I hope she will have less cause for anxiety soon. We leave this place on our way to Scotland probably next week. My wife will likely go by Manchester when I hope she will have the pleasure

of seeing you. She joins me in love to you & Mrs. Sutton. Lily sends her
love to Rose. She was asking the other day if she would see her again.

I am,
My dear Sutton,

Affectionately, your friend,
GEORGE MACDONALD

1. See the letter dated March 31, 1855 (p. 85).

To A. J. Scott   [Kingswear, Lynmouth]
                                                                     Lynton
                                                              June 17, 1856

My dear Mr. Scott,

What I have been able to write, I need not say I have written joyfully.
I thank you again and again for asking me, and shall be most happy if it
is worth printing. But please show your faith in me by throwing it aside
if you do not like it — you know I am not well and consequently stupid.
But if the Scotch precentor's recommendation be of any use to Jenny Lind,
it is a modesty self-defensive even to fierceness to refuse it. — I am sorry
that from a change from Lynmouth to Lynton, your letter was delayed a
post; and as our post arrives late, & leaves early I was not able to finish
the inclosed in time for yesterday's post. I hope it is in time to be of use,
if otherwise fitted for rendering any service. Surely you will obtain the
chair; if not, I can only say as you will say yourself — His will be done.

We are just leaving for Bristol on our way to London, where our
address will be, The Limes, Upper Clapton.

I am better, but not *very* sanguine.

A revised manuscript of my poems[1] is in the hands of Bogue who
expressed himself to a mutual friend as ready to peruse it. I do not expect
much from the introduction. But I will let you know the result.

I would rather not be styled Rev. But if you have the slightest preference for it in relation to the business in hand, do not hesitate a moment
to use the title.

My wife is too busy packing to send more than her thanks to Mrs.

Scott for her most kind note, and she joins me in love to you both and all your family.

> I am,
> My dear Mr. Scott,
> Most gratefully &
> affectionately Yours,

> GEORGE MACDONALD

1. His *Poems,* published in 1857.

To Mrs. A. J. Scott   The Farm, Huntly N.B.
                                               July 16, 1856

My very dear Mrs. Scott,

It *was* kind of you to send me your portrait — so good of you. I do not know anything else you could have done so kind. It gave me great delight as you would have seen had you been in a clairvoyant state when Louisa gave it to me. My best thanks for it, and for your care of my wife and family. They arrived here in safety but *very* tired on Friday morning, having travelled incessantly for twenty-two hours. The children are nearly recovered from their fatigue, but Louisa is still suffering somewhat from her exertions in Manchester.

I am so very happy that Mr. Scott was pleased with my letter. I had never done anything of the kind before, and the fear of the *untried* was upon me; for though in one respect it was easy, one could not help thinking sometimes of how it would look to others' eyes and being doubtful of the impression it would make. Now, by this time, I hope Mr. Scott is Professor of Logic and Metaphysics in Edinburgh College. But perhaps it was not decided yesterday. If it is postponed for any length of time, would you please let me know as soon as you can, if you should write nothing more. I think Mr. Scott will have his heart's desire, because he commits his way to the Lord. But you must not be too much disappointed if he should not get it, for you know nothing can go wrong, or be really a misfortune.

I thank Mr. Scott through you for sending me the copies of his testimonials. I shall, I hope, write to him soon, when I know that his anxiety is over, and the matter settled.

I have felt better since I came here, but the weather has been so unfavourable that I have not advanced so rapidly as I might have hoped. I cough very little, and can walk up hill without thinking of my chest. If I get through the winter comfortably, I can hope I shall be in some measure well again.

I thank you too for the letter in which you acted as amanuensis of my Lily. I wondered at your finding time for it. Will you give my love to Susie and Johnnie[1] and hearty thanks for their kindness to my daughter. Louisa has told me how sweet Susie was with her, and how manly and gentlemanly Johnnie was.

I do hope to see you in September sometime, if you are still in Manchester, but we have not yet fixed our plans for the winter. I am very glad Mr. Scott does not approve of Australia. The idea was most unpleasant to me. I should not mind a voyage there and back, after being scared with the idea of living there.

Louisa joins me in most warm love to you. She has found it difficult to write to you yet, and if she should yet delay perhaps you will allow this note to be a pledge for her gratitude and love to you.

I think you will not let us be long without hearing what the result of the election is. Louisa tells me you are looking so much better than when we saw you last. I am very glad to hear it.

You must keep young outside as long as you can, for you can never be but young inside.

I am, my dear Mrs. Scott,
Very affectionately yours,

GEORGE MACDONALD

1. The Scotts' children.

To His Father   Manchester, Aug. 29, 1856

My very dear Father,

I have again delayed writing to you for much too long a time, till it has made me too uneasy to let me delay longer. But I have several letters to write today, and being besides not very well, though nothing particular is the matter, this will be but a short one. I am glad to hear of John, and I enclose his letter which I had from Charles. Will you favour his going to Australia? I have sometimes thought of going there myself — but the thought is checked by the great doubt whether my wife would outlive the voyage, so grievously is she affected with sea-sickness. I think all my work is here. I have to do something for the young people of this country I think. I know I have had influence for good, and I hope to have more yet. But it will take a long time before this influence will be extensive if it ever becomes so. And I shall have much opposition and much abuse — for which I care little. What will it matter when all the generation has passed away into the region where men are judged by God's knowledge and not by men's fancies.

Lily is now in London. She went with her youngest aunt, Caroline, from Liverpool yesterday. With her and another of her aunts there — Angela — I feel her quite safe. The latter, however, is coming here on Saturday to await Louisa's confinement.

I am about to advertise my classes for ladies for the approaching winter, which I hope will add somewhat to our income. In time I hardly doubt I shall have a congregation which will support me, but I do not think about it much in that light. If I could live otherwise, I should not care for anything from that quarter.

By a mistake of the Printer my tale was not in the magazine last month, but you will find it this time. It is of a different sort from my previous ones, but I hardly know whether to like it or not myself.

Louisa sends her love to you and Mother. And so do I. And I shall see you sometime. Nothing·but impossibility could keep me away from you so long. Is the railway opened from Aberdeen yet?

> I am,
> my dearest Father,
> your loving son,
>
> George

To Mrs. A. J. Scott Marseilles
November 20th, 1856

[written by Louisa MacDonald:]

My very dear Mrs. Scott,

I am sure you will be glad to hear that we have at last arrived at our last stage before reaching Algiers.[1] We are looking towards that place as a promised land of rest and warmth. We have had a tolerably prosperous journey so far but at Palmer we were obliged to wait a week for George to recover from a cold which he managed to take somewhere and somehow between Paris and that place. By staying in doors for two or three days and getting a thorough rest he was soon much better and excepting a slight cough or remains of one he is as well as usual again. We were misled about the leaving of the Paquebots? from this plan and by it (a mistake in Bradshaw) we are condemned to stay here four days longer than we intended, which does not please us as we cannot manage long enough walks to get very far from the noisy bustle that is all round our hotel and driving is both wearisome and expensive. Yesterday however we had a very delightful drive along the coast of this very blue Mediterranean. The rocks and hills the sky and the sea delighted us much. It is a very remarkable coast, and to us everything about it has the charm of novelty. The sun was very hot for a November sun, and we looked across the sea with longing hopes that on the opposite shore so many miles further south we should find warmer winds with as hot a sun. I think my husband longs as much for rest as he does for warmth, and travelling fatigues him a good deal and he hates this hotel life so much. But still we get on better than I expected, knowing how very much he dislikes travelling even in England. I am happy to say he has been well enough to enjoy something of each place we have stopped at. Avignon was the place that most interested us. It was wonderful and strange and beautiful and so old! But I must get George to write to you a little bit to make this worth sending you, one thing more I must tell you — how kind your young friend "Laura" was to us at Paris. She spent a whole day in showing us what she could in the short time we had there, and she and Madame ? very kindly came to see us in the evening and stayed two hours. Her visit did us both good. They promised us further help if we stop there on our way back. I am still a little anxious about my dear father. His was a terrible accident. It has shaken him so much and injured one lung so as to make us very anxious for every letter and owing to some mistake on our part or theirs, we have not heard from my sisters for nearly a fortnight. I have written too much dear Mrs. Scott, believe us we often think of you and ever love you and my reverence and love for Mr. Scott always prevent my writing about him or asking how he is. He is too great to send messages to.

[written by George MacDonald:]

My wife has left me a page to fill up to you, my dear friend, (for that indeed I know you are). Yet I daresay she has told you all about our present condition. I am longing to get to the other side, and to sit down in a room that will be ours for more than a few days; especially that I may try to write again, for I seem to have a great deal to write, though I fear and hope it will be much better than the writer. May we hope for a letter from you soon after our arrival in the home you have got ready for us in Algiers? We expect to be there about noon on Monday. Indeed we should have been there by this time, but for too much confidence in our information, and not asking enough of questions. Do tell us all about Mr. Scott that you have time for, and Aunt Grace and Susie and Johnnie,[2] and my brother John, and do not forget your dear self. My wife says I must go to bed because I am coughing. So I shall not try to write more. Please tell my brother John if you see him soon that I will write to him when we reach the other side. The Mediterranean looks very friendly towards us at present. My true love to Mr. Scott and you from your friend,

GEORGE
MACDONALD[3]

1. Lady Byron suggested to MacDonald that Algiers might be a good place for wintering, especially because of MacDonald's weak lungs. Therefore, MacDonald and his wife left for Algiers on October 31, 1856, taking with them only their second daughter, Mary, who was sickly.

2. "Aunt Grace" was Louisa's sister Caroline. Susie and Johnnie were the Scotts' children.

3. A note is added: "Our kind remembrance to Mr. and Mrs. Ker and love to their dear daughters."

To Mrs. A. J. Scott Algiers, 28 Nov. 1856
Hotel de la Regena
Friday

My very dear Mrs. Scott,

[Louisa MacDonald writes:] As the post only goes out twice a week, I think I ought to send you word of our safe arrival here by this post, though perhaps by waiting another three days we might be able to give you a better account of what we expect our manner of life to be. We reached Algiers on Monday afternoon, all records of the passage had better be entirely forgotten, so I will only tell you how delightful it was to land in sunshine and sit with our window open looking out on the blue Mediterranean (toward which it must be confessed, however, I had not then any very friendly feelings) while we took our coffee; and it was such a charming change from the bitter cold we had at Marseilles that the bright sun made us feel quite happy. The climate at this season at least being all we can speak of from experience, is very delightful. The mornings and afternoons are like pleasant June days in England. At midday it is more like July. The effect of the change upon George has at present been very beneficial, he has almost entirely lost his cough, but he is not strong. We are longing to get more into the country, for the noises in the town are hideous, and besides the air cannot be so good as in some of the very pretty little villages that are scattered around Algiers in all directions. There are many of them built halfway up the hills in a gentle slope of the sea. We have been out in a carriage twice in search of a *petit champagne,* which they tell us we may get. The first drive was through very grand country, we had magnificent views from some of the heights and just went to the borders of some wild looking uncultivated land running along which were the Atlas Hills, the beginning of the Atlas range, but the rest of the country was very fertile, such strange hedges of olives, & hideous giant cactuses, many of these enclosing rich orchards of orange trees. There are also great numbers of coffee trees in that direction. But we did not succeed in our search for lodging. We saw one house *not furnished* which if you would come out for the winter would I am sure delight you. It looks like an old Moorish court in the middle of a delightful garden of delicious scented flowers and orange trees. The geranium roses & [?] were very rich. The chief room in the house is supported by pillars and the roof arched and the floor inlaid with mosaic tiles, but this is universal. The long arched passages leading from one room to another look romantic enough to our English eyes. This house we could have for £40 a year. But the furnishing made it come up to such a frightful sum as to render it impossible for us to think of it. We have seen one which might do but it is very small and very dear. Dear George would soon get tired there. He is rather out of spirits about our settlement. The place seems as far as we can judge to be little fitted for emigrants & those visitors who can afford to live in hotels, but we must hope to get on somehow. We wish sometimes we knew someone who could help us. The costumes of the various natives are very amusing. Our eyes quite ache with strange sights. The light is so intense that our fog-disposed minds can hardly believe it to be November. I must have George tell you about the Moorish part of the town. It is too extraordinary for me to attempt. [George MacDonald writes:] My dear Mrs. Scott I cannot fulfill my wife's promise, for I have been writing to my father, and I am tired. I can only wish you were here to see the strange sights. How we should scramble through the interminable alleys and archways and courts which combine to exclude the sun and form the city of Algiers! I enjoy wandering about them much, but I have not yet had half enough of it. Almost all the town is composed of places you would be afraid to go into in London, but though there are many idle people about, I have scarcely seen anything in the least disorderly. If I go on, I shall only write stupidly, which for your sake and my own I may as well not do. Oh, if Mr. Scott were here! I could get the people classified! But that's not why I want him. My love to him and you all. I am, my dear Mrs. Scott, most affectionately yours,

GEORGE MACDONALD

Tell Johnnie I never saw so many donkeys. And near long-legged fellows, if Arabs sit on them and wave their legs as if they were walking instead of riding. And there are numbers of beautiful little Arab horses. And yesterday we saw one camel walking patiently along with a man on its hump, but I will tell him more when I come home.

To Miss Caroline Chase Powell[1]   Algeria,
                                               Christmas Eve of 1856
My dear Sister,
     Our days move on without much variety, for I am not able for long walks or much exertion. . . . If I were able I should go to high mass at

midnight to-night, which I do not think would shock Archdeacon Wix[2] and his lady so much as they will be shocked when they find out, if ever they do, that I count *The Church* as much a sect as the Independents or the Mormonites![3] They are very kind to us and we like them. . . . I was interested to find when we saw the Miss Leigh-Smiths last that they expect a Miss Bessie Parkes, somewhat known as a poetess and a friend of our Mr. Sutton, to visit them this week.[4] They are rather fast, devil-may-care sort of girls not altogether to our taste, but very pleasant; and they seem to draw and paint well. One of them [Anna], who is in poor health, is more sweet and womanly. But what is all this for? I had better have told you of the silver-grey sea of this day, bounded by a narrow horizon-belt of intense and dazzling blue; over which silver-grey, immense lateen sails, with an enormously deep-reaching reflection, went crawling, moved not by the wind, for there was none, but the oars of the boat below. Meantime I have learned something of the face of Nature and the face of man — very little of the face of woman though! I look keenly through the thin Manchester stuff over the Moorish faces, but I see almost invariably a sickly, thin countenance — at least in appearance through the veil, with soft black eyes over it, and often made hideous by stained eyebrows, meeting in Moorish arches over the nose. The Jewish women, who expose all the face but the chin, are gorgeously dressed as to colour, but odiously as to form, and are invariably unpleasant looking — I would say *ugly* if I were not writing about women. But the men are often superb — the Arabs especially. I think the most beautiful arm for texture and form I have ever seen is the property of a negro, a right black one too; and he seemed to prize it, for he had on it, more than half way down the elbow, a pale-red flat tight bracelet, which set the black off well. This is certainly the place for the study of the human form. . . .

1. Louisa's sister.

2. "The Rev. Edward Wix, sometime Archdeacon of New Zealand, then vicar of St. Michael's, Swanmore, Ryde, and a frequent contributor to the *Gentleman's Magazine*" (*George MacDonald and His Wife*, p. 269).

3. MacDonald had little sympathy for organized religion, whether it was the state church (Anglican) or the Catholic.

4. The Leigh-Smiths were friends the MacDonalds met in Algeria. They were in Algeria because of their daughter Anna's ill health. Mr. Leigh-Smith was a Member of Parliament for Norwich. Bessie Parkes was s friend of Miss Leigh-Smith.

To Miss Smart[1]   January 12, 1857

My dear Annie,

(How would you like to buy oranges at 3 half-pence a dozen?) . . .
What shall I begin by telling you? First that if you were suddenly trans-
ported into the little room in which I am writing, my wife working, and
little Mary chattering like a Kalmuck praying-machine, you would stare
a little. . . . In the first place, the room is long rather, and would be narrow,
but for two deep vaulted recesses, in one of which stands a piano, in the
other a cupboard of ugly painted wood. On the other side are three small
windows of different sizes and elevations. The walls are 2½ feet thick, for
the roof is vaulted with crossing arches. The floors, and two feet up the
walls are covered with colored tiles, yellow and green and blue and black,
of somewhat varied but not very interesting patterns; and the absence of
red either pure or in combination gives to my eye a dingy appearance. . . .
We have only two or three little bits of carpet. Out of this room lead two
others, paved with red tiles — one of which is our bedroom, and the least
comfortable part of our interesting abode. A few steep steps lead up to the
kitchen, at which, from the paucity of utensils and the oddity of the
charcoal fireplaces, an English cook would be considerably puzzled. We
have a very stupid French girl from the Hautes-Pyrénées. . . . From our
windows we look out on the Mediterranean with its infinite varieties of
colour and shade, and for the last few weeks with plenty of ragged waves.
From our door we see eastward across the bay the distant snow-capped
peaks and the Lesser Atlas, towering over nearer ranges of lower hills. This
is, of course, the grandest part of our landscape. . . . You should have seen
how I made a conquest of the affections of an Arab horse to-day. They
are such beauties, but they do not use them well. . . .

1. Annie Smart, eldest daughter of Rev. and Mrs. John Smart, Vicar at Kingswear,
where the MacDonalds lived from early March, 1856. See *George MacDonald and His Wife*,
p. 262.

To His Father   February 4, 1857
                                                                  Algiers

. . . I feel with you in the fact that your sons have needed so much to be done for them.[1] For me, if it please God, I shall do better by and by. If not, I hope He will let me go very soon — for if I cannot provide for my family, I would rather not add to the burden. At the same time, some of what is given to me must be regarded in a very different light from charity in the ordinary sense of the word. True, it would not be offered to me if I did not require it; but if I contribute to make life endurable or pleasurable or profitable, I do not see why I should be ashamed of having that acknowledged in the way I need, any more than if I were paid for keeping a merchant's books. . . . You may hope that I shall not refuse to do anything that I can honestly undertake to provide for my family as soon as I return. I would far rather take a situation in a shop than be idle.

A new edition of *Within and Without* will be published in the spring; and I expect it will be accompanied by a new volume. . . .[2]

1. Greville MacDonald notes: "My Uncle Charles was leaving for Sydney after his father had settled his heavy debts" (*George MacDonald and His Wife*, p. 272).
2. *Poems* (1857).

To Mrs. A. J. Scott   The Limes, Upper Clapton
                                                             May 28, 1857

My dear Mrs. Scott,

I have been both ill and busy since we arrived here last Saturday week;[1] but now both the illness and the business are nearly over. I write only a note now with haste, to ask if you could take me in for a few days next week, to make me happy with you, and let me have some talk with Mr. Scott. Do not hesitate to say *no,* if you cannot, for I can imagine you without a square yard of room in this busy time at Manchester. I will not tell you anything more now; not till I hear that you cannot have me. My wife joins me in love to you and all your family. I am, my very dear friend, ever most affectionately yours,

                                                      GEORGE MACDONALD

1. The MacDonalds left Algiers at the end of April 1857.

To His Father   The Limes
                                                              [June 1857]

. . . I have been to see Lady Byron. She is the most extraordinary
person, of remarkable intellect, and a great, pure, unselfish soul. She has
made a proposal to me to edit a number of letters which she has at different
times received from distinguished persons. But this must not be mentioned
to anyone. Even if it is published, I presume her name will be quite
concealed. If all goes well, and she commits the papers into my hands, I
presume she will advance me a little money to work upon, which will
deliver me from immediate difficulties.[1] By the post preceding this, I have
at length sent you a copy of my new book, which I hope you will accept
— both in itself, and in its dedication to yourself. . . .[2] I wish I could
come and see you, but I have no money, and I cannot very well leave
Louisa just now.

1. Apparently the edition of letters was never done.
2. *Poems* (published in April 1857).

To Mrs. A. J. Scott   The Limes, Upper Clapton
                                                        Friday morning.
                                                           [July 1857]

My very dear Friend,
     I fear you will think I have been forgetting you, only you never seem
to think of yourself at all. I have been a good deal occupied, and have
scarcely had a pen in my hand. I preached for Mr. Ross on Sunday
morning, and baptized his baby, without being at all the worse for the
exertion. I went to see Lady Byron by invitation yesterday, and was very
much gratified with my visit. She seems a most remarkable woman. She
talked of Mr. Scott just as I could have wished, and you may think I was
pleased. She has two or three things in her thoughts for me, but she has
not yet told me what they are. She will not till she sees more about it. I
begged her not to be too fastidious for me. Perhaps she may find something
to suit me. I am going on horseback now to call on Mr. Chorley to whom
Mrs. Halle spoke about me. We saw Mrs. Halle, and were delighted with
her goodness and kindness.

Will you give my kindest remembrances to Mrs. Ker and her family; and please dear Mrs. Scott, I am sorry to trouble you, but I left a shirt and pair of socks in my bedroom there, and as I had not my bag at the time I poked them out of sight under the dressing table and forgot them. If you could get them for me, and keep them till they are called for I should be much obliged to you.

Louisa sends her love to you, and she does not want anything more out of the furniture-chaos. She can do very well now. I hope to send Mr. Scott a copy of my book next week[1] — it is advertised for the 3^d of July.

Now I must go. With love to you all, I am

> My dear Mrs. Scott,
> Most gratefully yours,
> GEORGE MACDONALD

1. *Poems* (1857).

To His Father The Limes,
August 27, 1857

We find it is useless to try anything till we have a house. We had a prospect last week of getting a young man to live with us for twelve months for which we hoped to have £100, as I would have given him three hours a day of instruction. But the fact that we had not a house was made the ground of postponement, though perhaps the real reason was that we were not Church people.[1] . . . Thank you very much for both your letters and for the *Scotsman*. It is a very gratifying review. We are anxious to get by ourselves again and have our children with us. If we could but get *bread literally* we should be content, and might perhaps thrive better on it than on dainties unearned. . . .

1. That is, members of the established (Anglican) church.

To His Father   East Hill, Hastings,
                                                        December 2, 1857

My very dear Father,

Thank you for your welcome letter. I sent you the other day the *Examiner* with a short notice of my last book. Will you please send it back as Louisa wants to have it. I have been very unwell since I wrote last, but I am now much better. The weather is milder, and I feel better than I have done since we came here. We are a little settled now in the house and feel pretty comfortable. We think we shall like it very much. My cough is greatly decreased. The doctor, who has been attending me ever since we came almost, at intervals of a few days, came this afternoon, & pronounced me very much better. I had hoped to have a fairy tale or something of the sort[1] ready by Christmas, but that has been quite prevented by my illness. I keep hearing now and then of my books, but nothing worth mentioning. I send you one of Lady Byron's letters in which she mentions it. You need not return it. Poor lady she is very ill. She sent me the other day the £50 she promised for Christmas, with just a note on the envelope that she was too ill to delay sending it. We shall lose a good friend when she goes, & I do not think she can live long. I am concerned to hear such a poor account of Mary Anne. Will you give my love to her. I wish I were able to ask her to come here for a while, but even if I were I do not expect they would permit her — it is so far from home. My father-in-law has not suffered, but they have met with considerable difficulty in helping others to keep going. Powell & Tiny are safe. They had their account on the right side when the Liverpool Bank failed — it being several thousands overdrawn. You must not lose heart my dear Father for your family. You have got through so far with great difficulty, & so shall we. We must all suffer & we all need it but as long as God thinks it worth while to let us suffer, it is worth while to us to suffer. If success in this life were an end, we might say all our family had failed, on all sides, but this life is but a portion & will blend very beautifully into the whole story. May the one Father make us all clean at last by his beautiful forgiving tenderness & his well-ordered sufferings, & when the right time comes, wake us out of this sleep into the new world, which is the old one, when we shall say as one that wakes from a dream — Is it then over, & I live? I for my part would not go without one of my troubles. I have needed every one, & I fear need many more yet. The only one I fret at is being dependent.

My Dear love to my mother & the children. Will you give my love

too to Uncle & Aunt & Miss Wilson & Dr. & Mrs. MacColl. How are
you getting through the winter?

I am,
My very dear Father,
Your loving Son

George

Louisa sends her love to all. I wish I could see you.

1. *Phantastes* (1858).

To His Father   Huntly Cottage,
                                                                January 2, 1858

. . . I am wonderfully better. The weather is very fine. Christmas Day
and New Year's Day were both fit for Algiers. . . . The house is pretty
comfortable now, but the floors are very open between the boards. Through
these the wind blows like knives. But I shall put the demon out by degrees.
I have pasted brown paper over the cracks in the floor in two rooms, and
we have two more that want it very much. . . . I am writing a kind of
fairy tale [*Phantastes*] in the hope it will pay me better than the more
evidently serious work. This is in prose. I had hoped that I should have
it ready by Christmas, but I was too ill to do it. . . . Louisa is very well,
and the children — except Mary, who constantly suffers from her eyes.
She has wonderful spirits, though almost too good sometimes. She is a
strange child. We think sometimes that she will not live long.[1] She is very
thin and delicate — a most elfish creature. We call her *Elfie* when she is
good and *Kelpie* when she is naughty.

Could you send us some more meal soon. This is not finished, but I
have taken to eating a good quantity every morning myself. Indeed, I take
nothing else but a cup of tea.

1. Greville MacDonald notes that "her death in 1878 from lung disease was the first
break in the family" (*George MacDonald and His Wife*, p. 18).

To His Father   [Undated]

I had a most successful visit [to London] — got some books I much
wanted at moderate cost — visited Mr. Maurice[1] and Lady Byron — put
a little MSS.[2] that took me two months to write without any close work
— a sort of fairy tale for grown people, into a new publisher's hands and
two days after had £50[3] in my hands for it. I likewise have plenty of work
on my hands for printing in one way and another. Indeed I shall now be
fully occupied for some time. I am going to give some lectures, too, here,
as I did in Manchester. . . .

1. F. D. Maurice.
2. *Phantastes* (1858).
3. Greville MacDonald explains: "This sum was paid for the copyright" (*George
MacDonald and His Wife*, p. 290).

To Mrs. A. J. Scott   Hastings, May 17, 1858

Hearty thanks, my dear Mrs. Scott, for your remembrance of me by
writing. I have felt accused and somewhat unhappy whenever I have
thought of you, because I had not written for ever so long. But it is such
a trial for me to write a letter, more specially because, if I have anything
else to write, I feel the little force of expression I had, greatly exhausted
and spent upon the letter. But it is very good of you not to measure my
love to you by the amount of my writing, which would indeed be an
untrue measure.

Here I am once more, turned back from my journey, & deprived of
the great delight of seeing my Master and you. I could not see my way
clear to accept your most kind invitation. For one thing, money has grown
scarce, seeing I had reckoned of what my work in the North would bring
me. But perhaps something else may lead me towards you before long. I
have been very busy while in London seeing people. I am charmed with
Mr. and Mrs. Russell Gurney,[1] whom I have at last succeeded in seeing.
I spent a few hours with them on Thursday. I have given eight lectures
here, which for a beginning were successful. But like Thackeray,[2] I feel
very like an imposter; only in my case, it is hardly a joke. I feel as if I had

good brains but not enough of them. I wonder if twenty of my old friends would take a new course in Manchester of eight lectures twice a week — I think of trying it in London. I have made yet a little more acquaintance with that old literature, and keep extending my poor knowledge.

I hope Johnny[3] goes on comfortably. I have not heard about him since he left. Thank you very much for saying Mr. Scott has something commendatory to say of my poems. Perhaps some day I may — not satisfy him — but something nearer it than now. I think I am really getting stronger and more likely to live than I was.

Will you remember me most kindly to all at Overstone Terrace. With much love to you all

> I am,
> My dear Mrs. Scott,
> Most affectionately yours
>
> GEORGE MACDONALD

I can hardly say whether John[4] is better or not. I fear the disease spreads. He may be able to go to Scotland, but I doubt much if he will get through the winter.

1. Lady Byron introduced MacDonald to Russell Gurney, Recorder of London, and his wife. Gurney's wife, Emelia Gurney, later organized lectures for MacDonald.
2. There is no record that MacDonald and Thackeray met, although *The Portent* (1860) was serialized in *Cornhill Magazine,* with Thackeray as its editor.
3. The Scotts' son.
4. John Hill MacDonald, who died July 7, 1858, at age twenty-eight, in Huntly.

To His Father   Hastings,
                                                              May 20, 1858

I returned last Saturday, having seen a number of different people in London. I spent some time with Lady Byron, dined with the Recorder [Russell Gurney], spent a day with Caleb Morris, etc., etc., and came home tired rather. Perhaps I may bring John home to you in a little while. . . . His cough seems to us less, and certainly the pain is *very* much less. He is decidedly more cheerful, and eats better, though doubtless he is in a precarious condition still. God's will be done. If He make your sons — after (it may be) a long time — good men, you will be satisfied that none of them had the success which on many accounts would be desirable. I have just had a note from Lady Byron announcing the sending of a mantle for my wear. . . . I am very well.

To His Father   Sunday evening,
                                                            [June 1858]

My very dear Father,

John has had a bad turn again since you wrote, but he is now almost over it again. He cannot travel yet, though. . . . Meantime I believe he feels quite at home with us, and all we can do for him we will. We both read to him when we can, but he is only able for a bit of a story at a time and is soon tired even of that. He is certainly in a very doubtful condition — but God's will is best. As to what you say in your last letter about giving up to the will of God, and then taking it again — I would just say that it is only by having wishes of our own that we are able to give up to the will of God. It is live things, not dead carcasses that must be brought to his altar. And then we do not know what his will is — it may be the same as our wish, for all that we know.

God is good to me. I have prospects of lectures in London that will bring me in the necessary money for another few weeks. If the plan succeeds I shall be the guest part of the time of the Recorder — whose lady is managing the affair for me.[1] I expect to go to London next week, and John bids me say that if he is able he will accompany me to London, and sail from there for Aberdeen. But *I* doubt it. . . .

1. "Thomas Erskine of Linlathen had written in July 1855 to Mrs. Russell Gurney thus of *Within and Without:* 'I like it better than any poetry and most prose that I have read for many years'" (*George MacDonald and His Wife,* p. 292).

To His Wife [Huntly, August 28, 1858,]
Sunday night.

. . . My mother seems a little more cheerful to-day. Charles and I went to see some poor people this afternoon. It is very pleasant to hear how they all talk about my father. You would almost fancy he had been a kind of chief of the clan. . . .

Now I have had your sad, sad letter.[1] I do love you, and am so grateful for the love you give me. I think God will show himself very kind somehow or other to us both — not that I deserve it, but you do. . . . Do not think I am unhappy. I am glad my father has got through. I love him more than ever. I am cheerful and hopeful. My love to Lily. Tell her I will pull her tooth out for her if she likes. My love to them all and to you, good, kind, beautiful wife. . . .

1. MacDonald's father died August 26, 1858. MacDonald's brother John Hill had died July 7, 1858.

To His Stepmother[1] [Hastings,
October 15, 1858]

. . . My new book is just out, and I am asking my publisher to send you a copy. I am very well, and have the prospect of a tolerable amount of employment. I dreamed last night I saw my father. I felt I loved him so much and was clinging to him, when to my surprise I found he was so much taller than I, that I did not reach his shoulder. There is a meaning in that, is there not? His great soul has already learned so much more than we know. But we shall all find him again, and that will be a blessed day. . . . Louisa joins me in warmest love to you. . . .

My chair and all my things arrived quite safe.[2] I will write you a few words every week. . . .

May God help you, dearest Mother, to go nearer to Him — that is the only thing that can comfort you for the loss of my father. There is no gift so good, but its chief goodness is that God gives it, and what he gives is not to be taken away again. Whatever good things we can fancy for ourselves, God has better than that in store for us. Even your sorrow is turned into joy, if you can say to God, "I am willing to be sorrowful, since it is thy will." . . . I am much obliged to Jeanie[3] for her little letter and the feathers, which are already planted in Greville's cap. . . .

1. Greville MacDonald notes: "From this time onwards my father wrote as regularly to his stepmother as hitherto to his father" (*George MacDonald and His Wife*, p. 295).

2. These were "things of his father's," notes Greville MacDonald: "His special chair, in which I now sit, was my father's study-chair for longer than I can remember. The only other thing remaining to me is a deep-mauve whisky decanter with silver-mounted cork. It always stood well filled on the sideboard at The Farm; yet, until the last few years, my grandfather never took any spirit, and then only one tablespoonful, always measured out by my grandmother, as a nightcap" (*George MacDonald and His Wife*, p. 295).

3. MacDonald's half-sister, Jane MacDonald Noble.

To His Stepmother   January 19, 1859

. . . I hope you will gradually be able to sleep better, dearest mother. May you know, when you are lying awake, that God is with you — our perfect good. My father is nearer Him now, and you will get nearer Him by losing my father. Even the bodily presence of Jesus in some degree prevented the disciples from finding God for themselves — the spiritual God, present to their hearts; and therefore it was expedient for them, as He said, that He should go away from them. . . . Louisa longs to have you with us. We should make you as happy as you can be now in this world, we think. And you would help us so much. . . . I am glad to hear Uncle and all of them are so kind. I should not wonder if they too learn more what my father was worth by his being taken away. . . .

To A. J. Scott   Hastings,
                                                                 July 2, 1859

My dear Mr. Scott,

I am ashamed of troubling you so soon again, and in the same way too as last time, but I know that you will think nothing too much trouble to you, that you can perform consistently with your duties, to help me

forward. You will see by the inclosed note to what I refer. I should like
the post at Bedford Square very much,[1] for I think in a little while I could
fulfill its duties well. I know there are many many parts of the circle of
which I am very ignorant, but I seem to myself to possess the key to the
whole, and I believe or rather *think* that I have considerably more than
the ordinary power of interesting young people. I can hardly doubt that
I should be useful and feel happily employed in this way. It is *very* much
to my mind. I know that the small salary would hardly overbalance the
increase of expenditure in London, but then I should be nearer other work
of every kind, and I think perhaps the benefit of steady and unavoidable
employment would partially counterbalance the injury of inferior atmo-
spheric influences. You will know at once what I ask you to do — to say
for me what you can in reference to this post. I shall not be greatly
disappointed if I do not gain it, for the advantages do not lie so much on
the surface as to excite one's hope in a very lively way, but for many reasons
I should be glad to have it.

You will see from Mr. Reid's letter that the Council will meet on
Wednesday. There is not time for you to communicate with me before
then, but if you think it necessary that your testimony should be in their
hands then, perhaps you would send it to Mr. Reid, or do anything else
with it that you think better. There are very few people whose testimony
would be of use to me — I can only think of Mr. Maurice, Mr. Crabb
Robinson, Mr. Llewellyn Davis, Mr. Masson[2] — the latter knows very
little of me. Could you suggest anyone? I presume the testimony of ladies
would be of little use, else I should ask Mrs. Barton to say what she knew
of me. Sure of your kind reception to my request, I am, dear Mr. Scott,

Most truly yours,
GEORGE MACDONALD

1. MacDonald was hoping to be elected professor of English literature at Bedford
College for Ladies, London, the first institute of higher education for women. He got the
post the same year.
2. All of these men wrote testimonials for MacDonald.

To Lady Noel Byron[1]   [Nov. 2, 1859]
                                              18 Queen Square, W.C.
                                                          Tuesday

Dear Lady Byron,

All that I know of the legend of the Sangreal is that Sir Galahad sought it and found it: at least that is all that is *non-original* in the poem.[2] Both the story, the mode, and the deeper meaning are original. The meaning of the 3rd part is that, ceasing to seek the central good in its highest manifestation, he failed to find the central good in the individual good thing. But finding God in Christ, he found God in all things — as certainly, though not so fully manifest.

I sent the poem to *Once-a-week*. It was refused on the ground that one of Tennyson's best poems is *Sir Galahad!*

You kindly ask me to tell you about my debts. I meant to do so, had I an opportunity. I am not in debt at all from having borrowed money — it is only some tradesman's bills at Hastings — amounting perhaps to £20. So far for confession!

Now about my drama.[3] You will be amused to hear, as showing how differently different minds are impressed with the same thing, that where you apply the epithet *flat*, Mr. Scott applied the epithet of *effervescent* — saying, that there was a fine effervescence about the conversation: that as conversation it was much superior to some successful plays which he knew; that in fact it had rather surprised him; but that the wit was too refined, and the intellect too much occupied with the edges of things for a play.

My best thanks for giving me your ideas about it. You will not mind my meeting them with an opposite impression. I hope to benefit by both.

---

1. Letters from Lady Byron to MacDonald can be found in *George MacDonald and His Wife*, pp. 308-10.

2. MacDonald's poem entitled "The Sangreal: a part of the Story omitted in the old Romances." This poem was originally published in *Good Words* (June 1863) and was reprinted in *Poetical Works* (London: Chatto & Windus, Piccadilly, 1893), vol. 2, p. 65.

3. MacDonald's drama "If I Had a Father," which Smith, Elder and Co. refused to publish. MacDonald eventually turned it into a story; it was published in *The Gifts of the Child Christ and Other Stories* (1882).

To His Wife   Edinburgh,
                                                January 6, 1860

Just a few lines, dearest Louie, for I have not time for more, as I am busy preparing for my lecture to-night. The evening before last I was a little annoyed by the presence of Lord B. ————— , a stuck-up Lord of Session — who is nothing but a Scotch Lawyer and a bad one, and makes out that God is just a Lord of Session. To hear how the wretched creature lectured Mr. Erskine[1] — the dear, good, humble, wise old man! His Stickship is one of the worst specimens of the worst phase of low Scotch — why they asked him I can't think — but certainly they want to give me the best society in one sense! I would rather take tea with an old washerwoman. . . . Will you tell Mrs. Reid [Principal of Bedford College] that I will make the trial of the Natural Philosophy. I have very little doubt I shall succeed. I know plenty for them and know it well, too. . . .

1. Thomas Erskine of Linlathen. He could not accept the Calvinist doctrine of election.

To His Wife   [Jan. 1860]

Dearest Wife,

I got to London rather tired, hurried to Lime Street, swallowed a chop whole, which was providentially ready, gulped — (don't you see gulp and gulf are the same word?) — down two glasses of wine, darted off against probabilities, bounded through Fenchurch Street like an India-rubber ball, and got in time to the station — with one minute to spare. . . . I was up and down before eight this morning to write some necessary letters. . . . I read *Ulf* and several other stories. They are all very bad translations. As stories they just want *the one central spot of red* — the wonderful thing which, whether in a fairy story or a word or a human being, is the life and depth — whether of truth or humor or pathos — the eye to the face of it — the thing that shows the unshowable. . . . How stupid I am, trying to be clever. "That's damned fine!" the sailor said to the horse that had just pitched him over a hedge. "But how are you to get over?" This is William's [Matheson] last find. . . . I am now waiting for my pupils; I have two lessons of two hours before I see you to-morrow. . . .

To His Wife   [London, 1861]

Dearest Wife,

    . . . My MSS. [*The Portent*] is in the publishers' hands. Mrs. Russell
Gurney[1] brought the children home [from 8 Palace Gardens] this afternoon. She is delighted with the upbringing of them. They look well.
Winny is so pretty.[2] She would have no one but *Man,* as she calls Mr.
Gurney, to carry her up to bed! . . . After leaving Court, Mr. R. G. had
just time to go and get them some toys before they left. . . . What a devil
the East Wind is! Certainly there is not much of the divine in it except
in the over-ruling. It takes all the hope out of a body — but not the faith.
Good-night. Welcome the antechamber of death!

    Do rest when you can, dear comfort. The children are very little
trouble. . . . Lily is just a mother to them all — seeming to think of
everyone before herself. . . .

    1. Russell Gurney, Recorder of London, was introduced to MacDonald by Lady Byron
in 1859. It was through the Gurneys that the MacDonalds met Mrs. LaTouche, and thus
MacDonald met Ruskin.
    2. Winifred Louisa, MacDonald's fifth daughter, born November 6, 1858.

To His Wife   March 7th, 1861

    Just a little chat before I go to bed. . . . I have been talking, penwise,
all this about my ugly self. Is it not strange that in the Christian law we
can offer to God the most deformed and diseased thing we have got —
ourselves? I have had a most strange, delightful feeling lately — when
disgusted with my own selfishness — of just giving away the self to God
— throwing it off me up to heaven — to be forgotten and grow clean,
without my smearing it all over with trying to wash out the spot.

    This evening I could relish nothing but a poem of Chaucer's. We really
have never surpassed him. He was a non-dramatic Shakespeare — not
un-dramatic. There is no greater delight in Coleridge or Keats at hearing
the nightingale than old Chaucer manifests. The man of genius may not
be a prophet but he is a prophecy: he forestalls what it will take ages to
bring around for the many; but theirs it will be one day. . . . You need

not be uneasy about us. Lily is a host of Gideon — and as sweet as any ordinary angel. But it will be very jolly when you come back.

To His Wife   [Tudor Lodge, London,
                                                                    April, 1861]

. . . The children are very good indeed. Gracie[1] most amusing in conversation with the rest. She was proving the superiority of her spoon both in material and manufacture over those of the lodgings, but saying how she would part with it for you, as you were very poor. They brought it in that you wanted a bonnet very much. This was amongst themselves. I generally listen in silence. . . . I have but two lessons more. You see how uncertain teaching is. . . . Emily[2] has just come for me to kill a rat, and I have happily effected it — the largest I think I ever saw. . . .[3]

1. Caroline Grace, the MacDonalds' third daughter, born September 16, 1854.
2. Probably a servant.
3. Greville MacDonald notes: "My father had a wonderful way of catching rats with his hand, thickly gloved" (*George MacDonald and His Wife*, p. 327).

To the Editor of   Tudor Lodge, Albert Street, Regent's Park,
Blackwood's Magazine   London, N.W., Jan. 18, 1862.

Sir,

I enclose a Scotch Ballad,[1] which may perhaps suit your pages. It was refused by *The Cornhill,* to which I am an occasional contributor, because it was Scotch. I presume this will not be an objection with you.

May I hope to have it returned if rejected by you?

I am,
Sir,
Your obedient Servant,

GEORGE MACDONALD

1. One of the thirty-one ballads and songs later published in *Scotch Songs and Ballads* (1893); see *Poetical Works,* vol. 2, pp. 365-423; possibly "The Earl o' Quarterdeck," which was published in the *Argosy* (Jan. 1866); see *Poetical Works,* vol. 1, pp. 145-48.

To William Cowper [Cowper-Temple,   Tudor Lodge, August 9, 1862
later Lord Mount-Temple][1]

My dear Mr. Cowper,

I am greatly self-reproached that I have not written to you before — long before now on the subject of the poem about which you wished my opinion. I had hoped to be able to breakfast with you; but one thing after another — amongst the rest, a new baby[2] — interfered to occupy my thoughts. Still I am not free from blame in the matter, such blame so often attaches to the repose superinduced by good intentions. Now I fear it is too late to find you at home, therefore I will venture to write my impression of the poem in a few words. I have read it over carefully more than once.

That the writer has a great deal of the poetic element, I have not the least doubt. Indeed I suspect that much more than that might be said of him; but experience, and the constant evidence of the capacity of the mind at his age to receive and *reproduce* impressions without the power of *producing* forms of its own, makes me cautious of making up my mind from a single specimen. But I am greatly pleased with many of the lines & likewise with the turn & return of some of the paragraphs. The similes too, whether or not always lying quite close enough to the idea, are often beautiful in themselves. The faults are such as practice will mend. First, and chief perhaps as well, an apparent confusion in the arrangement of the parts, preventing clear & easy perception of the meaning of the whole. I do not think that this confusion existed at all in the writer's thoughts — it is only in the form in which he has put them. But one of the most valuable lessons a beginner can have is that *utterance* is not necessarily *communication,* and that the object of all *utterance* is or ought to be *communication.* Therefore the less unnecessary difficulties the better. Now I found considerable difficulty in catching the *drift* of the poem, though the goal towards which it was driving was tolerably clear. The *chronology* of the story is obscure.

Then there is diffuseness rather — a lack of vividness of expression resulting from a lack of condensation. This is another needful lesson, and one of the hardest, I find, to learn. I would say — *condense* — *condense.* Be content not to say all you wish or mean, if you can only say forcefully & vividly the main thing you mean. The writer seems to me to yield too much to the temptation of saying what is beautiful, whether it exactly belongs to him there & then or not.

There is a little affectation I think — I mean of words only — a preference of a quaint mode now & then, which is not justified by any corresponding advantage to be derived from the words.

I am afraid he will think me a dreadful Philistine, but you asked me to say what I judged. All these are faults which belong & must belong to beginnings. There lacks that firmness of utterance in which one recognizes at once the practiced speaker. But how could it be present?

Now if I may give a few words of suggestion, I would say: Give up blank verse for a while. It can only be written perfectly by one perfect in rhyme. Milton's exquisite rhymed poems preceded his perfect blank verse. Besides, to write in a common short stanza with rhymes, compels as well as assists the condensation to which I refer. Blank verse is generally chosen by young writers because of the freedom it gives them; but it is with verse as with life — the difficulties always add to the value of the result; the thing is better itself from being produced under pressure.

I should be happy to be of any service to one who so evidently sees & loves what is true and good. If he knows anything of me so as to care for any help I could give him, I should be very glad to know him. His verses are not at all common ones.

I trust you are much better by this time, dear Mrs. Cowper. You will be pleased for my sake to hear that I have a novel coming out by and by.[3] It will give me the opportunity I have been longing for of sending a new book of mine to Mr. Cowper, just to let him know I value his kindness. But it will not be under two or three months.

Yours most truly,

George MacDonald

1. The MacDonalds met the Cowper-Temples (later Lord and Lady Mount-Temple) in 1867 at their seat, Broadlands, Romsey. William Cowper-Temple was the stepson of Lord Palmerston. Greville MacDonald quotes William Cowper-Temple's account of their meeting in his biography: "A tutor in our family lay in a dying state in our house in Curzon Street. Mr Davies [Rev. J. Llewellyn Davies] came and administered Communion to him, and brought also to the young sick man a fellow-countryman (for he was Scotch) to read *Saul* to him. It was George MacDonald; and from that time he has been one of our dearest friends and teachers" (*George MacDonald and His Wife*, p. 472).

2. Robert Falconer MacDonald, born July 15, 1862.

3. *David Elginbrod* (1863).

PART III

Novelist, Lecturer, and Editor (1863-1871)

INTRODUCTION

For the next ten years, from 1862 to 1872, MacDonald concentrated his efforts on building his career as a novelist and lecturer. Still thinking of himself as being primarily a poet, and having published two poetic works — *Within and Without* (1855) and a collection of *Poems* (1857) — he had attempted a new literary type in his fantasy-romance *Phantastes* (1858).

Next, hoping that he might gain a wider audience, he turned to drama, writing a play entitled "If I Had a Father," which he turned into a novel (*Seekers and Finders*, which was never published), but both were failures. It became obvious to MacDonald that he did not have the kind of talent that was needed for the stage. Encouraged by George Murray Smith, the publisher of *Phantastes*, to write novels, he published *David Elginbrod* in 1863. *The Times* called the novel "the work of a man of genius," and even the *Athenaeum*, which had been critical of MacDonald's poetry, gave the novel three columns in review.

But even with this small degree of success as a beginning novelist, MacDonald could not support his ever-increasing family. Thus he began taking all the speaking engagements he could get, lecturing sometimes four and five times a week, and tutoring — all while continuing to write novels, which left him very little time for his wife and children. His wife carried the heavy burden of taking care of the immediate needs of the home and children.

Both MacDonald and his wife were indefatigable in their efforts. But it was indeed exhausting work, as MacDonald wrote to his close friend, Professor A. J. Scott (March 29, 1864): "Till now I have been oppressed with work of one sort and another. I have a little breathing time now. I hope you will be able to find some relaxation in looking over the pages of *Adela Cathcart*," which was published in 1864 (see p. 144 below). In the summer of 1865, MacDonald went to Switzerland — without his wife, who was not able to travel — where, refreshed in body and mind, he marvelled at the spire of Antwerp Cathedral and "the mountains — God's church towers!" as he described them in a letter to his wife.

When one considers the volume of work MacDonald produced during these years, it is not surprising to discover that not many letters were written, except for occasional letters to friends to thank them for their financial help, such as those he wrote to the A. J. Scotts, or short letters to readers who wrote him for advice. One such noteworthy letter Mac-Donald wrote in 1866 to an unidentified woman who had written him about his belief in the Bible. To her he replied: "Though the Bible contains many an utterance of the will of God, we do not need to go there to find how to begin to do his will. In every heart there is a consciousness of some duty or other required of it: that is the will of God" (see p. 154 below).

Finally, in 1871, when he was forty-five years old, MacDonald got the opportunity he had been waiting for: an invitation to lecture in America. In reply to an invitational letter from the American editor and novelist Josiah Holland, MacDonald wrote that his so-called "Scotch clannishness" was "only one form of a rudimental form of love to all men" (see p. 176 below).

MacDonald soon discovered that his acceptance in America would be beyond his greatest expectations.

Significant Dates and Events

1863   Lewis Carroll asks MacDonald's opinion of "Alice's Adventures Under Ground"; Louisa MacDonald reads the story to the family while at Tudor Lodge. MacDonald publishes *David Elginbrod*. MacDonald meets Mrs. La Touche and John Ruskin.

1864   Maurice is born on February 7. MacDonald publishes *Adela Cathcart* and *The Portent*.

1865   MacDonald fails to receive professorship at Edinburgh. He publishes *Alec Forbes of Howglen*. Bernard Powell is born on September 18. MacDonald spends the summer in Switzerland. He receives a lectureship at King's College, London.

1866   MacDonald's friend A. J. Scott dies.

1867   The MacDonalds move to The Retreat, Hammersmith, London. George MacKay is born on January 23. MacDonald publishes *Unspoken Sermons* (first series).

1868   MacDonald publishes *Robert Falconer; Guild Court;* and *The Seaboard Parish*. He is awarded the L.L.D. degree from Aberdeen University.

1869   MacDonald accepts the editorship of *Good Words for the Young*. He takes a trip on *The Blue Bell*. He goes on a lecture tour of Scotland. He becomes friends with F. D. Maurice.

1870   MacDonald publishes *The Miracles of Our Lord*. Louisa MacDonald's *Chamber Dramas for Children* is published.

1871   MacDonald publishes *At the Back of the North Wind; Works of Fancy and Imagination* (10 volumes); and *Ranald Bannerman's Boyhood*.

To Mrs. David Matheson[1]   Tudor Lodge,
                                                January 14, 1863

My Dear Mrs. Matheson,

Accept my best thanks for your kindness in writing to me about the dear child who bore my name. Perhaps he has already a new heavenly name; but he will be to all eternity your own child. I know by thinking of anyone of my own, how dreadful the loss must be to you, but life at the longest is not so very long, and you will find him again by and by. He is only laid by for you — like a precious thought of God's goodness laid up in the mind, and known to be there, though you cannot call it up when you please and contemplate it. If God gave to take away again, he would not be the God that Jesus has taught us to know. The loss of the body is not more to his being than the loss of the little curl of hair would have been to his body, had that yet been alive. . . .

1. David Matheson was possibly the son of Greville Ewing Matheson, who became friends with MacDonald while both were at Highbury College. The letter concerns the death of Mr. and Mrs. David Matheson's son.

To Charles Manby Smith[1]   Tudor Lodge, Regent's Park,
                                                                N.W.
                                                September 7, 1863

My Dear Sir,

I meant to call and beg your acceptance of the accompanying volumes, but I cannot find time at present. I had intended one copy of the few the publishers first allowed me for you, but I found they would not go so far as I wished. Pray excuse the postponement of my offering. You gave me the Epitaph which was in a measure the germ of the whole. Please accept the result of its growth in my mind.

                                    With kind regards to Mrs.
                                    Smith,
                                    Yours very truly,

                                    GEORGE MACDONALD

1. C. M. Smith was responsible for the "Epitaph" that inspired MacDonald to write

David Elginbrod (1863). Greville MacDonald provides a full account in *George MacDonald and His Wife* (p. 320): "One evening at an informal supper of oysters, beefsteak pudding and bottled stout, he [Smith-Williams] and James Greenwood, my father and others were consorting, when George MacDonald's attention was arrested by hearing Manby Smith, the gifted journalist, then writing regularly for the *Leisure Hour, Chambers' Journal,* etc., reciting from a certain Scotch epitaph he had read somewhere. 'What's that, what's that?' my father exclaimed, as though catching sight of some living thing that might evade him: 'Say it again, Mr. Smith!' The latter repeated:

> Here lie I, Martin Elginbrodde;
> Hae mercy o' my soul, Lord God;
> As I wad do, were I Lord God,
> And ye war Martin Elginbrodde!

To A. J. Scott

12, Earles Terrace,
Kensington, W.
March 29, 1864

My dear Mr. Scott,

I send you today a copy of my new book.[1] The name of it is stupid, but that is my publisher's fault, not mine. It is made up of almost all the short things I have written (some of which have been published before) imbedded in another tale. Although slight, I don't think you will consider it careless, nor unworthy of filling a gap between the last and the next book which is on the way. I have dedicated it to Dr. Russell. Some day I hope to write a book good enough in my own eyes to let me ask you to allow me to dedicate it to you. I have long had one in my mind, for which I have some material ready — a life of the *Robert Falconer* who is introduced into *David Elginbrod.* For that I hope to be able to make the request.

Till now I have been oppressed with work of one sort and another. I have a little breathing time now. I hope you will be able to find some relaxation in looking over the pages of *Adela Cathcart.*

I have not heard of you for some time. If Mrs. Scott should be inclined to write by and by, she will be sure to let us know. Please don't think of writing yourself. It was very good of her to write to Lily.

Mrs. MacDonald is not at all strong yet.[2] But we are going to Hastings for a little while, in the hope of her finding some strength in the breath of the sea.

With warmest love from her and me to Mrs. Scott and yourself,

> I am,
> dear Mr. Scott,
> Ever yours

GEORGE MACDONALD

1. *Adela Cathcart* (1864), in which MacDonald published "The Light Princess" and other shorter tales.
2. The birth of Maurice in January had left her very weak.

To Mrs. A. J. Scott   [1865]

My dear Mrs. Scott,

Your kind letter was a great deal more than I deserved, for I have owed you a letter for a long time. But I have been dreadfully busy, in fact with a new story,[1] which I hope to be able to send you the week after next. But for an accident I wd. [would] have given your order the very day your letter came. I have done so today, and I hope it will be attended to. I shall do my best to have it done, and will send the photographs as soon as I get them. I thought it was safer to have them sent to me. I will call about them again, if I don't have them soon.

Any good news about Mr. Scott, however small[,] is greatly good to us. I trust he will get on a little now notwithstanding his work. I hope some Saturday to be able to run down for the Sunday, if you can take me in, and I find my pocket will stand it. I have been amazingly well all the winter. In fact I have turned a huge corner, and am past forty and invalidity. I can have a bad cold now without either bronchitis or asthma. I am amazed at myself.

Louisa is not very strong. She has too much to do, what with ignorant servants and children who, though not more ignorant than they ought to be, are nearly as dependent on her for mental nourishment now as they have each in turn been for corporal sustenance.

I shall be very glad to meet your cousin, and do not doubt we shall be friends at once, if I should have the pleasure.

I am tired and stupid and can't write more. My wife joins me in love to you and Mr. Scott and everybody yours.

> Affectionately yours
> dear Mrs. Scott,

> GEORGE MACDONALD

1. Possibly *Alec Forbes of Howglen* (1865).

To Professor J. S. Blackie[1]   [August 1865]

My dear Blackie,

That I have never written to you before is painfully evident to me from the fact that I hesitate over the liberty of calling you by your surname. But let my excuse be my love, ill as I have manifested that either in deeds or epistles. Well, have I the shadow of a chance for the chair of Rhetoric?[2] If not, let me know that I may not waste myself on it. I am writing to all my friends who can help me. I am sure you will do what your conscience will let you. Tell me what to do. I rely on you for any information *pro* or *con* the attempt.

> In haste and affection
> Yours,

> GEORGE MACDONALD

1. Professor John Stuart Blackie, who held the Greek Chair at Edinburgh.
2. MacDonald failed to get the Chair of Rhetoric and Belles Lettres at Edinburgh; it was given instead to David Masson.

To His Wife   [August 17, 1865]

My darling, I shall love you more than ever. I can hardly be sorry for
your sufferings, if they made you hear one word from Him which I do
think you would hear. Thank you with all my heart for trusting me in
sending me what you had thought in the night. Do not be in the least
anxious about me. I feel very fairly well now. . . . Simpson at Blackwood's
says it is absurd to hear Mrs. Oliphant's[1] worship (!) of me. "What is it
for her to be writing novels when such a man, etc." Isn't it funny? . . .

1. Margaret Oliphant (1828-1897), the Scottish novelist, who was influential in getting
David Elginbrod published.

To His Wife   Antwerp, [Summer, 1865]
                                                            Sunday night

. . . God be praised for that spire [Antwerp Cathedral]. I *would* go up
though my head ached and I seemed worn out. 616 steps, 410 feet! I made
the others go. I was on the point of crying several times with delight, only
I didn't. But just think of a man being able to sit at a finger-and-pedal
board — 250 feet from the ground and play any tune he liked on 40 bells
yet higher — play to the whole city spread below! Oh how I should delight
to build a cathedral — towers if nothing else. *God be praised!* was all I
could say — as the Arabs say when they see a beautiful woman. It has
filled and glorified me, and I could go home contented if I didn't see an
Alp. . . .

                                                              Antwerp
                                                        Monday morning

. . . If I hadn't climbed that tower and had a breath of divine air, I
should have been ill to-day. I went up ill and came down well. . . . Oh,
for the mountains — God's church towers! But I have nothing in me
to-day but weakness and hope. If I am ill again any time, that awful height,
though I soon got over the feeling, will haunt me with yawning depth. . . .
But I thank God for the tower. . . .
    . . . I did not sleep well, for there was thunder and lightening and a

tremendous fire flaring away right in front of my windows at some distance, and tremendous bell-ringing through the night, and watchmen's rattles. But I believe they were only ringing the bells to please God or drive away the devil. . . . Perhaps the best things we have seen since we left home were first the sight of the people pouring out of the cathedral at Antwerp as we entered, and then the congregation remaining or gathering afterwards. Many of the woman [sic] had caps with lace-bound lappets like rams-horns. . . .

Basel, Switzerland.

. . . The town at which we stopped [Weissenburg] is a French-German one in Alsace. We had seen nothing so interesting before. It lies off the railway. A policeman in a cocked hat and military clothes took us to a tavern, and took his share of a couple of bottles of wine with us. . . . But the lovely old town! with the water running through it, and the fine old church and the pretty women and the quaintest houses with rows of windows one above another in every roof. I *must* take you there for a month some day. It is just the place to write a book in and could be reached easily without going all the way we did. Will you come, sweet wife? Then we went on to Strasburg. And here again we found a glory of a city. I never saw anything to compare to it, except the old town of Edinburgh, and that is squalid and vile — this rich and ancient and glorious — rather smelly, of course, like the other. At eight o'clock yesterday morning we sat drinking champagne in a street planted with trees all over. And I think it did us good. Then the cathedral — far beyond Cologne in every respect — built of red stone — no glass but stained in it throughout — dark and solemn — nay, very dark with wonderful galleries which I will explain to you when I see you. I never saw such a huge organ hung against the pillars as if it had been only a kitchen clock — a blaze of colour — a clock full of moving figures and fantasies as big as a house telling everything that a clock could know about, even to the feasts of the church with women and cherubs and men that walk one leg after the other, and Goddesses and old Death, and chariots and horses, etc., etc., more quaint than beautiful. Then I did what the others declared themselves unable for — I went up the tower and up the spire. Oh, my dear, what would you think of such climbing and such visions, like out of a balloon! . . . I went up as far as they would let me without an order from the Mayor, and all my weariness and fatigue was gone. And, darling, I am sure the only cure for you and me and all of us is getting up, up — into the divine air. I for my part choose the steeple-cure for my weariness. How will it be when I get amongst God's steeples?

The roofs of Strasburg are dark with, some, as many as five tiers of windows! And the streets and the colours! Antwerp all white and same and tame compared with this. . . . Then we came here and soon found the town was beautiful too. Here the roofs all brown, rich brown, like that picture of Beauty and the Beast and great queer dormer-windows in them. Our hotel is right over the Rhine — a great, broad stream of bluish-green, purring and rushing down — the waters escaping in wild delight from the ice-prisons up there in the awful hills — a mighty deep stream as wide as the Thames at London Bridge. A long, wooden bridge close by constantly traversed by many feet puzzles you the first morning with its sounds.

Schaffhausen

. . . I like the look of this hotel better than any we have been in yet — perhaps partly because we have had a girl to bring us water, who talks broad, honest German and looks you full in the eyes. I hate hotels! I mean those great big brutes that only want to eat you, and lick your hands for what they can get out of you. Last night I could only bear the sheet over me and slept so all night, and there was a change towards morning and there was no watchful woman beside me to cover me up, and now [crippled with lumbago] I go about like an old man, and ashamed of being stared at. They will take me for a worn-out roué on his way to the baths. Yesterday I was twice up and down the upper half of Strasburg Cathedral-spire, and to-day the stairs at the hotel Basle — three tremendous flights — seemed Alpine. . . . But I must go to bed. . . . There is a piano going downstairs. That sounds homely. And there is a round thing of white porcelain in a corner of this room, reaching to the ceiling and begirt with brass which is not homelike at all. It is the stove and is lighted from the passage outside — and I have a basin to wash in the shape and size of a pie-dish, and an eider-down quilt on the bed, etc. — as you know. . . . I shall be awake before the sun most likely — for I can't sleep — at least I have not slept well one night since I left. But I am very fairly well — all but my back and that's only a bother. Good-night, darling wife.

[Thursday]

[A portion is missing here.] . . . giant shepherd-king sitting on the circle of the earth, the white-fleeced mountains, whose very calm looks like a frozen storm. And the highest of them is nearly twice as high as the highest in front.

And the little town below is gay as a doll's house. You never saw such decorations, for it is the time of an annual *Fest* which lasts for three days. What it means except that it is all for singing and that they give prizes, I don't know. We can't find out. The people come from all quarters of Switzerland. . . . We went to a meadow in the evening where they meet. It was like a fair — with dancing-places surrounded and half-hidden by boughs. We wanted to go into one of these, but were told that we must dance if we did, against which in my case there were two impediments, ignorance and lumbago. They were all of the people, drinking wine and beer. One or two were a little elevated, but there was no sign of excess of any kind, nor a woman with other than a womanly good face to be seen. . . .

Mürren

I am much better, dear, and have been out a good part of the afternoon. And if I had seen nothing else, I could now go home content. Yet I am not sure whether amidst the lovely chaos of shifting clouds I have seen the highest peak of the Jungfrau. It is utterly useless to try to describe it. . . . I hate the photographs, they convey *no* idea. The tints and the lines and the mass and the streams and the vapours, and the mingling, and the infinitude, and the loftiness, the glaciers and the slow crawling avalanches — they cannot be described.

Once to-day, looking through the mist, I said with just a slight reservation of doubt in my heart, "There that is as high as I want it to be," and straightway I saw a higher point grow out of the mist beyond. So I have found it with all the ways of God. And so will you too, dear love.

We have nice people, but I am not going to write about people. . . . I said to them to-day that I should not lie still in my grave if I had not brought you to see it.

I have been into a cottage to-day to drink some milk and had a chat in German with the people. . . . And perhaps I enjoyed the marvelous scene, not one instant the same, the more that I was alone. Sometimes in an instant the whole range is invisible from the mist which keeps boiling up almost constantly from the valley, and sweeps across the opposite mountains. . . . I rather want to get home, for I have got all I wanted here — at least I have as much as I can take in now. . . . I must bring you here next summer if I can.

To Mrs. A. J. Scott   12 Earles Terrace
                                                          Kensington, W.
                                                          August 25, 1865

My dear Mrs. Scott,

I write in great haste to save a post which is now of great consequence to me. My testimonies are just going to press, and they will be very incomplete without one from him whose opinion I value most. Would he not be able to let me have one without too much fatigue? Your letter I will show wherever I think it may correct the mistake with regard to Mr. Scott's condition to which you refer. It is good news to know that he is improving however slowly.[1]

My friends think I have a good chance, but I don't think I shall get it, for Dr. Hanna, Dallas, Masson, Dr. Daniel Wilson and three or four others are applying. I have some interest at head quarters — i.e. the Home Sec.y [Secretary] but I don't know that that will be of much use. I think I c.d [could] write better books if I had the post.[2] Forgive this selfish scrawl on the plea of haste. Love to all.

Yours affectionately

GEORGE MACDONALD

1. A. J. Scott died in 1866. The letter MacDonald refers to may have contradicted rumors about Scott's condition. See MacDonald's letter to Mrs. Scott, dated February 9, 1866 (p. 155 below), written in response to Scott's death.
2. The chair of rhetoric at Edinburgh. MacDonald did not get this post.

To the Secretary of a North London Congregational Church

If you have a collection regularly every Sunday, I have nothing to say; but I will have nothing to do with any special services, or any extraordinary collection. I am a member of the Church of England, but care neither for that nor any other denomination as dividing or separating. It grates painfully on my ears to hear of services for the sake of reducing debt. Debts must be paid, and I will see to my own; but I will preach nowhere for the sake of anything but helping my fellows to be true and trusting. Pray leave me out of your scheme, and in the confidence that you will regard my wish in the matter, I will preach for your pastor on the evening of the 30th September.

To Alfred, Lord Tennyson

12 Earles Terrace,
Kensington, August 25, 1865.

Honoured Lord Tennyson,

I am taking a liberty in addressing you now, but not one, I trust, beyond excuse. I am a candidate for the chair of English Literature & Belles Lettres at Edinburgh. How much you may happen to know about my writings I cannot tell; but I write on the chance that you may have read some of them, and may, in consequence, be able to say a good word for me in the shape of a testimonial. This mode of application may be equally unpleasant to all concerned, but it is the only mode available. At all events your human kindness will forgive me for the trouble I seek to put you to, and permit me without offence, to express the hope that some day you may at least feel no repugnance in knowing that, amongst the many who love you, I claim to belong to the necessarily smaller class of those who understand you.[1]

Yours most respectfully,

GEORGE MACDONALD

1. There is no record that Tennyson actually wrote the testimonial that MacDonald requested.

To Professor J. S. Blackie   November 5, 1865

My dear Blackie,

I am oppressed with work for a few days and I have not yet been able to do more than look over a part of the sheet you did me the honour and kindness to send. But I will do a little tomorrow and a little next day, and on Wednesday etc. I hope to post it if that will do. If not, I will sit up and do it on Tuesday night if I hear so from you. My corrections are to be minute ones. I am delighted to find it so spirited. But I will *correct* (!) points or anything I like — as you ask me — freely knowing them to be subject to your after correction.

That is, alas! all I am capable of.

The right man has got the chair and I am very glad, though I felt a wee bit disappointed for half an hour or so.

> Love to you both from us both,
> Faithfully yours,
>
> GEORGE MACDONALD

To A. J. Scott   12, Earles Terrace,
                                                            Kensington, W.
                                                            [1865?]

My dear Mr. Scott,

I am vexed and ashamed that you should have had to write about that book. I take it this morning to the library myself. I would have written to Mrs. Scott too, I ought to have done so long ago, but I have been so occupied with a new book, which after all, on account of my illness I shall not get ready in time, that any divergences to letter-writing was a labour of hindrance to me. Will you please tell her with my love, that I was only a few hours in Edinburgh, yet I did call on Lord Bareaple. I found the house being *done up* and his lordship absent.

I hope you will be able to read my new book, which I think will turn out better than anything I have done yet.[1] I wish I could think it good enough to ask you to let me put your name in it. Be sure if I do not do so it will only be that I hope to do a better and one more worthy of being dedicated to you. I will hope to have the pleasure though still I find it will not do.

I am much better, but unable to bear fatigue — I am getting fonder of writing and rather tired of lecturing, but I must go on. Ruskin is very kind to me in every way — begs me to apply to him when I want help and has helped me already. He is coming a little out of his troubles I think.

Yours most affectionately,

GEORGE MACDONALD

1. Probably *The Portent* (1864).

To an Unknown Lady [1866]

. . . Have you really been reading my books, and at this time ask me what have I lost of the old faith? Much have I rejected of the new, but I have never rejected anything I could keep, and have never turned to gather again what I had once cast away. With the faith itself to be found in the old Scottish manse I trust I have a true sympathy. With many of the forms gathered around that faith and supposed by the faithful to set forth and explain their faith, I have none. At a very early age I had begun to cast them from me; but all the time my faith in Jesus as the Son of the Father of men and the Saviour of us all, has been growing. If it were not for the fear of it's sounding unkind, I would say that if you had been a disciple of his instead of mine, you would not have mistaken me so much. Do not suppose that I believe in Jesus because it is said so-and-so in a book. I believe in him because he is himself the vision of him in that book, and, I trust, his own living power in me, have enabled me to understand him, to look him in the face, as it were, and accept him as my Master and Saviour, in following whom I shall come to the rest of the Father's peace. The Bible is to me the most precious thing in the world, because it tells me his story; and what good men thought about him who knew him and accepted him. But the common theory of the inspiration of the words, instead of the breathing of God's truth into the hearts and souls of those who wrote it, and who then did their best with it, is degrading and evil; and they who hold it are in danger of worshipping the letter instead of living in the Spirit, of being idolaters of the Bible instead of disciples of Jesus. . . . It is Jesus who is the Revelation of God, not the Bible; that is but a means to a mighty eternal end. The book is indeed sent us by God, but it nowhere claims to be his very word. If it were — and it would be no irreverence to say it — it would have been a good deal better written. Yet even its errors and blunders do not touch the truth, and are the merest trifles — dear as the little spot of earth on the whiteness of the snowdrop. Jesus alone is The Word of God.

With all sorts of doubt I am familiar, and the result of them is, has been, and will be, a widening of my heart and soul and mind to greater glories of the truth — the truth that is in Jesus — and not in Calvin or Luther or St. Paul or St. John, save as they got it from Him, from whom every simple heart may have it, and can alone get it. You cannot have such proof of the existence of God or the truth of the Gospel story as you can have of a proposition in Euclid or a chemical experiment. But the man who will order his way by the word of the Master shall partake of his peace, and shall have in himself a growing conviction that in him are hid all the treasures of wisdom and knowledge. . . .

One thing more I must say: though the Bible contains many an utterance of the will of God, we do not need to go there to find how to begin to do his will. In every heart there is a consciousness of some duty or other required of it: that is the will of God. He who would be saved must get up and do that will — if it be but to sweep a room or make an apology, or pay a debt. It was he who had kept the commandments whom Jesus invited to be his follower in poverty and labour. . . .

From your letter it seems that to be assured of my faith would be a help to you. I cannot say I never doubt, nor until I hold the very heart of good as my very own in Him, can I wish not to doubt. For doubt is the hammer that breaks the windows clouded with human fancies, and lets in the pure light. But I do say that all my hope, all my joy, all my strength are in the Lord Christ and his Father; that all my theories of life and growth are rooted in him; that his truth is gradually clearing up the mysteries of this world. . . . To Him I belong heart and soul and body, and he may do with me as he will — nay, nay — I pray him to do with me as he wills: for that is my only well-being and freedom.

To Mrs. A. J. Scott[1]   12 Earles Terrace, Kensington
                                                   February 9, 1866

My very dear Friend,

    May I come near you now just to let you know that my heart is with you? What else can I say? The best comfort is *in* what you know better than I do — the Will of God, and the next best, that he who has left us was the best and greatest of our time. Those who know him best will say so most heartily. But we have no more lost him than the disciples lost their Lord when he went away that he might come closer to them than ever. Life is not very long in this place, dear Mrs Scott. All we have to mind is to do our work, while the chariot of God's hours is bearing us to the higher life beyond.

    He was — he is — my friend. He understood me, and gave me to understand him; and I think I did understand him to the measure of my inferior capacity. All my prosperity in literary life has besides come chiefly through him to you, as I told your brother, Mr Stewart, last night, when he kindly called with his son.

    How glad and quiet he must be now the struggle is over! My heart clings to him. How I could have served and waited on him, had that been in my power or his need! Who knows but he may help us all now in ways that we cannot understand. But the best is, we are all going to him. The one God be with him and us.

    My wife joins me in deep love and sympathy for you all. I wonder if John[2] could come and see us. We *should* be glad to have him.

    Many words are needless. You will believe more than we say.

Yours, dear Mrs Scott,
Most affectionately,

GEORGE MACDONALD

1. This letter was written shortly after the death of A. J. Scott, in 1866.
2. The son of A. J. Scott.

To the Rev. Dr. MacIntosh 12 Earles Terrace, Kensington, W.
MacKay, at Harris   May 6, 1866

My dear Uncle,

Best thanks for your kind note. I think of the last visit you paid us
with much pleasure, more than normally belongs to such meetings, from
the strong and glad feeling produced in my mind that whatever might be
the difference of opinion between us, I had an uncle whom I could love
and honour. My hopes and expectations for the life to come are strong;
and one of the great sources of its expected blessedness lies in the enlarged
power we shall possess of seeing into each other's meanings, scopes and
aims, and doing each other that *justice* which is the rarest virtue on earth.
It is ever much easier to be kind than to be just. . . .

. . . I am quite content that you should think my endeavours worthless, so long as you don't think *me* worthless, or a mere literary adventurer.
Had I been capable of condescending merely to please, I might have been
in very different circumstances now — better outwardly; inwardly, how
much worse! But this may be mere boasting. . . . I am glad you found
some interest in my paper.[1] It is one result of much study of the poet.
Indeed, I have studied him more than any book except the Gospels. As
to his coarseness, one had only to read *any other* playwriter of his time,
he must be an angel of purity. And there is much difference between the
plays he wrote when first he began and the later ones, in this respect. Still,
knowing the customs of the stage of his day, I suspect that some of the
more objectionable passages — I could point to one in particular — were
put in by the actor to make the vulgar laugh, and are not Shakespeare's at
all. And mere coarseness put into the mouth of a coarse person is no more
objectionable than the recording of Rabshakeh's nasty speech to the people
of Jerusalem. . . .

1. An article in *A Dish of Orts* (1863); probably "The Art of Shakespeare, as revealed
by Himself" (1863) or "St. George's Day, 1564" (1864).

To Professor J. S. Blackie
12 Earles Terrace,
Kensington,
Sunday, October 28, 1866

My dear Blackie,

I am quite ashamed of such a beautiful and delight-full present. I do not deserve it. Only for that matter, I don't deserve any of the beautiful things I have. I was afraid that I had vexed you, or at least been annoying to you with the proofs, seeing you did not send me any more. I wish I were a Greek scholar that I might be able to judge and give my judgment publicly. I do expect to find it more poetic than any of the others; for you go into it with the kind of genius which it seems to me will understand Homer instinctively. What a handsome book it makes too! And the binding is nearly perfect. This is very like praising a poet for his handsome face and the way he brushes his hair! But first impressions are something even in the boards and type of a book.

I am dreadfully busy and getting on — working hard and getting better paid for it. My next story is coming out in *Good Words*.[1]

There is a very nice short notice of The Homer in *The Examiner* of yesterday.

Isn't it jolly news to us that [F. D.] Maurice is now Professor of Moral Philosophy at Cambridge? We ought to thank God and take courage.

My wife joins me in the expression of true love to you and your wife.

With renewed thanks,
Yours affectionately,

GEORGE MACDONALD

1. In 1866 *Annals of a Quiet Neighbourhood* was serialized anonymously in *The Sunday Magazine,* and in 1867 *Robert Falconer* was appearing as a serial in *The Argosy* (edited by Mrs. Henry Wood) and *Guild Court* appeared in *Good Words for the Young.*

To Professor J. S. Blackie   [ca. 1866]

Beloved Professor,

    I cannot dine or sup or any kind thing with you, for I am far from well — coughing much and spitting blood, and I have nearly a month yet of lecturing every night. I have telegraphed for my wife to come and take care of me. It is a real disappointment to me not to be able to call on you and Mrs. Blackie, but it is my best chance to avoid all I am not compelled to do — else I may and probably I shall break down quite.

    Love to Mrs. Blackie.

Affectionately Yours,

GEORGE MACDONALD

To an Unknown Man   12 Earles Terrace,
                                              Kensington, London

May 20, 1867

My dear Sir,

    Accept my warm thanks for your kindness in sending me such a valuable present. I will say this much for myself, that I doubt whether you could find a man in England to value it more than I do. I believe I understand and sympathize with our lamented Hawthorne as much as any man,[1] and, a man like yourself, who does not look at his work merely from the moneyside will care that the authors whom he brings before their fellows should be thus appreciated. I shall always prize the books you have sent me, not only as Hawthorne's, but as your gift, and they shall go down to my children as your gift.

I am, dear Sir,
Yours very truly

GEORGE MACDONALD

    1. Possibly MacDonald is referring to the copyright abuses of both Hawthorne's and MacDonald's books abroad.

Written in reply to a review printed in _The Spectator_   Kensington
                                                                July 11, 1867

I do not complain that your correspondent should say what he pleases
of my work, but that he should use the same freedom in representing what
I say of my origin, is hardly to be ceded. . . . Having the weakness to be
proud of my Celtic birth, I do not at all relish being represented as guilty
of "implicit repudiation of Celtic blood in the preface to _The Portent._"
Offering the little book to a grand old Celt who knew well that I had
been born in a border region whence the tide of Gaelic had ebbed away,
I used these words in apology for the imperfection of my work from a
purely Celtic point of view: "I can only say that my early education was
not Celtic enough to enable me to do better in this respect." Is there any
ground in this for your correspondent's assertion? . . . To one of a race,
the poorest peasant of which would be a gentleman, it is annoying to be
held up as guilty of what would afford just cause to his own people for
repudiating him. For surely it is one of the worst signs of a man to turn
his back upon the rock whence he was hewn.

To Professor J. S. Blackie   The Retreat,
                                                          Hammersmith, W.
                                                               [ca. 1868]

Honoured Professor,
     Your humble poet returns his hearty thanks for your kind hospitality,
but is sure that you will understand his sole reason for declining it when
he says that he could not accept it without giving pain to his old friends
the MacColls[1] — the more severe as they have just lost their adopted
daughter by an Indian marriage, and the poor poet hopes to revive them
a little in their solitude.
     Dear Blackie and Mrs. Blackie, I prize your invitation, but I do not
fear you will think I love you the less that I do not accept it, for the
above is just the reason for refusing it. My wife will not, I am sorry to
say, accompany me this time, for she cannot well leave her household,
and I shall hardly be two consecutive nights in the same place on this

visit. I shall be desperately hard worked, but it is a nice change from scribbling.

Yours affectionately,

GEORGE MACDONALD

1. Dr. and Mrs. Duncan McColl, the uncle and aunt of MacDonald's stepmother.

To Mr. Campbell   The Retreat, Hammersmith,
London, W.
February 11, 1868

My dear Campbell,

Conscious of a selfish reason for writing to you now, I will not make any bare-face attempt to hide it, but go to the point at once. When I told Sir Noel Paton that you were having a kilt manufactured for me, he insisted on my going to his kiltmaker and being measured for it, that I might send the measurement to you. So here it is — as set down by McIntosh of the North Bridge.

Length   26
Waist   32
Seat   43

I have agreed to lecture to the Philosophical Society in January and shall be glad if business brings me again into your neighbourhood, for I have a most grateful remembrance of you and Mrs. Campbell's kindness. I have been working very hard since I came home, and so I daresay have you. And I suppose you think some of my work had better be left undone. Never mind. We won't quarrel about it. Time will bring out the event of things. Meantime whether we agree or not, you are a downright good fellow, and I hope to know more of you. I hope too you will beg of me, as the man replied to the appeal of his dying wife — "On middlin', jist middlin'?"

My wife joins me in love to you and Mrs. Campbell and all of the family that care to have it. My wife says she must put a note inside this to Mrs. Campbell but I say she must write for herself. I wish you could send me a pair of hose with the kilt, but my foot is such a plaguing narrow one to fit, that if you can get them for me I had better send you the measure.

Yours in affectionate
contradiction,

GEORGE MACDONALD

To Mr. Campbell

The Retreat, Hammersmith,
February 26, 1868

My dear Campbell,

Best thanks for your good letter. I sent you the other day a volume just out,[1] in the opening poem of which you will find something of the process my mind has gone through. It is a kind of history, with a gradual development.

Could you find out for me the address of the secretary of the society which asked me to lecture for them in September. Two gentlemen called one morning while I was with you. You said they were good hands to be in — The Christian Instruction Society — or something of the sort. I had some papers of theirs, but have mislaid them, which would have given me the address.

I enclose the measure of my foot and calf. The broader of the two smaller strips is the exact measure of my calf; the smaller, the measure round the broadest part of my foot. The two black marks on the broadest piece give the length of my foot.

Mind I want the kilt made by *your kilt-maker* after the measure I sent you. I have had a present of a fine claymore[2] given I came home! You did quite right to order the belted plaid as well as the other. For all your kindness thanks and thanks again. If my wife were by me she would join me in love to you both. Please thank Gerty for her very pretty valentine. Tell her I am a dozy old bird now; but she'll get a young one some day if she's good.

Faithfully yours,

GEORGE MACDONALD

1. *The Disciple and Other Poems* (1867), the opening poem of which traces MacDonald's religious conflicts from his student days.

2. A large, two-edged broadsword formerly used by Scottish Highlanders.

To John Ruskin   The Retreat, Hammersmith, W.,
                                                                June 24, 1868

My dear Ruskin,

I do not know how to thank you for those beautiful books, so valuable and useful — if indeed that is not one and the same thing! And for the engravings from Turner[1] — I do not deserve such exquisite things. But I am indeed delighted to possess them. I shall understand them, I fancy, so much better than any engravings of his I have seen before, simply from their perfectness. We shall all enjoy them greatly, and thank you often and often.

My wife and I are troubled in our minds that in our anxiety to entertain the poor people, we neglected to make provision for our other guests.[2] I believe you went home half dead with unfed fatigue. It was our first attempt, and we shall do better next time, I hope. We ought to have one room in the house provided with refreshments, but everything was sacrificed to the one end, which I hope was at least partially gained. But you will forgive us.

With glad recollections of your most kind visit, and love and thanks from both of us to you and Joan [Agnew, now Mrs. Arthur Severn] who was a perfect picture of goodness.

                                                     Yours most affectionately,

                              GEORGE MACDONALD

1. Greville MacDonald describes these as "a set of proof steel plates after Turner's pictures. They were framed together in series and hung in the study. My father would talk to us about them, so that as children we came to understand something of Turner's genius" (*George MacDonald and His Wife*, p. 381).

2. Ruskin annually attended entertainment parties given by the MacDonalds at The Retreat for Octavia Hill's poor tenantry. At these parties the MacDonald children acted out plays for the company written by Louisa MacDonald (*Chamber Dramas for Children*, 1870), including plays based on Zola's *L'Assommoir* and Dickens's *Haunted Man* and *The Tetterbys*.

To Henry Sutton[1] The Retreat, Hammersmith W.
June 28, 1868

My dear Sutton,

I fear almost to begin writing this letter. I can hardly believe what I have heard. Should it not be true the very shock of its supposition would be a great wrong to you. But alas! I fear I must believe that your best human friend has gone away from you, and that you have now only to look out along the dusty road after her, gather up your garments, and trudge on wearily.

But friend it is towards the east. And the human God is with you. Even in the depth of your distress you have, I think, already felt the blessedness of saying "thy will be done." This concession is all we have of our own to lay in sacrifice on his altar. This something shall we not of free will offer? Then may we stand up glorified in purity & challenge the divine response to our human needs. Hath the Lord given and *shall* he take away? The child that knows the Father will fear no repulse.

But, dear Sutton, let the heart, in the petulance of its loss, scorn the words as it may, it is yet true that it is but for a little while. Already I feel the light shadows of the Evening are looking at me from over the western horizon. But I travel to the East in my soul, to leave them behind. Let us work well while the evening closes in around us, & when we lie down at last God will give a glorious waking to all our dreams; all that was lovely in them we shall find true.

The heart is sad when I think of your loneliness & grief, but God is in our hearts, friend. In him we will rejoice, because he is the life of our life, our Father, our Ideal All. In Him you will be yet nearer to her than you have ever been before. God nearer to Him than you have gone yet.

Yours most affectionately

GEORGE MACDONALD

1. Henry Septimus Sutton, a minor poet who published a collection of *Poems* (1886). This letter refers to the death of Sutton's daughter Rose.

To John Thorpe   The Retreat,
                                                Hammersmith W.
                                                  July 15, 1868

My dear Sir,

I can give you Nov. 30th. But before I go farther I must tell you that I have raised my terms to 10 guineas in London, because I had more lecturing than would favour more important work. In the country I must ask my expenses additionally. If this is of no consequence to you — and I know you will not make it such if it is not really so — for I have full remembrance of your liberality — I shall be at your service. I think I have lectured to you on Tennyson, Wordsworth and one or two of Shakespeare's plays. What do you say to John Milton, or "King Lear?"

                                          Yours very truly,

                                          GEORGE MACDONALD

To Macmillan   The Retreat
                                                Hammersmith
                                                  Nov. 18, 1868

My dear Macmillan,

I thought I should have been able to see you before now to thank you for your most kind letter. How cool you must have thought me when I saw you last, the fact being that I had not then received it! My wife had laid it, in a fit of absence, into her bureau, and I did not see it for some days.

I came home from Cambridge where I had been lecturing very unwell, & the letter then forthcoming was a great comfort to me. Most heartily do I meet the friendship which made you write so cordially. I was hardly fit to answer it then, and ever since I have, though unwell, been working hard at the last part, in the hope, now almost a certainty, of getting it out in good time & I think you will like it as well as the rest, though it would have been a better book, I think, if we had had more room.[1]

I should like sometime to do a book *Love Songs Poems* for your gem edition; at least it has come into my head several times, though when I could begin I have no idea. Still I should like you to turn over the thing to see whether it would be feasible or not. I should like to help young people to think a little more grandly & beautifully about love, the youth to chaff less and the maidens to giggle less about it. Not that I would part with its lighter moods either.

Now I am going to take a liberty: I want you to *give* me a copy of the Globe Shakspere and write my name in it[,] then I can't give it away. I can't keep one, & I want a travelling copy. This is a strange reason to give a publisher!

Next week I hope to be able to call on you & have a chat if you have time.

With renewed thanks for your lovingkindness — what a fine one word that is!

Yours most truly

GEORGE MACDONALD

1. Referring to MacDonald's book *England's Antiphon* (1868).

The Retreat, Hammersmith
Dec. 2, 1868

To Macmillan

My dear Macmillan,

Many thanks for your prompt payment.[1] I had no intention of troubling you for it yet because I did not want it, and I did not call *to suggest* it today. I think I never asked for money except because I was *in need* all my life, and I always do ask for it then when I think the man who owes it can pay it. But again many thanks, and more of a more delicate sort for the way in which you send it. Your words are better than the money. I return the acknowledgment.

Yours most truly

GEORGE MACDONALD

1. Probably payment for *England's Antiphon*, published in 1868 by Macmillan.

To Mr. Pattison   The Retreat, Hammersmith
                                                   March 7, 1869

Dear Mr. Pattison,

Your valuable gift arrived quite safe. It reposes with a first edition, a
quarto, of The White Doe,[1] & when that is bound shall be bound up
with it. Many thanks.

We have had rather a troubled house from an accident to Ronald,
who was knocked down by a chaise in the street. But he is now greatly
better, & needs only to be kept quiet.

I ought to have acknowledged your letter sooner, but I have been
unwell ever since I came home.[2]

With kind regards to Mrs. Pattison,

                                                Yours most truly,

                                        GEORGE MACDONALD

1. The reference is to William Wordsworth's poem "The White Doe of Rylstone; Or,
The Fate of the Nortons" (1815).

2. The reference is to MacDonald's lecture tour in Scotland. "Beginning January 5,
1869, he spoke during five weeks twenty-eight times, and never twice in the same town"
(*George MacDonald and His Wife*, p. 289).

To His Wife   [Summer 1869]
                            At Anchor in Campbell Town Harbour,[1]
                                                  Thursday night

It was a delight to see, the moment I set my foot on the deck of the
yacht, the perfect trim, the whiteness of the deck and everything that was
not varnished. You could lay yourself anywhere with perfect confidence
of cleanness. While we sat at breakfast we got under way, and so smooth
was it that we could tell by no motion that we had moved a yard. We just
crept along as softly as in a dream. In a little while, getting from under
the shelter of the greater Cumbray, the wind began to blow, and in a
moment the deck was like a small precipice, so much did the yacht lie
over. She was tearing through the water. So we held on for a while, and
then got becalmed again. While we were just washing our hands for dinner,

almost a squall struck us, and again she was off like a wild thing. . . . It got so rough at last that Mr. Stevenson thought it more comfortable to make for this quiet harbour, where we got about sunset, and are now lying motionless. I have enjoyed it greatly. I have not looked at a book all day, and although my knee is very troublesome sometimes, I am much better. I have eaten heartily, and feel that I shall sleep sound. The three clergymen are very kind and agreeable, and we have got on very well. Ker[2] is particularly attentive to me, doing everything he can for me. . . . The Captain is such a good fellow, reminding me much of the coastguardsman at Bude, only he is much bigger and rather ugly. . . .

I had a rather troubled night; indeed, I feared I should be ill, for I had a shivering-fit after I got into bed, but there is no fear of me to-night. To-morrow after the boat has gone ashore with our letters, we sail again round the Mull of Cantyre, and so northwards. . . . It is cold to-night again. But you don't mind the cold so much at sea. I have a nice cabin for myself. . . .

It is so fine to see the handling of the great sails — sometimes when they are reefing, you would think the men were fighting with a wild beast: the sail flaps and strains and cracks as if it would be off. . . .

1. Aboard *The Blue Bell,* bound for Norway. In June 1869 MacDonald took a cruise on *The Blue Bell* to Norway with three ministers. See *George MacDonald and His Wife,* pp. 389-96.

2. Rev. W. Ker.

To His Wife
Half-past three Monday morning,
21st I think,
[On board *The Blue Bell*]
June, 1869

Oh these dreary nights of pain and sleeplessness. I have not slept half an hour since one o'clock. And I don't sleep much in the day either, though the day is better than the night. We have been since Saturday morning crossing the North Sea, which has been wonderfully quiet — a good thing for my poor leg, though indeed the motion is not very irksome. We are approaching Christiansund on our way to Trondhjem, where we shall

arrive I hope this morning, for it is better to lie still. That is all I can hope
from it — except indeed I could get something I could eat. But I fear that
is not likely. It was a week last night since I took to bed, and have seen
neither sea nor sky since. Sometimes I have thought I must come home
to you — but it would be an awful undertaking, with a leg which I can't
draw up in bed, and no one to take care of me. . . . But the days are going
and will go. Probably from Trondhjem the rest will go on an excursion
into the country, leaving me on board with John, the steward, which I
shall like very much. There are good books on board, but I should have
liked a novel, and there is nothing but that awful *Vanity Fair*.[1] But I am
keeping up pretty well, and try to sing sometimes, but don't make much
of it. . . . If I only were on the way home to you! It seems likely Mr
Stevenson[2] will bring the yacht up the Thames — up to London — and
then you can come and take me home — and that will be joyful, and I
shall get some good out of it — perhaps I may have got some already —
though the means is very nasty. It is quite doubtful if I shall be out of this
cabin the whole time — whether I shall see the midnight sun or one
aurora. But I don't mind that a bit — that is a sort of thing that will keep.
How different it would be at home with you to take care of me and read
to me! But I have only to get through it as patiently as I may. . . .

1. MacDonald apparently did not appreciate Thackeray's moral sensibility in this
novel.

2. Alexander Stevenson. On their return, Stevenson kindly put MacDonald in a
wheelchair and assisted him in getting back to The Retreat.

To His Daughter, Lilia Scott MacDonald   Lerwick, Shetland
                                                             Wednesday
                                                             [June 1869]

My Darling Goose,

Will you send me a letter to the Post Office, Tondhjem, Norway, to
let me know how you and Gracie[1] are. I am confined to bed with my
knee. I have just had leeches on for the second time. Mr. Stevenson is very
kind. I have not seen much, for there is no window or port-hole, though
I have been moved into the best cabin — about as big as Irene's[2] room —
with the mast going through it. She is such a jolly yacht, and before my

knee got so bad as to drive me to bed, I enjoyed it — sometimes greatly. Here comes a poultice. By and by I hope to be able to be lifted on deck, and see the coast of Norway, but I have not begun to get better quite yet. We are going to Unst, a neighbouring island first. Mr. Stevenson has business about here with mines and ores, which will keep us a day or two. . . . I hope you are getting on with your riding. . . .

1. Caroline Grace, MacDonald's third daughter.
2. MacDonald's fourth daughter.

To His Wife

[July 1869]
Newcastle-on-Tyne,
Station Hotel

Darling, I have been dozing when I ought to have been writing. To-morrow the first end of my prayers will come at last. I shall be with you. Oh, I have gone through some of the folds of the shadow of death since I saw you, but the light has never ceased to shine. The train arrives at 9.40 to-morrow evening, but I will telegraph again. Alec Stevenson has been a true brother. I am lying at the Station Hotel now, nursed by the quaintest, handsomest old lady! My knee is bad still — a large abscess.
No time for more. Love to all my chickens.
A. Stevenson will bring me to London to-morrow.

Your Husband.

Tuesday evening. 3 weeks since I left home.

To His Daughter, Mary Josephine MacDonald

Dovedale
August 3, 1869

My darling Elfie,
I would have written to you before but I have been busy with a paper for the Sunday Magazine.

I will with all my heart try to answer your question. And in order to make it as plain as I can I will put the answer in separate parts. You must think over each of them separately and all of them together.

In order to anyone loving another, three things are necessary. 1st. That the one should be capable of loving the other, or loving in nature.

2nd. That the other should be fit to be loved or loveable.

3rd. That the one should know the other. Upon each of these three points respectively I remark:

1st. Now we are capable of loving, but are not capable enough, and the very best, the only thing indeed that we can do to make ourselves more capable is to do our duty. When a person will not do his duty, he gradually becomes incapable of loving, for it is only good people that can love. All who can love are so far good. For if man were to grow quite wicked he could only hate. Therefore to do our duty is the main thing to lead us to the love of God.

2nd. God is so beautiful, and so patient, and so loving, and so generous that he is the heart & soul & rock of every love & every kindness & every gladness in the world. All the beauty in the world & in the hearts of men, all the painting all the poetry all the music, all the architecture comes out of his heart first. He is so loveable that no heart can know how loveable he is — can only know it in part. When the best loves God best, he does not love him nearly as he deserves, or as he will love him in time.

3rd. In order that we should know God, & so see how loveable he is, we must first of all know & understand Jesus Christ. When we understand what he meant when he spoke, & why he did the things he did, when we see into his heart, then we shall understand God, for Jesus is just what God is. To do this we must read and think. We must also ask God to let us know what he is. For he can do more for those who ask than for those who do not ask.

But if it all depended on us, we might well lose heart about it. For we can never do our duty right until we love God. We can only go on trying. Love is the best thing: the Love of God is the highest thing; mean thoroughly right — until we love God. But God knows this better than we do, and he is always teaching us to love him. He wants us to love him, not because he loves himself, but because it is the only wise, good, and joyous thing for us to love him who made us & is most lovely.

So you need not be troubled about it darling Elfie. All you have to do & that is plenty is to go on doing what you know to be right, to keep your heart turned to God for him to lead you, & to read & try to understand the story of Jesus. A thousand other things will come in from God to help you if you do thus.

I am very glad you asked me my child. Ask me anything you like, and I will try to answer you — if I know the answer. For this is one of the most important things I have to do in the world.

Mama sends her dear love to you.

Your Father.

To Mrs. A. J. Scott   The Retreat, Hammersmith, W.
November 3, 1860

Dear Madam,

Some of us who honour and love Mr. Maurice as a teacher come from God, desire to minister to him of our earthly things, chiefly that he may be aware of our honour and love.[1] Will you help us in this by making it known to those of your friends who would be glad to have a share in the offering. I beg, however, that no one may be asked to give who is not under personal obligation to Mr. Maurice. I should be most happy to receive the money and account for it.

I have such a sense of the sacredness of money, and such a conviction that it is only the vulgar mind which regards it as an unclean thing — because in secret it worships it — that I would gladly prevail on Mr. Maurice, should the amount be large enough, to accept our love in the form of the gold of God's making, that he might do with it as he would. But if he should, for his own sacred reason, decline to accept it in this form, I should turn it into that of such books as should make him feel rich in their possession.

Should money be offered with the desire of its assuming any other form, I must decline to accept it. Let those who wish to present him with anything else, do it in their own way. If there should in consequence be more than one offering it will only add to the strength of the expressions.

Yours respectfully,

GEORGE MACDONALD

A Friend has already given £50 and my wife and I wish to give £10 between us.

1. Upon F. D. Maurice's leaving Vere Street, where "every Sunday" gathered "a handful of fine intellects and devoted followers," MacDonald "originated a testimonial to him" (*George MacDonald and His Wife,* pp. 398-99).

To Rev. William Harrison[1]   The Retreat,
                                                   Hammersmith
                                                   July 20, 1870

My dear Sir,

I am ashamed to see by the date of your note how long I have delayed my answer. How could you suppose I should have forgotten you? I still hope you will come & see us. The invitation stands for as long as I have a house to ask you to. I shall have a book on The Miracles[2] out soon which I should like to send you. If I should delay doing so after you see it advertised, be sure you remind me. I shall take it as a real favour.

I enclose an autograph *per se,* that you may use it as you please.

                                                   Yours most truly

                          GEORGE MACDONALD

1. Dr. Harrison was a friend of MacDonald's while he was at Renshaw Street. Dr. Harrison, says Greville MacDonald, saved his father's life in 1854. See *George MacDonald and His Wife,* p. 217.

2. *The Miracles of Our Lord* (1870).

To [Name Obliterated]   3, Reculvers, Hastings
                                             December 5, 1870

My dear [?]

As I know you are much interested in the welfare of our common friend George Cupples,[1] and are now making efforts to serve him by representing his case to the Duke of Argyll, I write to you now in the hope

Above Left: George MacDonald's father, George MacDonald, Sr., in 1822, at the age of thirty.

Above Right: George MacDonald's mother, Helen MacKay MacDonald, who died when he was eight, here shown at approximately twenty-two years of age.

Below: The house in Huntly where George MacDonald was born.

Top: The Noxman Castle in Huntly, which MacDonald knew as a child.
Middle: King's College, Aberdeen University; George MacDonald entered the College in 1840.

Bottom: College Bounds, Old Aberdeen, where MacDonald lived in student housing while attending King's College.

London, February 10, 1846.

My dear Father,

I have had no word from home
this long time, so I shall not wait longer,
but let you know that I am not forgetting
you. I have not much news to give you.
Every thing goes on much in the same way
as before. The boys are improving, but from
various circumstances, I fear I shall
never be able to make them behave as
I would wish.

I think God is leading me slowly on to know
more of him — What I most need is a deep
sense of its sinfulness, and the evil of it —
I think this must be very much the
reason why so many Christians are careless

Letter from George MacDonald to his father, dated February 10, 1846. The letter
is given in full on p. 14 in this volume. *(The Beinecke Rare Book and Manuscript Library,*
Yale University)

Above: George MacDonald's brothers Alexander MacDonald *(left),* 1852, and John Hill MacDonald *(right),* 1853. These two brothers, both of whom died before the age of thirty, served as models for the highlanders in MacDonald's novel *What's Mine's Mine.*

Below: George MacDonald, Sr., at a later age.

Above: The Farm, just outside Huntly, where George MacDonald spent his childhood. *(Courtesy of Christopher MacDonald)*

Below Left: George MacDonald in 1855.

Below Right: Louisa Powell MacDonald, George MacDonald's wife, at approximately thirty years of age.

Above: Independent Church at Huntly, where George MacDonald frequently preached when visiting Huntly.

Below: Louisa MacDonald and her children Greville, Mary, Irene, and Grace with Charles Dodgson (Lewis Carroll) in the garden of Elm Lodge, Hampstead, 1862.
(Courtesy of Christopher MacDonald)

Above Left: Greville Matheson MacDonald, taken by Charles Dodgson at 12 Earls Terrace (ca. 1863). *(Courtesy of Christopher MacDonald)*

Above Right: Mary Josephine MacDonald, taken by Charles Dodgson in 1863 in the garden of 12 Earls Terrace. Mary was Charles Dodgson's favorite of the MacDonald children; when she was ten he frequently took her to the theater in London. Mary served as the model for some of Arthur Hughes's paintings, and she later became engaged to Hughes's nephew Edward (Ted) Hughes. *(Courtesy of Christopher MacDonald)*

Left: George MacDonald with his oldest daughter, Lilia Scott MacDonald, taken by Charles Dodgson in the garden of 12 Earls Terrace (ca. 1863). *(Courtesy of Christopher MacDonald)*

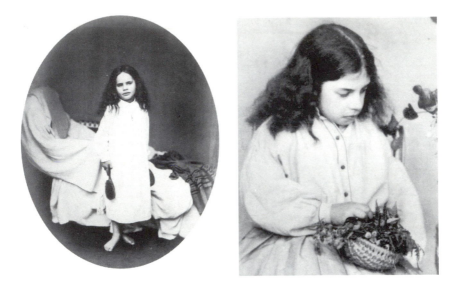

Above Left: Irene MacDonald, taken by Charles Dodgson in 1863. *(Courtesy of Christopher MacDonald)*

Above Right: Caroline Grace MacDonald, taken by Charles Dodgson at Elm Lodge (ca. 1863). *(Courtesy of Christopher MacDonald)*

Below Left: Winifred Louisa MacDonald, taken by Charles Dodgson, perhaps at Elm Lodge (ca. 1863). *(Courtesy of Christopher MacDonald)*

Below Right: Ronald MacDonald, taken by Charles Dodgson at The Retreat, Hammersmith (ca. 1867-68). *(Courtesy of Christopher MacDonald)*

Above Left: Robert Falconer Mac-
Donald, taken by Charles Dodgson
at The Retreat (ca. 1867-68).
(Courtesy of Christopher MacDonald)

Above Right: Bernard Powell
MacDonald, taken by Charles
Dodgson in 1876. *(Courtesy of
Christopher MacDonald)*

Left: George MacKay MacDonald,
taken by Charles Dodgson (ca.
1876). *(Courtesy of Christopher MacDonald)*

Right: One of the few surviving photographs of George MacDonald as a young man (ca. 1860s). *(The University of Nottingham)*

Below: Louisa and George MacDonald, taken by Charles Dodgson at Elm Lodge in 1863. This is the earliest photograph of the MacDonalds together.

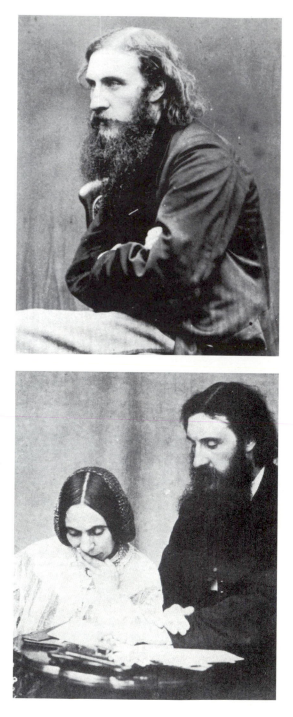

Left: The Retreat, Hammersmith, London, where the MacDonalds lived from 1867 to 1875. MacDonald did some of his best writing here, including *The Princess and the Goblin.*

Below: Louisa MacDonald with George MacKay MacDonald, taken by Charles Dodgson at The Retreat (ca. 1870). *(The Beinecke Rare Book and Manuscript Library, Yale University)*

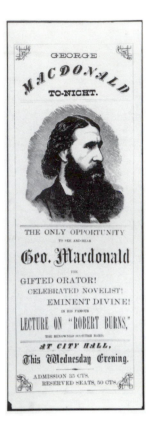

Above: Mary Josephine MacDonald in 1875.
Mary died only a few years later, in 1878. She
was the first of the MacDonald children to die.

Right: Poster advertising a George MacDonald
lecture during his American tour in 1872. *(The
Beinecke Rare Book and Manuscript Library, Yale University)*

Below: The MacDonald family in 1876 (with
Ted Hughes, Mary's fiancé)

Left: A Christmas poem written for William and Georgina Cowper-Temple (later Lord and Lady Mount-Temple) in 1877. *(National Gallery of Scotland)*

Below: Irene, Lilia, Grace, Winifred, and Louisa MacDonald in bathing hats at Porto Fino, Italy, in 1878-79.

Right: George MacDonald with his sons and Edward Troup in Porto Fino, Italy, in 1878-79. *(Courtesy of Christopher MacDonald)*

Below Left: Lilia MacDonald as Christiana in a MacDonald performance of *Pilgrim's Progress,* with four of her brothers and sisters (ca. 1877). *(The Beinecke Rare Book and Manuscript Library, Yale University)*

Below Right: George MacDonald as Greatheart and Caroline Grace MacDonald as Mercy in a MacDonald *Pilgrim's Progress* performance, ca. 1880.

Left: George MacDonald as Macbeth in a family production, ca. 1880.

Below: The original holograph version of "Going to Sleep," published in volume 1 of the *Poetical Works*. It was probably written in the 1880s and sent in a letter to the Mount-Temples.

Death.

Little one, you must not fret
That I take your Clothes away;
Better Sleep you so will get,
And at morning wake more gay—
Saith the human mother.

I who clothed with Body and brain
Now do you unclothe again—
But to clothe in better dress,
Even in everlastingness—
Saith the heavenly father.

I went down death's lonely stair,
Laid my garments in the tomb;
Dressed again one morning fair,
Hastened up, which me home—
Saith the elder Brother.

God is stronger than all pain;
Giveth courage in all fear;
Trust in him is purest gain;
All is well, for he is here—
Saith the witness-chorus.

George MacDonald.

Right: George Mac-
Donald, ca. 1900.
*(Courtesy of Christopher
MacDonald)*

Below: George,
Irene, and Louisa
MacDonald outside
Casa Coraggio in
the late 1890s.

that what I say may be of some service, however small, in backing your application.

Should his Grace succeed in procuring him a pension, he may be fully assured that rarely indeed does an opportunity occur of conferring one with such unexceptional fitness. Mr Cupples is no dabbler in literature, but a thorough workman. Neither at the same time is he a mere bookmaker: he is a man of rare & fine & delicate imagination as well as of plentiful invention. Long before I had the honour of his acquaintance, I considered his *The Green Hand* the best sea-novel I had ever read, not excepting from the comparison those of Michael Scott. I may add that I have always been so fond of sea stories, that I rarely let one escape that comes in my way.

For many years, as you know, he has suffered much — not merely from indisposition, but in actual & not infrequently I fear, exceeding pain, notwithstanding which he has struggled with more than natural effort to produce what lay in him, but which could not find fitting utterance under such conditions. Indeed he must long ago have yielded to the pressure of severe adversity, but for the quite heroic labours of his young and gifted wife, in whom a great talent has been developed for literary labour by the very pressure of circumstances. By her help chiefly, he has been able to do a great part towards the support of an aged mother, who is still alive, and to provide entirely for an invalid brother as well. But his wife's health has of late shown signs of failing and no wonder to one who knows the nursing and the writing by day and by night which are the ordinary conditions of her life; and if they do not have some regular aid, I fear she will break down altogether.

Indeed I do not know, and have never known[,] a case in which such strong claims exist for as large aid as it lies in the power of any administration to give. I trust I have not written more strongly than becomes me — more strongly than fits the matter in hand, I know I have not written. Courage and patience and self-devotion and laborious effort under the claims of literary excellence on both sides such as can hardly be surpassed.

Yours very truly,

GEORGE MACDONALD

1. George Cupples, author of *The Green Hand,* which MacDonald serialized in *Good Words for the Young* (1869). See also "The Tailors Cat" by Mrs. George Cupples, in the same volume.

To His Wife   The Retreat, Hammersmith, W.,
                                                    [February 25, 1871]

. . . I have a bit of bad news. The Magazine, which went up in the
beginning of the volume, has fallen very much since.[1] Strahan[2] thinks it
is because there is too much of what he calls the fairy element. I have told
him my story [*The Princess and the Goblin*] shall be finished in two months
more. . . . I know it is as good work of the kind as I can do, and I think
will be the most complete thing I have done. . . . Perhaps I could find a
market for that kind of talent in America — I shouldn't wonder. . . .

1. *Good Words for the Young,* of which MacDonald became editor in 1869.
2. Publisher of *Good Words for the Young.*

To Mrs. Grundy   3, Reculvers, Hastings
                                                    March 9, 1871

My dear Mrs Grundy,

I would have answered your letter sooner, but I have not been well,
and had, as indeed for some time I have had, an over pressure of work.

We have been here during the winter, in two small houses — very
small — in which we took refuge mainly to avoid the exhaustion of
visiting, and loss of time connected with it in London. We have taken a
house in this neighbourhood, in which it is likely we shall do the same
next winter, and there we shall be glad to see you, but we can hardly receive
anyone in either of these houses, they are so small. We return to our house
in Hammersmith about the end of the month, but my wife and I hope
to call upon you before we leave. I am not quite able for it at present.

I cannot hold out much encouragement to you about your translations. We do not favour such at all in our Magazine,[1] except they be of
stories never published before in any language. Indeed there is little to be
got by them. I do not know any magazine that takes such anywhere —
except of a lower class. Yes — I think the Temple Bar does sometimes —
although I should think you would easily find a publisher if that were the
sole object you had in view.

Please do not address me as Revd. It is many long years since I dropped
that always to me unpleasant title.

Hoping to find you well, and wondering how many you have about you still of the once numerous following — we have eleven —

> I am,
> dear Mrs Grundy,
> Yours most truly

> GEORGE MACDONALD

1. *Good Words for the Young.*

To Mrs. A. J. Scott   Hastings, May 15, 1871

My dear Mrs. Scott,

I will gladly read any manuscripts from Madame Colmache. You know I cannot promise anything, but if I can make use of it, I shall be delighted to do so, both as she is your friend, and as she is in trouble. I have not forgotten her kind reception of my wife and me in Paris many years ago now. If we were at home, my wife would be able to fix a day for asking her and you to come and see us, but we cannot do that just at present. However we shall be home soon — next week. We are only down for a few days. I am troubled that I have not been to see you for so long, but if I could set out before you all I have to do, and have had for the last two or three years, you would understand the difficulty.

My wife joins me in love to you all. I am struggling with asthma, but that is not the worst of foes.

> Yours affectionately,

> GEORGE MACDONALD

To Josiah Holland[1]   The Retreat, Hammersmith
                                        London, May 27, 1871

My dear Sir,

It is indeed high time that I should answer your most kind letter. I have
been and am oppressed with work — & kept putting off until I fear you have
begun to think me discourteous. It is nearly three years since I undertook a
revision of my poems for a new edition. I thought it would occupy me three
months, & they are still unfinished — although now the end is within sight.

I thank you heartily for your kind words, and I cannot but be very
glad that what I have been able to write has, under your pilotage, found
its way to so many sympathizing readers. I have only as yet peeped here
& there into your volumes, for which pray accept my best thanks, but I
have already found that our ways of thinking are so much alike as to be
to me almost amusing from the resemblance. I have especially noted what
you say on the *woman question*. It is to me very gratifying to read such
words from *fast* America. You are not always well represented here, & for
my part I should be very sorry [if] England, Scotland or Ireland should
be judged by some of those who crop to your hospitable shores. The day
may come when I may have the honour of saying in person to you how
much we think of you as our own flesh & blood — I find my Scotch
clannishness a most elastic material, & think of it as only one form of a
rudimental form of love to all men.

My serial[2] will & must lap over into the second year, for that is the
notion of the magazine for which I am writing it here. I hope that will
not interfere with your plans. I am afraid it cannot well be helped, except
I were able to finish it, and let you print double quantities for the rest of
the volume. I would make a push to do that if you wished it.

I do think of running over to America some day, & giving some
lectures. I am fond of lecturing on some literary subjects — poetry &
Shakespeare chiefly. What do you, in your friendship, think of the scheme?
It is the only way I, one of the Egyptians, can think of spoiling you, the
Israelites. I have never touched a cent of American money, and when I tell
you that I have eleven children, and no patrimony, you will understand
that it may be something else than love of money that would make me
wish to get something out of America in return for the books of mine
they have printed there to a much greater extent than at home.

By the way — if you should know of any publisher printing *Robert
Falconer* — I think he would do so from the three vol. edition and let me
make one or two slight alterations first. There are 100 pages more in that

edition than in the cheap one, & I am sorry I even consented to abridge it so far.

Forgive my egotism. What would complete sets of your standard American poets cost me? Please let me know.

With renewed thanks & best wishes, Yours, my dear sir

Most truly,

GEORGE MACDONALD

1. Dr. J. G. Holland, novelist and editor of *Scribner's Magazine,* who later met the MacDonalds in Philadelphia during their American tour in 1872-73. Holland had written in favor of women's rights, and MacDonald was sympathetic toward his views.

2. *The Princess and the Goblin* (1872), which was being serialized in *Good Words for the Young.*

To His Wife   [July 26, 1871]

. . . Mr. G_____ would have cut me yesterday in an omnibus, if I had let him. They say he thinks me just the devil. Poor man! He is always threatening his solicitor upon some one or other. I am more and more glad I am to be rid of the editing. . . .[1]

1. From 1869-72 MacDonald edited *Good Words for the Young.* The magazine failed, its publisher Strahan claimed, because it had in it too much of the "fairy element." The disgruntled "G_____" may be William Gilbert, who had contributed to the magazine.

To Charles Dodgson   The Retreat
                                                Thursday [August 31, 1871]

My dear Dodgson

I am very sorry my delay should have caused you the least inconvenience. I am dreadfully busy — in the hope of getting away for a while, & I laid your letter aside for a day, & then forgot how pressing it was.

There is not the slightest impediment in the way of my giving you

an introduction to Sir Noel.[1] I fear, however, that he may be out of town
at present. Arran is a favourite haunt of his.

Yours most truly

GEORGE MACDONALD

1. Dodgson was looking at the time for an illustrator for *Through the Looking Glass,*
after Tenniel had initially turned him down, and he decided to try Sir Noel Paton. In a
letter to MacDonald, dated May 16, 1868, Paton "describes in detail with great modesty
and good sense his reasons for refusing to undertake the task of illustrating the sequel to
Alice. . . ." (I am indebted to Prof. Morton N. Cohen for this note.)

To Rev. W. G. Blaikie   Antwerp, Sep. 14, 1871.

My Dear Blaikie,
    I am not so bad as I look. I had your last letter here two days ago, &
at once forwarded the proof with the alteration to Mr. Gellan. I trust you
will understand my position in doing so — I do not think any man bound
to say *all* he believes: he is only bound to say nothing he does not believe.
Also I have no right to compromise you with the public. Therefore I most
willingly did as you requested in such a kind & friendly way.
    But I have another apology to make for delay in writing. I have never
acknowledged your letter about my uncle. Here also however I was not
so bad as I seemed, for I attended to the directions in it at once. I got a
goodly array of M.P.s.[1] I could not ask the Duke of Argyll for as a member
of the government he could not sign it; but the Marquis of Lorne signed
it. Lord Colorsay refused — would ask nothing of Mr. Gladstone.
    We are on our way to Holland for a week or two.[2] I was nearly tired
out, & wanted a change much.
    I hope you are well & prospering in all that is worth praying for. Kind
regards to Mrs. Blaikie.

Best and friendliest
greetings from
yours faithfully,

George MacDonald

1. Members of Parliament.
2. In the autumn of 1871, MacDonald and his wife took a much-needed trip abroad.

To Rev. W. G. Blaikie   Halloway House
                                                                                          Hastings
                                                                                       [Undated]

My dear Blaikie,

When we had a little difference once before about a similar matter, I understood that any change that was desired should be referred to me — that I might make it myself according to the necessities of my conscience as well as the editor's. This does not apply to the reference to the old prophet who tempts the young one to his destruction, for conscience is concerned in that; but if I had the chance, I should simply have referred to I Kings, Ch. 13; and I am sorry that the reference to the obscure sermons of a dear friend should have been omitted, for they deserve to be anything but obscure.

In the second matter, however, my conscience is concerned in the alteration you have made. I believe that the phrase "for Christ's sake," conveys an utterly false meaning to most minds. The only two places in which it is used in our translation so far as I can find in the haste of reply are — Eph. 4.32. where the Greek is ὁ θεὸς ἐν Χριστῷ, and I. John 2.12. where it is διὰ τὸ ὄνομα αὐτοῦ; and "for Christ's sake" is to my mind a translation of neither, and I strongly object to the phrase.

It is late to refer to your former letter now, which I read very carefully, though I could not enter into a written controversy on the matter. But I must just remark that it was in great measure contained in this — that I denied the atonement, (which God forbid) because I refused the phrase that God was reconciled to us by Christ. Now there is, as far as I am aware[,] no such phrase even in our translation. God reconciles us to himself; Christ reconciles us to God, but nowhere is Christ said to reconcile God to us.

As it is not likely that there will be any more cause even for explanations between us, I need not go further. I wish this last had not taken place, for it makes me uncomfortable. But as we both want to do right, and both claim the one Lord as ours, we cannot cease to be true friends even if we would. In his name & heartily, I am & shall be

Yours most truly,

George MacDonald

To R. W. Gilder[1]   Halloway House
                                              Hastings, England
                                              December 10, 1871

Dear Mr. Gilder,
. . . I dare not believe that I deserve all that you and other kind American friends say of me; but in the sense of miserable demerit everyone may sometimes hope that he may be doing something beyond the reach of the fire, even as the saw and the plane did good work in the hands of the Son of the carpenter of Nazareth.

Till we meet, and I hope
before long,
Yours very truly,

George MacDonald

1. Richard Watson Gilder, assistant editor of *Scribner's Monthly Magazine,* who helped to make the arrangements for MacDonald's lecture tour in 1872-73 with Messrs. Redpath and Fall of Boston.

To Messrs. Redpath & Fall   Halloway House
                                              Hastings, England
                                              December 10, 1871

To Gentlemen.
After considerable hesitation, which, I presume, will not cause you much surprise, I have at length made up my mind to visit your hospitable country.
I therefore place myself with full confidence in your hands, with this

condition only, that I shall not have to lecture more than four times a week, lest I should break down. With thanks for the kind interest you have taken in my affairs,

> Yours very truly,
>
> GEORGE MACDONALD

To Helen MacKay Powell[1]   Halloway House, Hastings
                                           December 10, 1871

My Dear Helen,

   Many many thanks for your great kindness in sending me some things my brother wore. They are very pretty, but that is a small thing beside the fact of their being his. I shall have to wear them often next year in America, for there I shall have to dress almost every night, I suppose. It is now settled, as far as plans can be said to be settled, that I shall go in the autumn. Of course I take Louisa with me. We shall be away five or six months, I suppose.

   Your boy[2] looks well, & is very strong. He promises to excel in muscle at least. He said to me yesterday, "If you gave me more books to carry, I should be sure to let them fall — I'm so stodgy." I am dreadfully busy, and carry a conscience oppressed with letters unwritten. I should like to show you a book — a missal of the 15th century chromolithographed in Paris, which Strahan has sent me for today — the most magnificent book I ever saw — both outside and in.

> May God comfort you.
> With renewed thanks, & love
> from us both.
> Your affectionate cousin,
>
> George MacDonald

   1. MacDonald's cousin Helen MacKay, who had married Louisa's brother Alexander Powell. Alexander Powell had died in September 1870 after a long illness. Helen had recently sent some of her husband's things to MacDonald.
   2. Perhaps MacDonald's son Bernard Powell, who was then six years old.

PART IV

America and After (1872-1877)

INTRODUCTION

From the year 1872 onward MacDonald's reputation as a novelist and literary figure escalated. His lecture tour in America in the fall of 1872 with his wife and eldest son Greville gave MacDonald the wide public notice that he needed as a novelist. Upon their arrival on September 30, the MacDonalds were welcomed warmly by General Sherwin and James Redpath, who had arranged the tour along with James T. Fields and in whose home the MacDonalds stayed. Trying to keep the children at home abreast of their activities, Mrs. MacDonald and her son wrote lively letters describing their impressions of America:

> We had such a full day yesterday! Emerson, his wife and daughter came to lunch; after lunch we went to see Longfellow. He showed us his rooms and his pictures, and we saw one of his daughters. His house was Washington's headquarters — a hundred years old — which here is as wonderful as a three hundreder would be with us. Then in the evening we went to a severe tea and an elegant one — at the house of Mrs. Lowell's sister. . . . (See p. 203 below.)

On October 21, 1872, Mrs. MacDonald wrote to her children from Philadelphia: "It is very curious the way trains go right through a town so close to the shop windows some times that you can see the labels on the goods inside." And excitedly she described MacDonald's lecture in Philadelphia:

> We've just come back from the lecture. Such a house — a real theatre — the opera house here! Holds 3500 people supposed to

have held 3000 tonight. Papa says he never saw such an audience.
It made him rather nervous at first but he rushed into his subject
& he held their attention wonderfully. There was a bit of fun at
the close. He could not get off the stage. The curtain down behind
was so heavy he couldn't get out. He went from one side to another
to get an exit but not finding one & the people beginning to clap
him, at last he bounded into the stall box where we sat. It was
funny to see him stepping or jumping over the red velvet cushions.
They clapped him again & the laughter was hearty & cheery. (See
p. 215 below.)

The day after MacDonald's famous lecture in Boston, Mrs. Mac-
Donald wrote, in another letter to her daughter Lilia, that in spite of
having "two horrid headaches" they enjoyed a "most charming" visit to
the Fields's seaside summer house:

We had a glorious day, such a day! the one in a thousand one gets
in October. . . . the air is very exciting & of course all the kindness
& praise Papa gets is very exciting — quite enough to account for
today's headache. . . . (See p. 205 below.)

Of course, the MacDonalds had to make some adjustments to life in
America, such as different eating habits — the "severe teas" of ice water
and wafer-thin biscuits that had to last them until the next morning, for
example. And the diet, as MacDonald wrote to his daughter "Elfie" (Mary
Josephine) on March 25, 1873, did not always agree with him:

Give my love to Aunt Flora and tell her for pity's sake *not* to have
roast turkey for dinner the first day we come home. Turkey, turkey,
turkey for ever and ever here, and the very smell of it makes me
feel sick. Dear good kind people! it is a shame to complain but I
am getting off my feed again.

For MacDonald the trip to America was both exhausting and inspiring. Lecturing sometimes until he literally dropped from exhaustion, he
still found time to write to his daughter Lilia on her twenty-first birthday
about that "future home of eternal bliss" and about a "grander birthday,"
as he defined it in a letter to her. Writing from the home of Mark Twain's
mother-in-law, Mrs. Langdon, at Elmira, New York (December 22, 1872),

where the MacDonalds found themselves "revelling in lapsury's luck," he wrote affectionately to his daughter, "My Darling Goose":

> But may you have as many happy birthdays in this world as will make you ready for a happier series of them afterwards, the first of which birthdays will be the one we call the day of death here. But there is a better grander birthday than that which we may have every day — every hour that we turn away from ourselves to the living love that makes us love, and so are born again. And I think all these last birthdays will be summed up in one transcendent birthday far off it may be, surely to come — the moment where we know in ourselves that we are one with God, are living by his life, and having neither thought nor wish but his — that is, desire nothing but what is perfectly lovely, and love everything in which there is anything to love. (See p. 235 below.)

In the years ahead MacDonald would have even greater trials and would have many opportunities to test the validity of his belief in universal love.

Significant Dates and Events

1872   George, Louisa, and Greville MacDonald go on lecture tour of America. MacDonald publishes *Wilfrid Cumbermede* and *The Princess and the Goblin*.

1873   The MacDonalds return to The Retreat. MacDonald publishes *Gutta Percha Willie*. MacDonald visits Cullen and Huntly (background for *Malcolm* and *The Marquis of Lossie*).

1875   The MacDonalds leave The Retreat. MacDonald publishes *Malcolm* and *The Wise Woman*. MacDonald visits the Cowper-Temples.

1876   MacDonald publishes several translations: *Exotics; Thomas Wingfold, Curate; St. George and St. Michael.*

1877   The first performance of *Pilgrim's Progress* takes place. MacDonald is awarded a Civil List Pension. Mrs. MacDonald and children go to Palazzo Cataneo, Italy. MacDonald publishes *The Marquis of Lossie*.

To an Unidentified Woman   Halloway House, Hastings
                                                     February 7, 1872

My dear Madam,

Your invitation is most kind and welcome,[1] but I cannot accept it before you know what it would involve to you. I am going to bring Mrs. MacDonald and my eldest son, a boy of sixteen with me, and that is rather a formidable invasion, which it may not be at all convenient for you to meet.

I must therefore keep myself disengaged until I hear from you again, begging only that you will not allow any desire to be hospitable to interfere with the comfort of your family.

Hoping at all events to make the further acquaintance of you and your husband.

                                          Yours, dear Madam,
                                          most truly,

                                          GEORGE MACDONALD

1. Reference is to the MacDonalds' intended visit to America.

To Mrs. Cupples   The Retreat,
                                                  Hammersmith, W.
                                                February [12, 1872]

My dear Mrs. Cupples,[1]

Many thanks for your kind letter, & for the trouble you take in sending me so long an extract.

I have told Mr. Strahan[2] about it, & he is going to open communications with Messrs. Lee & Shepherd on the matter. I think it is possible something may be done, though I cannot tell till they make a definite offer. What they offer me for a new book is only two thirds of what I get ahead from American magazines.

It will be enough if you just say to your nephew that Mr. Strahan will for me open communications with Messrs. Lee and Shepherd, & that I am much obliged to him for sending me the message through you.

I hope your husband is suffering less than some time ago. Give him my love. I haven't forgotten him though I don't write. I can't write: for one thing I am working very hard to get things ready for going to America in the month of Sept. with my wife & Greville — to be away six months on a lecturing tour.

My wife has been very poorly but she is better though far from well. We are up here for a little while only.

Perhaps we may see you in April. We are going to Edinburgh & further north.

Yours most truly

George MacDonald.

1. Mrs. George Cupples was a contributor to *Good Words for the Young* during MacDonald's editorship. See her "Tappy and Her Chicks," *Good Words for the Young* (Nov. 1, 1869), pp. 52-56.

2. Publisher of *Good Words for the Young.*

To Susan Scott[1]

56 Ludgate Hill,
London E.C.
March 5, 1872

My dear Susan,

Will you accept the accompanying books — already known to you, but in a new dress? I cannot feel quite at ease without someone belonging to your father having them, and this must be my excuse for sending them.

We were much concerned to hear from Miss Leitchild of your aunt's illness. We do hope she is coming round again now. Mr. Maurice also has been giving us anxious thoughts.

In haste, but with much love to you all, and the best of wishes from both of us,

Yours affectionately,

GEORGE MACDONALD

1. Daughter of A. J. Scott; the "accompanying books" were probably MacDonald's ten volumes of *Works of Fancy and Imagination.*

To Mrs. A. J. Scott Halloway House,
Hastings
March 22, 1872

My dear Mrs. Scott,

Your lovely sister has left you for a time. I know you do not need words of comfort, for the God of all comfort is with you. I only write to let you know that my heart feels with yours. We are all going. May I, in the great beautiful somewhere — for there must be such a *somewhere* — be admitted, with mine, to share sometimes in the blessedness of your re-united family, as in the old days when you all so comforted us in our troubles.

My love to you all. My wife is in London, or she would join in messages or written words. I have only just heard of your loss, and do not know when it occurred.

God be with you.

Yours affectionately,

GEORGE MACDONALD

To Miss Zimmerau Halloway House,
Hastings
March 24, 1872

Dear Miss Zimmerau,

I am concerned to see the date of your letter. I was ill, and it got put on one side. Not that it would have made any difference practically, for I was and am too far off at present for you to come to see me. I am not aware that I expressed a *wish* to give you any hints, though I may have said that I should be willing to do so if you desired it. The fact is I have read very little of yours, and the only thing I read, I cannot say I liked — Mr. Strahan had accepted them either before I was editor, or at all events without showing them to me. I spoke to him about them lately — that is, since Miss Blythe spoke to me — and I cannot tell anything about when they will appear, for he manages all the details himself. Besides you have talked with him on the subject, and can do so again. My impression is that he intends to use them by degrees.

I shall be in London for one week — that between the 8th and 14th of next month, and not again for some time. If you would like to see me, I will try to find an hour for you in that week — only, lest I should forget for I have many things to think of — will you let me hear from you again at the commencement of it — addressing to the Retreat, Hammersmith. If I can be of any service to you, I shall be very glad; but you have no idea of the difficulties and impossibilities that lie in an editor's path, nor the multitudes who for various reasons cannot find the literary work they desire.

Yours very truly,

GEORGE MACDONALD

Mr. Strahan retains *Good Words for the Young* in his own hands.

To His Wife   Huntly,
                                                 May 20, [1872]

I must try to work on my proofs in the trains, or I don't know how I shall get through with the last of the *Vicar*[1] which is now being lugged from me. I am going to preach here tomorrow evening. The sun is just breaking out of the stormy clouds in the west and shining through thin falling snow. . . . A long letter from Rose [La Touche]. . . .[2]

1. *The Vicar's Daughter* (1872).
2. MacDonald met Rose La Touche's mother at one of the lectures at Tudor Lodge in 1863, and throughout the Ruskin–La Touche trouble he and Louisa were confidants of Ruskin and Rose La Touche. MacDonald's involvement is reflected in *Wilfrid Cumbermede* (1872).

Helen MacKay Powell to Louisa MacDonald[1]   8th June, 1872

My dearest Louisa,

I thank you very much for your pleasant letter & the invitation you gave me to visit you — you will have enough to do to prepare for your absence from home & to arrange your household for a long transatlantic sojourn — without my money I trouble you.

. . . I will send the thing to George — do you know of any [train] arriving from Liverpool to London?

. . . Yes — indeed, I know 'the old house of Troup' well — did George never hear any of the terrible stories about it? The old Banff folks used to mention it and the 'Pirate Wullie' with mysterious whispers. I had to scramble up some rock behind it once to save my life — being caught by the tide and all alone — my father and dearest Alex and others having gone through the headland of the cleft called 'needle ee' and came out the magnificent cave on the other side. The rocky headland just before you come to Troup's head is higher than it — 900 feet to the height — the highest sea rock in Britain — perhaps may be a very little higher — it is called the 'Moor of More' and from Banff looks like this. [A sketch of the place follows.]

Yes it is a wild sea and some times — oh how still it is and lovely sometimes too in the beauty of very early morning. There is an old farm house in a glen on the way to Troup called the house of Melrose — and [of it] strange tales are told. Some of them connected with a terrible and true story — my grandmother knew well the truth of the story and I have heard from people who have lived in the house and one odd thing which may have been the result of the story! My father used often to go to Melrose House in the days when 'Lady [?]' was the tenant — a relative of our own now dead — '

1. This incomplete letter written by MacDonald's cousin and sister-in-law Helen Mackay Powell to Louisa Powell MacDonald suggests places MacDonald may have known about or visited as a young boy in Huntly. It may have been "the old house of Troup" here referred to that MacDonald visited instead of some mysterious mansion "in the far North," as Greville MacDonald suggests (see *George MacDonald and His Wife*, p. 73n). Many castles during the period had impressive libraries, and there is no real evidence that MacDonald ever spent any time as a young man at Thurso or Dunbeath Castle — or at any other mansion — cataloging a library.

To Dr. Hodgson   The Retreat
                                                            Hammersmith W.
                                                             June 21, 1872

My dear Dr. Hodgson,

I am afraid you must think me very careless if not discourteous, seeing I have not long ago replied to your kind note of the 16th of last month. The fact is it arrived when I was away in the north, and only yesterday did it reach me, for it had got mislaid. What is worse is that I have not seen the M.S.[1] that, I hope, may yet show itself somewhere in the house. I cannot account for it, as my daughters are very careful in keeping or forwarding any papers or letters that arrive. There has been a slip here, but I hope to recover the missing paper soon. The worst is I have no assurance that it is in the house. But I think the probabilities are strong on that side.

I am almost on the wing for America, and have a great deal to do in clearing off and beginning work as well before I go; therefore please forgive my brevity, and accept my best thanks for your kind invitation to the seaside. We pass every winter now at Hastings, where I have a small house which we shut up when we don't want it, and so oscillate between Hammersmith and Hastings. I will let you know soon what success I have in regard of the missing M.S.

Please remember me very kindly to Mrs. Hodgson.

                                                      & believe me
                                                      Yours very truly

                                                      GEORGE MACDONALD

1. There seems to be no record of the missing MS, which was probably something Hodgson had sent to MacDonald for *Good Words for the Young*.

To Mrs. Norman McLeod[1]   The Retreat, Hammersmith,
                                                          July 7th, 1872

My dear Mrs. McLeod,

I almost dread drawing near you with a letter. It seems as if all one could do, was to be silent and walk softly. Yet I would not have you think me heedless of you and your sorrow. And yet again, what is there to say? Comfort, all save what we can draw for ourselves from that eternal heart, is a phantom — a mere mockery. Either one must say and the other must believe that there is ground for everlasting exultation, or comfort is but the wiping of tears that for ever flow.

The sun shines, the wind blows soft, the summer is in the land; but your summer sun and your winter fire is gone, and the world is waste to you. So let it be. Your life is hid with Christ in God, at the heart of all summers — so "comfort thyself" that this world will look by and by a tearful dream fading away in the light of the morning. I do not know how I may bear it when similar sorrow come[s] to myself, but it seems to me now as if the time was so short there was no need to bemoan ourselves, only to get our work done and be ready.

And, dear Mrs. McLeod, if you will not think me presuming, may I not say — Do you not find your spirit drawing yet closer to the great heart that has seemed to leave you for a while? I ask this, because I think the law of the spirit is really the law of the universe; that as, when the Lord vanished from the sight of his friends, they found him in their hearts, far nearer then than before, so when any one like him departs, it is but, like him, to come nearer in the one spirit of truth and love. . . .

1. Dr. Norman McLeod, H.M. Chaplain in Scotland and editor of *Good Words for the Young,* had recently died.

To Mrs. Fields[1]   The Retreat,
                                                     Hammersmith, W.
                                                     September 11, 1872

My dear Mrs. Fields,

I write a hurried line to let you know that we sail from Liverpool on the nineteenth, on the *Malta,* direct for Boston. Perhaps Mr. Fields would be able to meet us when we arrive, for we shall be so lost in your huge country if left to ourselves.

I trust we shall not repay your kindness in offering us your hospitality by proving very troublesome guests. We are not very merry now, much as we expect to enjoy our visit[,] for it is not easy to leave ten behind us. Perhaps however it would be harder to leave only one.

With kind regards from both to both.

Yours very truly,

GEORGE MACDONALD

1. Wife of James T. Fields, who was making arrangements for MacDonald's lecture tour.

LETTERS FROM AMERICA

Telegram from Mrs. MacDonald, The Malta, off Queenstown

Arrived at Queenstown. All three well. Our cabins very comfortable. Sick yesterday. Very fine morning now. We have written.

Lying in cabin within an hour of Queenstown.   Sept. 20th

Dear Children,

I must just tell you that we have got on so far quite endurably. I never moved after I once lay down & slept a good deal all night. Of course I have been properly sick & felt disgusted with food etc. but I [ate] some of Uncle William's lovely grapes early this morning & now have drank some tea & eaten a bit of toast. Interesting information! But to me a promissory note. Grev. [Greville] was very bad last night, but he is now as bright & lovely as a May morning & has eaten a good breakfast. He has a very kind cabin fellow. We have a very nice steward & a queer jolly kindhearted stewardess, very attentive & kind. The steward calls papa "Professor." He comes in "Well, Professor, you'll be thinking I've forgotten you." - - - -[1]

¶Don't go to Hastings before you like — if it is fine weather & you are all well you might wait till last week in October or 1st in November. Isn't it nice that I can open my eyes enough to read this. Stewardess says we shall be worse tonight but I'm not afraid of being too ill. The cabin is very comfortable.

1. All of the letters in this section, from September to November 16, 1872 (with the exception of the letter to Longfellow dated October 8, 1872), were copied by Lilia Scott MacDonald. When she recopied these letters, she did not include their original paragraphing. In her MS, a series of dashes or a large space at major topic shifts seems to denote that a paragraph change has taken place. For the sake of readability, I have begun new paragraphs at these places, and have denoted these changes with a ¶ symbol throughout this section.

From Greville MacDonald to His Sister Mary   On board the Malta
                                                  September 20ᵗʰ 1872

My dear Mary,

I am writing under difficulties — a hard wind blowing as hard as it well can & doing its best to blow the paper out of my hands: then again, the screw joggling as hard as it can & gloves on my hands, for if I took them off my hands would be pretty nearly frozen. I am on the upper deck above the state-room, because one does not feel the rocking of the vessel so much as in the saloon. But it is not very bad as it is much calmer than yesterday. - - - -

¶Do you know, I am the least ill of us! I was only ill for three or four hours yesterday but slept nearly the whole of the afternoon & like a top all through the night. I ate like a horse at breakfast this morning. At table I sit next the Captain & "the Professor" as everyone calls Papa & Mama sit on the other side, a place or two lower down. Mama & Papa have not been out of their room yet, & neither of them were able to undress to go to bed: but I undressed last night & had a lovely bath this morning. I have such an agreeable fellow for my companion in the cabin. He tucked me up in bed last night & did not come to bed till after everybody else because he saw I was asleep! We have had the Irish coast in view ever since the morning & are now nearing Queenstown. It is now a quarter past ten. I see we are just going into Queenstown, so I must make haste. It is a heavenly day — it rained in the early morning but now "Small clouds are sailing, Blue sky prevailing," "The rain is over & gone." The scenery is perfectly lovely "quite too much so" to describe but the sea is sparkling like so many diamonds & we are within a quarter of a mile of the coast & swarms of sea-gulls are following us. We are going to take on board here a number of steerage passengers[1] & a few cabin ones. There are a great number already — nearly all Irish — & some of the women going about without any stockings or shoes, & petticoats no lower than their knees. No time to write more. I send as much love as will not weigh more than one ounce.

---

1. Steerage passengers paid the lowest fare and thus occupied the lower-class sections of the ship.

From George MacDonald to His Daughter Irene   Near Queenstown
Friday morning,
September 20th 1872

My great Goblin,

Mama having written to Lily, & Greville having gone on deck to write to Mary, I mean to have a gobble with you. I mean, *gabble*. We are doing wonderfully well. I never saw Mama so little ill before, though it is something bad enough for all that, & we *may* be worse yet. We shall be into the grand natural harbor of Queenstown — a place I was at or near for two months a year or so before we were married — in half an hour or so, & there we shall remain for a few hours, quiet. Our cabin is very nice for we have lots of fresh air. The wind blows about us so strong that it keeps Mama much better & makes me sit comfortable in both my fur coats — one over the other. Fur is to my body what faith is to my soul. Yesterday, some time after we had started, I thought to amuse Mama by shewing her the bracelet I had got for her, & so proceeded to open a parcel which James had gone to the railway to get for me; for I had had a telegram from Clerke to tell me it was sent. To my dismay, when I opened it, I found nothing but some underclothing & some coarse towels like kitchen cloths. Looking at the direction I found it had been sent some days before, & was addressed to W. J. MacDonald. So I am sending it back from Queenstown & hope to get my own sent out next week.

From Louisa MacDonald   The Malta
Thursday, September 26th 1872

The first day that I have been able to raise my head even lying down. I won't say anything about the misery, only I know I wont [sic] ever go to Australia — nor a second time to America. However, I am alive! & have had some soup today — and they say we have had a lovely voyage so far. We are in our eighth day, that's a blessing. Papa & Greville are both on deck today. They were both in their berths yesterday. That was our worst day. But she — the *Malta* — is not rolling us about & pitching us up & down as she did yesterday, & God is giving us lovely weather & cheerful hopes. If we go on like this we shall be in on Monday night. So I hope, I hope, but oh! the nights are so weary! Papa sleeps beautifully, & I worry my brains with all sorts of things to amuse me but the time moves slowly in the nausea of sickness. If I were up, there is plenty of amusement on board. The stewardess (such a jolly creature) wanted to get me out today, but I preferred letting well alone & keeping on the couch with the window & door both wide open. It is very bright & cheery. I hear people talking all about me. The nasal twang is predominant & not lovely but I don't think it is as bad as a common girl's laugh & ugly cockney pronunciation. She is one of my daily worries — hearing her odious voice above every-one's. The ladies (Americans) some of them have very sweet mellifluous voices. There are two professional musical ladies & a young man singer. One, Miss Liebe, a violinist, the other Miss Fairman, a contralto singer. The first night I heard her voice, like an angel's in the night. It was delicious as I lay miserable & sick, & I couldn't believe it came from anywhere on the ship at first. But she has been too ill herself to carol again. They propose having a concert some evening for the benefit of the sea mans [sic] society & Papa is asked to read at it. He will, if he is well enough. Tickets are to be two shillings each. I should like to be able to go in but I'm afraid I shan't. Oh! the noises! all round one! Some young fellows are playing shuffleboard under my window. I like that better than hopping races which they have over my head. I can't tell you what that's like — bullets on the brain is what it leaves behind. Greville has a very nice cabin companion — a young Devonshire swell — been to Oxford — meant for the church but couldn't go into orders, not thinking himself fit for it — has a yacht of his own & is travelling — with a gun — for six months in America. He's such a nice fellow. There is one other gentleman a young Dixon from Ireland & I think that's all but I really don't know from observation. I only went on deck the day we stopped at Queenstown. There is a fat woman with two daughters, who have long hair tails down their backs. She (the mother) told Dixon that they "belonged to the educated classes" — but Greville says they talk about "am & heggs."

Sunday

¶I'm going to try to scribble a little note — but I don't know. Friday was a lovely day; the one day of enjoyment I have had. I was on deck *all* day & because it was so lovely & we saw *land!* & the sun shone & it was warm, we fancied it was going to be a pleasure trip for the rest of the voyage, but I believe I have heard before of the sea being treacherous & now I understand it. Not that it was very bad, only it was so rough again

on Saturday that all my sickness began again & I have been flat on my
back ever since though not nearly so miserable this time & though I can't
sit up or go out again I can take some nourishment & eat lots of apples
or French plums. Tell Jessie B. that I found a nice ripe apple was almost
the first thing I could eat. But I have never been able to go into dinner
though I have had one good one & that on deck. Excuse so much about
food but it is an immensely important & interesting part of our lives here
I assure you. I have had a bill of fare brought me every meal! though for
more than a week my only answer was *Gruel* — fortunately that was very
nice — gruel & ice bags. They had the concert the day that I was up on
deck so I heard it though I couldn't go into the room. Miss Fairman the
singer, lives in St. Peter's Square, Hammersmith, dined with us at the
Walkers once & sang then. Greville has stood the voyage better than I
expected. This time tomorrow we shall be all on shore. I have just heard
a man's voice say, "Oh joyful news!" I don't think anyone can be as glad
as I am. They all seem so merry. But they are not an interesting set of
people. There is one nice American lady Mrs. Holmes, Wendell Holmes'
son's wife. She is pretty & pleasant, rather like Mrs. Tilbrooke. Grev. will
tell you how the Americans (ladies included) eat. It's marvelous. He de-
clares they must have hollow legs — he cannot else imagine where all the
food goes — he says he should like to dissect a Yankee to find out. Young
Dixon, an Irish young gentleman, is Grev's pleasantest companion — he
has left ten brothers & sisters behind him. I have not felt nearly so cold
as I expected. I have had the windows open, blowing on to my couch
every day long & almost every night — except one very stormy day. Papa
was sick one day & has felt often very poorly but he keeps quite cheerful
& is very good friends with several people on board. There's an immensely
rich American — of an English family — who is very kind to us all — an
old man — so good & kind — he is not literary but he heard Papa read
at the concert & says he thinks he will make a great success in America[;]
"He never heard Tennyson read right before." This is Monday & we shall
be in in two or three hours. You will sing a Te Deum the morning or
evening after you get this, won't you. We have indeed to Praise Him.

From Louisa MacDonald   Boston Thursday morning
                                              October 3ᵈ 1872

My dear Elfie[1] (& all angels),

I can hardly believe we have been here three days — it seems like nearly as many weeks — such a sense of newness & strangeness, clearness & brightness! all about & round us. I don't know where to begin telling you. I'll try & fancy what questions you would ask me if I could get home tonight. Well, you'd want to know how I & Papa are. "Very well, thank you dear; all of us flourishing apparently, both by the way we walk, talk, look, eat & sleep — though as to the latter *I* hope to improve in that function as my head gets steadier & as we get used to our not having anything substantial to eat after three o'clock, unless you call tea & their wafer biscuits & iced water substantialities. They are *very* charming people that we are with. Mr. Fields is quite a gentleman — has made himself so, I think, a polished, genial, kind, well educated man. His wife a thorough lady — a nature's lady — refined, delicate, largish & kind. He is, & evidently has been a lion hunter but it seems to me that this is because of his love of the lions more than for the reflected glory he gets by it. His autographs & letters & books, first editions, authors own copies, presents of the M.S. copies etc. etc. are really something to boast of, something to count oneself rich to possess: but he does not boast a bit, he only seems to rejoice in them as a schoolboy might dance about prizes he might get for athletic sports. He is very simple hearted & clever in his own way. He tells a story *"first-rate"* & had lots of most excellent ones to tell. He is very dramatic in his telling & with great appreciation of humour & a good deal of pathos, he is really what people call *capital company.* The house is furnished much as ours might be, had we money & no children. They have travelled a good deal & collected no end of charming things — a great many engravings & some nice pictures, but her taste is evident everywhere. She strikes me as simply delightful. I wish Mrs. Russell Gurney might come to know her. I thought her a little stiff & grandiose at first but she is really great & no end of kind. Her mind seems *full* — not too full to grow though — of beautiful & best things — verse & prose. Her sister has been here this morning — a lady a little like Mrs. Lowes Dickinson — an artist-amateur — very clever & nice too — with a touch of a fashionable English drawl which mixed with the American nasal is somewhat amusing. Her sister has scarcely a touch of the American, perhaps a little pedantic — like Miss Pipe a little — not her face, but a very sweet voice. They keep a most hospitable table & if we/you could but eat enough at once — or rather at twice, we should do excellently but it is difficult for us to manage at first. They have a sumptuous breakfast at 8, dinner at 3, and coffee & tea with thin biscuits & iced water at seven. If we go to a lecture or the theatre which we are going to do tonight, it's rather difficult not to be hungry when you come back — but still, modified, we think we should like to do something like it at home.

¶I meant to write much more today but the callers & callers & callers — one after another or rather in twos & threes after each other have prevented me. Everyone is very kind & all say heaps of polite & complimentary things but Mr. Redpath[2] says that Papa's popularity goes very much in strata — very much, I think as it does at home. Those who care for him care very much — others can't endure his writings. So they can't tell till they try whether he will take. They have sent in a list this morning of forty engagements. It reaches till December but there are many more than that, only the times & places are not yet arranged. Did you hear that the very first person we saw in Mrs. Field's house was Mrs. [Harriet Beecher] Stowe! It was hard lines to be introduced to her & have to shake hands with her before one had time to draw one's breath in the new country. However, we had to be civil & so we were. We heard her read publicly last night. She read about Topsy & other bits of stories. Of course people all like to see her — but her voice is not strong. She is very amusing — not sweet, stern looking — not gracious — very humorous, altogether she is rather fun, but her voice & Yankee tones are to me horrid. We shall tell you more about her when we get back. I only wish I could remember half the funny stories I have heard since I came into this house.

¶Mr. Spaulding's son & his wife called today — the leather S. I mean — she is *such* a pretty American girl — *so* pretty & so beautifully dressed. The first I have seen that is like what I expected them to be — all the other people I have seen — Mrs. Fields' friends etc. are more like what we are used to in nice literary people — dress quite a secondary — manners & speech like our own — of the Mrs. M. style — only perhaps more quaint in their manners & old fashioned politeness. This has been the worst day for being interviewed but I don't think any of the visits have been of that nature.

1. Affectionate name for her daughter Mary Josephine.
2. James Redpath, who helped to arrange MacDonald's lecture tour.

From Greville MacDonald   148 Charles Street
                                                       Boston
                                                October 3ᵈ 1872

My dear Lily,

I wish I might describe characters well as you might derive a good deal of fun from some of our fellow passengers. Some of the Yankees were the most beastly creatures — to see them eat & to hear them talk about it — it was pretty disgusting! I don't believe some of them can do anything but eat. I declare they eat at breakfast twice as much as I do in the whole day. And they will eat everything on the same plate; for instance, marmalade with beefsteak! If you see a group of Yankees standing together on the deck you may be sure they are talking about "clams" or chowdars" or some such dish & how they are cooked.

¶I have just been talking about the Yankees eating so much; but don't imagine that all do so to such an extent. On the contrary, we literally have only two meals a day except tea, at which we only eat a biscuit. So at dinner (3 p.m.) we have to lay in a store that will last us till 8 o'clock the next morning. (Greville's modesty wouldn't tell, I will. Yesterday Papa & I desiring to lay in a stock were both obliged to retire after dinner, he to unbutton his waistcoat, I my dress, my new black silk. Mrs. L. M.D.) This city of Bawston[,] as they call it, is a most delightful place. There is such room & space about everything. The streets are so broad, & the shops so light & airy. All the cabs, or hacks, as they call them[,] are large roomy carriages with two horses invariably; but you pay for the luxury of it two dollars per hour about 8/6 [8s. 6d.] of our money.

¶We have had a very jolly time of it up to the present. We have been to two lectures — one about Grant & Greeley by one Curtis — a very eloquent man, & another by a Mr. Gough on Temperance but we did not stop to the end of it but went off to hear Mrs. H. B. Stowe read. The Temperance man is a most dreadful chap. He was a fearful drunkard himself & murdered his wife — all which he tells you with the greatest cold bloodedness — & the frightful delirium tremens he has experienced. We did not stop to hear all this thank goodness! but this is what Mr. Fields tells us. Do you know we do hardly anything but laugh here. Mr. Fields is forever telling us funny stories & we roar with laughter. I am going out with a certain Charles Putnam for a drive this afternoon — a youth about my own age, I suppose. There are several young fellows who say they are desirous of making my acquaintance. One is Scribner the publisher aged 22. Does not it sound odd? A publisher wanting to make *my* acquaintance!

We have the most glorious sunsets here every evening I have ever seen. I wish you could see them. I believe we are going to the play tonight.

From Louisa MacDonald   Boston,
                                                                  Saturday, October 5th

Dear Lily,

This seems such a long week!

¶I have such a sweet quiet room to write in. They gave us a suite of rooms — a little library for Papa, our bedroom, a dressing room, a bathroom for Greville & then a bedroom for him, it is the top story but one in the house. We knew directly we got in that they knew & followed *Morris*. Pomegranate patterned curtains, black curtain poles, red rings, Morris pattern oil cloths round all the rooms, old oak chairs & quaint furniture, cabinets etc. pictures & books & Wardour Street looking furniture all about made us feel at home at once — & such nice people. She [Mrs. Fields] is one of the most charming women I ever met with. She frighted me a little at first with her stateliness but I soon got more at ease with her and I *"feel like"* loving her already. She is true through & through — much educated, but no false polish — not French tarnish you know but real genuine crystal clear polish. He [Mr. Fields] is very amusing, full of anecdotes & exceedingly kind — a great mimic evidently & tells his stories most dramatically. They give themselves up to us most kindly & keep invitations & albums of Papa in grand style. We had such a full day yesterday! Emerson, his wife & daughter came to lunch, after lunch we went to see Longfellow. He showed us his rooms & his pictures & we saw one of his daughters. His house was Washington's headquarters — a hundred years old — which here is as wonderful as a three hundreder would be with us. Then in the evening we went to a severe tea — & an elegant one — at the house of Mr. Lowell's sister. (*He* is in England just now.) She is a very interesting person. I should like to tell you all about our two hours there, but must wait till I see you, if I have not forgotten by then. One amusing chapter in the evening was my talking to a youth as I thought a college student — a tremendous big boy with large open eyes who had travelled a good deal & talked charmingly I thought for so young & so big a fellow. I thought perhaps he was going into the navy, thought he would make a jolly captain. I thought I was talking very kindly to him & encouraging him to speak his mind about things. When I heard afterwards that he is *the* great preacher of the town — as an episcopalian clergyman, & is run after tremendously, crowds rushing to his church etc.[1] I was more flabbergasted. However, all that's not worth writing about but I wanted to tell you about our day. Then, when this wonderful tea was over, we went on to another great big immense house — such rooms! such enormous reception rooms, but they look so bare — just handsome tables & couches & mirrors, & nothing else in them — but fashionably & otherwise dressed women. The attraction to me in the company — in fact *the* reason why we went was Miss Cushman[2] being there, & it was a reception evening for her. We are going to hear her read this afternoon, & *we* are to have a reception for her this evening — every day next week is full. I am very well & so is Papa — he is in good spirits too. Grev. is well & gets on nicely with the girls & everybody.

1. The Right Reverend Phillips Brooks, a famous American preacher of the time.
2. An actress.

From George MacDonald to   148 Charles Street
Henry Wadsworth Longfellow   October 8, 1872

My dear Mr. Longfellow,

It is most kind of you to ask us to sup with you, and more than I could have looked for. We will do so with very great pleasure.

Will you allow me to enclose two tickets for the lecture. I hope I shall not give a very bad one, else I shall feel that I do not deserve your company afterwards.

Yours most truly

GEORGE MACDONALD

From Louisa MacDonald

148 Charles Street
Boston
Thursday October 10th

I've stolen this bit of paper from Mrs. Field's table to try & go on with my last letter which wasn't finished. This is the only way I can write but you won't mind if the notes have neither beginning nor end, nor any letter shape. I shall just chat to you whenever I can just what comes uppermost & you must remind me of anything I don't tell you that you want to know.- - - - -

¶Papa keeps wonderfully well & ditto Grev. I have broken down rather with two horrid headaches. Yesterday I would not make much of it because we were to go out to spend the day at Manchester — their Hastings — not that it is like it — it is more like Oban but it is the Fields' seaside summer home, & it *is* a most charming place. We had a glorious day — such a day! the one in a thousand one gets in October but we have had several here (though it has been wet some few days & just as wretched looking as England) but when the sun shines — How it shines! & it has been so hot we could scarcely bear the heat. I think I trotted about walking too much when I first came — the air is very exciting & of course all the kindness & praise Papa gets is very exciting — quite enough to account for today's headache — no. 2 — which has kept me in bed all the morning & from making a heap of calls which I was destined to so I ought to be grateful to said headache. Mrs. Fields is a darling — she really is one of the few — I was going to say — but it would doubtless be nearer the truth to say the *many* that one feels thankful to have known and seen as giving you a new feeling of the divinity of grace & graciousness. I was too ill to go to a party last night & she staid with me & I had such a delightful evening with her alone. I think this will be the best bit of our visit to America — the rest will be much harder work, moving about daily. This ten days has been a delightful preparatory holiday. Did I tell you of the reception on Saturday night here? Such a roomful of people. Mrs. Whitney & her daughter & Wendell Holmes were the most interesting people in the room. There were two people from England friends of Mrs. Craik's but I did not speak to them. Mr. Alger & wife & daughter, & Mr. & Mrs. Rufus Ellis — the marmalade lady — & her daughter & two other Unitarian clergymen, & the Governor of Boston & his daughter. They had invited us to their country house. Such a pleasant Mayor kind of man. His daughter plain but so enthusiastic about Annals & Seaboard & Vicar's D.[1] likes the last the best — has 3 little children, & she *was* so sweet & kind to me. Next Saturday there is to be another reception & Miss Cushman is

to come. I wore (this is according to your order, my dear Mademoiselle) my
— your — black silk with the white lace. Mrs. Fields praised it & so did he
more than anything I have put on. They are too polite of course to criticize
but they are very artistic in their tastes & she dresses very charmingly but
with very little variety. She *is* so sweet looking. Fancy a very pretty Mrs. W.
rather younger without her eccentricity. Her hair is black & grizzly in the
short bits but goes into rich smooth coils in the long places. She never wears
a scrap of lace nor ribbon nor pad nor false hair, but morning & evening it
always looks full dressed. I know you would like her. He is just our age. She
is ten or twelve years — perhaps 15 years younger. I wore my red spotted silk
skirt & the soft white china silk over it at the house where we met Miss
Cushman — my new black silk out of doors when we called on Longfellow.
We are going there to tea — severe teas are the fashion here — before Papa's
lecture. I mean to have my brown velveteen & silk. I have plenty of dresses
but I was very stupid not to bring a black jacket or cape like Pattie's —
something cooler than my sealskin. I can't buy one here the prices are so
hideous. I wrote to Mrs. Gurney directly we came but she has not answered
it — but . . . one can't tell how she is engaged. If I had time I could tell you
lots of things that would interest you much more than what I have written
but I am very stupid today & so you must forgive me. Every body seems
charmed with Greville. We have plenty of invitations to the different towns
but not nearly all yet — so perhaps we shall go to hotels sometimes which
would be a great help I think to get out of company now & then.

    ¶Here they *are* so kind — they shield us from every body unless we
ask to see people & turn albums & autograph collections away without
even letting Papa see them. Mr. Fields gave a lecture on Tuesday, & Papa
tonight — so they have had great fun about hearing each other. They joke
too about which shall wear the finest neckties & studs & rings. Mr. Fields
has some Dickens gave him. It is great fun to hear them. He is very droll
& simple hearted too — with a great appreciation of genius & really is
very clever himself. I like him better as I get to know him more. There is
no end to their kindness. Have you heard that Mrs. Scott Siddons has
given up coming here — illness is specified as the reason. People here are
as sorry for her as we are[;] they say they were never asked again where he
had stayed in a house once — people couldn't do it — i.e. in good houses.
Poor little woman. Papa & Mr. Fields come in. Dinner time.

    1. MacDonald's *Annals of a Quiet Neighborhood* (1867); *The Seaboard Parish* (1868);
and *The Vicar's Daughter* (1872).

From Louisa MacDonald   Boston
                                                              Sunday, October 13th

Dear Lily,

    Such a bad headache and this is my fourth. I am beginning to be afraid of their lasting too long. I have been in my room all day nearly out of my senses with it, but now (5 o'clock) it is getting a little better. Papa is lying down. He was too tired to go to church. I did not tell you (did I?) that last Sunday Papa[,] Grev & I went to the Episcopalian church here & heard a really lovely sermon from the Mr. Brooks whom I had talked to & been so kind as to encourage to speak his mind. I thought him 22 or 23 & he is 42!! We had such a refreshing service & he is a very powerful preacher. We stayed to the Communion. Mr. & Mrs. Fields went to their own church — a Unitarian. They have a wonderful preacher there & I've promised to go there today but I couldn't move & Papa stayed because of his cold & fatigue. I find it difficult enough to keep engagements off for him — there are so many kind people who want to see Papa — & the Fields forget sometimes & make engagements for us without asking us when they are their friends. I have however had to make myself very disagreeable & break up some excursions into the country or Papa would not be fit for his lecture on Wednesday. This last one was dear Mrs. Gurney's doing. She called on Friday with Mr. R.G. [Russell Gurney] when we were at Mr. Spaulding's son's house (leather S.). So in the evening we all called at their hotel & found that they had come to Boston for a week or ten days. They said they wanted to be here the first time Papa lectured. So Mr. & Mrs. Fields gave up their tickets to hear Miss Cushman read & we went together on Saturday afternoon. Greville went with two young ladies from the country who are staying here for a few days. It seemed so strange for us four — the Gurneys & we two — to be driving together in this new world — just as if it were the most natural thing in the world. I must say I don't think she looks quite altogether in her element but she is very dear & quite as stiff & quite as *really* loving & kind as ever. He looks as lovely & genial as ever. Enter my tea — Grev. the bearer. Oh! I'm so pleased to see some tongue & some toast with my tea. I had some soup etc. at their dinner time — 2 o'clk & now I'm a little better & I have got hungry & I was dreading our usual third meal & last — a cup of tea & a biscuit of the wafer order. It is trying sometimes. I believe yesterday's was partly the forerunner of my headache. We dined at 1.30 & had to run away before it was quite over to go to Miss Cushman's then in the evening they had a grand reception — at 7 o'clock. We had tea in elegant Japanese cups & little biscuits as big as lozenges — there was sweet cake too — but you know I can't eat that — at 9.30 we had an ice & sweet cakes handed about. We had a delightful evening — the Gurneys & Miss Cushman were here & lots of nice people & talk besides readings & recitals & storytellings — it was charming but we should much have enjoyed a good substantial supper of bread & cheese or cold mutton & ale & claret after it. Papa & I had to content ourselves with some wafer biscuits in our bedroom one of you — I think it was dear Goblin [Irene] or Mary [—] got us from Austen's [and] some ginger Aunt Flora gave us for the voyage, but which we did not touch then. It came in delightfully last night. You must not think they are not hospitable — quite the contrary — only they cram all their feed into two meals. Such breakfasts! & then dinner — only we have not learnt to eat so much all at once. They have fish & bird & meat & omelets & hominy or porridge & potatoes & beans & other vegetables & four or five kinds of bread & tea & coffee & iced water & Vichy water & wine if you like & then a regular fruit dessert just like dinner with finger glasses & doilys in due form; all at eight o'clock breakfast — then if you can manage it cleverly of course you can eat gorgeously, but I haven't got into the way yet of not getting hungry again.

¶I wonder whether I told you about our day in the country last Wednesday. We got up at 5 o'clock — that was the first of my headaches. We had breakfast at a quarter to six & then went 30 miles into the country by train or "in the cars" as they say. Then we went to a Dr. Bartol[']s — a unitarian minister's house. Such a dear lovely old man full of sweetness & deepest religion & devotion to Christ. The Unitarians seem very different sort of people here from those we know. His house he has lately built on a rock high up close to the sea, with a lot of land all round about it — meadows and trees & flowers & lumps of rock. Such delicious foliage — the maple trees red & yellow all glorious just now — the vines, as they call what we call American creeper, winding & climbing about everything — then round the house are covered walks — piazzas or verandahs; all their country houses seem blessed with these. Oh! such a morning it was. The sea & sky reminded us of the Mediterranean — but that fiend the headache kept me in thraldom all the while & I was conscious of making everyone uncomfortable. Two sweet girls met us on the piazza; one lovely & graceful, bewitched me directly — a Miss Oakey, Dr. Bartol's niece — the other Miss Bartol, I should have known for a Unitarian all the world over but she was very kind & good & clever. They took us into the house & into Miss Bartol's studio. I thought I should like to be able to give you girls such a room for painting. Then we had a long drive in a "pic-nic wagonette" they call it — & we went to see a family in another beautiful house — all new, on a rock looking out to sea — with the piazza, polished floors, Indian mats, Persian carpets; all things bright & pretty but not a mouthful of anything to eat till half past two when we got back to Dr. Bartol's. Then such a dinner & how they *stow away*. Oh! how I should have enjoyed that day without my head. We had a long walk too before dinner along the shore zig-zagging up rocks, through sandy swampy places, climbing about seeing such charming views — strange flowers, strange butterflies, & creatures insectile quite new to us & such, such foliage. But every bit I looked at was small torture. Miss Oakey is half Irish & has a wonderful gift for telling Irish stories dramatically. She was here last night & though Miss Cushman was here too, they persuaded her to tell us some, which she did in the most charming artless way. She is so bewitching & simple you i.e. I can't help being charmed with her — & she dresses in the most maddeningly artistic way, not a bit fashionable but in a *perfect* artisto-fashionable way — looking all the while as if she has come up to & had not attempted anything. Her mother's first husband was *Newton* the painter — she was quite young when he died & then she married Mr. Oakey. They say she was a real beauty which this girl is not. Her fascinating manner is so different from Rose[1] & yet she reminded me of her somehow. But she looks as if she never thought about herself. I daresay that is part of her art — it may be, I don't know. When Papa thanked her for her stories she told him in the most bewitching way "That she owed him everyone she could tell him & a great deal more — he had told her so many," but she had not said a word before of adoration & admiration. She mended *my* gloves & was so kind to me. She is the first girl I have longed to import. She was making a little oil painting of Miss Spartali from a photograph which we saw. It seemed strange to us to see her face there & all sorts of beautiful things of first class beauty out in that new half-furnished unfinished sort of a house. I wish I had my best wits about me, dear, that I could give you a general sort of idea of the niceness of everything — but having a headache I have only mooned on & on about nothing.

We like almost everyone we have seen. But Mrs. Russell Gurney says I have not seen America at all yet — she says Boston & all the people we have met are so English & intelligent & the town is so like a continental one. We think it exceedingly like the Hague. There is a very large public garden & walks through it & trees & seats — so like Holland. In this

Charles Street there are tall Elms all down the street & the houses are big
& high, red brick, flat, & green shuttered. I like Boston very much — the
shops are grand & pretty but the things in them are awfully dear. I have
asked Aunt Flora to get me a little black mantle. I am most uncomfortable
for want of one — those little colored shawls don't take its place. Is it not
stupid? I have got yours or Mary's purple shawl as well as my own. I wish
I could send it you. Another vex is that all those gloves bought at Planterose
are too large. They are *bags* on me — at least you would say so. Is it not
provoking[?] So many of them — they are only 6 ½ too. But then I have
really got so thin I can hardly keep my rings on my fingers — so perhaps
the gloves will fit me better when I get my — like proportions again. My
legs are very genteel, but none the stronger for it — & Mrs. Gurney says
I'm a great deal too white — certainly, in that blue dress last night I did
not look much like what I usually do at home. Oh! I [am] going to tell
you how she helped me out of a water party. She told me as she was going
away "My dear, they are getting up a water party for you on Monday &
I'm sure you're not a bit fit to go & Mr. MacDonald would be much
better at home — go & stop it." Was it not kind of her? So I did — but
it had been made & they had to write letters & put it off. We are going
to Mrs. Whitney's (The Gayworthy's) in the evening & I have to make a
lot of calls with Mrs. Fields in the evening — if I am able. So I imagine
that will be enough for one day. Tell Gracie [Caroline Grace] that I wore
her pretty blue beads with my blue dress last night & the blue velvet riband
trimmed with lace. I can't quite wear my little caps here — they look so
peculiar — I do in the day but I can't in dress. Tell Gracie it was very dear
of her to send me those beads but I was very shocked at having them —
they are too young a great deal but Papa enjoyed them. Grev. was rather
shocked at my putting on another dress[.] "Was it necessary to have one
on I had not worn before?" he said — you know his way.

   He gets on in company better than he did. It will be brighter for him
at New York at Dr. Holland's where there are young people. We go to
Philadelphia on Friday. You must "all the time" write to Redpath & Fall.
If you were an American girl you'd say "Yes, I know it." They say "I know"
to everything or, "I know it" to shew they understand your sentiments.
Ten o'clock strikes. I go to bed. . . .

1. Possibly Rose La Touche.

From Greville MacDonald   Charles Street Boston
                                                                      October 15

My dear youngest sister,[1]

We are having such a gay time here that there is really very little time
to do anything but go driving about the country watching the marvelous
colours in the trees. It is so beautiful! Sometimes you see a tree just one
blaze of carmine or rather blood colour then all this variety of foliage with
the exquisitely graceful form of the American elms — a tree which we
have nothing like. Tulip trees seem rather plentiful here; but they have
hardly begun to change yet.

I went to the play last night with a Mr. Strout who knew Mother
before she was married & Uncle Alex & Aunt Helen. We first dined at
one of the hotels — the one at which Mr. & Mrs. R.G. are staying — &
then we saw a romantic, sensational melo-dramatic, rather good drama —
all about gipsies stealing little boys, sliding panels, murders, & everybody
& everything turn[s] out to be somebody & something else. It lasted four
hours! Is that not tremendous? Papa & Mr. Fields are both going a good
distance to lecture tonight but both of them different ways, & neither
Mother nor Mrs. Fields nor I are going, & "as the mice will play," etc.
Mrs. Fields & Mother are going to have rare larks & are going to lock me
up in a cupboard. Today I went to see Miss Peabody. She is a nice old
lady & always called Papa George Falconer!

The day after tomorrow Mr. & Mrs. Fields leave for Chicago on a
lecturing tour & the day after we start for Philadelphia & after that we
go to New York.

Mrs. Fields has a reception on Saturdays. Last Saturday was a most
delightful evening. Miss Cushman was here & there was a most charming
young lady [Miss Oakey] who told Irish stories to the whole company &
made us all roar with laughter & yet she is so simple & quiet. I wish you
girls could see her!

Mother has just been reading to me Lily's letters & all of yours. It is
so nice to hear about you all.

1. Winifred MacDonald.

From Greville MacDonald   Charles Street
                                                              October 17

My dear biggest sister Irene,

I often wish I had you to go out for walks with me before breakfast
& after tea when this glorious sun is setting. It seems as if it hardly could
be the same sun — the colours are so different & the colours seem to
arrange themselves differently from what they do at home. But of course
it is the same & it is so nice to think so; that after it has lit your side of
the world up till you are tired, it comes to us to tell us it has been looking
after you all & you are all right. There is a lot of nonsense for you! but
Mother & Father are out & Mr. & Mrs. Fields are gone to Chicago & I
have nothing to do but write letters. They are calling on Professor O. W.
Holmes.

¶I think I must get a photograph there is here of Papa. You cannot
imagine a more brutal thing. It is photographed from the engraving there
was of him in "Scribner's Monthly" & with his autograph. You can't think
what a brutal effect it has! It is beginning to get rather cold here, though
the sun is as bright as it can be but the delightful furnaces they have make
the house so beautifully warm — they have air pipes going up from the
furnace all over the house. They have grates in most of the rooms besides
& they burn hardly anything but wood in this country & it is so pleasant.

From Louisa MacDonald   Philadelphia
                                                          Sunday October 20th

My darling Irene & all children,

It is a whole week since I wrote to Lily with a fierce headache & I
was up in my room all day — since then I have not had a comfortable
half hour to write you but I know Greville has let you know that we have
not ceased to be or to love you all. I should have written a scrap now &
then but for my headaches — they have not been so very bad but when
we have been visiting or driving or receiving visitors or mealing, an escape
to our own room is of necessity spent in resting or trying to rest or often
I read Papa to sleep — for the more he sleeps *you* know the better. I wish
I could tell you all about our adventures since Monday last. No great
adventures certainly but everything is so new & big & handsome & the
people are so kind & glad to see Papa. I can't tell you how very happy it

seems to make some people to look at him. The most *dissolved* people in this respect were a company we met at Mrs. Whitney's. They were all more religious people I think than those we met at Mrs. Fields & not so fashionable — literaryly [sic] fashionable I mean, & not so rich but it was very pleasant to hear the different people tell of the way Papa's books had come to them & the good & the comfort they have been to them. I hope we shall see Mrs. Whitney some day at Hammersmith. There was Papa's lecture at Boston on Wednesday that was the great event of the week to us. Papa had two lectures in the neighbourhood besides, but that was *the* night. It was a time of great excitement. There were two thousand eight hundred & fifty ticket holders besides a few that got in as friends. Such a hall! far bigger than St. James Hall with two balconies all round it. They say Papa was heard in every corner of it. Was it not delightful for me? There I sat between Mr. & Mrs. Russell Gurney — one of the *"proudest moments of my house"!* & to sit there with them & see all those earnest eager faces listening — almost breathlessly sometimes (we sat on the platform where we *could* see) was a sight I shan't soon forget. I suppose there will be nearly as many people tomorrow here — at least the hall will hold as many but we do not know the people here & I do not know whether there are as many people who know the *great man* here. The family we are with are very kind. Mr. Lippincott[1] is a publisher but I don't think they care much personally about Papa's books & he won't be spoiled or sickened with flattery here. There might be a danger of both at New York where we were for a night on Friday at Dr. Holland's[2] house. They were outrageously kind & flattering & we had hosts of people to see us there. But Papa does not lecture there till the 18th of November. We go there on Thursday to a grand reception evening to which Mr. Froude[3] has been invited & has accepted the invitation. He will certainly be the most interesting feature of the evening. Tell Lily I am going to wear my soft black silk. It is such a grand reception I ought to have my velvet with me but I would not put it in the smaller box & Mrs. Fields besought me not to take the big one on this very shifting tour. I might just as well have had the big one & shall another time but I don't mind — that black silk is *so* pretty & comfortable though doubtless this will be the biggest reception we shall have — but I don't think it will be the *swellest* (this is to comfort Lily). I shall take it to Washington on the 2nd December. Mrs. R.G. is going to give a dinner party for us & if we come here again I will bring it. The ladies here are more splendaciously attired in this house than any I have visited. All their dresses are sent from London — West End

dressmakers — every six months they have a fresh relay — mother &
daughter. The mother is a very fine handsome woman, the daughter a very
pretty reminder of J.B. They are very cold in their manner but I like them
much better on acquaintance & after being two days in the house we find
they do know & like very much P.'s books. (I mean always to write Papa's
name thus — it will save time in the end — P & Grev G.) They took us
for a drive yesterday afternoon in an open carriage. Mr. Lippincott has six
carriages — a lovely one lined with rich golden brown satin fetched us
from the station. He is enormously wealthy — all made out of the publishing business! This house we are in he built of Italian & Pennsylvanian
marble — white marble & white marble steps up to the house. I may have
"dreamt that I dwelt" but never before slept in marble halls — but such
a house for size & length of rooms & height & staircases we only see in
noblemen's dwellings & I fancy not often so big even there. Grosvenor
etc. Squares are almost cottages to them & then think how nice — in the
long cold winters they have their houses *perfectly* warm, every corner of it
— one corner is as warm as the other, bedrooms & halls all quite warm[,]
all the winter through they sit with open doors just as we do in the summer
& never have, as a lady said to me "You English people always have your
backs cold in the winter." That was true enough, wasn't it? They never
have their backs colder than their faces.

21ST.

We are going to see the handsomest house in Philadelphia this morning. It is built of white marble outside, coloured marble exquisitely
polished floor & pillars, ebony doors. Well, I'll tell you more when I've
seen it. It belongs to people whose riches are something incomprehensible
— they've no children & neither of them a relative in the world. Then we
are going to see Mr. Lippincott's "store" that is, the publisher's shop &
warehouse & then we dine at three — tea & coffee before the lecture &
after the lecture a little supper to which no one is invited as a special mark
of kindness to P. They really are so very kind. They were Quakers & I
suppose that accounts for their undemonstrative manner but they are very
warmhearted behind all that stillness. The girl — perhaps 22. I thought
haughty & rather cross at first, I think now she is shy & perhaps not
goodtempered but very kind & perhaps with all their riches & lovely
possessions a little discontented about something. She has translated some
German books which her father has published but she is exceedingly

modest & unpretending. She is going out in the carriage with P. & me (her mother is an invalid & can't go). G. is gone down to the store with the young men. There are two sons in the business, one is married & has a very handsome sweet rich wife — who looks like a Spanish girl — has a little 8 months old baby. Walter the unmarried brother I like very much — he is like a larger & handsomer Mr. Moore (the Huntsman). We are going back to Dr. Holland's tomorrow. I'd rather stay here, they are so sweetly quiet. We did not go to church at all yesterday — my head was so tired.

1. Joshua Ballinger Lippincott.
2. Dr. J. D. Holland, editor of *Scribner's Magazine*.
3. James Anthony Froude, a famous Victorian historian.

From Louisa MacDonald   Monday, October 21st.

We've just come back from the lecture. Such a house — a real theatre — the opera house here! holds 3500 people supposed to have held 3000 tonight. Papa says he never saw *such* an audience. It made him rather nervous at first but he rushed into his subject & he held their attention wonderfully. There was a bit of fun at the close. He could not get off the stage. The curtain down behind was so heavy he couldn't get out. He went from one side to another to get an exit but not finding one & the people beginning to clap him, at last he bounded into the stall box where we sat. It was funny to see him stepping or jumping over the red velvet cushions. They clapped him again & the laughter was hearty & cheery. But this is only a prospective diary I thought you would like to know where we are likely to be as far as we know. The bear's keeper[1] has not lengthened the chain of our vision beyond the 23[d] of December. Tomorrow, Tuesday a reception at Dr. Holland's (*sotto voce.* Don't like *'im.*) Wednesday 23[d] Springfield Mass. to be housed at a Mr. Atwater's. Thursday Worcester, Mass. (Hotel). Friday Lynn nr. [near] Boston. Friday night we go to Mrs. Ellis — the marmalade lady & stay there till Monday. Sat.[?] rest. Sun[,] ditto. Monday, 28th Amesbury stay at Whittier's the Quaker Poet — he is a real poet & a great one among the Americans. Tues. 29th Providence, Rhode Island. Wed. 30th Lowell, to stay with Revd. H. Blanchard. 31st

Thurs. Dover. Rest till Monday. Nov. 4th Hanover. 6th Andover near Boston. Frid. 8th Leominster. Rest till Mond. 11th Fitchbury Mass. Tues. 12th Charlestown, Boston. Wed. 13. Westboro, Boston. Thurs 14. Albany, New York. Rest till Mond. 18th New York 18th 19 Hartford. 21 Brooklyn. 22. Wilmington (to stay with a Scotchman from near Huntly — Dr. Cameron, a jolly man — he spoke to us tonight after the lecture.) 25th Jersey City 26. Plainfield. 27. Newark (stay with Mr. Gilder a young lover of P.'s. I have cottoned to him — a fine fellow with *such* black eyes.) Nov. 29. New York. 30. Go to Washington 1512 H. Street.————.

1. James Redpath, who helped to arrange the American lecture tour. MacDonald referred to himself as a "tame bear" on a chain and to Redpath as his keeper. See the letter from Greville MacDonald dated November 4, 1872 (p. 225).

From Louisa MacDonald   Bay State House
                                                    Worcester Mass.
                                          Thursday, October 24th 1872

My dearest Winnie,[1]

    We go on travelling & travelling & I am longing every day to write to you all & can't — but we have to talk & look & make new acquaintances so often. It is very amusing but it does not leave much time for rest or writing. This is the first time we have been at a hotel & we have been here nearly a month. Is not that very kind of the American people. Last night we were at the most amusing house we have visited yet. I was very sorry to leave them. It was quite a country house & I am sure you would be amused if I could just pop in & tell you about them all. Their name was Atwater. They are Mr. & Mrs. A. & two daughters 18 & 16. & an old mother 89. Such a dear old lady who entertained Dr. Matheson when he was in America — Uncle W.'s[2] father. And aunts & uncles & a cousin & their clergyman & his wife & son & daughter & last not least their steward or butler as he would be called here [in England]. Such a swell! he walked in like an affected dancing master — he bowed & bent & waited so kindly & attentively — brought me flowers & lovely coloured dead leaves — he had a long rose coloured necktie, satin, extended down his shirt front drawn together with what looked like a lady's gold bracelet with a cameo in the middle. Then he had very curly light yellow hair parted down the

middle, a delicate yellow moustache & a smiling mouth — always showing
pearly white teeth glistening through the long delicate moustache.

    1. Winifred Louisa MacDonald.
    2. William Matheson.

From Louisa MacDonald   Boston October 26

    But here we are in Boston again & somehow I feel at homer like here
& nearer to you. We have been travelling every day & I am sick of the
cars (the railroads) & the motion of travelling is still in my head. Papa is
wonderfully well — he lectured delightfully last night on Tom Hood —
a change for him. The critiques in the papers are generally very complimentary about the lectures but there are some annoying ones. We are with
such nice kind people. Mr. & Mrs. Ellis. They came to see us at the Retreat.
They have one grown up son at home, one daughter Lily's age & a little
boy Bob's[1] age. He & Greville are gone to the theatre afternoon performance to see *Ours*. Greville went to another theatre yesterday evening while
Papa & I went to his Hood lecture about 10 miles from here. Letters from
home this morning.——They were most delightful.———

    1. Robert Falconer MacDonald.

From Louisa MacDonald to Her Daughter   Sunday October 29th
Lilia Scott MacDonald   106 Marlborough Street
                                         Boston

My dear Goose,

    As I can't write every day I *must* write every Sunday to you. Being
here we went this morning (of course) to Mr. Ellis' church — a beautiful
church! a lovely organ, sweetly played with an excellent choir, who sang
the Te Deum & an anthem with real taste. 1st Sop. has a lovely voice but
no congregational singing. Lovely church windows from England but I
could discover no other life in the service — that might be my fault

though. "An admirable sermon" says everyone[;] "an excellent essay" I thought. I hope Papa will preach next Sunday for a Mr. Wright, a congregationalist, a very pleasant & loveable man. All the Unitarians have asked P. to preach but I was so glad he said he *would* preach for one of our own faith first & then he can more willingly for our *weaker brethren* as I cannot help feeling them to be. But Mrs. R.G. told me that the most spiritually minded clergymen she has met told her that most of the *life* of religion here is amongst the Unitarians. I don't think this morning[']s service bears out that statement as compared with the Mr. Brook's church[1] I went to this day fortnight — no, 3 weeks ago. We have been here a month tomorrow. I was going to say, so we've only 5 months more, but we can't tell yet. We may go to Canada after we have done here & we may not finish here till March.

The paper I sent you yesterday about Tom Hood we found here on arriving yesterday but P. had not been told anything about it — so you see the Bear has to dance when the keeper shakes his chain. Last week was the first week of a journey & a lecture every day, and we were really all three very much tired by Friday night. I did enjoy yesterday very much. We sat indoors all day. There were *people* in the evening but they were all very kind & pleasant. I was very sorry to leave the Lippincotts. They were very interesting & hospitable people. We left on Tuesday morning. Had one vex — I lost Grev's new umbrella. I suppose it was taken by someone in the cars [train] — however, it's gone. When we arrived at New York a Mr. Smith met us with his carriage which went on the ferry boat & we were over the river in about 10 minutes. He drove us to Dr. Holland's & after, for an hour in the park. At Dr. H's they were high busy for this reception — nominally to receive G.M.D. [but] *really* to make a great hullahbaloo over the 2nd year of *Scribner's Monthly.* One Miss Holland was in bed, ill — the other, the most delicate, was decorating their rooms with leaves & flowers. It looked very charming for a dance, had there been one, but to us — Papa & me — it was woefully dreary. Nothing but standing squashed up against walls & being introduced to people all the evening — answering these questions over & over again till you hadn't got a thought left to ask any questions back. "Is this the first time you have been on this side? I won't ask you how you like our country for I daresay everyone asks you but I should like to know the impression we have made as regards the difference of the countries." "How long are you going to remain?" "Have you any more children than this son? Is he the eldest? No! really! but you don't look like it & really Mr. MacDonald (or often

The Doctor) bears his years wonderfully — but I expected quite a young man. I thought he had only just come out." "Have you seen our autumn foliage? ah! but you don't really know what it is generally like, the colours are so pale this fall." or "Oh! you've only been *there*! ah! you ought to see such & such a place" — miles away of course from where we are going. "How far West are you going?["] St. Louis. "Oh really! we scarcely count that West." "How far South are you going?" "Have you seen Mr. Froude? I suppose you know him in England." "Do you know Miss Faithful?" "Do you like her?" " Which do you like best, New York or Boston?" "Boston." "Oh! yes, Boston is so much more English of course you do." etc. etc. These are all very well for once but when you are very tired & have to stand hours & don't care *that* for one of the people, you can fancy the night was a trial.

At 11 we had a grand supper stand up one of course with 200 or 250 people. After supper P. was seized with a minor attack of asthma which became a major one in my mouth after he disappeared to his bedroom. He would have been quite ill the next day had he not abstracted himself. There were two or three pleasant bits in the evening — one a long chat with Mr. & Mrs. Lathrop née Miss Hawthorne, of course we talked of Ted Hughes.[2] He did not know that his brother had been to Bruges with Ted. He had not heard of him for many months & was very glad to hear good things of him. She was very bright & interesting & appeared immensely glad to see P.

It seems but a poor lookout for two such young creatures. She wants to go & live in England. He would rather stay in America. He thinks it so wrong of young men of genius to throw their talents away or rather give them to another land. Then we were introduced to Mr. & Mrs. Bret Harte[3] but we were so pushed about one could not get much beyond the first stiff moments of a new acquaintanceship with anybody. Mr. Froude did not come though he had accepted. Mr. Gilder I liked again very much. Did I tell you about him. He met us some 30 miles off New York when we first went there. He is young-ish (30 I daresay) subeditor & real *worker* of the magazine [with] sallow clear cut features — coal black eyes — a very impetuous boylike manner — came & sate [sat] on a little stool by me & talked eagerly to me all the way to New York. He is like a big bright good boy. You would all have laughed immensely if you had seen the fits of ecstatic delight he went into over the big Elliot & Fry's group.[4] I *never* saw anything like him. It was real fun. You must know he has been a real student of P.'s books for years & his devotion is as great as Mr. Davies'.[5]

"I declare" he said after looking at *it* or rather at every face for more than ¼ hour. "Mrs. MacDonald I'd rather have seen this, yes I would! it's better than a new poem of Tennyson's!" He brought his two sisters to the party — one is a very beautiful girl. They had not been introduced to P. when he went to his bedroom — so I let him & his 2 sisters & a lady staying with them come into our room & we all five sat round the bed (P. lying on it with his dressing gown on) talking to him. That was the best bit of the evening. I was very glad I had my black velvet on. I wore my soft black silk & the H. lace shawl — it was so intensely hot. Oh, how they heat their rooms. I think we shall like it in winter tho'. They had some delightful glees after supper. They were very deliciously sung & some good pianoforte playing.

   1. The Right Reverend Phillips Brooks. Greville MacDonald notes: "In 1877, this preacher, lecturing to the Divinity School of Yale College, incidentally referred to my father: '. . . Among the many sermons I have heard, I always remember one by Mr. George MacDonald, the English author. . . . It had his brave and manly honesty. But over and through it all it had this quality: it was a message from God to these people by him. . . . As I listened, I seemed to see how weak in contrast was the way in which other preachers had amused me and challenged my admiration for the working of their minds. Here was a gospel. Here were real tidings. And you listened and forgot the preacher'" (*George MacDonald and His Wife*, p. 423n.; citing Brooks, *Lectures on Preaching* [1904], p. 16).
   2. Edward Hughes, nephew of MacDonald's artist friend Arthur Hughes, who later became engaged to MacDonald's daughter Mary.
   3. Bret Harte, a well-known American author.
   4. Perhaps a group of photographs of a number of authors, including MacDonald. See *George MacDonald and His Wife*, p. 353.
   5. William Carey Davies, who acted as MacDonald's secretary at The Retreat.

From Greville MacDonald   106 Marlborough Street
                                                    Tuesday, October 29

My dear Lily,

   I am here alone at least I mean without Father or Mother. They went off today to Providence Rhode Island & left me behind as they are coming back next Friday, for Saturday there is to be a "MacDonald Matinee" at the Music Hall. The papers announce that this is in consequence of the "great sensation" father made by his last lecture here. This time it is to be on Thomas Hood[,] "universally acknowledged to be his most popular lecture" (vide newspapers). Since I wrote last we have been consecutively to New York, Philadelphia, New York, Springfield, Worcester, Boston, Lynn, Amesbury. We returned from Amesbury this morning, that is where J. G. Whittier lives & we stayed at his house last night. He is such a dear old gentleman — a quaker — as I suppose you know & it sounds so pretty his "thees" & "thous" & "thy" etc. He has two nieces living with him who keep house, & there is also a baby, some relation of the old gentleman's, but its mother is not there. The audience Father had last night was really the best that he ever has had, though Amesbury is only a small town, scarcely larger than a village. But they clapped & laughed quite in the right place[,] but what proves most that they were a sensible audience was this. In all the other halls there has been a burst of laughter at two words which invariably come in the Burns lecture viz. Devil & drunk. These two words generally act like magic on the dullest audiences; but last night no more notice was taken of them than any other words except for the one or two silly girls who giggled. After the lecture two Scotchmen made Father a present of Whittier's works in two volumes & this morning Mr. Whittier said to him "It is not fair that thee should get it all" so he made Mother a present of "The Pennsylvania Pilgrim." I don't know whether you have heard of the horse disease that is raging all over this country. There is hardly a horse to be seen in the streets, & men have to drag about the carts, sometimes 20 to one cart. They use oxen in the city sometimes & it does look so odd. But the disease is not fatal; it is a kind of influenza — coughing, sneezing, crying &c.

   I am getting very fond of Boston; it is so much nicer than any other of the large cities I have seen; it seems quite English & so I feel quite at home in it. New Yorkers & Philadelphians complain of its crookedness & say they can never find their way about, this is because these cities are so very regular — all the streets are so very parallel or at right angles to each other. It is quite painful to me. The box of jewelry has just arrived. They will be so surprised when they come back. Tomorrow there is to be a grand republican demonstration here. The city will be illuminated & torchlight processions will go about the city all the evening. I have not the slightest idea what its object is. It is on the side of Grant who is the republican candidate for the Presidency.

From Louisa MacDonald   South Farmingham,
                                                         October 31 (or 30)

At a station on our way to Lowell — a little country station — from Providence, Rhode Island where we lectured last night. On Monday we left Boston. I got your letter & Graces's & Aunt Flora's[1] on our way. We were staying at Mr. Ellis' but we have our boxes at Charles Street. Mr. Fields, P. & I went to fetch some things & there were our letters. Greville is staying with the Ellis family while we go this little round. On Monday we arrived at Amesbury, at Mr. Whittier's house — such a sweet country like — the most thoroughly country place we have been to. A real poet's cottage, not an elegant villa, but a real, primitive, white wooden low house. We dined in the room that the roadside door opens on. Then through that was the little sacred study of one of the sweetest most dignified loving, humble & gentle of men. He was very good to us & he reminded me of Mr. Erskine[2] in manner & look & kind of talk. He is a Quaker Poet. He was never married — a niece keeps his house & another niece was there as a visitor — both sweet New England girls. The whole visit was sweet & elevating. The hall in which Papa lectured was full (They all have been as yet). Some of the Scotch men present made P. a present of 2. vols. of Mr. Whittier's poems. In the morning Mr. W. [Whittier] said that "friend G.M.D." should not be the only one to have all the presents, & he gave me his latest volume only published this year, with my name written in it & his own. He is a most loveable holy man, but full of fire & enjoyment of all things good. He is very wide in his beliefs & I know you will all enjoy his poems — real poems — when we get home. Last night at Providence we went to a Mr. Weedon's house — large, handsome, expensively furnished. A little man is Mr. W. — a large woman is Mrs. W. — both very kind, children 3. Twin boys of 4, little girl of 3. Papa breaking down a little, bad headache. Hall closely packed, fearfully heated & so much gas made the room stifling for Papa to speak with any ease.

Nov. 2nd back at Boston. This feels like our house now — we must write & congratulate Tom on such a happy engagement. I am *delighted*. P. quite well again. We went to a dinner party after the lecture last night & young people in after. Very nice people. Mr. & Mrs. Silsby. She has grandchildren, but she is the jolliest girl, heart & manner I have seen in Boston. I don't mean in America. But of course I suppose we don't get hold of the jolliest people. One lady, a nice tall youngish person, talked a good deal to me last night. I got on with her famously about all sorts of things[;] at last she said "You do remind me so of an English lady I knew last year, I think you are so like her." "Indeed, was it in England?" "No, in Washington — she is the wife of the Recorder of London[;] they are over here again about the Alabama" &c. &c. I thought it was very funny as you say so sometimes, some of you, & I daresay the English manner & speech are partly what made her think so. Grev. says I get like Mrs. Fields, but that's a fancy of his I think.

Nov. 1.

On our way, Friday morning to Boston from Dover, where we were at an Inn, only the 2nd since we were on the tramp but the people were all so kind & cordial — it was the great wonder we were not invited to any house. One man, a Mr. Bracewell, an Englishman born, met us & was very sorry he said he has not known the Mr. MD's [MacDonald's] wife was with him, he would have been delighted to have entertained us. Funny! His wife was very nice & his sister a nice girl from Manchester — had heard Papa before there on Tennyson. She was, I should think, the first person who has heard him lecture before, that we have met. It's so curious to hear the names of the places we stop at called out. They rarely have the name written up at a station. Exeter, Plaistown, Acton, Chelmsford, Westfield, all on the way to Dover! The people — lecture-hearing people I mean are so cold & undemonstrative. There were about seven clappers last night at the beginning, & eight at the end of the lecture — but they are very intent listeners & so I suppose they like it very much. Also heaps stay to "clasp him by the hand." Two girls came for a repetition of this operation at the Inn this morning while Papa was at breakfast. I made them wait. One greatly desires to be a poetess. But it is really most gratifying to find the number of quiet earnest & grateful readers of the Sermons, Poems & novels. R.F. [*Robert Falconer*] is the greatest favourite of those who have really learnt from him. The foliage has been most beautiful for reds & bright yellows — we never saw the like. They are going off now. Oh! there is such a pokey man talking to Papa now. I have been very X [cross] to him. He wants to introduce "a very celebrated lady" to P. & make him talk all the journey through. I did *bark* about that & prevent it. He has just come now for an autograph for her!! Oh, these cars are so hot. Two stoves, one at each end make yr. [your] head hot & your feet cold.

1. Louisa MacDonald's sister, with whom the rest of the MacDonalds' children were staying.

2. John Erskine, an American writer.

From Louisa MacDonald to Her Son   Monday morning
Robert Falconer MacDonald   November 4ᵗʰ
                                                            In the train.

Papa & I off again, leaving Greville behind at the Ellis'. I think he gets on very well with them. He & Gertrude Ellis get on famously. She is about Lily's age & a very nice quiet & sweet girl, but not at all like the fast chattering you hear of American girls being, generally. I think we have seen as many of the one kind as the other. We go back to Boston tomorrow[;] as it is my birthday & Papa has no lecture he is going to take Greville & me & his own self to the theatre to see *Macbeth* played. Lady Macbeth is to be played by Miss Cushman — Lily will tell you she saw her at Bude. P. & I are travelling very comfortably today. They have only one class of carriages. They are all velvet seated benches with half backs — but you may happen to get a tipsy man or a dirty man spitting out tobacco juice. You can't help yourself if the cars are very full. But on some lines they have what they call drawing room cars which are very comfortable & today, as we have a long journey from 8 in the morning till 2.30 we have taken a whole compartment which consists of a couch & two easy chairs, large handsome windows, curtains & blinds, footstools & [a] valuable & refined addition a — spittoon! The greatest reason for liking the drawingroom cars is that they are not so hot. In the other cars there is a large stove at each end of a long car which they heat up most fearfully & this (is) mixed with odours of peppermint & garlic — & then when you go out what can you do but take cold? They made my head ache. The sun is so bright this morning. Yesterday it rained all day long but it does not seem to keep wet here so long as it does in our land.

From Greville MacDonald   106 Marlborough Street, Boston
                                                        Monday, November 4th

My dear Lily,

Tomorrow is Mother's birthday, so I shall wish her many happy returns for you all. I saw them off this morning in the cars [train] for Hanover, but they will return tomorrow morning. In the carriage going to the station I told them that Miss Cushman was going to act Lady MacBeth this week in Boston, so they told me to get tickets for tomorrow: but when I came home I found that Mrs. Ellis had invited friends & some that she had invited for Sunday evening but had to put off, because of Father's preaching, so she cannot put them off again. Saturday afternoon is the only chance, but that is Guy Mannering — & perhaps there is going to be another MacDonald Matinee.- - - -

¶Father preached last night at Mr. Wright's a congregationalist & I think he will preach again next Sunday very likely for Mr. Ellis.- - - -

¶Mr. Redpath was in an awful way about it [the preaching] & Mother says he gave her a scolding such as she has not had since she was twelve years old, just because he is afraid he will break down. You know, I go down to the bureau every morning I am here, to see about letters, etc. & Mr. Redpath when he sees me rushes forward & seizes my hand & enquires "How's your father this morning?" Father says he is a tame bear & Mr. R. is his keeper. But for all this the keeper is a very pleasant fellow, not quite a gentleman, I suppose. All last week I went sight seeing with Miss Ellis. For one place Bunker's Hill Monument where the first battle of the Revolution was fought & the only battle where we thrashed the Yankee rebels.

We are going back to the Fields on Thursday. Here is a recipe for lovely sponge cake. 8 eggs, the same weight of sugar & half as much flour, the rind of a lemon & half the juice. It is lovely!

From Louisa MacDonald to Her Daughter   Marlborough St.
Winifred Louisa MacDonald   November 6th 1872

I am pleased to have time to scribble to you, because the most of most of our days are spent either "in the cars" or in company — or in bed which we hail as "oh bed! oh bed! delicious bed!" not that we get so much of it — for *everyone* wherever we go has breakfast at 8 o'clock or 7.30.

¶Imagine our feelings when they tell us after a reception, after a lecture, after a six hours journey & a lot of talk, at 12 o'clock at night that they breakfast at 8 & have prayers before that! That was at Hanover yesterday at a congregationalist minister's house. Dr. Holland's of New York is the only other house where we have had prayers. This [is] a minister's house — a Unitarian [minister] — but they don't have it here. But I was going to tell you how it is I have time today to write to you. This morning after breakfast I was going rather rushingly upstairs to pack up my yellow box & Papa's portmanteau because we go back to Mr. Fields tomorrow, & then I was to go out with Mrs. Ellis to buy another trunk, because my big one is too big to take about everywhere, & my tin one is too slight to go to New York, Washington, Chicago, & St. Louis, Niagara, etc. etc. when I caught my foot in my dress (tell Grace I suppose the consequence of having it too long) & fell upstairs my whole weight came on my leg afore my knee & gave a terrible pain. I can't tell how it was exactly but the consequence is a tremendous bruise which leaves me very lame & very much shaken, so badly that I cannot go with Papa to Andover tonight. But it is not far & he is coming back here tonight, having written to the Superintendent to ask him to have the last train stopped to pick him up at Andover — which he has since said he will have the greatest pleasure in having done for him. Then tomorrow the lecture at Roxbury is only a very short way from here, so I shall leave Greville to go with him there & I hope I shall be all right again by that time. Meantime the pain is not pleasant & it is worse to have anything the matter with you when you are not at your own blessed home. Mrs. Ellis here is so awfully kind. She looks very grave & rather dull but there is no end to her kindness & thought for us. When I fell on the stairs I was so afraid she & lots of others would rush to me but when she saw I was really hurt & faint she left me to Papa & only sent me Eau-de-Cologne & cold water by Greville. Was it not sweet & thoughtful of her[?] Gertrude, her only daughter — she is about Lily's age — is a nice sensible good looking girl — so very retiring & modest but as kind & cheerful as can be. She & Grev. get on very well together, in fact, he told me this morning people must be saying things about them — they have been out together so much! Wasn't it funny of him to think of it? People do admire him so very much. There was one lady told me she thought he was the loveliest youth she had ever seen — just like the Apostle John! He is very sweet to people & of course I am very proud of him — in a way you know. All this while I haven't told you the great pleasure I had when I came in last night from Hanover. We had a very tiring railroad journey & when we had dined Grev. gave me such a bundle of letters that had come in my absence[,] one from Lily & the large packet from you all, which I did get on my birthday. It could not have been better timed. After all, though a fortnight seems a long time, when you think of those thousands of miles of sea & land the wonder is that we get it so soon. I am very glad you like the new schoolroom. I hope the housewarming passed off to the satisfaction of the hostess & the butler. How did the young lieutenant in the navy amuse you with his sea stories? How kind of an Honble. [Honorable] lady to patronise your juvenile academic halls!

¶The birthday letters & pictures were the best treat I could have. It was a very lovely morning at Hanover — very cold — & though we had to get up so early we were with very nice people, Revd. & Mrs. Leeds. I think Mrs. Leeds is the next sweetest woman I have seen to Mrs. Fields. She was very lovely to us both — it was a surprise to us, because we expected to go to an Inn but she sent to meet us & when we arrived she met us at her door & said she had been looking to this day ever since last February — but she had not written to us & we did not know there were such people in the world. But to go back to my birthday — after prayers, very, very nice pleasant prayers & breakfast, we went over the Colleges there & saw the spots on the sun through the telescope in their observatory. Then we walked to the station through the prettiest country we have seen yet, and after that came the long weary journey that took all the good spirits out of Papa. He lost his pencil & pen case too, & that troubled him — but he is better today, only he has a stye. He is correcting proof now[1] (it is quite a treat for him to be indoors) which is to be sent to England when ready. We have a fire in our bedroom — an open fire as they say here, with nice logs of wood. - - - -

¶I forgot to tell you that Papa gave me that exquisite aqua-marine pendant yesterday. I suppose you saw it before Papa left. It is very beautiful. People admire all my pretty things so much. And, for the group![2] it is the amusement[,] amazement & admiration of all beholders. There was a company of people here last night, after our fatiguing journey & I was not in a [mood] to shew off my cubs, but I had to come up & fetch my pictures & the old bearess had to receive a great many congratulations & compliments.

Now I must shut up or "dry up" as they say here. Dear Louisa the Young, I am your loving mother Louisa the Old.

1. Possibly for *Good Words for the Young*. See *Once a Week* (Nov. 2, 1872) for the famous caricature of MacDonald.

2. Probably a photograph of the MacDonald family.

From Louisa MacDonald   November 6th

Oh, about bonnets "well I guess I keep some of 'em pretty well on the trot" I have tried & discarded the brown hat that I am keeping for Mary or Goblin [Irene]. The *Paris Smoke* is my & P's favorite. I have worn the black lace with pink roses, but I couldn't like that large rose. I have worn the white & pink one oftener. I did the night I sate [sat] on the platform here with Mrs. Gurney. She said something about how nicely I was dressed, but I do wish I had brought a black cloth or merino jacket. The cars are too hot for sealskin & yet the draughts oblige me to have something warm & with arms. I have found a very good way of dressing well & yet carrying only my bag. Old black silk dress, red satin petticoat, take white silk polonaise in bag — then I am ready for company or otherwise. It is so convenient as it does not crumple & looks prettier than anything. Then at breakfast I put on that blue flannel jacket I got in Regent Circus. My blk. [black] lace bonnet does well for travelling.

November 7th

We have to go off sooner than we expected today to Mr. Fields. Poor P. cannot get time for his proof & it bothers him so. My leg is very much bruised but it is better today — it is good for me that we are having a restful week, but you should see the elegance of my gait in going up & down stairs!! We are trudged off now to Mr. Fields where we are going to stay till Tuesday because they are having a lunch at which are to appear Mr Longfellow, Sothern (Lord Dun dreary) & some other actors. So we have to budge & I have to pack — so I can't write more or I shall perhaps not be ready. It is pouring like a regular London rain, so I shan't have to walk a step, so much the better for me. I am very sorry to leave these dear Ellises. They are so deliciously kind to us & more homelike than the other delightful people we are going to. There is a little too much *full dress talk there* — all good but a little more than makes me perfectly at rest. These people are of such *dear plain brown goodness*. You know, don't you?

From Louisa MacDonald   Boston, dear Charles St.
                                              Monday, November 11th

Not such good news today. Papa is very unwell.

¶Tuesday. I had to go to him yesterday, dear. He has had a tremendous gumboil & swollen face & neck — could scarcely open his mouth to utter a word, then came the *tremendous fire.*

Wednesday. Nursing & visiting & having to see our hostess' visitors & to repack, are not compatible with letter writing, however, Papa is better today, though he has had enough bloodspitting just to make me very anxious. We are going to Mrs. Cunningham's today. She came on Monday morning & entreated me to persuade P. to give up all this week's lectures & to go & stay with her at Milton. She lives in a sweet place they say, about 8 miles from Boston — she came with Mrs. Gurney one day — did I tell you about her? She is large & stout [or sweet] — knows Nannie Smith — lived close to her in Algiers one winter — knows *Mary Garth* & the Munros[1] I think another winter at Cannes. So I fancy it is just the place to go. She came like a ministering angel on Monday morn for we had had a terrible night of anxiety — Papa ill — fire raging within sight all night — rumors that Charles St. was in danger. In the morning terrible news of everybody's property being gone — clean burnt away — among them, the Field's & her mother & all the Banks broken & Insurance Offices. The dismay was fearful. These dear people more dismal than I can describe. She trying to smile, but fancy my distress — should I hurt them by proposing to go to a hotel & yet to be here, & locusts eating up their little all. "This house," said he at breakfast, "& 3 lectures, are all I have in the world." So you can fancy I welcomed Mrs. Cunningham with her kind message & promise of shelter & entreaties to go to her, as a true

God sent woman. But since Monday it has been discovered that the Banks have not broken, that the Ins. [Insurance] Offices are paying in part & though some of their houses are burnt down these dear people are not at all in so penniless a condition as they feared they were going to be. But yet they have a great anxiety upon them & I cannot help seeing that it will be as much rest for them as it will for us to go to Milton for a few days. We have got so fond of Boston, that it is a small *grief* to leave it. There is already a home feeling about the place to us that is very nice. But we must go forth again amongst strangers. If we were both quite strong it would be no end of amusing & funny. I must go now & pack for Milton. I have had to buy another box, such a nice one. Tell Mary we mean to give it to her when we come back if it has its ribs intact at the end of the journey. The yellow iron one was stabbed through, the partition came out, & 2 of my favorite bonnets were pancakes at the end of the journey — & I cannot have the face to travel with my gigantic apparatus box.

1. Alexander Munro, the sculptor, and his daughter Annie.

From Greville MacDonald   Milton, Mass.
                                                    November 14th 1872

My dear Winnie,

I suppose Mother has told you all about our coming here & why & everything, so I will only say it is a most delightful place & Papa has a study all to himself & Mrs. Cunningham is delightful & so is Miss Dobney, who plays the guitar & sings charmingly. Of course you have heard of the terrible fire we have had in Boston, & I suppose have been wondering whether we were there at the time & whether it was near us & if so, whether we were burnt out, so I will do my best to tell you something about it. To begin with we were in Boston during the whole time the fire lasted — we were not near it & therefore not burnt out.

¶On Saturday night Mrs. Fields had a reception — not many people, but among them Miss Cushman, whom we had seen as Meg Merrilies in Guy Mannering the same afternoon. Well, about nine o'clock we heard that there was a terrible fire raging. Miss Cushman hurried off at once because it was near her hotel, though it never reached that. Of course everybody went off. And with them a Mr. Wild, an artist — but before he could reach his studio the flames had seized his building & the fire was licking up his oils & paints & smacking its lips with great relish over all the finished & unfinished pictures & sketches he had ever done in his life.

Mr. W. Hunt, about the most celebrated painter here, whose studio was in the same building, also had every mortal & immortal picture burnt. Of course we were all in a tremendous fright, not knowing but what it might reach us before morning. Mrs. Fields, I believe, packed all the silver up, & Mr. Fields stopped up all night as well, but made us all go to bed. He & I went out about 11 o'clk to see how it was looking. This will give you some idea of the intensity of it. When we were nearly half a mile off the fire, on the common & the moon was nearly full & shining as bright as it ever did, the glare of the flames obliterated a shadow the moon would have made & cast one right in the opposite direction! Any stranger would say that their fire system was perfect. When there is a fire anywhere you go to a "fire box" — of which there is always one within five minutes walk — & turn a handle round as many times as the handle of the box represents, so that all the stations know at the same time where the fire is, & turn out at once. Yet with all this they let the fire get to such an extent that the streams of water which were played upon it were not of the slightest avail. It was just like squirting water out of a small syringe into a large furnace. The cause of the whole thing, apparently, was bad management. When they wanted to blow up buildings the mayor would not give his consent because the city would have to pay for those that were blown up. After the fire had been raging for seven hours & a half, he at last gave his consent, but only after more than half the mischief was done.

¶Mr. Robert Collyer, who did so much for the Chicago fire & went through it all, was staying with us at the Fields' at the time.

All the very finest business places in the city are now burying their heads in the mud & dirt as though ashamed of ever having dared to stand so high that the water could not be reached up to them. On Sunday I did nothing but go about the ruins & the burning buildings the whole day. There is something most touching & sad about it all; nearly a hundred acres which the day before were worth millions of money, are now lying in burning masses & smoke, & not worth a cent. Over all this vast extent of ground you can't distinguish one street from another & here & there are poor Irish women guarding their few old chairs & ricketty table with an old Dutch clock & a few other little ornaments. But there are very few people burnt out of house & home; there are only about a hundred poor tenement houses burnt down where the very poor Irish live — for there

are no poor Americans — & subscriptions are coming in so quickly &
plentifully that there is a fear that we shall not know what to do with it
all & there are poor hurrying from all parts of the country who are going
to pass themselves off as having been burnt out of home. There fire raged
from 7.30 on Saturday night till 2 p.m. on Sunday, & it was only then
that they began to get it all under & it is still burning in places, cellars
etc. & I suppose it will for several days more though of course it will not
spread. As to that, Chicago is still burning & it is more than a year ago
that the fire took place. Mr. Collyer tells us that if you want to light your
cigar you have only to thrust a match into the smouldering debris & it
will flame up immediately. But at Chicago (pronounced Shicawgo) all the
houses were built of wood & here there are — *were* I should say the finest
granite & marble — most palatial buildings, & yet now they are none the
better off for that; they say that the buildings alone were worth
$20,000,000 that is £4,000,000. But [what] is the worst loss is the mer-
chandize which was stored as tight as it could be in all the warehouses, &
the impossibility of moving it because there were no horses. The whole
loss together is estimated at 20,000,000 £'s & I suppose they would have
it all up again, were it not for the frosts which soon will be setting in.
Why, fancy! Mrs. Fields who has just been to Chicago says it is three times
as large now as ever it was, & all built with marble & granite & stone. It
is ten miles long. Nothing but these splendid houses for ten miles!

From Greville MacDonald   Milton, Mass.
                                                    November 16th

My dear Mary,

I have just escaped from the drawing room where are assembled about
six people who have come in to see Father & Mother. Everybody is related
to everybody here, though it is a pretty big place & every other house is
either a Forbes or Cunningham. We dined this afternoon at Mr. Forbes,
a brother of Mrs. Cunningham, a man with a most unfortunately big nose
& just like a beetroot. He has two daughters the youngest of which marches
me off for walks in a most amusing manner. She is rather like Grace —
snubs me on every opportunity — or rather, tries. After dinner of course
she marched me off & kept me going till it was quite dark. She is quite
a character, though I do not much like her.

¶Last night we went to a children's party here at Mr. Edward Cunningham's & of course all the children were cousins or something. He has been a great part of his life in China & Japan & we saw some of the most wonderful things — some of which he says it must have taken a man 20 years to make! He has a crystal ball of the very purest sort, without a streak in it & about half the size of an air ball: he says there is only one larger in all the earth & in England. You cannot think how small the "Old Country" seems to me now — after this immense space. Why, people think nothing of taking their whole families to California which takes 7 1/2 days & steam all the way. I know you will all think I have turned Yankee for saying this; but it is an undeniable fact that you could cut England out of the United States & they would scarcely miss it! There is some brilliant dance music going on.

I am sorry for you, having such rainy weather — here it is lovely, & I think freezing. Miss Forbes & I went down this evening to see about flooding a certain meadow for skating; & of course she brought me home the longest possible way!

Tell the boys they did not put me in a cupboard, but changed their minds & went to hear [Tyndale] lecture & left me standing outside! it is worse, is it not?

From George MacDonald to His   [America, December, 1872]
Daughter Mary Josephine MacDonald

My Darling Elfie,
     . . . I am much better, and have just written these verses to send to my chickens for the Little-Baby time [Christmas Day]. Would we were all the holy babies of our Father in heaven — out and out, I mean. My love to Lily and everyone. I have thought you all over.

                                        Your loving

                                        Father

A Song for Both Sides of the Atlantic

Fur-footed, slow, for all thy gracious charms,
　　We pray thee, dear December, to depart;
We kiss the Child thou bearest in thine arms,
　　But all the year he dwelleth in our hearts.

Young January, with the wrinkled face,
　　Follow thy sisters on their starry way;
Sweep on, we beg thee, with thy snowy train;
　　When next thou com'st, we'll give thee leave to stay.

Make, February, few steps o'er the floor,
　　Nor linger by the hearth when thou should'st cross;
Haste thee, nor turn to courtesy at the door;
　　Pass through, and make us richer by thy loss.

Nor best thy robes, O March, nor clutch the hair
　　That hither, thither, all about thee flies;
O let thy dusty winds afar thee bear,
　　That thy sweet sister come with smile and sighs.

And yet we care not whether sigh or smile
　　Shall, April, on thy fair face win the day;
We love thee, girl, but thou hast not a wile
　　To move a prayer except — oh, haste away!

Come then, dear May; lead o'er the sea-waves dull
　　The eager ship, the angel of the boon;
And when our arms are as our full hearts full,
　　Then go or linger, dear and perfect June.

From George MacDonald to His Daughter   Elmira, [New York]
Lilia Scott MacDonald   December 22, 1872

My Darling Goose,

This will hardly reach you on your birthday. Neither did I think of it for that but just for the sake of writing to you. But may you have as many happy birthdays in this world as will make you ready for a happier series of them afterwards, the first of which birthdays will be the one we call the day of death down here. But there is a better, grander birthday than that, which we may have every day — every hour that we turn away from ourselves to the living love that makes our love, and so are born again. And I think all these last birthdays will be summed up in one transcending birthday, far off it may be, but surely to come — the moment where we know in ourselves that we are one with God, are living by his life, and having neither thought nor wish but his — that is, desire nothing but what is perfectly lovely, and love everything in which there is anything to love.

I am greatly better. I thought as I lay in bed last Thursday night after a lecture that I should have to give up. My chest was so bad and I could not rest. The stove, which had been burning like a demon, and making us miserable with red-hot heat, for we could not control it much, went out, and the room grew cold. A great storm of wind, mixed with small snow, was roaring outside, and I felt it blowing on my face as I lay, and everything seemed against me. But what do you think? I grew easy and calm and restful, and fell fast asleep, and woke indescribably better, and have been better ever since. For there had come a change, and it was a great South wind that blew into the room and all about me. Like so many of God's messengers, it had looked fearful to my ignorance, when it was full of healing. Mamma, too, who had had such a frightful headache the day before, so bad that she had to let me go to the lecture alone, was so much better, that we got up and dressed in half an hour, put up our things, drank a cup of tea, and hurried off to the station for a five or six hours' journey here, and were nothing the worse, and in this house, belonging to the Mother-in-Law of Mark Twain, we are revelling in lapsury's luck.

In a few days I will send you some more money. Mr. Davies will let you know when it arrives.

I have had your letter and those of all my darling chickens for my birthday [December 10th]. You must all take my thanks in a lump and divide it amongst you. I hope to write to you all before I return, but I have very little time. . . .

Mamma has reminded me that it is your 21st birthday. I send you a little poem I wrote in the dark in one of our railway journeys a few days ago going to Buffalo.[1]

1. For this poem, "To My Goose, on Her Twenty-first Birthday," see *George Mac-Donald and His Wife*, p. 433.

From George MacDonald to James T. Fields[1]   Elmira [New York]
                                                          December 22, 1872

My dear little Jim,

Your old uncle never dreamed of deserting you and leaving you to blossom in rainbows unbefriended. All he thought of dropping was a pair of crystal buttons because they were taken for diamonds. I think Dr. Bellows owes me a diamond pin though.

I am everlastingly obliged by your devotion in the offer of your breathing and travelling physique; but I am glad to be able to give my small nephew all the credit without any of the inconveniences that would of necessity result from the carrying out of his plan; for I am amazingly better. The very night — that of last Thursday — when I feared more than ever I had feared, that I must give up my engagements, healing came on the wings of a "good south wind," and I am now very hopeful. We are most comfortable and hospitably entertained here by Mrs. Langdon, the mother-in-law of Mark Twain. They are all gone to church but me. And I am trying to ease my conscience of a load of unwritten letters, of which yours comes first.

And now I am going to ask you to do a piece of business for me. First, will you pay this cheque for $500 into the bank for me. Messrs. Lee and Higginson. Then will you take this cheque of my own for $2222 to Mr. Curtis of Mesr. Brown Brds. & ask them for a bill at sight for £400, payable to the London and County Bank, just such as they did for me before. Any difference I will make up after, this being just double (all but 20 cents) what I paid for a bill for the half of the amount some time ago to them, but the rate of exchange will have varied. Then will you send me the bills to the care of Mr. Gilder, Messrs. Scribner and Co. Publishers, 654, Broadway, New York, and your petitioner will ever pray.

We had our first sleigh ride yesterday and enjoyed it much.

My wife joins me in love to you and Dame Fields, the lovely. It will
be jolly to see you once more — perhaps in February.

Meantime, all Christmas love & joy be yours.

Your affectionate uncle

GEORGE MACDONALD

1. James T. Fields made arrangements for MacDonald's lecture in Boston and meeting
with a Christian preacher named Dr. Bellows. See *George MacDonald and His Wife*, p. 453.

From George MacDonald to His Daughter   Boston, U.S.A.
Lilia Scott MacDonald   March 20th, 1873

. . . Seriously I am inclined to try how it feels to be a murderer, I find
I can learn Macbeth's part very easily for me, and before we come home
expect to be complete in it, as far as the words go. Whether I can act it
is another thing, but if you will be Lady Macbeth I will try. What made
me think of it, and Mamma too — was seeing the latter done pretty well
and the former very ludicrously the other night. . . .

From George MacDonald to James T. Fields   Chicago, April 12, 1873

My dear Fields,

Once more I trouble you with money to deposit for me £800. Will
you favour your old uncle with a note addressed to the care of Rev. W. Fisk,
Ann Arbor, Michigan, where I shall be from the 17th to the 20th — to let
him know if it all arrives safe.

This is the most wonderful city in America — in some respects the
most wonderful in the world. One can hardly believe it. Its resurrection
is like something out of the Arabian Nights. It is surely destined to be one
of the first in the world.

On the sixteenth I shall begin to work my way back towards Boston.

And hope to lecture on Saturday the third of May, if nothing comes between. By the way, will it be against the law to take that edition of De Quincey you were so generous & kind as to give us, to England? Is it copyright there? I fancy not. If it is, I do not feel at liberty to take it however much I should like.

It seems I am probably going to give some of the Vermont lectures after all.

With various vicissitudes, I am, I think, really better now than when I left home, & confidently hope to return in better health than when I left home. Hoping to see you in the beginning of May, which I fear will be for a goodbye, & with love from both to both

Your affectionate Uncle

GEORGE MACDONALD

LETTERS WRITTEN
FOLLOWING THE MACDONALDS' RETURN
TO ENGLAND

To James T. Fields   The Retreat, Hammersmith
                                                          London, June 20, 1873

My dear Fields,

I would have written to you long ago, but I have been ill & laid up since my return, & unable to do anything without great effort. I am now getting well again, however, & I have need for I have a great weight of arrears of writing to encounter.

This is no letter, only a whistle across to let you know I love you, & shall always. If my wife were by me, she would (& does) join me in love to you both.

I do not know if you will like these carbuncles.[1] If you do not, & would prefer a nice setting round them, just send them back, & I can easily change them. I rather liked nothing to be seen but the stones. If you do like them, please think of me when you are putting them in your shirt. They are a poor thing to offer, but I hope to be judged by what I would do if I could. I have taken a step or two towards the ring, but have not yet had time to be successful.

How you would, both of you, have enjoyed yesterday with us in a boat all day — on the Wey, a sleepy, lock-restrained, willow-garlanded, green, meadow-banked tributary of the Thames! You have far grander views, but they don't go to sleep like some of ours, as if they never wanted to leave the grass & the flowers & the overhanging trees.

May the day come, ere long when we can enjoy something of the kind together!

                                                          Your loving old uncle,

                                                          GEORGE MACDONALD

1. For shirt studs.

To Mr. Cleveland[1]   Hastings, Jan. 5, 1874.

Dear Mr. Cleveland,

    Tomorrow the watch will be in the hands of Mr. Samuel Clemens (Mark Twain) who sails on the 13th from Liverpool — addressed to the care of the Rev. S. W. Swimney, 20, Cooper Union, New York City. As you gave direction in your last. I have time only to wish you and yours all good things in this New Year.

Most truly yours,

George MacDonald

    1. Mr. Cleveland is possibly Connecticut State Senator Edward S. Cleveland. Mark Twain attended a testimonial dinner for MacDonald in New York City, 19 May 1873. The novelist Bret Harte and the painter Thomas Moran also attended. Two months later, when Twain was in England, he attended a garden party at the MacDonalds's. There is much debate on the subject, but it has been suggested that Twain's best-known novel, *Huckleberry Finn* (1884), is an American adaptation of the popular novel MacDonald based partly on his own boyhood, *Robert Falconer* (1868).

To James T. Fields   The Retreat, Hammersmith
August 13, 1874

My dear Fields,

    Best thanks for your most kind letter. I have given up the thought of visiting America this coming winter, but if I find they want me, I think it very likely I shall venture again next year.

    I heard from Gilder some time ago that he had written to you, but I suppose it did not reach you. I am not very sorry, for on going over my plan I find great fault with it, and I have also had a few hints from an actor, and I know I can greatly improve it — whether I can make it worth acting is another thing.

    So, if you have done nothing, do nothing till I write to you again, with a corrected copy.[1]

    Do think of coming over next summer — early — with your lovely dame, and then you could go back with us in the autumn. I know we should make you happy with abundance of young life, which your endless youth would enjoy. I know it is a risk for me to try the lecturing again;

but I mean to manage better next time — courses in large places, with a few between to fill up, would at least not be so hard, and I get very tired of writing.

In haste
Your loving uncle,

GEORGE MACDONALD

1. Possibly MacDonald still had hopes of producing his play "If I Had a Father."

To Helen MacKay Powell   The Retreat,
                                                        March 24, 1875

My dear Helen,

Tennyson came here uninvited to the boat-race and was with us two or three hours. He seemed delighted with my little library which he did not think a little one:[1] there seemed so many books he had never seen. . . . What do you think he borrowed? A splendid copy of the Gaelic *Ossian,* which I bought at Uncle's[2] sale, that he might read the prose Latin translation, which seems to be a literal one. He had never believed *Ossian* was a reality, but seemed a good deal more ready to believe in him when he had read a few lines, with which he was delighted. . . .

1. Tennyson had come to see the Oxford-Cambridge boat race.
2. MacDonald's uncle, MacIntosh MacKay, who was a Gaelic scholar.

To General Wilson   The Retreat, Hammersmith
                                                        May 9, 1875

My dear General Wilson,

I would have written to you sooner, but I have been both ill and very busy. I now send you, at the long last, the copy of the poem I promised you, but in copying it out it seems hardly worthy of your acceptance.

Best thanks for your kind letter. I shall be very pleased to be in your book, and give you full permission to use any of the poems you think proper. I would only venture to ask whether, as it is a book of Scottish poetry, it would be well to have some at least of the poems Scotch, of which I have written a baker's dozen or so.

The 10th of December 1824 was my birthday.

They say the cuckoo is Michael Bruce's, but it is such a dreadful charge to make on Logan that I dare not say — though truly I have never gone into the question.

[James] MacPherson is surely rather the paraphraser than the translator of Ossian. You would have been amused to see our poet laureate [Tennyson] the other day carry off from my shelves three quarto volumes of the Original Ossian that he might read the literal Latin translation annexed. Then first a belief that there had ever really been an Ossian seemed to dawn upon him. My wife joins me in kind regards to you and *yours* — God be with you.

Yours most truly

GEORGE MACDONALD

To R. W. Gilder[1]   The Retreat
Hammersmith, London,
May 15, 1875

My dear Boy,

. . . I have been more or less ill all the winter, now in bed, now hard at work. It is summer weather at last, and although I can yet bear no fatigue, I am much better and working hard at my story. . . .[2] As soon as I get it finished I shall bethink myself about your story — on whose tail, when I have once caught sight of it, I shall not be long in casting salt. I lean to a wild one [story], into which one can put so much more, but I cannot tell yet. . . .

Is your volume ready yet? I wish I had time to write verses! Perhaps I shall have when I am too old to write stupid prose — and feel the husk splitting away to let out the leaves of the new life. . . .

1. Richard Watson Gilder, assistant editor of *Scribners' Monthly Magazine*.
2. *Malcolm* (1875).

To John Ruskin[1]

Great Tangley Manor
near Guildford
May 30, 1875

My very dear Ruskin,

I want just to speak a word in your ear. I do not know what it shall be. I only want you to know it is my voice. Do not turn your head to look at me, or stop what you are doing to think a moment about me. Go on.

But the Psyche is aloft, and her wings are broad and white, and the world of flowers is under her, and the sea of sunny air is around her, and the empty chrysalis — what of that?

Now we are all but Psyches half awake, who see the universe in great measure only by reflection from the dull coffin-lid over us. But I hope, I hope. I hope infinitely. And ever the longer I live and try to live, & think, & long to love perfectly, I see the scheme of things grow more orderly and more intelligible, and am more and more convinced that all is on the way to be well with a wellness to which there was no other road than just this whereon we are walking.

Let us thus call a word now and then through the darkness as we go. There is a great sunrise behind the hill. But that hill Death alone can carry us over. I look to God to satisfy us all. It cannot be but that he will satisfy you to your heart's content. You have fought a better fight, I think, than you yourself know, and his gentleness will make you great in the Kingdom of love.

For Rose, is there anything fitting but gladness? The growing weight is gone; the gravestone heaved from off her; the light with that which was and yet was not herself is over. It may be she haunts you now with ministrations. Anyhow the living God does. Richter says it is only in God that two souls can meet. I am sure it is true.

My wife's heart is with yours in your loss. She sends her love. If we could do anything for you!

Your friend ever,

GEORGE MACDONALD

[P.S.] I have just bethought me of the enclosed. Perhaps I may have sent you a copy before. They are the fruit of bereavement in one of the loveliest thinkers of last century. I have spent immense labour on their English dress — extending over more than twenty years — because I love them so much. The more you read them, even in a translation, the more I think you will like them.

G.M.D.[2]

1. This moving letter, written four days after Rose La Touche's death, was enclosed in a copy of *Alec Forbes,* inscribed to "John Ruskin in faith & love from the author, May 1875." It is printed in part in Greville MacDonald's *Reminiscences of a Specialist* (London, 1932), p. 122, addendum, and again in part in Derrick Leon's *Ruskin: The Great Victorian* (London, 1949), pp. 500-501. The book MacDonald refers to in the postscript is his translations of Novalis, the *Exotics* (1876).

2. Greville MacDonald adds a note: "Apart from its intrinsic beauty, the letter is a fitting end to a story that has no end. The opening paragraph suggests that, as Ruskin had evinced a certain coolness towards my parents after their failure to serve him and Rose La Touche, my father felt some reluctance lest he should be obtruding. Otherwise I do not quite understand it. The book referred to must have been 'Exotics,' as it begins with a series of translations from Novalis. Its imprint never-the-less is given as 1876; but it was a frequent custom then for a publisher to anticipate by a year such a date. An earlier and privately published version of these 'Spiritual Songs,' done at Arundel in 1851, had been so far improved, and some faulty rhymes rectified, that I do not think my father would have now, in 1875, sent these less perfect versions."

To Mrs. William Cowper-Temple   Boscombe, Bournemouth
                                                December 7, 1875

Dear Mrs. Temple,

Don't think me faithless or heartless. It would have been at great risk if I had gone to you today. Indeed I was not able, for I have not been so unwell since I came down as today. But the beauty of this place is that I can be positively ill, and I hope, notwithstanding the bitter weather, to be no worse if I am careful. Not for a long time have I been able to work so steadily, and I hope my work will turn out better for it.

Mary[1] has not been quite so well the last few days, but there is no serious relapse. She is so cheerful — immeasurably more so than when she came down. It may indicate nothing as to the disease, but it is better to be happy than to live.

We have taken such a pretty house! The fact that I can do twice the work here seemed to justify it, as well as the prospect of having two girls to take charge of; if we came here, which will pay the first year's rent at least. The clock says stop, and my work says *stop,* and another letter I must write says stop — so I must.

If Ruskin is with you, give him my love — and please give my love to your dear husband.

We all love you and him — but that is no news to you.

Affectionately yours,

GEORGE MACDONALD

1. MacDonald's daughter, Mary Josephine.

To Macmillan   Corage, Boscombe, Bournemouth,
Feb. 15, 1876

Mess. Macmillan & Co.
Gentlemen,

I have now a book on hand, more than half-finished, for which I wish to find a publisher in the 3 vol. edition. It is appearing in Mess. Strahan & Co's magazine *The Day of Rest.*[1] If after I have stated to you my terms, you should be inclined to see it, I can send you about the half of it already in print.

For the entire copyright — that is with the understanding that it is already arranged for in America — and only America, I want £500.

For the right to print as many copies of the 3 vol. ed. as you please — then the copyright revert to me — £400.

For the right to print 1000 copies £350, with 50 more if that number is exceeded.

I should want half the price down on delivery of the half and the rest when the whole is handed over to you.

I am, Gentlemen,
Your obedient servant,
GEORGE MACDONALD

Should any other proposal occur to you as preferable to either of these, I should like to hear it.

1. *Thomas Wingfold, Curate,* published in 1876 by Hurst & Blackett.

To Mr. Furnivale   The Retreat, Hammersmith
                                                             April 17, 1876

My dear Mr. Furnivale,

Best thanks for your kind wish that I should take the chair, but at present I have neither leisure nor strength for that kind of thing — not to mention a disinclination toward it sufficient to destroy my pleasure the meeting itself might give me — or the prospect at least. Until I get through with certain work which weighs on me I must undertake nothing. It is only this very week, that having been persuaded to conserve, to take the chair of a half-private assembly, I had to telegraph on the day itself that I was unable to attend.

But perhaps things may get better before the summer is over — If I should get a paper written out for publication on any of the plays, I should feel inclined to offer you a reading of it, but that I have never done yet — I always speak extempore.

> With all good wishes,
> Your most truly,
>
> GEORGE MACDONALD

To Dr. J. D. Holland[1]   Hastings
                                                             October 5, 1876

My dear Holland,

It is very pleasant to see your handwriting once more. Do not judge of my regard for you by the length or rather brevity of my reply, for I am in one of my periods of occultation, or more properly *eclipse,* which the medicine man is doing his best to drive away.

I cannot undertake the charge of a youth: it would be to put a stop to all my other and perhaps more important, certainly more necessary work. But my wife has room in the house for a girl or young woman — we have one such now — who would share in what is going on in the family, and to whom I would give lessons in English along with my own daughters. But we cannot promise anything beyond English for a girl of the age mentioned without external aid, for which it would be necessary for her to pay beyond the £120 we should require, though doubtless we should be able to give assistance in preparing for the master or mistress.

The best thing to be got in the house from the intellectual point of view, is an impulse towards thought, and some enlightenment towards the intelligent use of books. While there are always things going on, and often talk started, that helps to moral development and strength.

To know my wife's influence with girls, you ought to know my daughters; but that cannot be just yet; and it would not become me to praise either her or them. But I may say this for us both that we care, with our own, infinitely more for the moral and spiritual development than for the merely intellectual, and anyone with whom the latter is the main point, need not, and I hope will not send a daughter to us, for the result will appear at first to be a disappointment, whether in reality it be a failure or not. For *accomplishments,* regarded as a means of display, we care less than nothing, but the more should we value and encourage all effort after mastery for the thing's own sake. My wife will write by next post. What I have said applies to a girl of eighteen. A child could be taught everything needful for some time by my own girls, under Mrs. MacDonald's supervision.

I am glad that Arthur Bonnicastle has done so well. I read it with so much sympathy and conscious approval that I cannot but be pleased to hear that many read it. It cannot fail to do good.

> With much love to you all
> Yours most truly

> GEORGE MACDONALD

1. Dr. J. D. Holland, a novelist and editor of *Scribner's Magazine.* He and his family became friends with the MacDonalds during their American visit.

To Mr. Strahan[1]   Corage
                                                      October 11, 1876

Dear Mr. Strahan,

Will you give my friend Miss Macirone a kindly reception for my sake. She has been a friend of all of us for very many years — and a true one.

Not knowing at all with what special object she has asked me for an introduction, I may be mentioning what may lead you to wrong conjecture, when I say that she belongs in music to the class *genius*. I would rather hear her play also, than any one else I know. And yet more, she is a born teacher, and I, having the vanity to believe I can myself teach, believe also that I can recognize such better than most.

If I knew what she wanted, I could write more to the point. Altogether, she is worthy of any assistance you may find yourself able to give her.

I am, dear Mr. Strahan,
Yours very truly

GEORGE MACDONALD

1. MacDonald's friend and publisher of *Dealings with the Fairies* and other of his works.

To Henry Wadsworth Longfellow   Corge, Boscombe,

Bournemouth, England
December 21, 1876

My dear Mr. Longfellow,

Your kindness to me and my wife, on our ever-memorable visit to your country, emboldens me to comply with the request of a very dear friend to make mention of her to you — for a very simple reason, which will presently appear when I have introduced her.

She is Clara Macirone — Italian on the father's side — a pupil of the blessed Mendelssohn, and a dear friend besides. She is one of the very few women who have shown originality in musical composition — while under her fingers the piano becomes like a living thing of sound — for her execution, which to better judges than myself leaves nothing to be desired, is but the slave to her feeling and expression. Now she has set one or two of your lovely songs to music — *her* music — and she wants to send you copies. But there is one thing in your house she is afraid of — a thing which cannot be spared from a house any more than a limbo of vanity from the universe — the waste-paper basket. In the hope that my mediation may save them from fluttering over the verge of that hopeless abyss, she has asked me to write to you — and herewith I beg — not for mercy — but for justice; for, to a sister in art, a kind reception of her be nothing more than justice. My wife joins me in best wishes for you and yours. May the good will of this holy time be yours, and may God be more and more your strength.

> I am,
> dear and honoured Mr.
> Longfellow,
> Yours very sincerely,
>
> GEORGE MACDONALD

To Dr. Hay[1]   Corage, Boscombe,
                                                        Bournemouth
                                                       March 4, 1877

My dear Dr. Hay,

How can I comfort myself suitably when I am borne by the postman to your presence! Could I tell you all my excuses without boring you or wearying myself who have no time to be weary — comprising illness, and such busy-ness as the fact that, although this is Sunday, I have been hard at work, as upon any other day, will show, I think you would at once forgive me — and, were I present with the bodily needs of the race, offer me a share of what was going at your table. I am glad to hear you have one to sit at the head of it now, and two to crawl under it as well. God bless you all.

That you should have often thought of your kind promise was better than fulfilling it offhand, except indeed it gave me the disadvantage of seeming to plague you about it. A thousand thanks for the book. It is a beautiful edition, and looks so tempting. Add to the kindness by telling me some book that will give me such an idea of the pronunciation that I shall not get into bad habits before I may get a better instructor. The language will have no difficulties — great ones, at least — for me — but the pronunciation is not to be gathered by linguistic intuitions.

Do not, please, address me as Reverend. I am not a clergyman, and cleave with tooth and nail to the liberties of the layman. Hoping to see you some day yet again in the flesh.

I am,
My dear Dr. Hay
Yours most truly,

GEORGE MACDONALD

1. Perhaps related to Sir Andrew Leith Hay of Leith Hall near Huntly, one of whose sons was Robert Bruce in *Alec Forbes of Howglen*. See William Raeper, *George MacDonald* (London: Lion Publishing Co., 1987), p. 190.

To Mrs. William Cowper-Temple   Corage [Boscombe, Bournemouth]
April 1, 1877

My dear Mrs. Temple,

Sometimes I do not know how to thank God for a special gift, because from him it is all and equally gift. But I can thank him for making me the surer that he is and that he does care for the sparrows. This kindness of yours also is only just like you, and your goodness to me and mine has been just a part of the Father's, and in thanking you I thank him.

You can hardly know how much you give me; and I do not think it will do me the harm now it once might have done, for I feel my stay here so short that I shall not begin to love the world now — if for no other reason, yet because it is no use. It may be good for me however to have a few years in a house we can call our own, and therefore I think that, as God has sent me this towards one, he may be meaning that I shall be able to add to it in the years to come so that I may be able to build or buy someday. The portion you allow me to use takes a load off me. What better gift can you give a man than a taste of peace? I hoped in God, and will hope in him even if that worst of earthly evils, debt, should overwhelm me. But I do not think he will punish one in that way, and it does not now look like it. I have never been left long in great embarrassment of the kind — only I would gladly owe no man anything but love. And for this which you and my other friends have given me I do not feel that I owe anything but love. What is given me is mine, and love to boot. If I did not believe in the love, however unmerited, I could not take the money.

It is the love that not only makes you give it, but makes it possible for me
to take it. It is a lovely thing to be obliged to you and your friends. I hope
I shall be and do and write better for it. When you let me know the names
of my friends, I shall be able to write something to all, I hope. My wife,
I need not say[,] is with me in my words. And of course I say all this to
your husband too.

> Dear daughter of God,
> Therefore dear Sister,
> take my love and thanks,
>
> GEORGE MACDONALD

To Thomas Carlyle   Corage, Boscombe,
                                                                  Bournemouth
                                                                April 23, 1877

Honoured Mr. Carlyle,

I am driven to trouble you.[1] Hear my story and bear with me, for I
come in humility. Some little time ago, an old friend of mine, Henry
Cecil, wrote to you, telling you how he and his wife, upon her deathbed,
had been reading together your *Frederick the Great.* I did not know of it
when he wrote, and am not now sure whether it was before or after his
wife's death he received from you, with your own signature, a very kind
note which he, I need not say, prized very highly — alas, that I have to
use the past tense!

A few months ago, he showed me this note, and I begged to be allowed
to keep it a while that I might show it to a friend of mine who, unknown
to you, owes you the greatest thanks a man can pay to his fellow man. I
did so with all satisfaction to him and me. But the sequel is of another
sort. This evening Cecil asked me for the note. A misgiving crossed me
even then. I have searched for it everywhere, in vain, and my distress is
greater than I should like to set forth in words. For the knowledge of the
loss will be to him a keen pain, as it is to me. He is but a middle-aged
man, and I will trust, for his children's sake, live many years yet — be yet
in the strife and the cloud of the battle when you have had the *well done*
from the lips of the Master, and all the time your note would have been
a possession. My heart is sore for my fault and his loss. I am not a careless

man, but here is carelessness. I have lost my evening's work, which to a man who works steadily, is no little punishment. But the loss of tomorrow's is threatened also by my mental disquiet, and the only thing that has brought me relief is the thought of troubling you — happily not with the heartache I beg you to take from me. Now to put my request plainly — a cry to my big brother to come to my help. Will you, out of your humanity, dictate again a few words to my friend, founded on the contents of this letter, and send it with your own autograph signature to me, that I may give it to him instead of the other. Then I shall have courage to confess my Failing. Do not write a word to me; I do not deserve it. I am ashamed of thus troubling you. But some day, I trust, on the other side, I shall thank you for a kindness which lightened a real burden, when our life here has become the dream which real as it is, Novalis says perhaps it ought to become.

Sincerely I pray you to pardon me for thus intruding myself on you, but sorrow is told. The God you have served be with you.

> I am, my dear Mr. Carlyle,
> Yours not the less
> respectfully
> that I venture to say
> lovingly,

> GEORGE MACDONALD

1. See G. E. Sadler, "Unpublished Letter from George MacDonald to Thomas Carlyle (and a Missing Note?)," *Scottish Studies* (Fall 1972): 125-27.

To Mrs. William Cowper-Temple   Corage, May 3, 1877

Dearly beloved helper of pilgrims,

I have ploughed this garden and dug it over with my shade, and disfigured it to the eye, but if I now walk therein, more will find strange flowers, and right lovely, peeping through the broken clods. How gladly would I be a helper of thy faith, as thou art of mine. Yet let me tell thee this, that almost every day I see lovelier things and think stronger things, and could that which is life to my very soul come forth of a lie? I ask. Be thou patient with the giver who withholdeth the less that he may give the greater.

As to this my offering to thy love, we shall have things to say when we meet. I would it were done more fairly, but time is so precious now for over-neatness of work.

Salute my brother William, who is dear to my heart. I and my wife and all of us love thee and him.

I write like them of old time, but my meanings are fresh as the new flowers, while old as the Spring that leads them back to us once more. The father of his children be with thee.

Thy servant,

GEORGE MACDONALD

To His Wife

[The home of the
Cowper-Temples]
Broadlands, Romsey
[August 4, 1877]

Thanks, dearest, for your letter. You would have liked to see the angel's [Mrs. Cowper-Temple's] face as she gave it me back after reading it — for I did what I never did before, I think, gave one of my wife's letters to another to read. She said "What a wife she is to you!" or something more lovely. . . . They are all so sweet about Mary,[1] and they all prayed for her under the beeches yesterday. . . . But might you not come? Just for Sunday. . . . Probably Mr. Russell Gurney is coming down to-morrow. And do you know, I quite like Lord Radstock, and I have learned a good deal; and much this afternoon about St. John's Gospel from Mr. Duglass the Jew. . . . Love to Elfie [Mary]. I hope to nurse her a bit on Monday. . . .

1. His daughter Mary Josephine, who was ill.

To His Wife   [Palazzo Cattaneo]
                                                   Nervi [Italy}
                                                   [Autumn 1877]

. . . You would like to hear the way G. [Greville] talks. He is a boy
no longer however. One thing he sees plainly — the elevating power of
suffering even on these poor women. . . . I have once or twice been
tempted to feel abandoned — in this messy and struggling house. . . . But
it is only a touch of the Valley of Humiliation — of the Hill of Difficulty
rather. . . . My love to my little sick dove [Mary]. Tell her to keep a big
heart for God to fill for her. When I was a boy my desire was to be loved;
but now my prayer is to be made able to love. . . . What a little we know
yet! And how much is to be known. . . . Don't be anxious about me. I
shall soon be well. . . . How comfortable I am compared with the last time
when I didn't have you — on board the Blue Bell! . . .

I dare not attempt to pay for the horses' keep while we're away.[1]

1. Greville MacDonald writes: "The ponies being a gift, could not be sold, and they
were taken charge of by Mr. Cowper-Temple; the mare was sold for £50 — my father
offering to take less if that proved beyond her value" (*George MacDonald and His Wife*,
p. 475).

To Mrs. Russell Gurney[1]   The Retreat, Hammersmith
                                                   October, 1877

VERY DEAR FRIEND, — Mr and Mrs C.-Temple are coming up
to-morrow, and are going to take me to Stanhope Street on Thursday. If
you will come and see me there I shall by that time be able to talk a little
better to you. I had when you left me the disappointed feeling that I had
answered one or two things you said very unsatisfactorily. I knew I had
gold (for I had thought much about them), but I could only lay my hands
on coppers. I am better, but don't feel better yet. What poor trustees we
are! Sometimes, when we have a whole subterranean lake of blessed hope,
we are yet fearful about some mere trifle.[2] But at least I am learning to
obey, by refusing to be care-full.

I think, perhaps, the last few years of my life, when I am quite old, I shall be allowed to speak to people about these things. What God will. —

Affectionately yours,
GEORGE MACDONALD

1. This letter was published in *Letters of Emelia Russell Gurney,* edited by her niece Ellen Mary Gurney (London, 1902), pp. 230-31.

2. The symbolism here is interestingly like the "dark lake" that "reflected the rose-coloured clouds in the west," in MacDonald's parable *The Castle,* first published in *Adela Cathcart* (1864) and reprinted in *Works of Fancy and Imagination* (1871).

To William Cowper-Temple The Retreat, Hammersmith, W.
October 1, 1877

Dearest friend,

Where are you? I am here, but want much to be where you are for an hour or two before I get back to Boscombe. I want some advice from my brother, and love from both of you.

Nothing but good news from the travellers as yet.[1] The last I heard of them was near Toulon, and looking on the Mediterranean on their way to Mentone where they will remain for a week. That was Sunday morning. I had it this morning. When will you be at Broadlands again? I shall be returning somewhere between this week and next, but could visit you from there if you are not back before.

I am longing to see you.

The Retreat is almost empty. My study looking a desert — even the bookshelves removed. But there is the blue sky — there are the gold stars above. And if all this world had grown a desert, there would only be the more stars in heaven.

In haste yours right lovingly,

GEORGE MACDONALD

1. Mrs. MacDonald was traveling in Italy with her daughters Lily, Mary, and Irene and her son Ronald.

To Mrs. William Cowper-Temple   The Retreat,
                                                Hammersmith, W.
                                                October 5, 1877

The messenger of Satan has got me by the lungs again, dearest sister, and thrown me into bed, where I trust God will have his will with my heart, and then my lungs may go to dust for what I care. So tell my Temple I can't run to his refuge just yet — and thank him for his good true letter. Indeed I don't quite know when I shall get away, for I am trying to dispose of my next novel,[1] of which I have two volumes written and on which in a great measure depends our going at all — on that and letting the house.

But isn't it good to hear of their getting so much pleasure — especially Mary.[2] If she dies now, she will go with a more delightful feeling about the world — and that is worth even troubling you for, you dear — I send you the card received this morning — also the letter Ted[3] had a day or two ago — you see it is all things in common with us. Only I hope you won't be too shocked at the carnage described in it. It was not written for the eyes of Lady Clementina's mother. For me I must have been through the insect world once, for the buzz of a gnat or a fly sometimes is enough to put me in a rage with a sense of insult yet.

Don't be unhappy about me — I have my youngest daughter and my eldest and youngest boys to take care of me — and a nice middle-age cook, a good-hearted creature. Did I ever tell you about my illness at sea once — not sea-illness? I should like to tell you, if I haven't —

Please send the letter and card to Grace at Corage — or get Annie Munroe[4] to do it. Please give her, I mean Annie, my love. If you have a minute anytime, make me glad with a letter, if only three words.

                                                Yours lovingly

                                                GEORGE MACDONALD

1. *The Marquis of Lossie* (1877).

2. Referring to his wife and children traveling in Italy.

3. Edward Hughes, nephew of MacDonald's artist friend Arthur Hughes, who became engaged to MacDonald's daughter Mary in 1873.

4. Annie Munro, the sister of Alexander Munro, the sculptor, was serving as the Cowper-Temples' governess. She was also godmother to MacDonald's son Robert Falconer.

To Mrs. William Cowper-Temple   The Retreat, Hammersmith,
                                           October 7, for October 8, 1877[1]

God be thanked for your birth, my sister. A blessed day it was for me
and mine. Surely our angels turned and looked at each other. I began to
make some verses for you — but this is all I got to — Don't blame heart
or imagination that I got no further for the devil is only in my right side
— now I must turn the leaf even for the poor one stanza

> Up the hill of years
>   To the peak of youth!
> There the mist of fears
>   Veils no more the truth;
> There we children all shall meet,
>   And play about the Father's feet.

If we can build castles of air, God can turn them into granite.

It came to me today, thinking about you, and the growing birthdays,
that there was one thing Jesus had not borne with his children — old age.
Therefore it cannot be looked on as any evil by the heavenly eyes. They
see the dawn of the divine flower of which we see only the withering calix.

No I cannot say that is all that we see, for you are more beautiful than
you were twenty years ago — I too see some glimmer of the heavenly
flower. May you be as much more beautiful still twenty years after this;
and you *will* be, for you will a haunt the trail of his garment till he turns
and looks at you. He will, I think, lay his hand on my head one day, but
he will give you a kiss.

But William is the one to whom my congratulations ought to be
offered. Here, brother, is my wish for you: May you and your Georgina
live as long as God pleases, and die the same day.

The grapes and the cream have been my food today — chiefly —
Thanks for everything, and the glorious magnolias, and the roses, chiefly
the red one — I hope Annie was not over tired. I will come to you as soon
as I can.

                                           Your loving

                                           GEORGE MACDONALD

1. Presumably Mrs. Cowper-Temple's birthday.

To Mrs. William Cowper-Temple   The Retreat, Hammersmith, W.
                                                    October 11, 1877

Not much nearer coming to you yet, dearest sister. But the doctor says I am better, and I believe I am. Indeed the pain in my side is better, there seems to be a little pleurisy with the bronchitis this time. Until I am able to get up I can't say when I can go to you.

Good news still from the pilgrims as I may still call them, for though they have found an *ideal* — a House Beautiful[1] they do not enter it till Monday. Mary has her variations of course. They must be now at Genoa. So they intended when I heard last. Mary got tired of seeing nothing but the sea.

I suppose William has left you for four days now. He will be back I hope by the time I can come to you. I am not very able to write.

Pardon stupidity.

Yours ever lovingly,

GEORGE MACDONALD

1. Alluding to John Bunyan's *Pilgrim's Progress.*

To Mrs. William Cowper-Temple   Bed, October 1877

This is the tenth day I have been in bed, and that is the usual time with these attacks: tomorrow I do hope to get up for a while. I am *much* better tonight. How glad your letter, not to speak of the enclosed ones, made me. I had begun to be — not afraid exactly — but it seemed as if some evil mist had crept in between us. I had been so longing to see you — and no word would come. But I know all about it now, and am quite content.

And now I feel as if — oh! if you were only at Stanhope Street,[1] and it were not such a long way to ask you to come! I do want to see you. I would not say so before; it seemed so greedy of good. But no — I will not have you come except you could do this for me — without dreadful trouble — could you take me to Stanhope Street for two or three days? I cannot hear about my book till after Thursday, and I may have to go to some places. It would be like a fairy story to have you to take care of me.

I would pay you with things out of the New Testament. It is much much to ask, but what are you my sister for if I am going to be doubtful before you. This you see is hardly a house now for an invalid — it is so cold and draughty — beyond this room — and when I was away Winnie[2] could soon finish what remains to be done in the clearing out. But if you cannot, dear sweet sister, only say it, and I shall know it. It is so grasping to take you from William for days. But then he is as good as you, and I owe it to him not to be afraid of his grudging you — if only it can be done. I have expressed myself stupidly, but it must stand.

It was so nice to have those letters through you — and read by you first. Ted[3] was here when they came.

Your loving brother,

GEORGE MACDONALD

1. The Cowper-Temples' house in London.
2. His daughter Winifred.
3. Edward Hughes, Mary's fiancé.

To Mrs. William Cowper-Temple   The Retreat, Hammersmith, W.
October 16, 1877

A fear has laid hold of me, dearest friends, that I have asked too much — not for your love — that is safe, but for your comfort. A thousand thanks for your telegram. I do not think I could well have ventured before Thursday, so your plan will suit me exactly — but oh! if I have perplexed you, and perhaps put you to much needless expense. It is done now though — and you must try to think as excusingly as you can of my — I *can't* find the right word, but it is rather a bad one. Don't take the trouble to answer this. Even my trouble at bringing you up will be gone when I see your dear faces, I know.

Your loving brother,

GEORGE MACDONALD

Accounts of Mary a little variable, but on the whole much better than when she left. All else is delightful except delay in getting into the villa.

To His Wife   15 Gt. Stanhope Street, W.,
                                              October 18, 1877

. . . To-morrow surely I shall hear something of my affairs. Dear love, trust hard in God, for he is our rest and our peace and our love. . . . I want to be able to say — and not only mean it but be able to stand to it — "though he slay me yet will I trust in him!"[1] . . . Surely I shall be allowed to come to you. . . . Love to "all my pretty chickens and their dam, at one *sweet* swoop." . . .[2]

1. Job 13:15.
2. Alluding, of course, to Shakespeare's *Macbeth,* act 4, sc. 3, l. 216.

To His Wife   15 Gt. Stanhope Street, W.,
                                              October 29, 1877

. . . I am so glad you like the little Song. It was only meant to be like the baby-verses I wrote for Lily when she was a wee, white thing. . . . Dearest, here came a gap, and I read your letter to the angel-sister. Then William the brother came in, and she went out. He said he wanted me to do him a favour: I was so pleased, thinking he really wanted me to do something for him. Then I cannot tell you how sweetly he begged me to take "a few of his slates" — which were represented by a cheque for £200. I tried to refuse it — but it wouldn't do. Then she came in and kissed me, and laughed at me. So here is the cheque, and I shall be with you soon now, my love. . . . This ought to make me gooder. . . .

> If to myself — "God sometimes interferes" —
> I said, my faith at once would be struck blind.
> I see him all in all, the lifing mind,
> Or nowhere in the vacant miles and years.
> A love he is that watches and that hears,
> Or but a mist fumed up from minds of men,
> Whose fear and hope reach out beyond their ken.[1]

1. See *A Book of Strife in the Form of the Diary of an Old Soul* (privately printed [by Unwin Brothers], London, 1880), the entry for January 9.

To His Wife   Corage,
                                          November 2, 1877

. . . We are now getting ready to start, though we cannot be out by your birthday. My love and thanks to you for being what you are and have been to me. May your birthday be hopeful, for hope is sure to come right if only we go on hoping long enough. My love to my Mary on her mother's birthday [November 5th]. I never forget the lark's nest I found the morning she was born. . . . [Here comes a letter] from Lord Beaconsfield's secretary, telling me that the Queen has given me £100 a year. Isn't it nice? I must send you the news for your birthday. . . . Mrs. Temple *thinks* it is the Princess Alice's doing, but Mr. Russell Gurney rather thinks it is Lord Beaconsfield's, moved by late reviews. . . .

To Mr. and Mrs. Cowper-Temple   Nervi,
                                          Christmas 1877

ANTHEM FOR MY FRIENDS

They all were looking for a King,
    To slay their foes, and lift them high:
He came a little baby thing
    That made a woman cry.

O Son of Man, to right my lot
    Nought but thy presence can avail;
Yet on the road thy wheels are not,
    Nor on the sea thy sail.

My how or when thou wilt not heed,
    But come down thine own secret stair,
That thou mayst answer all my need,
    Yea, every by-gone prayer.[1]

[This was written for William and Georgina Cowper-Temple, Christmas Day.]

GEORGE MACDONALD

1. Printed as "That Holy Thing" in *Poetical Works,* vol. 2, p. 323.

PART V

Living Abroad and More Novels (1877-1887)

INTRODUCTION

Upon returning to England, MacDonald found himself exhausted from his very successful eight months in America. On June 20, 1873, he had written to James T. Fields: "I would have written to you long ago, but I have been ill & laid up since my return, & unable to do anything without great effort" (see p. 239 above). That MacDonald did not write a novel based on his experiences in America is indeed regrettable. In 1878, however, he wrote and published a curious fictionalized letter of appreciation for the hospitality he and his wife and son had received in America, which he entitled "A Letter to American Boys."[1] Although the meaning of the parable in this letter is not totally clear, it may suggest the kind of story he might have written. Much in it is reminiscent of his *Double Story: The Lost Princess or The Wise Woman,* published in 1875 in England and America. The mother figure in the letter-parable reminds one of the parental role of the Wise Woman in *The Lost Princess,* and the differences between the two cultures (the palace and the country) in that story may be analogous to how MacDonald felt England and America could learn, like obedient children, to understand each other better. In both *The Lost Princess* and his letter-parable, MacDonald attempted to put into fictional form his belief in an universal parenthood of love.

As MacDonald continued to gain an ever-increasing audience on both sides of the Atlantic, he held firmly as a novelist and a poet to his positive

---

1. This letter can be found in *The Gifts of the Child Christ: Fairytales and Stories for the Childlike,* ed. Glenn Edward Sadler (Grand Rapids: William B. Eerdmans, 1973), vol. 1, pp. 10-16.

approach to life. Repeatedly in his letters to family members and friends, MacDonald expressed his visionary "message" of hope. On November 2, 1877, he wrote these words to Mrs. William Cowper-Temple: "Oh how easily God can send his wind through the heart of our griefs! Fancy the sorrows flying before it — 'Yellow and black and pale and hectic red!' "(see p. 268 above).

There is hardly a letter written by MacDonald during this period in which he does not depict his visionary hope in the life hereafter. In a moving series of letters to the Cowper-Temples (who later became Lord and Lady Mount-Temple), MacDonald offers some of his most intimate thoughts on death and dying. In these thirty-eight previously unpublished letters, written by MacDonald in the 1870s during the height of his fame, he shares his own sorrow as a father anticipating the approaching death of his second daughter, Mary Josephine.

MacDonald seems to have had a special fondness for Mary. He called her "my blackbird" because of her dark hair and sprightly personality and beautiful voice. He also nicknamed her "Elfie"; for her second birthday he wrote:

> I have an elfish maiden child;
>   She is not two years old;
> Through windy locks her eyes gleam wild,
>   With glances shy and bold.
>
> (George MacDonald and
His Wife, p. 243)

Born on July 23, 1853, Mary was Lewis Carroll's favorite of the Mac-Donald children. When she was about ten he frequently took her to the theater in London. As a little girl, her health had been robust, according to Wilfred Dodgson, who had "taught her to box" and "used to call her the 'Kensington Chicken' " (*George MacDonald and His Wife*, p. 466). At the age of twenty she became engaged to Edward R. ("Ted") Hughes, the nephew of MacDonald's artist friend Arthur Hughes, who had — as his photograph reveals — an "Apollo appearance." But nearly two years later, in the winter of 1875, while the MacDonalds were staying in Hastings at Halloway House, Mary became seriously ill. She contracted scarlet fever, and her lungs were affected.

Finally, in the autumn of 1877, it was decided that Mrs. MacDonald would take three of their daughters (Lily, Mary, and Irene) and their son

Ronald with her to Italy, while MacDonald remained at The Retreat in Hammersmith in order to lease the house and keep a close check on the sales of his latest novel, *The Marquis of Lossie* (1877), and finish the final volume of *Paul Faber, Surgeon* (1879). Separated from his family, MacDonald turned during this critical time in his life to his friends the Cowper-Temples, whom he had first met in 1867. From the confinement of his home at The Retreat, MacDonald wrote in gratitude to Mrs. Cowper-Temple for having made it possible for Mary to be taken to Italy. From his bed, MacDonald wrote again to Mrs. Cowper-Temple on October 5, 1877:

> The messenger of Satan has got me by the lungs again, dearest sister, and thrown me into bed, where I trust God will have his will with my heart, and then my lungs may go to dust for what I care. . . .
>
> But isn't it good to hear of their [his family members traveling in Italy] getting so much pleasure — especially Mary. If she dies now, she will go with a more delightful feeling about this world. . . . (see pp. 256-57 above)

There followed for MacDonald a series of favorable events: his novel *Paul Faber* was sold to Strahan for a three-volume edition at £400; he received a Civil List Pension for £100 per year from the Queen; and his health gradually began to improve, making it possible for him to join his family at Villa Cattaneo at last.

Upon his arrival, he wrote to Mrs. Cowper-Temple in November 1877:

> I found Mary better again a little. I fear she is a little thinner, but she is so cheery, and so funny. She said this morning: "I feel just like a badly cut nine-pin. When I try to stand up, I tumble over before the ball touches me." The worst symptom has for the time ceased. Every other is better. But the wasting — that I cannot say for. (p. 269 below)

Unfortunately Mary's health continued to deteriorate. Several months later MacDonald wrote of Mary's condition in a letter to Mrs. Cowper-Temple, depicting her impending death with his favorite "mother and child in the nursery" image (February 17, 1878):

So much is better, but all is not better, and she does not get stronger, I much fear. The perfect will be done. Why should we be like the little child that would snatch her sick kitten out of the lap of her mother? When I look forward and think how I shall look back on my folly, I want to have some of the wisdom now. If Jesus was born, and said such things, and died, and rose, and lived again, can I trust my God too much? Am I in danger of losing my human tenderness if I say — Let the Lord do as He will: I shall only hope and look forward the more. (p. 276 below)

On April 28, 1878, not long before her twenty-fifth birthday, Mary died at Nervi, Italy.

The year 1878 and the several years following became for MacDonald and his wife, as Greville MacDonald notes, "the heaviest burdened of all the twenty-seven years, with sunshine and blue sea, palms and oranges all about them" (*George MacDonald and His Wife*, p. 483). Less than a year after the death of Mary, MacDonald's fifteen-year-old son Maurice died on March 5, 1879. Maurice's sister Caroline Grace followed on May 5, 1884. In one of MacDonald's most moving letters, he wrote to William Cowper-Temple: "How real death makes things look! And how we learn to cleave to the one shining fact in the midst of the darkness of this world's trouble, that Jesus *did* rise radiant!" (p. 293 below). Much of the sorrow that MacDonald experienced, as he tried to console his wife over the loss of their daughter and son, he records poetically in *The Diary of an Old Soul* (1880); for January 4th he wrote hopefully:

Death, like high faith levelling, lifteth all.
When I awake, my daughter and my son,
Grown sister and brother, in my arms shall fall,
Tenfold my girl and boy.

Almost as a reaction to their losses, however, the MacDonalds adopted two young girls named Joan and Honey, who had been orphaned. But for all of MacDonald's optimism and hope in the face of sorrow, he had yet to face the final test of his faith: the trials of old age.

Significant Dates and Events

1878   Mary Josephine dies on April 28. The MacDonalds arrive at Porto Fino, Italy.

1879   Maurice dies on March 5. MacDonald publishes *Paul Faber, Surgeon* and *Sir Gibbie*.

1880   The MacDonalds arrive in Bordighera, Italy. MacDonald privately publishes *A Book of Strife, in the form of the Diary of an Old Soul*.

1881   The MacDonalds take in two young girls, Honey and Joan, whom they later adopt.

1882   MacDonald publishes *The Princess and Curdie; The Gifts of the Child Christ* (fairytale reprints); essays entitled *Orts: Weighed and Wanting;* and *Castle Warlock*.

1883   MacDonald publishes *Donal Grant; A Threefold Cord;* and *Poems by Three Friends,* edited by MacDonald.

1884   Caroline Grace dies on May 5.

1885   MacDonald publishes *The Tragedie of Hamlet;* Preface to Valdemar A. Thisted's *Letters from Hell;* and *Unspoken Sermons* (second series).

1886   MacDonald publishes *What's Mine's Mine*.

1887   MacDonald publishes *Home Again*. The MacDonalds experience a major earthquake at Bordighera, Italy.

To Mrs. William Cowper-Temple   Corage, November 2, 1877

I must send my beloved sister one word to tell her I shall sleep tonight — thanks to her and my brother. Oh how easily God can send his wind through the heart of our griefs! Fancy the sorrows flying before it — "Yellow and black and pale and hectic red!"[1]

I have another letter, but I have no time to send it now, as the hour of post is come, and I must glance it over again. I will send it tomorrow.

All my chickens are well and happy.

I have seen Mrs. Grundy. She came in — but I had left the nosegay for her while she was out.

> Haste
> Love love
> Yours ever,

GEORGE MACDONALD

1. The Cowper-Temples had been helping the MacDonalds financially and had made it possible for Louisa MacDonald to take her children Lilia, Mary, Irene, and Ronald to Italy.

To Mrs. William Cowper-Temple   Corage, Boscombe, Bournemouth
November 3, 1877

Here is another letter, best of sisters. You need not send it back: I hope to see you on Tuesday, but it *may* be Wednesday, with the Z's.[1]

I found this little poem in an old pocket-book, will you take it?

How I should like to offer you a little think-bud every morning! But I may be able to do something better than that. Love to my William.

I took Mrs. Gurney [for] a drive this morning with your ponies — she is going with me after church again tomorrow — and Mr. Gurney on Monday. We think we *may* get away on Monday week. Oh if you could come out! Don't answer my letters except when you *want*. So I may write as often as I like. And don't be vexed with my little wife for always calling you God's messenger. I haven't told her yet you do not like it.

> With a heartful of love,
> Your

GEORGE MACDONALD

1. A pair of Shetland ponies that had been a gift to Louisa MacDonald. (See the note on pp. 254-55 n. 1.) The Cowper-Temples took care of the ponies while the MacDonalds were in Italy.

To Mrs. William Cowper-Temple   Villa Cattaneo, Friday Afternoon,
[Nervi, Italy, November 1877]

At last I am set down at my table to write to my great-great princess grandmother.[1] We got to Genoa at midnight on Wednesday. My wife and Ronald[2] were there to meet me, and we passed the night in Genoa. When we came here yesterday, there was so much to see and say that, not knowing the hours, I let the post-time slip. And now I wish I had time to fill all this sheet to you my dearly loved sister. My heart, if it had its way, would just tumble over at your & William's feet, and empty itself like a cup of wine. I found Mary better again a little. I fear she is a little thinner, but she is so cheery, and so funny. She said this morning: "I feel just like a badly cut nine-pin. When I try to stand up, I tumble over before the ball touches me." The worst symptom has for the time ceased. Every other is better. But the wasting — that I cannot say for.

Now I want to get one thing off my mind. I found my wife a little troubled that I had showed you the letter in which she expressed her wish about Ted.[3] She had written it only for me, as she could only write to me, and I in my perfect faith in you had done such a thing as I had never done before — showed it. But then I know that there is not a thought or feeling about such things in my wife's head or heart which would not bear the light of your dear eyes. I know there is not a *common* thought even; and for the child [Mary], she is as white and clean as a baby. Therefore I can hardly repent showing like to like, nor can I fear your reading anything there which was not there. You see I got in the way of talking to you about anything and everything, and I feel certain she will not mind it long, and I know she does not mind it very much. So I send you, for her sake, the next letter she wrote, which has followed me here. And after this I hope we shall not trouble you again with the sensitiveness of either of us — for a while.

But oh! if you would come here! We could receive you and William quite comfortably in this large house — palace they call it here. A few minutes ago, the sea was all purply black, except a gold sweep on the far horizon. For I brought English weather with me. As soon as we were through the great tunnel, it was cold, and then came rain, and the face of Italy when I met her first was savage rather than lovely. For greater desolation than the slopes this side of the tunnel I have never seen excepting the African desert bordering the Atlas mountains. We have had only a little sunshine today. I am well-pleased with the house. It is larger even — in extent — than I expected. But after all that Louisa wrote I will not trouble you with more — only that they made me shut my eyes last night, and led me to the secret that you knew of before. When I opened them — there I was looking into a little cold chapel through a lattice opening — with a marble altar in front and the madonna upon it, while one of them played "Abide with Me," on a harmonium behind. I was delighted, you may be sure. It is such a lovely idea to have a little core of rest in the heart of the house — a chamber opening out into the infinite. Only it is all useless, except there be just such a chamber in the heart of the heart itself, where, instead of an altar, is a common hearth, and instead of the madonna above, sits the son of man below, tending the fire, and making it burn with the words of the eternal love and tenderness and courage and patience. Ah if you could only come over by *old* Christmas Day, we would keep it over again in our white oval hall, with all the candles lit in the huge, too big chandelier. I could play the prince in this house very comfortably, and I know my wife would keep it always full.

It is more stately than comfortable — yet not *very* stately, and quite comfortable to our minds. Only I do wish I could turn Irene and Grace[4] loose in it with paint pots and brushes. The decorations are all bad — yet I would rather have them than not. I do not know all the house yet — nor the garden. The dining hall is splendid for music. In my study where I am now, I have only to open a shutter and I look into it from almost at the ceiling. I could see all my family, all my guests, hear every word they said, myself unseen, like a benignant gnome, or evil jinn. Yet it is not very big — not big enough to feel proud in, *if one wanted*. The house is on the middle of a hill, not too steep to have houses scattered over it and be covered with olives. Our garden is just an orange grove, where not content with old thick trees, they have them standing along the tops of the low walls in big pots as well.

The people were so pleased to find we did not want the chapel shut up, or the crucifixes removed from the rooms. There are many of the latter. We think we should like to cover some of them with a little curtain. Even the word must be hid in the heart that it may be potent. I have not quite come to myself yet. But I hope to begin work tomorrow. When I write next, I may be able to say something you will like. The bottle of wine is set aside for Christmas. The Russells [Russell Gurneys] are coming to us that day, and if we have all our own out, we shall have a time of hope and thanksgiving. My blessings — the blessing of the poor — be upon you; beloved sister and brother. My wife joins me in this love and thanks, with all her heart, which is somewhat of the volcanic in loving. My last words with William seem so strange now — in the middle of the lovely road — nearly eleven o'clock at night. Our own God be with you — and with all men and women. Ever and always your loving brother,

GEORGE MACDONALD

1. An allusion to his book *The Princess and the Goblin.*
2. MacDonald's son.
3. Edward R. Hughes, nephew of Arthur Hughes, who became engaged to Mary Josephine on January 24, 1874.
4. MacDonald's daughters.

To Mrs. Russell Gurney[1]   Villa Cattaneo, Nervi, Genoa,
November 12, 1877

VERY DEAR FRIEND, —

What would you think to see the weather, and hardly anything but weather, on which I am looking out? Ever since I entered Italy last Wednesday nothing but rain, grey sponge squeezed by the hand of the wind.

But I have a jolly wood fire, the smell of which would be enough to make one feel at home either in the cave of a hermit or a palace of gold and ivory. There must be a home-heart to the universe, seeing so many things tend to soothe and comfort us, and say, "All is well."

I have not got to work yet. It takes much longer to get over fatigue than it did twenty years ago. When will our youth return? This is hid with Christ in God, and is safe. When He shall appear, that will come with Him. Eternal youth is the redemption of the body.

What would be the most dreadful thing, do you think? To me it seemed the other day that it would be for God to let any fault or wrong in me pass; for Him not to mind, not to care about it. Better hell a thousand times than that. Let Him forgive, splendidly, tenderly, but let it be forgiveness, and not *never minding*. Let Him make every excuse, every honest excuse for us, for that is but fair; but let not our Father be content that one spot should be passed by, or one shade less than His righteousness satisfy Him in us!

M. [Mary] is no better for this weather, but she is only on the wheel of the great potter. Oh, what will not come out of it all? What a good — a good so great that I need faith to give me the courage to face it. It is not death alone that is awful without faith; but life is to me so vast and unknown, that one might well fear that more than death, but for faith in Him who loves us and is our life.

Will you give our love to your husband. I hope he is pretty well. Blessed be the God that makes us love each other. Is not that part of the meaning of *the God of Love?* It is the one thing He cares about. I see more and more into the religion there is in our relation to our fellow-men. I come nearer to understanding that if a man does not love his brother, he cannot love God.

Happy are we that we are utterly in the power of the Father; helpless against Him as the struggling little pulpy thing is in the arms of his strong mother. Sometimes one is tempted to say, Would it were all over, and we altogether in the great thought room beyond! How one is tethered by the heavy chain of gravitation! But I do not say it. Let me be just as He wills, for His will is my will. Until we're ripe it is not good we should drop; then we shall hang no longer.

I am so glad you enjoy the sound the wind makes in the leaves among which I hang. On the other side I send you a sound of a going, that this letter may be a pleasure as well as trouble to you. — Dear sister Emelia, yours lovingly

GEORGE MACDONALD
AND WIFE.

O wind of God, that blowest in the mind,
    Blow, blow, and wake the gentle spring in me;
Blow, swifter blow, a strong, warm, summer wind,
    Till all the flowers with eyes come out to see;
Blow till the fruit hangs red on every tree,
    And our high-soaring song-larks meet Thy Dove,
Bringing Thy harvest home, hearts laden with Thy love.

Blow not the less though winter cometh then;
    Blow, wind of God, blow hither changes keen;
Let the spring creep into the ground again,
    The flowers close all their eyes, not be seen;
All lives in Thee that ever once hath been:
    Blow, fill my upper air with icy storms;
Breathe cold, O wind of God, and kill my canker-worms.

1. This letter was published in *Letters of Emelia Russell Gurney*.

To Mrs. William Cowper-Temple   Villa Cattaneo, Nervi,
                                                                   January 6, 1878

It was but yesterday, my bountiful sister, that Ted, long hoped for, arrived. He brought us your parcel of embodied love. Shall I not be proud of the delicate handkerchiefs, which surely are fine enough now to satisfy my extravagant sister! I shall never go to lecture or do anything better, without one of them, and they will make me think of you often, for the thought of you is always so near coming, that a sight of one of these will always be enough to bring it.

My wife will tell you herself how delighted she is with the shawls as indeed so am I too. And you will be glad to know that I had been wishing, seeing the book was to be thinner than we had formerly supposed, that I had suggested it should be interleaved, for you will remember we gave up that only because of the too-thickness. So that is more than all right.

This morning came your right welcome letter. I fear you are tired with doing so much. We enjoyed together what you say about the Christmas and the decree — and the baby coming in the midst of tumult. I wonder if we shall need solitude as much when we rise into higher regions of life. I doubt it. Only we shall have it if we need it. Oh how solitary one could be yet in the universe! Railways and factories and dirt and smoke don't go very far after all. It is delightful to think that even in this world the precious sea keeps a wide solitary space for us; and that the very garment that wraps the world about and is our life is a consuming fire, in which no foul thing can have more than the momentary existence necessary to its dissolution; that as it sets on fire and dissipates the cosmetic fragments that reach it before they can reach and strikes, so also the evil things that come out of the world itself are consumed by it. It is so like God — who not merely wards, but frustrates with utter change of evil into good. And well this atmosphere in motion — the wind may be the type of the cleaning spirit of our living Father![1]

But what I was going to say was something quite different. The sunset here is different every night of course — but *so* different! And one wants to keep some record which is impossible. Nay so impossible that one shrinks altogether from the attempt. Last night was a specially gorgeous one — part of the sea a still lake of gold under a red canopy. They are different from the sunsets either of England, America, or Algiers — the prevailing characteristic being the soft blending of dull tender colours as if every hue were wrapped in a twilight of its own — a twilight made of thoughts of other colours — like the hues, rather, of a Roman scarf — but before our hard bright colours ruined the taste of the weavers there. Especially I delight in a brown smoky green that prevails here. Now this profusion of passing, untreasured, never-repeated, unrecorded splendour, makes me wonder whether *all* our recordings are not a heaping up of treasure after a worldly sort. When we are well up the hill, we shall no more — perhaps — think of treasuring a poem, or a drama, or writing a book, than my brother William thinks of heaping money together. We shall share our poems and our music, like eloquence, fresh from the heart, and let them go, no more to be recalled than last night's sunset, and no more to be mourned over, there being no time because of expecting the sunset of tonight. The musicians will get up their concert, and when it is ready, we will gather to heart be blest, but the sounds will float away into the infinite of God in golden ripples, and when the concert is over, all that will be left will be the loud trumpets no longer uplifted, with the other instruments of strange loveliness, waiting for the new life that is already throbbing in the eager heart of the master Musician — where all is vivid burning life. No one will think of storing its results any more than of drawing off the water of the perennial fountains into Heidelberg tins. There, I have done & I leave my wife to tell you about Mary. She seems to me better since Ted came. Ellen Gurney[2] is coming to us at the end of the month. I don't like being without my beautiful book so long, but I would rather wait than have it entrusted to the post.[3] I wonder if there is such a thing as a lexicon for the New Testament which faithfully gives the meanings of the words as used by heathen authors as well. I have no great faith in any lexicons for the New Testament I have seen, and always use a big one. Still the great sweet book, so wise, so simple, so daring, yea — infinite — grows upon me. But I have not been reading so much of late. I have of course been thinking a good deal; but even in thinking, the mind needs its seasons of fallow now and then. The only thing that it is ruin to intermit is *obedience*. We are so glad the Z's are not a pure trouble. They are willing little dears. What a sweetness lies in being *willing!*

But I will not meander away more lest I should meander into maundering.

My dear love to my brother William. I don't see how, but for him, I should be here now. Well, I hope I shall live so that it may turn out to have been worth his while to be so good to me and I hope the same for all of us.

Give my love to Annie[4] too, please — and no end of it please take to yourself.

from your right loving brother,

GEORGE MACDONALD

1. This is a recurring theme in *At the Back of the North Wind* (1871).

2. The daughter of Russell and Emelia Gurney, close friends of the MacDonalds.

3. Possibly Mrs. Cowper-Temple was going to send MacDonald a Greek New Testament.

4. Possibly Annie Munro, sister of Alexander Munro, the sculptor. She had been governess of the Cowper-Temple's children.

To Mrs. William Cowper-Temple   Nervi, Riviera di
                                                     Levante, Italy
                                                     February 17, 1878

My very dear Sister,

I have long delayed thanking you for my lovely New Testament, but
there is this comfort that where people do trust each other they may be
silent without change, and meet the same as if they had never parted. I
am writing all I am able, and I fear letters come badly off. But then I write
very few of the friendship letters: my wife takes the most of that labour
in addition to the rest. The book is all right and more than right, except
the device — the hand instead of offering the cross, is keeping it to itself,
and the mouth ought to be saying *Meum est* instead of the sweet words
Quum est. But oh! the madness of the disobedience of humanity, which
will always prefer doing the other thing from what it is told. This is only
a small instance of the great evil principle. Munro[1] could not get his carvers
to cut the marble according to his clay. I need not go on to the application.

I think my wife will be telling you about Mary. So much is better,
but all is not better, and she does not get stronger, I much fear. The perfect
will be done. Why should we be like the little child that would snatch her
sick kitten out of the lap of her mother? When I look forward and think
how I shall look back on my own folly, I want to have some of the wisdom
now. If Jesus was born, and said such things, and died, and rose, and lived
again, can I trust my God too much? Am I in danger of losing my human
tenderness if I say — Let the Lord do as he will: I shall only hope and
look forward the more. The present in no way satisfies me, least of all the
present in myself. I want to be God's man, not the man of my own idea.
I look forward — God grant I press forward too. Parent would not have
more comfort in his children than he gives me in mine: shall I be oppressed
because he may choose to take one before the rest? Who knows how soon
the turn of her parents may come, and then they will be very glad she is
there and not here. But of course it will or would be much harder for
those whose whole being almost is taken up with watching and ministering
to her. Even they however would, I believe, be more anxious that she
should not suffer greatly than that she should stay long with us. But all is
unknown — save that it is well with the child.

I am much better. I have a walk almost every day now. I never *felt*
walking to do me good before; but then I always walk up the hill, climb
with effort and some weariness into the clear air, and am better all the day
after it. (Application understood.)

What a different life yours must be! — but we all have our work set us, and we all can retire into the presence. I don't know when I shall be in London, except I heard of some lectures, which is not very likely. Please don't think I want you to do anything: *I do not.* Probably we shall find some inland place in Piedmont, where we can live much cheaper than at home. If we could but let Corage! I fear I shall have to go to America next winter, but the mention of it makes Mary so sad that I will not do it if I can well escape it. If it were to please God to take her, it is possible we should all go. But I am learning very slowly to trust him. "Ye cannot serve God and Mammon; therefore take no thought for the morrow." Here is a little prayer I made lying in bed. All my verse now — almost — is made in bed, but I do not think there will be any more than what I have now got till I am ill again —

> Still am I haunting
>   Thy door with my prayers;
> Still they go panting
>   Up thy steep stairs:
> Wouldst thou not rather
>   Come down to my heart,
> And there, O my Father,
>   Be what thou art?

My dear love to my true, great-hearted brother William. May God do what I cannot, thank him fitly for his goodness to us.

I have nothing to say about the state of affairs but just what you say: The Lord reigneth, and neither the Russians nor the Germans nor the English.[2] Is there no talk of occupying Egypt? That would surely be a good deed to do, and would stand us in good stead. I hear they want us there. And now the Khedive[3] seems falling away from what truth he had. But I know more of the politics of the kingdom of heaven than I do of those of this world — at least, if I do not, I am in evil case.

Please give my love to Annie Munro. Ask her if she knows the wild narcissus: it has walked right into my heart.

My love to you. Sorella
pietosa —
Your Friend and brother,

GEORGE MACDONALD

Our dear Ruskin has been behaving very naughtily to Octavia, and has troubled her much at a time when she seems little to need more trouble. See last *Fors*,[4] which has not all the correspondence. I have not thanked you for your last letter. This I say just to let you know we have it. Do you have one from me, thanking you for the lovely handkerchiefs?

1. Alexander Munro, the sculptor, who did a bronze medallion of MacDonald in 1858.

2. Reference here is to Britain's involvement in world affairs. From 1874 to 1880, Disraeli purchased a controlling interest in the Suez Canal, made Queen Victoria empress of India, defended Turkey against Russia, and joined France in an effort to administer Egyptian affairs. For all this, MacDonald took little interest in politics.

3. The title of the Turkish viceroy of Egypt from 1867 to 1914.

4. In *Fors Clavigera* (monthly letters to working men of England, from 1871 to 1884), Ruskin had said some harsh things about Octavia Hill, a pupil of Ruskin's who became romantically involved with him. See *George MacDonald and His Wife*, p. 486.

To Mrs. William Cowper-Temple   Villa Cattaneo, Nervi,
                                                  Riviera di Lavante,
                                                     April 7, 1878

It is time, sister beloved, that you heard something of your people here. Surely the father is with us, and the shadow that seems to deepen is but the shadow cast from his hand by the light of his countenance. I can hardly trust myself to write about our Mary. But God is with her, and she clings to him. Surely he will take her as easily as may be consistent with her good entrance into the more abundant life. She is very weak now — and nothing on her dear bones. But we shall all be glad to change this lowly body for a better one day. And we hope in the Lord, who *is my* resurrection, for surely I have *risen* in him — a little already — I have got my head up and my heart too — and my body will follow.

What do I not owe you for my New Covenant! I use it every day, and had no idea before how useful the Greek would be to me. Oh how much more precious already even than before is the word of it to me! Some difficulties are quite cleared away by the Greek — or it suggests possible explanations where I must ask a scholar before I am certain. The English is vanishing from me as inadequate — and so will the Greek by and by, and nothing be left but The Word. The Father will take us all home by and by, my sister, and then — how good we shall all be and never know it!

Do you remember the Tauchnitz Greek Testament that was sent to show you it would not do for interleaving with the English one? Would you send me one of those please. I think it contains at the end the different reading of those Mss. Or if that does not, the *last* edition of Tischendorf's Greek Testament does, I know. My edition has not the Sinaitic. Only when quite convenient, dear sister — and I know you will not like me to make apologies for troubling you.

I am well into another story,[1] but I do not know when Strahan is going to bring out the last. I cannot write tonight; but I will make my letter more worth to you by copying a poem I made some little time ago. When I am well, I write prose — when ill, verse. But the verse is better than the prose. The verse is mostly made in bed.

Shall the dead praise thee?[2]

I cannot praise thee. By this instrument
    The organ-master sits, nor moves a hand;
For see the organ-pipes o'erthrown and bent,
    Twisted and broke, like corn stalks tempest-fanned!

I well could praise thee for a flower, a dove;
    But not for life that is not light in me;
Not for a being that is less than love —
    A barren shoal half-lifted from a sea.

And for the land whence no wind bloweth ships,
    And all my living dead ones thither blown —
Rather I'd kiss no more their precious lips
    Than carry them a heart so poor and prone.

Yet I do bless thee thou art what thou art,
    That thou dost know thyself what thou dost know
A perfect, simple, tender, rhythmic heart,
    Beating thy blood to all in bounteous flow.

And I can bless thee too for every smart,
    For every disappointment, ache, and fear;

For every hook thou fixest in my heart,
    For every burning cord that draws me near.

But prayer these wake, not song. Thyself I crave.
    Come thou, or all the gifts away I fling.
Thou silent, I am but an empty grave:
    Think to me, Father, and I am a king.

Then, like the wind-stirred bones, my pipes shall quake,
    The air burst, as from burning house the blaze;
And swift contending harmonies shall shake
    Thy windows with a storm of jubilant praise.

Thee praised, I haste me humble to my own,
    For love not shame shall bow me at their feet
Then first and only to my stature grown,
    Fulfilled of love, a servant all complete.

Good night, sweet sister. My wife, I think[,] is now writing to you. Lest she should not be able, I take upon me to send you her heart's love. And the same from both of us to William, the Faithful —

Lovingly yours,

GEORGE MACDONALD

1. MacDonald had finished *Paul Faber, Surgeon* (1879), and was half-finished with *Sir Gibbie* (1879).

2. See *Poetical Works,* vol. 2 (1893), p. 326. Also published in *A Threefold Cord: Poem by Three Friends* (1893).

To Henry Cecil[1]
Villa Cattaneo, Nervi,
May 12, 1878

My dear Cecil,

. . . Ah, my dear friend, we better understand your mental condition and feelings than we did before. Our child is gone from us,[2] but we are following after, and I shall hold her yet again to my soul. . . . The dreadful thing would be that some died and others did not. The only cure for everything is Christ in us. If he be our Saviour, then why should even my own faults and miserable parvitude [littleness] render me at all hopeless, or even cast down; for these are but the skins that the ever newborn eternal serpent is casting from her; and there is in me the everlasting will, the living thing that hates these and prays against them, and will one day emerge pure and clean and loving entirely. . . .

We do not return to England this year. We live cheaper here, and another winter of Italy will do much for me and perhaps make me able to encounter another [tour] in America. . . .

1. Henry Cecil was a fellow-master with MacDonald's brother John at Sheffield Academy and became his best friend; he had high regard for George MacDonald's poetry, and in middle life MacDonald and he were close friends.

2. Mary Josephine, who died April 28, 1878.

To Mrs. A. J. Scott
Villa Cattaneo Nervi
Riviera di Levante
May 12, 1878

My very dear Mrs. Scott,

I write for my wife and myself to thank you for your most kind letter. You could not have done better than send us a word from the "High Countries," in the handwriting of our beloved friend.[1] Ah! one day — we shall talk with him again. My faith in his Master and ours makes one bold to cling to such hopes. But for Him who conquered death by dying how few and how feeble hopes of any kind should I have! and but for the Father of him and us none at all.

My wife suffers much still. I trust she will feel more by and by that death is but the shadow of life. But she sorely wants her child to talk to

just for a little. I think we have all learned a little through the sorrow —
and will more and more look forward.

My wife joins me in love to you all. The God of their father be with
his children. How soon we shall all go — thank God. Dear Mrs. Scott,

> Yours gratefully and
> lovingly,
>
> GEORGE MACDONALD

1. An old letter written by A. J. Scott (d. 1866), which Mrs. Scott had enclosed.

To Mrs. Russell Gurney   Porto Fino
                                              June 5, 1878

My Sister Emelia,

You have been a happy wife, and now you will be a patient widow.
The noble man is gone to his kind, and may we all come near him again
some blessed day of the eternal age.[1]

The world will be like a dream to you after this, a constant waiting
for something at hand. Your dearest are nearly all out of sight now; but it
is not visible proximity but love that is the bond, the oneness. Well as you
knew him, greatly as you loved him, you will know him better, love him
better now. Be sure of this, the grandest thing in England, the justice of
her administration of the laws, is a purer, grander thing yet, because Russell
Gurney has had a share in it. And the Lord who loves justice as his own
being will know how many cities to set him over.

Age was drawing near him here, but he has escaped from it to the
land of youth. All there is impenetrably hidden from us for a time, lest
we should by the glory of it miss the door into it. . . . And there is your
old warrior gone after our young maiden. . . .

1. MacDonald's friend, Russell Gurney, had just died. He left MacDonald £500, which
greatly helped him with his debts.

To W. C. Davies June 19, 1878

. . . Yes, I have never known such a time. Friend after friend going — more than one not dead, but more or less deranged. But our hope is in heaven. God comes nearer and nearer. If only we went as fast as he was drawing us. . . . If we would but understand that we are pilgrims and strangers! It is no use trying to nestle down.

Things look much better for me now, I thank God, in money ways. He will keep me short, I daresay, as will probably always be best for me, but he will enable me to die without debt, I do think. Mr. Russell Gurney has left me £500, which will go far to clear me off, I hope — would almost, if I were not straightened[1] for will be out in 3 volumes in October, and a new story *[Sir Gibbie]* begun in *Glasgow [Weekly] Mail* in September, which is more than half done. . . .

1. That is, in straitened circumstances.

To Mrs. William Cowper-Temple Porto Fino, July 7, 1878.

How long it seems since I wrote to my true sister and friend! But she understands how one who has been writing all day as long, generally as strength can labour, recoils from trying to say what he feels in a letter. Perhaps if my working were not of a kind that let me get my heart out, I should be readier to write to one whose door is always open to receive the words of love and faith.

I wish William had a yacht, and could come here. It is the loveliest little harbour — all round with hills — and is certainly the most beautiful place I was ever in. Our only carriage is a boat (and a canoe). To the west we look out to sea over the top of a little isthmus, & to the east we almost see Spezzia — only it is round a corner. The sea is a perfection of blues & greens — and we have miles of terraces, with plenty of shade from better trees than olives — which as yet I admire without liking. How you would enjoy the warmth too! We have not yet had any too great heat, though we have to go lightly clad. I am able to work more steadily than ever I did — I mean I am less laid up than ever before — and so shall be enabled to make up for the loss which my increasing popularity in America brings me. That sounds strange — but it is simply so: where I used always to get £300, I get now — for this book I am writing, only £110 — because they have begun — pirates, that is to publish my books at 20 cents or so. But we live much cheaper here. We have but one servant — to cook, and never were so comfortable before. The girls & boys do everything else almost. I hear the piano, and that means that I must go and give them their little Sunday sermon. Oh what a good your gift of the Greek Testament has been to me! I read no other — read it everyday, and I am almost in despair at being quite unable to say the things I am learning. Truth comes & goes in a thousand shapes like the sunsets & sunrises. There is no truth one can keep but The Truth. It grows better and better — the main of things, I mean — this life that is in God, with its eternity and its all things. But I cannot write about it now.

What good news we hear of dear Annie![1] It is good to think she is really likely to be better. We have been sending now and then to get news of her.

We cannot believe she ever had anything of the sort, or the least like it before. We should surely have heard of it — and we never did.

Louisa sends her love with mine to you both. Dear Sister Emilia [Mrs. Russell Gurney] is now in the shadow of death, but the end is the sunrise. It is weary waiting, but we must learn to share in God's patience. She has been divinely good to us, but of that another time.

I must close in haste.

> God bless you both —
> with himself.
> Yours
> Most lovingly
>
> GEORGE MACDONALD

1. Possibly Annie Munro. See p. 275 n. 4 above.

To Mr. Ireland   Porto Fino, Riviera di Levante,
                                                    July 20, 1878

My dear Mr Ireland,

It was a real pleasure to me to hear from you again, though I wish you had said a word about yourself. How the years flit past, and lives flit with them out of our sight. We have lost a loved daughter[1] since we came here last year — but I do not mean *lost,* for I live by hope of all kinds. I hope things are well with you. Tell me when you write again.

I am pleased also that you would like me to write a story in your paper. I could not undertake it just at once. I have a book coming out in October,[2] and a story to begin in September in *The G. Weekly Mail [Glasgow Weekly Mail]* — a Glasgow paper, two volumes of the latter are nearly ready but the other book will take two months work over the proof. The story in the *Mail* will run for six months — that is, it will be over in March.[3] I suppose it would not do to begin yours before that was finished? but you see I could not begin to print with a good start much before January and later — How dreadfully this paper has beguiled me — but I have no time to do more than beg your forgiveness for the trouble it will give you — would be better. I like writing in a newspaper because it reaches more people whom it may help, and Mudies[4] can't bind up the newspapers, as he does the magazines, and lend them instead of the book.

I do not myself think the newspaper hurts the book, but for the last one Hurst & Blackett gave me £50 more because it has not been through any periodical.

The *Mail* pays me £300 and did so the year before last for one, which they told me themselves sent the paper up 5000 a week. Of course I should be glad some day if I could get more, but that would quite content me from you. But times are rather hard on me through the increase of my popularity in America which has brought in the pirates. I have always got £300 for a book in America — going through a magazine first — till this last when I got only £110. They can't give so much they say when these pirates bring out an edition at once for so many cents. I think my last was published by them at 20 cents.

Other matters may remain till I hear from you again. It is late for our early times and I am working hard.

With kindest regards,
Yours very truly

GEORGE MACDONALD

1. Mary Josephine, who died April 28, 1878.
2. *Paul Faber* (1878).
3. *Sir Gibbie,* serialized in the *Glasgow Weekly Mail* (January 4–March 15, 1879).
4. Charles Edward Mudie was the proprietor of the famous "Select Circulating

Library," to which thousands of families in England subscribed. He was a strong evangelical, and his acceptance or rejection of a new book could make or break an author's career.

To Mrs. Russell Gurney[1]   Porto Fino, September 1, 1878

DEAREST SISTER EMELIA, —

I would have written to you long ago, but I have been pressed with work that has a set time to it, and so have put off too long. I am now seeing a book through the press which I think you will find sympathy with.[2] It is another like "Thomas Wingfold," and will be out in the beginning of November, I think. I do not know that I shall write any more of the sort. The whole thing is beyond writing about; it is only fit for living. Sometimes the change that must come in me seems so immense, it is nothing less than a birth from above. But if there be One who could call us into thought, He is able for this too. We have but a poor glimmering notion of what life means. If we were *one with* the life eternal, the delight of mere consciousness of being would, I think, be something unspeakable. The greatest bliss is just the one thing we cannot do without. As often as we get a little glimmer of truth, we are ready to feel as if now we could get on and be at peace a while; whereas it is every moment a breathing of God's breath, a walking with God, a thinking of God's thoughts, a consciousness of His presence as our deepest being: this is what we need, to live other than a broken, half-slavish life. Every breath we draw, that, for all we feel to the contrary, might have come from a dead law of existence, and is not the wind, the air, the breath of God to us, is but a kind of death to our deepest self. Only He is behind the death even, and is bringing life out of all death.

How is your conscious world moving now, dear, lonely sister? You are now like the creature spinning its chrysalis. That is the use of the world to you. Have patience, and let your wings grow. There is no food for feathers like patience. I have been learning a little about patience lately. Ah, what lovely quiet we have here! But it only gives the room for severer battle. It is in desert places that the real battles of the world have been first gained. And who can tell? nay, I think I can almost tell, that now in your loneliness, now that the noise of the surf of the tide of the world has receded, and will recede yet further from your dwelling, you will find more unexpected doors opening around you, and will learn more clearly than ever that you are all the time in the heart of the Father, where your beautiful husband is also.[2] It cannot be very long. We will go on cheerfully. Our life might be a call to those beyond: "We are coming friends!" Christ be with us and teach us. I am generally, I think, perhaps always, sooner or later sent back to Him when I get into a hedge. That He knew God and was satisfied is a lovely comfort. If He lived really, all is well, and we will trust even when we cannot get things all right in our thoughts. To what a bliss we are called — to be the heirs of God! I shall one day live in the universe as God lives in it, with a pure, potent, perfect existence, at home with every form of life, because one with the Heart of all life.

You see I have been talking rather than writing to you. You will take what truth there is in it. How I should like to talk to you many times a day. I should get very sick of myself if I hadn't got God to refer the thing to. I think the moment we feel not near Him we should make haste to lay hold upon Him. It is not my books nor your convalescents that is the first business of the day, but that God should have His own in us, and we, what we cannot live without, or do anything without, our own in God. Yours, ever lovingly,

GEORGE MACDONALD

1. This letter was published in *Letters of Emelia Russell Gurney*, pp. 233-34.
2. *Paul Faber* (1879).
3. Russell Gurney died in the spring of 1878, at the age of seventy-four. See *George MacDonald and His Wife*, p. 487.

To Henry Cecil[1]   Porto Fino, Riviera di Levante
                                        September 23, 1878

My dear Cecil,

Best thanks for the good news, and God be praised. He takes a long time, but he does not forget. I have had few such keen troubles as that was to me, and now that is over, with the result at least that your kindness and generosity to me in the affair has drawn my heart nearer to yours. Forgive brevity and even neglect. You can hardly know how closely I am at work. *Paul Faber* going through the press, and being as good as rewritten in the process, and *Sir Gibbie* being printed for the *Glasgow Mail*. So bear with me, and let us look forward to the time when we hope all to meet. John and Charles and all. Love to your bairns. We are all well.

Yours affectionately,

GEORGE MACDONALD

1. Henry Cecil and his family lived near the MacDonalds at Boscombe. When Cecil's wife died in 1876 of consumption, he gave her two Shetland ponies, "with a chaise and harness," to Mrs. MacDonald, who had the animals for a while at The Retreat, Hammersmith. When the MacDonalds went to Italy, the ponies were taken care of by the Cowper-Temples.

To William Cowper-Temple   Porto Fino, January 13, 1879

My dear William,

I need not tell you that I call you by your own name not that I honour you less but that I love you more. And well I may!

Many thanks for your most kind letter, which gave me great pleasure. I am so glad you were not annoyed by my dedication.[1] It is very kind of you to take it just as I meant it. And your letter says of my books just what I try to go upon — to make them true to the real and not the spoilt humanity. Why should I spend my labour on what one can have too much of without any labour? I will try to show what we might be, may be, must be, shall be — and something of the struggle to gain it.

I would have written to you before but I was last week in the final effort of finishing another book[2] — a very different one from *Paul Faber*, and much easier to read.

Now about your guests the highly privileged ponies. I am sorry to hear they have so little to do for that shows they have not been so useful as I had flattered myself they might be. It has become pretty clear that we are not to be allowed to have any farther use of them, and therefore I am sorry, only we could not tell, that you have had the burden of them so long. I wish they had been useful and then we could have *begged* you to keep them. Now we can only ask you whether you know of any one who would buy them or accept them. There is this difficulty about selling them, that Zephyr is really worth nothing, and the other though not eight quite, I fancy is not worth much without her. I should not like to part them, and much rather than do so I would give them to anybody who would be kind to them & would not sell the old one. Zephyr must be nearly entering her 32nd year. If any one who would be good to them would prefer buying them, I would take anything he pleased to give. I fancy the whole affair, carriage, harness & all[,] is not worth £40 now. But really if they were only well placed we would take £20, or anything, or nothing. If you do not know of anybody, we will write to see if we can find anybody to take them.

It is very doubtful — the balance leans quite the other way — that we shall be home this year, and if we were I do not now see how we could keep them. Sir Henry Wolff[3] has made us take down our little stable.

What a mercy our coming here has been. We have lived on so much less — and I made not half my usual amount last year. Had we been in England — I was going to say I should have been in despair, but then it would have been managed differently for us. As it is we have done a little better than usual. And this winter I have had neither bronchitis nor asthma except one slight attack of the former — and have worked more steadily than any winter, I think, for thirty years — nearly.

You have sore times in England. I cannot come to understand what should be done with people who strike, and come upon others for bread.[4] People willing to work who cannot find work ought of course to be helped to the very uttermost, but in the other case, if it were not for their families, I do not think they ought to be helped. And yet when it comes to seeing them in want — one's theories will certainly break down.

I doubt if any combination but one of pure love, that is, the body of Christ, will work for good. And these combinations of workmen have surely done more evil than good. But I may be wrong, for I am very ignorant of these things.

My wife joins me in truest love to you both. Do let us know when there is any better news of Annie Munro. Who can tell what God is doing with her under the veil of that cloud?

Yours most lovingly and gratefully,

GEORGE MACDONALD

1. MacDonald dedicated *Paul Faber, Surgeon* (1879) to Mrs. Cowper-Temple.
2. *Sir Gibbie* (1879).
3. Probably the MacDonalds' landlord in England.
4. Referring to the rise of trade unions and events leading to the last Reform Act of 1884.

To His Son Greville MacDonald   [March 1879]
[Porto Fino]
Monday, half-past two.

. . . Our Maurice is alive, but that is nearly all I can say. . . . He has been sleeping a good deal to-day, and it seems as if he was gently gliding into the land where all is well. He is angelic — a poor word, but at least not too strong to express his patience and sweetness; and for his intellect, that is as marvelous as the disease. Yesterday he played a good game of draughts — and a long one, with Ronald.

I fear your mother will have a terrible illness when it is over; the fatigue is great, great, and she never goes to bed now, but gets a nod or two when she can't help it. . . . His brothers and sisters are just like strong angels tending a weak one; and for his mother, one can't say more than that she is a perfect mother to him. God is with us and will help us to hope on and on beyond all sights and sounds. . . .

Tuesday evening.

. . . The doctor says there is just the smallest star of hope. His lungs are as bad as they can be. He is a wonderful boy, with an energy incredible — moving about in the bed in a way you could hardly believe, and now and then making us all laugh in the midst of his terrible restlessness, and much misery, though no unhappiness. . . . That telegram was sent in a time of much dread, and although there is as much doubt still, we are not in such distress. Then we naturally cried out for help, and, as I said, I am very glad to know you were only prevented by a doubt of your duty.[1] But take care, my boy, lest you should ever lend ear to the advice of any with whom *prudence,* so-called, is the first thing. We have had a letter on the subject from [————] which is just as worldly as it is prudent, as careful for the life it would save as careless for the life it would ruin. Fancy telling our boys and girls not to nurse their withering brother for fear they should develop the same fell disease hidden in themselves! She is most kind, however, and does not know better. Oh, these wise people that look down on the simple.

I am glad to say your mother had an hour and a half's sleep this evening while I nursed, with plenty of needful help. This morning she was beginning to talk nonsense herself from fatigue, but then she got a mouthful of rest, enough to restore her senses. God grant the "little star of hope,"

which Schetilig [the doctor?] confessed to this evening, may grow a sun
— and, if not, give us strength to help the darling to die.

1. Greville MacDonald writes: "A word of explanation may perhaps be allowed, even
if, in this case at least, love ought to have been the only mentor *ruat coelum*. I was to stand
in April for my final M.R.C.S. examination, and had been thrown back so much by illness
that it was a question whether I could pass. If I failed, it would postpone my qualifying
for six months; and I was naturally keen to relieve my father of my own necessities. But
the account of my brother's sigh and turning of his face to the wall when he heard I would
not come, has never left me" (*George MacDonald and His Wife*, p. 491).

To Rev. John Smart

Porto Fino,
March 11, 1879

Dear and Honoured Friend,

You know why I have not written to you before — that while you
were mourning the loss of the much loved lady who had so long helped
you to live, we were watching our boy, and helping him to die.[1] Dear
friend, let us hold fast by the Resurrection and the Life. Life looks very
short to me now — or rather I should say — Life is drawing very near. . . .

Dear to me is the memory of your sweet, generous, hospitable, gracious wife — a pattern of Christian ministering. Great has been the kindness of both her and you to me and mine, and it shall never be forgotten. . . .

1. Maurice MacDonald died March 5, 1879.

To W. C. Davies

Porto Fino,
March 19, 1879

My dear Davies,

. . . He was quite a child by himself[1] — in the eyes of his brothers
and sisters as well as ours. Though not so strong as his elder brothers, he
was the most active, and the best swimmer and diver of them all. He had
been weakly and had what seemed a cold for part of the winter, but was
better, when one Sunday morning about 3 o'clock he was seized with severe

hemorrhage. That ceased but was followed by inflammation of the lungs, and on the 18th day he died. We had hoped almost to the last hour. He was just over fifteen. It is a sore affliction, but though cast down we are not destroyed. Jesus rose again glorious, and to that I cleave fast. My boy is of course dearer to me than before, and we shall find him again, with his love as fresh as the life that cannot die. Not a murmur escaped him. His contentment was lovely and his soul strong to the end — his obedience perfect — and his rest in God marvelous.

1. Referring to his son Maurice, who had recently died at the age of fifteen.

To Mrs. William Cowper-Temple   Porto Fino, March 20, 1879

I hardly know how to begin a letter to you, my dearly loved sister and friend. My wife says if we get this house we are looking after now she would like to put up in the hall "And they confessed that they were pilgrims and strangers on the earth." That is our mood, and may it last until we shall be no longer strangers or pilgrims but at home. There are so many things that belong to home here — they must be strangers and pilgrims too somehow. Nothing comes to perfection — there is no time for anything but getting ready to go. But my faith and hope grow stronger. I seem very hard to teach. Imagination must be sent out of the throne of Faith, and taught to sit lowly on the footstool. A thousand things have to be set right. I have to be simply the child that tries to be good, and keeps close by his father. One day the door will open and we shall find ourselves at least started for home and the finding of our own. Meantime I must try to be better for the love of my children whom I cannot see, and that will bring me nearer to them.

Still I have the old story to tell you — more and more delight in my New Testament. I had no idea how inadequate was the English of the Epistles, nor how much I should learn from the Greek. Some day God will, I trust, reveal himself to me as he has never done yet, and I shall be as sure as St. Paul. I must try not to stand in the way of his redeeming will with me — for he is doing his best for me as for us all. Once I repeated to my lovely child — "Let patience have her perfect work that ye may be perfect and entire, wanting nothing" — and I delight to think that he asked for it again a minute after. Patient indeed he was — I think as quietly trusting as boy could be. May God make me a better father by the time I find him again, for my boy he must be to all eternity.

I am writing stupidly but where is the good of a sister if I may not let my thoughts run out to her as they come!

My dear love to William — I thank him for his sympathy and love. God bless him and you with your hearts['] desires.

Ellen Gurney[1] has kindly accepted the ponies. She is having a place got ready for them, and will soon be prepared to take them. I am very glad they will go where they can be of more use. I do not know how to thank you for all the care and expense you have laid out on them. Will you kindly say a word to her about them, as she may be shy of speaking first.

I do hope we shall be able to get home for the summer. My wife and most of the children greatly need the change. I think I am about the best of the family except the three elder boys.

I am hard at work on a new book. Can you tell me if anything has been done or is likely to be done about my animal sermon? — because I have had another application, perhaps, I do not know, from a different society from Miss Cobb[']s and yours. I referred the applicant to Miss Cobb. It was a good many weeks ago, and I have heard nothing more.

Yours most lovingly,

GEORGE
MACDONALD.

1. Daughter of Russell and Emelia Gurney, friends of the MacDonalds.

To William Cowper-Temple Porto Fino,
April 9, 1879

My dear William,

How real death makes things look! And how we learn to cleave to the one shining fact in the midst of the darkness of this world's trouble, that Jesus *did* rise radiant! I too have noble brothers to find where the light has hidden them, besides my faithful children, girl and boy. And you, beloved friends, will find your dear ones also, and when your hearts are filled with love and embraces, you will perhaps turn to us to help you to endure your bliss. My wife and I look for and hasten unto the coming of our Lord, whatever that means in words — we know what it means to our hearts.

He alone who invented the nursery and its bonds, can perfect what he began there. I for my part, cry more for a perfecting of my loves than perhaps for anything else. That does make him a real God to us when we feel that he is at the root of all our loving, and recognize him as the best love of all, causing, purifying, perfecting all the rest. Our perfect God! and perfect — making —

We have made up our minds to return to England for the summer. We have the prospect of more than enough employment in acting the pilgrims to pay our travelling expenses, and we all feel we *must* have a change — that another summer here would be too much for us. I ought almost to except myself, and yet not quite, for I have troublesome head-aches, although *no* bronchitis or asthma — not even when I catch a little cold. But we have been very little out this winter — my wife & I partic-ularly, for the rain has been such as would be almost incredible to one whose acquaintance with the coast has been of the usual kind. About the middle of next month we hope to see our own country again, and our beloved friends.

I don't think I mistook you about the ponies. I did not wrong your big heart, but I did get a little frightened at the thought of how we had used you. But it is well Ellen[1] should have them. If only they would frisk some of her weary prayers out of her! It is sad to see people praying like that, and yet I know they have true hearts, and I love them dearly. But oh how I hate forms and love St. Paul for the way he tells us to let no man burden us with them, even when he himself loved and kept those he had been used to from his childhood.

My wife joins me in true love to you both. What a delight it will be to see you and hear your loved voices again. I am well into another book, name uncertain, and next month a new one will be out, called *Sir Gibbie*. I never wrote so steadily for so long I think.

God be with us all —
Yours affectionately

GEORGE MACDONALD

We have heard a report of Annie Munro being at Broadlands: is it indeed so? We want much to hear something about her. Have you read *Catherine of Siena*? A lovely book.

1. Ellen Gurney, daughter of Russell and Emelia Gurney.

To Mr. Horder   39, Longridge Road
Kensington
June 15, 1879

Dear Mr. Horder,

I want to arrange[,] if agreeable to you and Mr. Toms, for preaching for one of you in the morning and for the other in the evening, for opportunity will be getting scarce soon — I mean I shall have as much to do in that way as I can well manage. I will write to Mr. Toms by this same post to the same effect. I could do so on the 29th of this month, or on the sixth of next month, only I should like to know before next Saturday.

Yours very truly,

GEORGE MACDONALD

P.S. This is with my wife's permission!!

To Dr. J. D. Holland   The Retreat, Hammersmith
July 7, 1879

My dear Dr Holland,

I am sorry to hear you are ill. I trust it is but a passing indisposition, and that when I have the pleasure of seeing you in the autumn, I shall find you well and enjoying all kinds of life.

As to the request with which you honour me, I am sorry I cannot undertake it. I am at this moment busy with a three volume novel,[1] which I cannot finish before leaving for your world,[2] and I must not load myself with fresh labour. Besides a short story is almost as difficult to do as a long one — it is quite so in everything but the mere time required, and does not renumerate one at the same rate by any means. And where all one can do will not make both ends meet, this is a consideration of importance. But the main thing is that I am so far overworked that I am getting sick of it.

I have partly ready a translation of fifteen hymns — Spiritual Songs, he calls them, of Novalis.[3] I have been at work upon them over a period of twenty years, ever trying to please myself with them, so much do I love them, and so severe are my notions of what a translation ought to be. Three of them have appeared in *Good Words*.[4] I do not mean them to have any more of them, for they have vexed me in more ways than one of late. I send you the first and longest though not the best that you may see the tone of them, and think whether they would do for you. I spent far more labour on them than on originals. I think I ought to have £5 apiece for them. I mention this to help your judgment in the matter.

With a thousand thanks for your kind offer of hospitality, and hoping that your illness at least may not be the cause of our failing to be your guests — for if you take one, you will have to take three.

Believe me, dear Dr
Holland,
Yours most truly

GEORGE MACDONALD

1. *Mary Marston* (1881).
2. MacDonald was considering doing another lecture tour in America.
3. *Exotics,* which contains "Twelve of the Spiritual Songs of Novalis" plus three additional hymns; reprinted in *Rampolli* (1897).
4. *Good Words for the Young,* of which MacDonald was editor for a time.

To James T. Fields   Corage, Boscombe,
                                                          Bournemouth
                                                          August 8, 1879

My dear Fields,

It was a great pleasure to me to see your letter, for I feared that my neglect of writing had made you think I did not care for you. What then was my disappointment on reading it to find that you requested something from me which I could not give you. I have refused such a request again and again, because I dislike the thing so much — partly on personal grounds, partly on principle.[1] A man should keep his shell till he gets his coffin instead — and for my part I trust the outer life of one who has written a good many volumes tending to reveal most that is worth knowing of his inner life, will be forgotten in this world, after he has left it.

At all events, my dear Fields will believe that it is for no reason whatever relating to him that I decline to do what he asks of me. On that I am settled and firm. Honestly I do not like or approve of this way of publicizing live people. If anything is left after a hundred years, accompanied by a desire to know, *then* is soon enough.

We have had great troubles since we saw you, losing in one year two of our children. But faith and hope, and I trust charity also, are stronger than before, and we go on, expecting one day ere long to find those whom we have lost.

How I should like to see you again! We are pilgrims and strangers without a home at present. We have been two winters in Italy, and expect to return again in October. There only I am well.

I hope things go well with you and Mrs. Fields. Give & take our love. We shall never forget your great kindness to us. Sympathize with me: all my books have been in boxes for nearly two years!

                                          Yours, dear Fields
                                          Affectionately,

                                          GEORGE MACDONALD

1. Fields had requested that MacDonald consider writing an autobiography or having a biography written.

To His Stepmother   Bromsgrove,
                                                          August 18, 1879

. . . If I did not hope in the risen Christ, where should my life be
now? But I desire to hasten on my way that I may find my children again
— and all my dear ones who have gone before me. Neither Louisa nor I
knew much about death till those two were taken from us within the year
— and now we know its terror and its comfort.

You know we have been acting with considerable success in London
and other places.[1] We have gained friends by it and lost not one. Now we
have a little rest till near the end of September, when we have a month or
five weeks of acting and lecturing before we set out again for Italy, where
we are still hoping to buy a house before the winter. . . . I am wonderfully
well. . . . No bronchitis for nearly two years now. . . . And so Jeanie[2] is
married also! . . .

1. The MacDonalds performed dramatic adaptations from Bunyan's *Pilgrim's Progress*
during the summers from 1878 to 1887 in England and Scotland. See *Dramatic Illustrations
of Passages From the Second Part of the Pilgrim's Progress by John Bunyan. Arranged in the
Year 1877 by Mrs. George MacDonald* (Oxford: Oxford University Press, 1925).
2. Jane MacDonald Noble, MacDonald's half-sister.

To James T. Fields   England, August 21, 1879

My dear Fields,

I hope you are not too vexed with me to read this note. I send you
with it a pamphlet in which what seems the true Yorkshire descent of your
great Washington is set forth by Colonel Tewsome of the Royal Engineers
— the brochure will speak for itself, but hardly, I fancy, for the labour
needful to produce it. Would not the *Atlantic Monthly* be interested enough
in the matter to take some notice of it? I add two notes given me in
manuscript by the author.

We are resting for a week or two in Worcestershire, for the sake of
the salt baths in Droilwich, a town where the houses are absolutely comical
with the twisting and unlevelling caused by the sinking of the earth from
the pumping up of the salt water from the saltsprings. We are now, as you

may have heard, turned into a sort of company of acting strollers. I mean strolling actors — and have a good reception and tolerable results. We have really hardly tried the country yet though. People seem a good deal interested in our attempt. In the beginning of November we set out again for Italy where by that time we hope to have a house of our own, in which to rest for that and a few following winters till we are called, I hope, to the high countries.

In haste, with love to you both,

Yours affectionately

GEORGE MACDONALD

To Mrs. William Cowper-Temple   Corage, Boscombe, Bournemouth,
Christmas Eve, 1879

Very dear sister Georgina,

I must write just a word or two with my Christmas offering. Strange to think of you on that side and we on this! but that is the way, and God is on all sides. There is no end to his content — which is the rest of Christ, and will be ours if we hold on. We send our love and greetings in the hope which the child brought with him from the father.

I cannot write more. I have been prevented.

Yours and brother William's with true hearts both of us,

GEORGE MACDONALD

Christmas, 1879

Great-hearted child, thy very being *The Son!*
   Thou know'st the hearts of all us prodigals;
or who is prodigal, but him who has gone
   Far from the true, to heart it with the false?
   And who but thee, that, from the animals,
   Know'st all the hearts, up to the Father's own,
   Can tell what it would be to be alone!

Alone! no father! at the very thought,
    Thou, the eternal light, wast once aghast;
death in death for thee it almost wrought —
    How thou didst haste, about to breathe thy last,
    To call out *Father* ere thy spirit passed!
    Exhausted in fulfilling no hard vow,
    But doing his will who greater is than thou.

That we might know him, thou didst come & live;
    That we might find him, thou to him didst die;
The son-heart, brother, thy son-being give,
    We too would love the Father perfectly,
    And to his bosom go back with the cry,
    Father, into thy hands I give the heart
    Which left thee but to learn how good thou art.

There are but two in all the universe —
    The Father and his children — not a third;
or all the weary time tell any curse,
    Nor once dropped from its nest a fledgling bird,
    Never old sorrow in new heart has stirred;
    But a love-pull it was upon the chain
    That drags the children to the Father again.

O Jesus Christ! babe, man, eternal son,
    Take pity: we are poor where thou art rich —
Our hearts are small; and yet there is no one
    In all the sad and noisy nursery, which,
    Merry, or mooning in its narrow niche,
    Needs not the Father's heart this very now,
    With all his being's being, even as thou.

For my beloved Brother and Sister William and Georgina Cowper Temple.

                                        GEORGE MACDONALD

To Mrs. William Cowper-Temple   Corage, Boscombe, Bournmouth,
                                                                           January 26, 1880

Very dear sister Georgina,

I would have written to you long ago, but I have been a good many days in bed, and only today have I got to my study.

I send you at last a copy for yourself of my little book.[1] Where shall we send the twenty copies you were so kind to order? Looking over it with more interest than I have yet felt for a book of my own, I think it is not a failure, but a great deal will depend, not only on the degree and kind of spiritual training but on the mood of the reader. That you will be with me in it I have every hope.

Would I could say any word to touch the sorrow of your dear Lady Joscelyne; but God alone can comfort real heart-pain. I could say many things with which I could comfort myself, but the things God says to you come in mostly at the back door, and what others say, at the front. I have some notion of her pain, and God knows it quite, yet lets it go on. This I will dare to say that it was more, whether she knew it then or not, to the widow of Nain, to have looked in the face of Jesus, than to have had her son restored to her from the dead. Jesus is always the same — therefore he has mothers and sisters on the earth still.

Perhaps you may find a little bit here and there in my book that may make her glad for a moment. I will not presume to send her a message. A mother's grief folds her round like an aureole, and one would not speak aloud.

We may perhaps see you. We are going, some of us, at least, to Bordighera — if we can. I find I am not to live here, for I cannot work for illness — though I have not been so ill as before we went to Italy. It looks as if there was some chance of being useful as well as well at Bordighera, and a house, probably, within our reach.

My wife has taken two baby girls deserted by their father, a Frenchman, and with a dying mother. The mother is come with them, and after she has been a little while here, Louisa hopes to get her into one of the homes at Bournmouth. They have but just arrived.[2]

Would it be possible, without giving anybody too much trouble, to get the Septuagint brother William has for me? If it is not easily accessible, do not think anymore of it at present. When I heard that you were gone and he was going, I telegraphed to him to Stanhope Street, saying I could send there for it, but I had no answer, and a nephew called twice, but the house was deaf and dumb as old Baal.

My love to William. I hope he is all the better for the lovely air and less biting winter. Louisa is overwhelmed with things to do.

She sends her love to you both.

> Yours right lovingly,
>
> GEORGE MACDONALD

1. *A Book of Strife, in the Form of the Diary of an Old Soul* (1880).

2. Honey and Joan Desaint were the young daughters of an Englishwoman who had been deserted by her French husband. The two girls rapidly became part of the MacDonald household, while Louisa MacDonald arranged for Gertrude, the mother, to go into the Firs Home to rest. See William Raeper, *George MacDonald* (London: Lion Publishing Co., 1987), p. 349.

To James MacDonald[1]   Corage, Boscombe, Bournemouth
                                                  Jan. 28, 1880

My very dear Cousin:

The blessed woman has gone to her own at last — God be praised. I will not say *her memory* is dear to me, but *she herself* is dear, and shall be, I trust, dearer yet, in the holy time coming. I always adored her, for she was like a mother to us also. It were hard to find a lovelier type of Christian service than that embodied in her.

I am troubled to hear that she suffered much, but it is over. We are in the foremost rank now, or very nearly, and our time is coming. But we shall not die by chance or the will of man, for he who makes strength perfect in weakness will be with us also.

It was well for all that Louisa[2] should go early, just as it was well for all that your mother should linger and long to go. Our life and its needs are known only to the Father, and he has his own best teatment for each. Now you, my dear fellow, are left alone in the silent house. Seventeen that I have known the dwellers in it are gone into the world we call unseen — but we shall see them all again, and be blessed. I wish I were able to go to you, but I am quite invalided just now — so much so that we are going to start for Italy if possible as soon as we can — not for a fortnight yet however.

May God be with you in your loneliness, and that will make it full of life. I wonder what you will do, and should like much to hear from you again.

This world is a terrible thing if the materialists were right. But my faith & hope grow.

Your very affectionately,

GEORGE MACDONALD

1. This letter was written by MacDonald to his cousin James MacDonald on the death of James's mother, Jane Duff (Grant) MacDonald. The father of George and James together built the house at The Farm and brought up their two families all together there — eight and six children respectively, of whom only three lived to be over forty.

James inherited The Farm. He did not marry, and at his death The Farm passed to his nephew, Robert Gordon Troup.

2. One of MacDonald's half-sisters.

To Mr. Blunt   The Tarn House, Ilkley
                                                                                    Aug. 3, 1880

My dear Blunt,

I am sorry to hear that you are not so well, and hope you may get away sooner than you expected. Alas! I do not see the possibility of my getting away. I am now so pressed with the finishing of this book, and the necessarily immediate commencement of another, that although it seemed to me essential to the latter that I should breathe the Scotch air for a few days, I don't see how I am to have it, and have ceased to hope for it.

It is a strange thing that however long I may have been about a book, I am always compelled to finish it in a hurry — and that does not mean carelessly. But all these things are ordered, *managed* would be the better word, by the all-pervading Life — *in* more than *around* us, if there be any more and less to be said about *him*.

I hope it will not disappoint you much, or trouble your plans at all.

We are very comfortable here after our rather close quarters in London, but, though we came on Saturday, I am too busy to have had a walk yet.

My wife joins me in love to you & yours. Do not take the trouble to answer this — though I should be glad of a word from some one — *any* one to say how you are.

Yours affectionately

GEORGE MACDONALD

To Sir Henry P. Craik, M.P.   Casa Coraggio,
                                                      Bordighera
                                                      May 13, 1881

My dear Craik,

The bearer of this letter, Miss Julie Sutton,[1] is a particular friend of mine, for whom I have a great regard, and I shall be personally grateful to you for anything you can do to further her views.

It is possible you may be aware that I have paid a good deal of attention to translation, though I have not done a large amount of work in it. I remind you of this merely to establish a sort of right to an opinion. Of very little translation that I have read could I say it was well done; of most, I think it abominable, but I knew some translations that are as translations works of art. Amongst these is one of *David Elginbrod* into German by the lady I now use the right of friendship to present to you. I think she spent more earnest labour turning it into German than I did in making English (or Scotch) of it. So much pleased was I with it that I gave a copy of it to Prince Louis of Hesse Darmstadt.

I do not think magazines make sufficient use of *good* translation. Perhaps they cannot get it. I wish Grove would look at a short tale which Miss Sutton has now ready. I do not believe her English will be more than a very slight degree if at all defective, and if he likes I will undertake to set all that right. But please have a little talk with her. She is a woman of real education and insight and faculty.

Pardon abruptness — I am just beginning to work after a fortnight mostly of bed.

                                            Yours most truly
                                            George MacDonald

1. Julie Sutton, sister of Henry Sutton, who was a lifelong friend of MacDonald.

To George Rolleston, M.D., F.R.S.,   Casa Coraggio, Bordighera
Linacre Professor of Anatomy and   June 16th, 1881
Physiology, Oxford[1]

Beloved Friend,

Do not start at the warmth of my address, for brief as was our opportunity of knowing each other, it was more than long enough to make me love you. I write because I hear you are very ill. I know not a little about illness, and my heart is with you in yours. Be of good courage; there is a live heart at the center of the lovely order of the Universe — a heart to which all the rest is but a clothing form, — a heart that bears every truthful thought, every help-needing cry of each of its children, and must deliver them.

All my life, I might nearly say, I have been trying to find that one Being, and to know him consciously present; hope grows and grows with the years that lead me nearer to the end of my earthly life; and in my best moods it seems ever that the only thing worth desiring is that his will be done; that there lies before me a fullness of life, sufficient to content the giving of a perfect Father, and that the part of his child is to yield all and see that he does not himself stand in the way of the mighty design.

But why do I write thus to you who may know all this, tenfold better than I? Just because I want to come near to you in your illness. . . . Christ speaks of the world's goods as not ours — as things that cannot be ours, but are in their nature foreign to power of possession. Our own things are the riches towards God. What I may have in this kind I offer you, in love and sympathy with you and yours.

May the great life whose creating power is Love be with you and make you strong and comfort you. One moment's contact between his heart and his child's makes of that child a young God. "I said ye are Gods."

May he make you triumph over pain and doubt and dread, and restore you to perfect, divine health. . . .

1. This letter was written the day Rolleston died.

To Messrs. A. M. Black   121, Harley Street
                                                          July 18, 1882

Dear Sirs,

Great pressure of work has prevented me from personally applying to you for permission to reprint in a volume of essays now nearly ready the notice of the Poet Shelley which I wrote for the last edition of the *Encyclopedia Britannica*.[1] I can hardly take it ill if you should decline my request for I have not the smallest claim on you, but I should be greatly obliged if you could allow me. My productions in that kind have been very few, and I should like to include that one.

> I am
> dear Sirs,
> Yours truly,

> GEORGE MACDONALD

P.S. My friend Mr. Watt, who manages all my publishing business, has already written to you, but I see that I ought to have written myself, only I am oppressed with work of various kinds at present.

> G. MCD.

1. See MacDonald's article on Shelley in the eighth edition of the *Encyclopedia Britannica* (1860), vol. 20, p. 100, signed "G.M.D." It was reprinted in *A Dish of Orts: Chiefly Papers on the Imagination and on Shakespeare* (1893).

To W. C. Davies   Casa Coraggio,
                                                      January 19, 1883

Dear Davies,
     . . . In my illnesses I sometimes make verses. These times I have taken to Rondels and Triolets. Here are three of the latter —

> I'm a poor man, I grant,
> But I am well neighboured;
> And none shall me daunt,
> Though a poor man, I grant,
> For I shall not want —
> The Lord is my shepherd!
> I am a poor man, I grant,
> But I am well neighboured.[1]
> — — — — — — —
> When I wake from sleep,
> Lord, I am still with thee;
> For while I slumbered deep,

Nor could wake from sleep,
'Twas thy storm waves did sweep
So softly over me;
And when I wake from sleep,
Lord, I am still with thee.

— — — — — — — —

Lord, what is man
That thou art mindful of him?
Though in creation's van,
Lord, what is man,
Who wills less than he can,
Lets his ideal scoff him!
Lord, what is man
That you art mindful of him?[2]

All King David's, you see! . . .

1. *Poetical Works,* vol. 2, p. 410.
2. *Poetical Works,* vol. 2, p. 331.

To Mr. Marston   Bordighera
                                              March 11, 1883

Dear Mr. Marston,

When I asked to see the proofs of the cheap edition of *Weighed and Wanting,* it was not that I could read and correct them — I have no time for that, but only to make one or two little changes. I send back the two sent me. There is nothing in them I want to change. But I am anxious it should not be supposed that I have read them over through. I have marked one blunder I chanced to see. The execrable way in which some cheap editions are read; the utter obscurations of the author's meaning I have seen occasioned by false printing and polishing — for I never read a sentence without trying to understand it myself — is enough to make some wish they never might be popular enough to reach cheap editions. I have sometimes thought of writing a paper on that and kindred subjects.

I should be obliged by having the other sheets sent me. The changes will amount to next to nothing either in number or size, but still are of some little importance.

>With kind regards,
>Yours very truly,

>GEORGE MACDONALD

To Mrs. William Cowper-Temple   [Bordighera]
>Saturday, April 3, 1833 [1883?][1]

Dearest sister Georgina,

Today I have had your letter, and must tell you how glad it has made me to hear from you again. I have been, though not very ill, far from well for some time; but your letter seemed to do me good, and I am now feeling better than for many weeks, and have got some work done today. I am learning a little to be quiet and wait when winter blocks the way between this and the high countries.

Winter is needful as spring and summer for our poor hearts. I know I am very apt to forget in the summer day. But God comes nearer and nearer *I think*. How can I be sure till he actually comes, and I know as I am known! Dearest friend, yours must be the kingdom of heaven, for you are poor in spirit. You feel yourself like the Publican, poor. It is coming to you, and when it arrives you will wonder that you doubted, for you will see that it must have been all the time. It seems to me that the passage about the unjust judge, and God's elect, and the help he is making haste to give them, applied specially to such as you.

God help and keep and rejoice my dear brother William. Where should I have been now but for him or if you say God would have sent some other angel to help me, then I say thank God it was he and not another. When we cannot climb the ladder of prayer, surely God comes down to the foot of it where we lie. I think God will make us content infinitely content with him. We are his and he is of our kind — only all that is infinitely better. Wife was very glad of your letter too. We have several angels hovering about Bordighera at present — none quite alighted — Sister Emelia [Mrs. Russell Gurney] — Lady Ducier, & Miss

Seward who called today and interested us very much. Your loving grateful brother,

GEORGE MACDONALD

1. This letter, which was written on small notecards, was apparently misdated; it was almost certainly written in the 1880s.

To Helen MacKay Powell[1] Casa Coragio, Bordighera, Italy
December 24, 1883

Dearest Helen,

I am so often laid up, and my work put behind that I put off letters again & again. Best thanks for yours — and for the beautiful book. It is extraordinarily well done. The various places are full of interest. You will be the more pleased you gave it me when I tell you that a little drawing of Tilguhillie Castle, which place I had never even heard of, was the sole and only germ whence sprang my story of *Castle Warlock*.[2] It was in I. I. Stevenson's book on House Architecture — the architect Bob[3] is with now.

The widow of the late owner of Fyvie Castle is a good deal here. She comes often to our house, drawn chiefly by the likeness she sees in me to her late husband, Colonel Cosmo Gordon.[4] By the way the main staircase in that castle, of which staircase she gave me a photograph, is one of the finest things I know in that kind, & I have a passion for stairs of all sorts, especially spiral ones. I thought of it in my last story *Donal Grant*.[5] Of the etchings, my favorite is Barra Castle with the snow on the roof. Huntly Castle is the least satisfactory, I think. I wish I could see all these places. I am often terribly hampered in my stories by sheer ignorance. I have seen so little of Scotland or any other place. Aberdeen, Banff, Cullen, & Huntly are the *only* places I knew when I left at the age of twenty, & I have never been but once for as long as months in Scotland since. I have a shocking bad memory too. So I'm just driven back on bare-faced *leein'* [lying] — only I gar't tell trowth.

How gladly we would welcome you here! and how amused you would be with things we should have to tell you!

Grace[6] is a little better. But we are very doubtful about her sometimes. Her child is darling. They are all in the house with us now.

I saw Louisa showing great satisfaction over your delightful shawl yesterday. But she will be telling you about it herself. So I must not take the words out of her mouth.

> Love & Best
> Wishes from us all
> for Christmas & New Year
>
> Your loving cousin,
>
> GEORGE MACDONALD

1. This letter provides an interesting commentary on Greville MacDonald's explanation of why his father missed the 1842-43 session at King's College — the "fact" that "he spent some summer months in a certain castle or mansion in the far North" (*George MacDonald and His Wife*, p. 72n.). MacDonald probably lacked sufficient funds to return to Aberdeen for the 1842-43 session, and it is possible that he had to work instead at The Farm, or he may have visited his pretty cousin Helen at Stamford Grove, Upper Clapton, London. Possibly the "castle-in-the-far-north" story was told to make it less embarrassing for MacDonald and his family when he returned to Aberdeen for the next session. It seems highly unlikely that MacDonald would not have recalled (in spite of his "shocking bad memory") being at such an outstanding place as Thurso or any other castle "in the far North." Had this event actually taken place, it seems very probable that MacDonald would at least have mentioned it when recording "the *only* places" in Scotland he recalled seeing, or that there would be some mention of it in his letters, which there is not.

2. Published in 1882.

3. Robert Troup.

4. General Charles George Gordon, who was killed at Khartoum in January 1885. Greville MacDonald notes: "My father had met General Gordon several times and it was inevitable that they should love one another. That greatest among military evangelists had given my father the chain mail of a Crusader he had himself found in the Sudan" (*George Macdonald and His Wife*, pp. 530-31).

5. Published in 1883.

6. MacDonald's daughter, Caroline Grace MacDonald, who had married Rev. Kingsbury Jameson. On March 17, 1883, she had given birth to Octavia Grace Jameson, MacDonald's first grandchild.

To His Son Greville MacDonald   Bordighera,
                                                          April 6, 1884

My dearly Loved Son,

It puzzles me a little that you, to whom God has given more insight than many have into the necessities of the spiritual relations, should be so changeable and troubled by the appearances of things.[1] "In quietness and confidence shall be your strength." "Wait on the Lord." You are so impatient! You will hardly give him time to do anything for you! As you are so easily troubled, as your faith in him seems so much in the abstract, and when it comes to the matter of next month or next year you are full of doubt — as if what the day was to bring forth must be evil and not good, notwithstanding that perfect goodness is at the head of your affairs — this being the case, I see why you should be troubled and tossed about as you are. Do not be always speculating on your future and thinking what you shall do. You are not a bit nearer knowing for that; and it is a great waste of brain tissue, to say nothing of spiritual energy left dormant. . . . There is more action in dismissing a useless care than in a month's brooding over the possible or the probable. When the hour for decision arrives, one moment's clear untroubled thought will do what weeks and weeks of brooding beforehand will only make more uncertain and difficult. . . .

1. Apparently Greville, like his father, had concerns about his future and choice of vocation.

To A. P. Watt[1]   Bordighera,
                                                          November 7, 1884

. . . I cannot but think I could get it [my price] easily after what Ruskin has been so late saying about me. . . . Business people are not quite within the scope of my understanding and I should be very sorry to misjudge them — only what I have been told about them! At the same time people say worse things of myself which I know to be false. Let God judge between me and any I have a quarrel with. . . . So if the information as to Mr. Ruskin's speech concerning me at Oxford[2] does not influence Mr. ——— to go farther, I will take what you can get for me from him. But it must be put in the agreement that no copies are to be sent for review. . . .[3] I cannot and will not have those cuttings used for advertisement. I did not send them for any purpose but to encourage Mr. ———— to venture. . . . Besides, the description is false: there is not one sonnet in the book. If I would use such, why should I not supply my own critics? . . .

1. MacDonald's literary agent.

2. Ruskin said of MacDonald's *The Diary of an Old Soul:* "perhaps the days which have given us 'Hiawatha,' 'In Memoriam,' 'The Christian Year,' and the 'Soul's Diary' of George MacDonald, may be not with disgrace compared with those of Caedmon." Reported in the *Liverpool Mercury* (October 28, 1884); included in Ruskin's *The Pleasures of England* (London, 1898), pp. 313-14; also cited in *George MacDonald and His Wife,* p. 497.

3. Referring to *The Diary of an Old Soul* (1880), which he had recently privately printed.

To Charlotte Powell Godwin[1]   Bordighera, Last Sunday of 1884

My dearest sister Charlotte,

I thank you for your most kind letter which gave me much pleasure. I wrote at once to Bently to have the mistake corrected. Apparently the word *Preface* had got dropped out. Two thousand I hear have been sold. In Germany 20000 were sold in a year.

Yes, we are growing old; but the Ancient of Days cannot be old; and Jesus Christ is not old; his body must always be about thirty three, for it is embalmed with the light of life. He is child and man and one perfect friend. He is accountable for me, else I should not like to live. I look to the origin to make life worthy my having to all eternity. I can conceive by glimmers a vision of such worthiness, but such as I am I would rather be and cease altogether. He is my life and in the good to come I rejoice — in the hope of the glory of God. That the life in me should be of the same kind as that which makes God willing to live and be himself, can alone satisfy me — a life of absolute love and self-forgivefulness — from which at present [I] seem thousands of years away.

I believe in nothing but Jesus Christ, in whom are all the mysteries of reality. Less than the story of him could not satisfy me, though less might give me hope. But if he be such as that story says, then all is well. If God be indeed such a God as satisfies Jesus, then hail to the world with all its summers and snows, all its delights and its aching, all its jubilance and its old age! We shall come out of it the sons and daughters of life of God himself the only Father.

I entirely feel with your husband that a house of your own with *any* climate is better than being in a hotel. I would rather encounter all the winter at home except I had at least a part of a house to ourselves. I hope you are able to keep warm.

I have been told that Annie[2] does not lose flesh, that she is not thin, and does not grow thin: if this be true, I cannot see such reason for your anxiety. That is a strong likelihood of the victory of life.

I have just been out — for the second time only since I came — to hear the carols in the church. They were very good, and it was a pretty sight too — only the ladies ought to have been in surplices — and the few gentlemen too. It is very difficult — I ought to say impossible to tell where the spectacular should stop. I delight to think of St. Francis' live [?] and [?] in the church though. They at least would be genuine actors and unaffected. But that I see any of that in our church.

I am too tired to write much more — not that I have done anything today, but it is one of my tired days; and I have to find something to read to my little company this evening, for I always read a little bit of verse or perhaps prose, and a chapter of the Bible, besides preaching, or rather talking to them.

My *Hamlet*[3] and a new volume of *Unspoken Sermons*[4] are both ready to come out, and I am well into a new novel. I don't find my brain worse than it was. I seem to understand better than hitherto. I forget words rather, but I can read a book better than I used. I may forget the word for a meaning, but I do not forget the meaning of a word.

Louisa sends her love to you. You would not wonder she does not write very often if you saw how busy she is from morning to night.

Thank you for remembering my birthday, and sending me the wise tortoise that carries light inside him. I like it. My love to you and yours.

Your loving brother,

GEORGE MACDONALD

1. Louisa's sister Charlotte, wife of Professor J. H. Godwin.
2. Possibly Annie Munro.
3. *The Tragedie of Hamlet — with a study of the text of the Folio of 1623* (1885).
4. *Unspoken Sermons* (1885), second series.

To A. P. Watt   Bordighera,
                                                        January 10, 1885

My dear Watt,

. . . I don't know that ever I *seemed* worse off. I say *seemed* because I
do not acknowledge the *look* of things. I am spending borrowed money
now, and *see* no way but to borrow more. If I had a good offer for my
house I would sell it. . . . You see I have only one son off my hands yet
— that makes it so heavy with two of them away from home.[1] However,
they cause me no other burden whatever — thank God, as I hope you will
find with yours. . . . What do you think? It is very odd how those who
have plenty seem to stick to their money when others are most in want
of it. But business is a strange country to me. . . .

I think it [*The Elect Lady*] will turn out well. It is a Scotch story
without any Scotch and *touches* on Highland affairs not in detail but in
principle. . . . I am very glad you have got another place for the story.
What should I do without you! . . .

1. Greville was already a doctor. Ronald went to Trinity College, Oxford, in 1882 to
read history.

To A. P. Watt   Bordighera,
                                                        February 26, 1885

. . . As I expected, the critics are down on my *Hamlet* on all sides. Of
course! They are just of the class which I say cannot understand him or
his inventor. How should there be anything in common between me and
the — *Review,* for instance — a paper I have looked upon with literal
repugnance almost since its first appearance! . . . I am not in the least
surprised. It shows me the more how desirable it was that the coming
generations should have what help I could give them to start with, some
notion of what Shakespeare meant in his *Hamlet;* for the interpretation
commonly given makes a poor thing of it compared with what I see in it.
But how should the commonplace understand the best that the highest
intellect of the country could produce? But the truth will stand. . . .

To Miss Frances Martin[1]
225 Bath Street,
Glasgow.
September 17, 1885

My dear Frances,

I have only this day got your letter with its very welcome news. Our love to the regained companion of your life, and may you live more and more blessedly, and when you part, part peacefully and confidently. There is an endless union, such as we have no idea of now, in store for all lovers.

I fear I must beg you to excuse me speaking to your dear women. I fear I should disappoint you. I am far from well, and have very heavy work before me almost up to the 17th.

We have just yesterday heard of the death of our sister-in-law, Mrs. George Powell. I forget if you had met her. She is much beloved, and was a friend to many. We hope to be in London on Saturday week. We are acting four days this week.[2]

In much haste,
Yours affectionately,

GEORGE MACDONALD

1. Greville MacDonald notes that Frances Martin, a close friend of the MacDonalds, was, "till her death in 1921, the mainstay of the Working Women's College in Fitzroy Street, to whose students my father often lectured" (*George MacDonald and His Wife*, p. 370).

2. Scenes from Bunyan's *Pilgrim's Progress*.

To an Unidentified Friend
Hillfield, Hampstead,
September 30, 1885

True and kind friend,

The money I owe you ought to have been paid before now, and would have been but that I found myself unable, with all our acting added to a certain pain in my back, which the doctor said came from overwork, to get on nearly so fast as I expected. I am anxious that you should understand my position. The story[1] was all in print before I asked you to advance the £200 on the coming price; and I expected to get it quite ready for the book-press rapidly. But I found it needed so much done to it in the way of simplifying, strengthening, and shortening, that even now it will not be ready for perhaps six weeks after our imminent return to Bordighera. I am so full of lecturing work that it takes my whole strength till I go. My wife precedes me by a fortnight because of her duty as an organist.

Now, dear helper of your brother-men, I want you to tell me if you are in any *immediate* need of the money, because I could borrow it to send you. This would not be difficult, seeing the repayment is now nearer at hand. Please do not scruple to tell me if you would like to have it at once.

I hope you and your visible soul are both in peace and hope. God lives, and our unbelief cannot kill him.

Your loving friend,

GEORGE MACDONALD

1. *What's Mine's Mine* (1886) was then in proof copy.

To an Unidentified Friend

Hillfield, Hampstead,
N.W. October 18, 1885

Very dear Friend,

Your telegram and letter followed me to Leicester, where I could not write as I was just starting to come here. The letter which was spirited away from you was written to explain how it was that I had not repaid the money you so kindly lent me a few months ago, saying that I had been, as the doctor said, overworked, and could not go on doing much at my proofs while in Scotland. The story[1] is all written, and was before I wrote to you asking the loan, but part of it still wants the many final touches, which have so much to do, not merely with the finish but with the general impression of every work of art. These I cannot now finish giving it before my return to Bordighera, which, I hope, will be next Saturday.

I could not send you an ordinary letter of condolence with your loss, but I have been trying to write something for Lady Mount Temple which I hope to send in a day or two. It is but a little thing, but better than a letter. Alas, I cannot come to see you. I have been lecturing night after night, and need to get away. I have still two lectures on hand, and tonight I go to preach in a very humble place in Rotherhithe. If it was a bit well-to-do chapel I would not go, for I have had very hard work.

We were four months in Scotland, and were very kindly received — with our Pilgrims. Though we cannot say we made any money exactly, we kept ourselves, and that is much, for it is the daily bread.

I hope my delay in sending the money will not plague you. I could borrow elsewhere to repay you if you wanted it at once, but if you do not mind, I will yet delay till I sell my book. With much love to you both.

Your loving friend,

GEORGE MACDONALD

Wife is gone home to her new church organ, which fills her full of delight.

1. *What's Mine's Mine* (1886).

To James MacDonald Bordighera, March 28, 1886

My very dear Cousin,

I thank you heartily for your kind letters, and for the newspaper with the report of your lecture, which I need hardly say I read with interest — though I should have liked much better to hear you give it. The meal[1] is at Genoa, where it has been for a week before they let me know it had arrived. I suspect it is nobody's business, and so he does it! I enclose a cheque for the carriage with real gratitude.

You have a wrong notion of the relation of my life and work to my occasional acting. In the first place, it has been a welcome rest for the much harder labour of writing. In the next, seeing you regard it as interfering with my work — is not forty-two books, all told, enough to have wirtten in thirty years! Then once more, look upon the art of acting as a very high one; and when I tell you that both Burne Jones and Robert Browning have spoken of our, or rather of my wife's work, for the arrangement is entirely hers, as near perfection as they could wish, you will not think that we have any doubt about the dignity of the endeavour.

I have been laid up, almost for the first time this winter, or I would have written to you sooner. We have had a severe winter for us, as everybody else has had. I suppose weather does go in cycles, else we should be compelled to say that fine weather is gradually departing from the earth.

I shall have my next story[2] out very soon now. It is out of my hands. I think you will see some of the signs of our little talk about Sutherland-shire in it.

I wonder what you think about Ireland! I have been long of the growing opinion that nothing else will do but re-conquest, and fresh constitution; and towards that things seem to be tending. But the Irish have from the first been used abominable, and I confess to a great sympathy with the malcontents. They do well to be angry, but very ill to be angry after such mean & cruel & unjust fashion. Of course I would have the government wait for such provocation — sure to come — as would render it imperative for self-preservation.

I hope things are looking a little better for you.

Winna 't be gran' whan a' this is ower, an' we're wi' the auld fowk again? Man, I expec' awfu'!

Yours lovingly,

GEORGE MACDONALD

1. MacDonald is here thanking his cousin James for a consignment of oatmeal from The Farm (which James was in the habit of sending from time to time to impecunious relatives, as readers of some of the Scots novels will recognize).

James MacDonald was an authority on place-names in Western Aberdeenshire, which may have been the subject of his lecture.

2. Probably *What's Mine's Mine* (1886), set in the far northwest of Scotland. Some passages near the beginning deal with the derivation of a character's name — for example, Peregrine Palmer, "pilgrim," and those of his children: Christian, Mercy, Grace, and Hope, from *The Pilgrim's Progress*, one of Mrs. MacDonald's dramatizations, which the family was at that time presenting frequently both in Italy and in Britain, and in which MacDonald sometimes played the Evangelist or Greatheart.

To John Ruskin   52, Welbeck Street, London
                                              June 23, 1886

Dearest Ruskin,

I thank you most heartily for your two most kind letters about my last book.[1] I am indeed glad you like it. There is no man alive whose sympathy and approval could give me so much pleasure.

You think my highlanders impossible: they do not seem so to me; my own brothers [Alec and John], who died both before thirty, were in my mind as I wrote. They were capable of all I say.

Then there is only *one* bad Englishman [in the book]; the Palmer family belongs to Glasgow.

I am dreadfully busy lecturing — almost every day, and some days twice, so write a shabby letter.

My wife, whom you used to call "Mother-bird," missed a message from you, and would like to send her love.

God keep you in his very heart.

                                    Your loving and ever
                                    grateful friend,

                                    GEORGE MACDONALD

1. Ruskin had written to MacDonald (May 15, 1886) after having read part of *What's Mine's Mine* (published in 1886): "I like all its refined philosophy and principles of resurrection. But I don't see why half or ⅗ of the people should have been vulgar. Why wouldn't one vulgar girl have been enough? I'm only in the 1st vol yet — but a first vol ⅗ vulgar is too much." Ruskin also criticized the "technical bricks" in the story and suggested that MacDonald read *Robinson Crusoe* and *Gil Blas* and good French plays.

To John Ruskin   52 Welbeck Street W.
                                              July 20, 1886

Dearest Ruskin,

I have been so hard worked that I have had to delay much longer than I meant the sending of the accompanying little volume,[1] which I do with reference to the younger of the two highlanders in my story.[2] All the poems with the title underlined in red are by my brother John, who died at six or seven and twenty, but the poems were written before or about one and twenty. The rest are by myself, and a dear friend also long dead. I hope you will like some — only please remember how young my brother was. In haste but in much love,

Yours always

GEORGE MACDONALD

1. *A Threefold Cord: Poems by Three Friends* (1883). This privately printed collection of poems, edited by MacDonald, contains poems by him, by his brother John Hill MacDonald, and by Greville Ewing Matheson. Although Ruskin's "underlined in red" copy seems to have disappeared, an autographed copy presented by MacDonald to Charles Edward Troup is now at King's College Library, Aberdeen. For authorship of the poems in this collection, see Appendix A in Glenn Edward Sadler, "The Cosmic Vision: A Study of the Poetry of George MacDonald" (Ph.D. thesis, University of Aberdeen, 1966).

2. The character Ian in *What's Mine's Mine* (1886) is, according to Greville MacDonald, "a very true portrait of my Uncle John" (*George MacDonald and His Wife*, p. 166).

To His Son Robert Falconer MacDonald   C.C.B.
[Casa Coraggio, Bordighera],
August 29th, 1886

. . . We have no boys with us at present; perhaps we may never all meet again together in this world. God knows: but I have all my life, I think, been attended (I would call it *haunted*, were it not that the word has the atmosphere about it of the undesired) by the feeling of a meeting at hand. It must come one day — the hour when our hearts, all of them, will come together as they have never come before — when, knowing God, we shall know each other in a way infinitely beyond any way we have now. But the new way will fold up the old way in it. The Kingdom of Heaven has come near us that we may enter into it, and be all at home together. Kingdom and home are one. . . . Lily has just taken me on the loggia to see two broad, faint-red rays shooting up into the blue from the far-down sun, while all the mountains and the towering clouds are a misty gray. They say this is the hottest day there has been. . . .

To Mrs. William Cowper-Temple
Casa Coraggio
[Bordighera]
December 20, 1886

Dearest Sister Georgina,

I send you this new old song for Christmas Day.[1] If the story were not true, nothing else would be worth being true. Because it is true, everything is lovely-precious. Wife and I send our love to you and William, and our never ceasing gratitude for your divine goodness to us. The kingdom of heaven has come near to us, and we are all striving to enter in. Thank the Father that we are! that we exist, with this eternal fate before us — to know him!

May you have a trusting, restful birthday — the birthday of us all!

Pardon my childish love of colour in the song-paper. I meant to send it in your handkerchief which you so sweetly lent me when I was with you last; but when I remember the prevailing suspicion of lace in letters, I think it better to keep it till I come again, lest all should be lost.

Do you know last time was the only time I ever left your house without a goodbye from you! Is that a presage of your coming here before the winter is over? We have not heard about you for some time.

Belonging to you both with
endless love,
Yours,

G.M.

1. See "An Old Story," *Poetical Works*, vol. 1, pp. 302-4. This may be the Christmas Day poem to which MacDonald refers here. Another possibility is the poem "Christmas Day and Every Day," *Poetical Works*, vol. 1, p. 309.

To His Son Greville MacDonald[1]
Christmas 1886

When a man comes to feel quiet confidence and hope, even when the life he *feels* is indeed not worth living, then he is getting ready fast. When one in a dream can welcome the thought of the sun and the active day, he is worth waking. But many of us will not consent to leave our coffins till we have made them tidy. I don't think Jesus folded his death garments:

the angels did that after he had gone out of his three days' chamber. This is not quite coherent, but I may make *thinks* in you. May you have a divinely good Christmas.

1. This letter and the letter that follows (dated January 19, 1887) are in answer to Greville MacDonald's questions regarding thought and feeling and how they are related.

To His Son Greville MacDonald   January 19, 1887

. . . Many good birthdays be yours, as many will surely be, if only we let our Lord have his way for and with us. More and more I see and feel that what the Father is thinking is my whole treasure and well being. To be one with him seems the only common sense, as well as the only peace. Let him do with you, my beloved son, as he wills. Be hearty with his will. Submission is not the right feeling when we say "Thy will be done." This will is the only good. . . .

Mrs. George MacDonald to   Casa Coraggio
Miss Anna Leigh-Smith[1]   [Bordighera]
                                                         February 24, 1887

My Dearest Nannie,

. . . Have you had tidings of the great trouble that has fallen upon Bordighera in the last two days? An earthquake yesterday morning, about six o'clock, surprised us out of our beds.[2] I remember some slight ones we had at Algiers, but I never knew the real terror of one before. The poor people here have suffered the most — their houses came tumbling about their ears, some buried in the ruins. Our plaster cracked and ceilings and vases and jugs broken — but our walls, so well built, stood firm — the only danger to us is from the stupid stucco tower that I dare say you remember vexed us so — George having ordered the tower to be of the same stone as the rest of the house. However it received such a shock yesterday that it will have to be taken down. Yesterday there was such a panic that no one would do anything — besides it was Ash Wednesday and no one would lift a finger to work. So the night was spent by all the poor camping out, and some terrified women from the cracked hotels would not accept any shelter and sat all night in carriages on the high road, or under the olives all day. We had one family to meals, their kitchen and roof having fallen in, and another came to camp out in our big room for the night; but we had also to pack all the top story into the ground floor, and away from the unsafe tower. So an immense amount of packing and coaxing and a little manoeuvring had to be exercised to keep our large household in good spirits and to keep off faints and hysterics, besides being very tired and sick with the motion and alarm. . . .

I remain ever and always your loving friend,

Louisa Powell MacDonald.

1. The MacDonalds became acquainted with the Leigh-Smiths while they were in Algiers in 1856. The Leigh-Smiths were in Algiers because of their daughter Annie's ill health.

2. Greville MacDonald describes it thus: "At 5:30 in the morning of February 23, 1887, the terrible earthquake began, lasting till 9 a.m., and beginning again in less severity the next morning. Its center was Nice, and it extended from Milan to Marseilles; so that Bordighera, distant from Nice only a little more than twenty miles, was trapped in its fellest grip" (*George MacDonald and His Wife*, p. 513).

To W. C. Davies   Bordighera,
March 8, 1887
Our wedding day 36 years ago.

. . . We have had the most extraordinary time — terrible indeed in its awfulness.[1] That one shock was worth having lived to know what power may be. You knew it must be none other than God. No lesser power could hold the earth like that, as if it were "A very little thing," and shake you as if your big house were a doll's fly. . . . Don't be anxious about us. We are all right. . . .

1. Referring to the earthquake that occurred in Bordighera on February 23, 1887.

Mrs. George MacDonald to W. C. Davies   Casa Coraggio,
                                                             March 20, 1887

. . . I am so surprised to hear that your parson was so alarmed by the earthquake that he ran away in an expensive carriage. It was only the old fogies that did that here, and the poor nerveless creatures — but I suppose when a man sees every one else running he runs too, if he does not know better. Well, I hope he is better now. . . . Such will be as frightened and try to rush off when they are told they are going to die. . . .

To His Cousin James MacDonald   April 12, 1887

My dear James,

I am ashamed of myself that I have not answered your kind and welcome letter sooner. I can hardly tell you how I shrink from letter writing. Perhaps with the kind of work I have to do, it is as well. For what small amount of steam I have might escape in letters instead of books. But when it pleases God that I stop writing stories, I shall be glad, for I never *feel* that it is my calling by nature, though it is. I hope by a yet higher command I have one short story which will be out in book form in the summer,[1] and another on the stocks,[2] besides a long one about a third written,[3] that I don't yet know how to work out.

Your lecture interested me much. I should like to have them all — this is marked 2, I think. There again your calling seems philosophy or something in that direction. God has called you to other work — *in the meantime* and when we go up, we shall see into the *hows* and *whys*.

The earthquakes seem to be over now for awhile. Though it often seems as if one must be coming — shaping train, a cart, a foot overhead — anything raises the mental ghost of one, and makes you feel as if it might be on you in a moment. It is a strange and memorable experience, and one we are always exposed to here.

This is partly by keeping as much as I can indoors even here, and wearing flannel at night. But I look now the picture of health. Still age tells, and I feel it good that a time is set for deliverance. In three years I shall be the age of my father when he died.

I heard from Frank[4] the other day — with a splendid drawing of the door of Huntly Castle. He works beautifully. He hopes to get back to London before very long. Somehow nobody who has once lived in London, likes any other place so well.

I wish you to give my very kind regards to W. Pillam, who kind of wrote to me, and say I wish I could send him a subscription, but I positively crack my income in trying to get the edge together.

Your very loving cousin

GEORGE MACDONALD

[note added to letter:]

I wish you would time your London visits more to my advantage. Is there any chance of you being up in June or July. I hope to be there then.

I have had a wonderful winter — no bronchitis even — the best I have been for nearly forty years. Yet the weather has not been up to *our* mark though we have never had anything much before since we came. The top of the tower of our house has had to be taken down; the arches were so cracked that another shock as strong must in all likelihood bring it down, when it would have fallen through the house.

I have had an invitation to subscribe to your cottage hospital — but I *cannot*. I have not anything of margin whatever, and must leave Huntly to take care of itself. I do for others as much as I think is required of me. We have four dependent on us who are no relation and two of our boys are at Cambridge. Not one fairly started in life yet. Though there is not fear from them.

1. *Home Again, A Tale* (1887).
2. *The Elect Lady* (1888).
3. *A Rough Shaking, A Tale* (1890).
4. Frank Troup, the son of Robert Troup.

To Helen MacKay Powell   Bristol, September 7, 1887

Dearest Helen,

I have been so dreadfully occupied that I could not do anything more at present to the verses. But I must just write to tell you so. By and by I shall be able to look at them again, and at the new one. Except I can get the former one to my mind as well as to the composer's I cannot let my name go with it. At present it is not mine at all.

W. Bjornsen did not turn up. So I could not hold any conference with him. I lectured an hour & three quarters last night in the Victoria Hall here. I preach tonight and lecture again tomorrow night. Louisa is at Shanklin on a visit. I left her and Winnie[1] there yesterday & go to them on Friday.

I wonder how you are. I hope well, though I am a little afraid you are not. We shall be at 47 Queen Anne Street on Saturday.

I am afraid the Song of Songs will prove very difficult to get right, but I mean to have a try.

                                    Yours lovingly,

                                    GEORGE MACDONALD

No, I haven't seen the Castles of Aberdeen.

1. His daughter Winifred Louisa MacDonald.

To John and Antoinette MacKinlay   October 6, 1887, Bordighera

My dear John and Antoinette,

We got here last night, and having no black ink I am reduced to — not my heart's blood, but the colour of it — the fitter, I hope, for the song I have made for you. I think you will find the rhythm very correct, but if any word does not suit, let me know, and I will do my best to meet the singing — necessity. This is the measure: —

$$-\smallsmile\smallsmile/-\smallsmile\smallsmile/-\smallsmile/-\smallsmile/$$
$$-\smallsmile\smallsmile/-\smallsmile\smallsmile/-\smallsmile/\ -/$$

‑˘˘/‑˘˘/‑˘/‑˘/
‑˘˘/‑˘˘/‑˘/ ‑/

The third foot in every line may be / — / instead of /‑˘/‑. In the first two stanzas the two first lines should I think be minor; the second two major. In the third and fifth the lines should be minor and major alternatively. The fourth should be all in the major key. Perhaps I am writing something absurd, from my ignorance of music; but you will know what I mean. If you should use the song, and print it, I should like a proof, for my distrust of printers is profound.

I presume that you would leave me the right of publishing the verses elsewhere? But if you would rather not let me know. At all events it would be *after* you had begun to sing them — if you do. But if you do not think them suitable for you, just say so. There is no harm done, and I have had *my sing* out.

We are all well, and love you.

Yours ever,

GEORGE MACDONALD

SONG.[1]

Hark, in the Steeple, the dull bell swinging,
Over the furrows ill ploughed by Death!
Over his young ones the loud lark singing
Pours out his soul in triumphant breath!

Wild in the pine-wood, the wind complaining,
Moaneth and murmureth: *Life is bare!*
Caught in the organ, the wind, out-straining,
Bursteth to freedom in soaring prayer!

Sit on the ground, and hold fast thy sorrow;
I will give freedom to mine in song;
Haunt thou the tomb, and deny the morrow;
I will go watch in the dawning long!

For I shall see them, and know their faces!
Look in the depth of the eyes of old!

Clasp the same self in the old embraces,
Tenderer, sweeter by many a fold.

Tell for the burying, Sexton tolling!
Sing for the second birth, angel Lark!
Moan, ye poor Pines, with the fast condoling!
Burst out, brave Organ, and kill the dark!

GEORGE MACDONALD

1. MacDonald added this note: "Written for the heart and voice of Antoinette
MacKinlay, at Aosta, October 1887."

To His Cousin James MacDonald   Bordighera, Nov. 5, 1887

My dear James,
   Once again I come a beggar to your door for my handful of meal!
Could you let us have your usual kind gift this year. I should gladly pay
for it but the offer to do so has become such a form by your always refusing
to accept it, that it comes easier to beg for it right out.
   We are trying a new dodge to get paid in America for our work, we
poor authors, whose brains are picked with so little compensation.
   Pardon my brevity. If I thought I must write you a long letter, I should
not, to use an American idiom, feel like writing at all.
   A man whose business is writing is seldom fond of letters. I hope you
are pretty well, and as usual, looking forward.

Ever yours lovingly

GEORGE MACDONALD

To an Unidentified Woman Bordighera
December 8, 1887

Dear Madam,

I return you my best thanks for your kindness in writing to me. I had just been wondering how I could hear of Mrs. Gordon.[1] I am glad to know that her end as to this life was without suffering. As to death itself that is not in any sense an evil, for it is not the thing it looks to the eye that looks on. I can well imagine the freed one exclaiming "Is this what they call death!"

Her kind good heart will have found love and comfort waiting her. It was good of you to write to me.

Yours most truly,

GEORGE MACDONALD

1. Possibly the wife of General Charles Gordon.

To Mrs. Russell Gurney Bordighera, December 11, 1887

DEAREST SISTER EMELIA, —

I thank your loving heart and generous hand. . . . Only now the days are growing very short, and the night is at hand. But, is it the night? At worst it will be a sweet twilight, full of hope. Or, even if I find that still I need the purification of loneliness and pain to free me from the phantom of life by me imagined, instead of accepting God's intention of my life, it will yet be full of the hope of sunrise, and I will hope now in the Living One, by and in Whom I live.

My true love and gratitude are bending and holding out arms to you. Your loving brother,

GEORGE MACDONALD

PART VI

Last Years — Bordighera (1888-1901)

INTRODUCTION

At the age of fifty-seven George MacDonald tried to summarize the meaning of his own life in a letter he wrote to his close friend Professor George Rolleston. To his "Beloved Friend," MacDonald wrote (June 16, 1881):

> All my life, I might nearly say, I have been trying to find that one Being, and to know him consciously present; hope grows and grows with the years that lead me nearer to the end of my earthly life; and in my best moods it seems ever that the only thing worth desiring is that his will be done; that there lies before me a fullness of life, sufficient to content the giving of a perfect Father, and that the part of his child is to yield all and see that he does not himself stand in the way of the mighty design. (See p. 305 above.)

For the last twenty years of his life MacDonald had to live out the meaning of these words. He was forced to endure increased pain and suffering, the loss of his eldest daughter Lilia and finally of his wife, and he had to cope with decreasing mental powers as his career as a writer came to an end. Finally, the death of his wife in 1902, when MacDonald was seventy-eight, left him with very little to hope for beyond experiencing death itself.

The letters he wrote from 1887 to the end of his life are characteristic of MacDonald's lifelong attempt to keep his hope in God alive and his insistence that real happiness is to be found only in the life to come. As the MacDonalds enjoyed a few golden years of retirement at their villa,

331

Casa Coraggio, in Bordighera, Italy, where MacDonald became a patriarchal literary figure, he continued to write letters of comfort to his friends, such as the one he wrote just before his sixty-fourth birthday to Georgina Cowper-Temple after the death of her husband William (Dec. 9, 1888): "This world, if it were alone, would not be worth much — I should be miserable already; but it is the porch to the Father's home, and he does not expect us to be quite happy" (see p. 340 below).

In spite of such letters of encouragement, there seems to be little doubt that MacDonald's desire to participate in life was decreasing. At age sixty-nine he wrote to his agent-friend A. P. Watt: "My memory plays me sad tricks now. It comes of the frosty invasion of old age — preparing me to go home, thank God. Till then I must work, and that is good" (June 11, 1893; see p. 355 below).

According to MacDonald's son Greville, the death of MacDonald's eldest daughter Lilia was a terrible blow for MacDonald. He "could hardly leave the grave: he came back twice after all others had left, and it was with difficulty he was at last led away" (*George MacDonald and His Wife*, p. 526).

From what we can determine from MacDonald's last letters, he gradually came to accept his own approaching death and even in some sense looked forward to it. In a letter to Mrs. William Cowper-Temple, MacDonald declared: "Some day God will, I trust, reveal himself to me as he has never done yet, and I shall be as sure as St. Paul. I must try not to stand in the way of his redeeming will with me — for he is doing his best for me as for us all" (March 20, 1879; see p. 292 above).

Whether MacDonald truly believed these words to the end of his life is uncertain — and perhaps inconsequential. According to his grandson Colonel Maurice MacDonald, who recalled as a very young boy seeing his grandfather at Casa Coraggio, Italy, and later, just before his death, at St. George's Wood, Haslemere, in England, MacDonald was silent in the last years of his life because he had had a stroke and found speaking difficult, if not impossible. He would be seated near the window in Casa Coraggio, where he enjoyed watching the children playing in the street. Later, at George's Wood, after his wife's death, whenever the door opened he would look up with expectation, and seeing that the person who entered was not his wife, would lapse back into contemplation. The death of his wife was a blow from which MacDonald really never recovered.

In perhaps the last letter that Louisa MacDonald wrote, a letter written at Casa Coraggio to Lady Mount-Temple that contained a photograph of

MacDonald taken at their golden wedding anniversary, she describes lovingly her husband's condition: He "is still but sadly — not always, and I believe rarely is the sadness deep down in his heart — but he has not had much power to converse with *it* — his heart — the fearful irritation of the nerves, prevents *comfort* — but I know nothing could stir the absolute obedience of the will to the Lord Divine — the Will of God — still it is only by a few words here & there & by the lovely smile & the pressure of the hand that we see the peace behind all the disturbance of nerves" (see p. 369 below).

In 1894, MacDonald had written to a "dear old friend," probably Henry Sutton: "We shall get home to our father & elder brother before very long — at least we shall somehow get a little nearer to them. But The Father of Jesus lives and we shall *know* that he lives because he is more than with us, he is in us" (see p. 360 below). Whether or not George MacDonald finally believed in all he had written to his family and friends about the life of eternal brotherhood hereafter will probably never be known for sure. That he never ceased trying to maintain his faith even in old age is, however, certain.

Significant Dates and Events

1888 MacDonald publishes *The Elect Lady.* MacDonald's friend Lord Mount-Temple (William Cowper-Temple) dies on December 9.

1889 MacDonald publishes *Unspoken Sermons* (third series).

1890 MacDonald publishes *A Rough Shaking.* First draft of *Lilith* is completed.

1891 Lilia Scott MacDonald dies. MacDonald's granddaughter Octavia dies. MacDonald publishes *There and Back; The Flight of the Shadow;* and *A Cabinet of Gems* (quotations from Sir Philip Sidney).

1892 MacDonald publishes *The Hope of the Gospel.* The Mac-Donalds spend the summer in Switzerland.

1893 MacDonald publishes *Poetical Works* (2 vols.); *Heather and Snow; Scotch Songs and Ballads;* and an enlarged edition of *Orts.*

1895 MacDonald publishes *Lilith.*

1897 MacDonald publishes his last novel, *Salted with Fire,* and a collection of translations entitled *Rampolli.*

1898 MacDonald publishes in *The Sketch* "Far Above Rubies" (MacDonald's last published work). MacDonald suffers a stroke.

1901 The MacDonalds celebrate their golden wedding anniversary.

1902 Louisa MacDonald dies on January 13 at Bordighera, Italy.

1905 George MacDonald dies on September 18 at Ashtead in Surrey. He is cremated, and his ashes are buried beside those of his wife in Bordighera.

To Susan Scott[1]   Bordighera,
                                                        January 21, 1888

My dear Susan,

You will be missing your mother more now than when first she went away! As the days go on and the common look gathers again upon the things round you, and the kingdom of heaven seems no nearer, we are apt to feel more a separation. There seems sometimes to be nowhere beyond, because no voice comes back from the beloved. This parting seems so complete at times. Why is all so dumb? Why no personal relation of the world to which they are gone?

God knows and cares, and uses for us a means of education for our hearts and spirits which we do not ourselves understand. It is not needful that we understand the motive power in the processes that go on within us. It is enough to him who believes it that the Lord *did* rise again, although after that he was hidden from their sight. Yes, I will believe that I shall hold my own in my arms again, their hearts nearer to mine than ever before. It is a blessed thing to be children and to be parents of children. So God binds us all together. You and I have much to thank God for that we came of such parents. And we shall see them again and our hearts shall rejoice. For what is true of the Lord is true of all his, for they are one with him.

I need not say to you that I owe your father & mother more than I can tell. I looked up to your father more than to any man except my own father, who did not know half so much, but who was worthy of knowing whatever God taught him. We *shall* see them all and love them more & more to all eternity.

My wife joins me in all expressions of love & sympathy. We wish you could sometimes pay us a visit here. There are things that would make you glad. Please give our love also to your dear aunt and to John,[2] and our sympathy in their loss — for a time.

                                        Yours affectionately

                                        GEORGE MACDONALD

1. Susan Scott, the daughter of Mr. and Mrs. A. J. Scott. Her mother had recently died. See *George MacDonald and His Wife*, p. 446.
    2. John Scott, Susan's brother.

To Lady Mount-Temple   St. John Lee — but last day there.
(Mrs. William Cowper-Temple)

G. H. Powell
Cedar Lawn
Hampstead Heath
September 30, 1888

Dearest Sister Georgina,

I must come directly to the point in answering your letter. You will think me hard, but you know I cannot go by your conscience nor you by mine. And if, in doing what seems to me right, I do what in reality is wrong, I shall at least, thank God, have merited the suffering that may be necessary to put me right.

You ask me to forgive; but that comes nowise within the province of one against whom is no offence. I have only to order my own behaviour according to what I am able to believe, or to abstain from action where I have not ground enough to go upon. In this case, I tell you frankly, I do not believe in the lady or in her repentance. Neither would anything she could say make me able to believe in her. The very fact of her seeking to place herself with her former friends as she was argues with me against her. There is no word in the English language, and certainly in no other, so far as I can think, for the crime of which she has been guilty, and one who could commit it could not claim to be believed after. She may have seen her own vileness and repented, God only knows, but even then he cannot require of me to act as if I had this insight and knowledge. That he will restore her at last, I believe, but I see nothing that he requires of me to do in the matter. If I were to go to see her, or to receive her, I should be false, as I much and deeply suspect her to be — so false that she does not yet see the utter horror of her wicked selfishness. Things cannot be smoothed over. God himself could not & never will do that. If she knows that he has forgiven her, that ought to content her till it be possible that others should know it. She ought to be content to bear her shame. Nothing can remove that but the lifting of her up into a region where sin is no more possible because she loathes it. While she cares for the judgment of society, her worship of which demon-idol cast her into the gulf, she can rise above nothing.

I know, dearest sister-friend, you will think me hard, but I must say what I feel. The one thing I strive against is falsehood, and here I could not be false. While I do not believe in her, I must not knowingly meet her, for I am not her judge, and should have to act so as to seem to judge her.

But whatever you think of me, I love you, and look to the Master to make all things right at last.

Wife and I are always yours
Lovingly

GEORGE MACDONALD

I could write on and on, but you will allow this is enough.

To Lady Mount-Temple   Sunday night

My beautiful sister,

If I were to write what is in my heart, it would be to tell you how lovely yours is, but as that is a study for your friends and not for you, I will not. Let it be all understood between us now, and when the time comes that I can flash all colours and sing no end of new songs, perhaps I will try to thank you. Now I will only love you, and my great hearted generous brother, to whom please give the opposite leaf.

Yours, please God, forever,

GEORGE MACDONALD

William, a Temple of the God of grace! From the loud winds to me a hiding place.

GEORGE MACDONALD

To Lady Mount-Temple   [Casa Coraggio, Bordighera, Italy]
                                            December 2, 1888

Dearest Sister,

I have not time to write a letter worth sending you. But when two ships pass in mid ocean, who would not feel the silence deathly strange if no shout passed from the one to the other? So even an inarticulate sound may be a greeting of eternal import. It says you are and I am, and there is something in which we live and move. And so if I only call to you across France to say "Here I am this loving Sunday, and I am thinking of you," it will not go for nothing. I look out of my window on a dark salty sea, with a border of dark cloud, and then a ghostly shadow of soiled roses above it, and a region of dingy thin green above that, and then the blue with the one lonely glorious evening star in it. There is no one beside it to keep it company, but all the sky is its own, and is all company. Oh the great Father is enough! — enough surely to keep us company while we wait! And what would the best beloved be? Would he or she be enough without the eternal inside? But the thing is unthinkable for all love is God.

So let us lift up our hearts — and another will take them. Do you not sometimes feel now as if the Father had taken his child into his arms, and was having her to himself, and nursing her, and getting her ready to go to sleep, and have her new clothes tomorrow [for her] birthday? My love to you in sign of love from all of us.

                                            Your brother

                                            GEORGE

DEATH[1]

Little one you must not fret
    That I take your clothes away;
Better sleep you soon will get,
    and at morning wake more gay —
Saith the human mother.

I who clothed with body and brain,
    Now do you unclothe again —
But to clothe in better dress,
    Even in everlastingness —
Saith the heavenly father.

I went down death's lonely stairs,
    Laid my garments in the tomb;
Dressed again one morning fair,
    Hastened up, which welcome —
Saith the elder Brother.

God is stronger than all pain;
    Giveth courage in all fear,
Trust in him is purest gain;
    All is well, for he is here —
Saith the witness-chorus.

GEORGE MACDONALD

1. Published as "Going to Sleep," in *Poetical Works,* vol. 1, p. 348.

To Lady Mount-Temple   [Casa Coraggio]
                                       December 9, [1888]

Did you ever think, dearest sister, what kind of mourning is meant where the Lord says "Blessed are they that mourn"?[1] It is simply and specially those that are mourning for the dead. The Greek word means that. Then the Master says you are a blessed woman, for there is comfort coming that will content you. When it comes, perhaps you will say to yourself, "If I had known it was anything like this, it would have made me happy even then when I missed and wanted him." Then might not he say, "You might have expected something good when I told you that such a comfort was coming that I congratulated you even in the midst of your sorrow!" "Will they never trust my Father!" I imagine him saying sometimes.

Yes, dear, it is a hard time for you, but he is drawing you nearer to himself. You will have, I think, to consent to be miserable so far as loneliness makes you miserable, and look to him and him only for comfort. But the words that the Lord speaks are spirit and life. We are in a house with windows on all sides. On one side the sweet garden is trampled and torn, the beeches blown down, the fountain broken; you sit and look out, and it is all very miserable. Shut the window. I do not mean forget the garden as it was, but do not brood on it as it is. Open the window on the other side, where the great mountains shoot heavenward, and the stars, rising and setting, crown their peaks. Down those stairs look for the descending feet of the Son of Man coming to comfort you. This world, if it were alone, would not be worth much — I should be miserable already; but it is the porch to the Father's home, and he does not expect us to be quite happy, and knows we must sometimes be very unhappy till we get there: We are getting nearer. I need sorely to be got ready and die to myself.

Your loving brother
George.

1. Matthew 5:4.

To Lady Mount-Temple   [Casa Coraggio]
December 19, 1888

Dearest Sister,

I would not have failed writing last Sunday but that I was — not ill, for it was only lumbago and exhaustion, but in bed. Not that I can be of much use to you, for there are times when all that one can say must be only words, words, words. But other times words are at least the rolling of pebbles in the tide of the eternal sea, and if they don't say anything they bear some witness that there is a sea outside, and that it rolls into some bays. The universe would be to me no more than a pasteboard scene, all surface and no deepness, on the stage, if I did not hope in God. I will not say *believe,* for that is a big word, and it means so much more than my low beginnings of confidence. But a little faith may wake a great big hope, and I look for great things from him whose perfection breathed me out that I might be a perfect thing one day. The more we trust, the more reasonable we find it to trust.

I will go on sending a
word at a time.
Your loving but
unprofitable brother,

GEORGE MACDONALD

To His Son Greville MacDonald Bordighera,
January 20, 1889

This is your Sunday birthday. My love to you, and the desire which is sure to come true, that you may have all the good that may be gathered in the world to which the Lord of souls sent you through us. That existence is a splendid thing I am more and more convinced, while, at the same time, but for my hope in God, I should have no wish for its continuance, and should feel it but a phantasmagoria. But Jesus Christ did come, for no man could have invented him; and he thought our being worth giving himself for; and he was perfectly satisfied with his God and Father. And so I am content in God. Rather than believe in the popular God, I would believe in none, but the agnostics. . . .

To Henry Cecil[1] Bordighera,
March 3, 1890

Dear Old Friend,

What can I say to you, for the hand of the Lord is heavy upon you. But it is his hand, and the very heaviness of it is good. . . . There is but one thought that can comfort, and that is that God is immeasurably more the father of our children than we are. It is all because he is our father that we are fathers. . . . It is all well — even in the face of such pain as yours — or the world goes to pieces for me.

It is well to say "The Lord gave and the Lord hath taken away," but it is not enough. We must add, And the Lord will give again: "The gifts of God are without repentance." He takes that he may give more closely — make *more ours*. . . . The bond is henceforth closer between you and your son. . . .

To give a thing and take again
Is counted meanness among men;
Still less to take what once is given
Can be the royal way of heaven!

But human hearts are crumbly stuff,
And never, never love enough;

And so God takes and, with a smile,
Puts our best things away awhile.

Some therefore weep, some rave, some scorn;
Some wish they never had been born;
Some humble grow at last and still,
And then God gives them what they will.

1. This letter was written on the occasion of the death of Cecil's eldest son.

Written for a lady in sore distress
because her daughter had lost her reason.

June 1890

A wind puffs out the lantern of the child;
    Yet think not therefore no live cloud of wings,
Tent-like moves with her through the darkened wild,
    Instinct with love, and vague sweet murmurings:
God minds his sparrow, nor forgets his child.

'Tis dark, and she is walking in a dream;
    The dream is not all true — but God is there —
Else nought at all could either be or seem:
    The air is dark, and yet we breathe the air;
The child but dreams: God wakeful sees her dream.

Wrapt in her darkness, she is yet with God,
    And in her dream may foil the evil powers.
Dream-skies above, and underneath dream-sod,
    Her bare feet treading thorns or sunk in flowers,
She may be walking hand in hand with God.

GEORGE MACDONALD

To His Daughter   C.C.B. [Casa Coraggio, Bordighera],
Lilia Scott MacDonald,   January 4, 1891 [her birthday]
at Asheville, North Carolina,
U.S.A.[1]

Dearest Child,

I could say so much to you, and yet I am constantly surrounded by a sort of cactus-hedge that seems to make adequate utterance impossible. It is so much easier to write romances where you cannot easily lie, than to say the commonest things where you may go wrong any moment. . . . I can only tell you I love you with true heart fervently, and love you far more because you are God's child than because you are mine. I don't thank you for coming to us, for you could not help it, but the whole universe is "tented" with love, and you hold one of the corners of the great love-canopy for your mother and me. I don't think I am very ambitious, except the strong desire "to go where I am" be ambition; and I know I take small satisfaction in looking on my past; but I do live expecting great things in the life that is ripening for me and all mine — when we shall all have the universe for our own, and be good merry helpful children in the great house of our Father. I think then we shall be able to pass into and through each other's very souls as we please, knowing each other's thought and being, along with our own, and so being like God. When we are all just as loving and unselfish as Jesus; when like him, our one thought of delight is that God is, and is what he is; when the fact that a being is just another person from ourselves is enough to make that being precious — then, darling, you and I all will have the grand liberty wherewith Christ makes free-opening his hand to send us out like white doves to range the Universe.

Have I now shown that the attempt to speak what I mean is the same kind of failure that walking is — a mere, constantly recurring recovery from falling? . . .

I have still one great poem in my mind, but it will never be written, I think, except we have a fortune left us, so that I need not write any more stories — of which I am beginning to be tired. . . .

My dear love to Ronald. I could not bear you to leave him any more than you could yourself. Tell him from me that Novalis says: "This world is not a dream, but it may, and perhaps ought to become one."[2] Anyhow it will pass — to make way for the world God has hidden in our hearts.

Darling, I wish you life eternal. I daresay the birthdays will still be sparks in its glory. May I one day see that mould in God out of which you came.

Your loving
Father

1. Lilia was visiting her brother Ronald, who was serving as headmaster at an Episcopal school there.

2. Throughout his life, MacDonald quoted this epigram from Novalis, which appears in *Phantastes* and at the end of *Lilith*. He frequently compared human life to a dream.

To C. Edmond Maurice   March 1, 1891

... We are a house of mourning afresh at present, though by no means crushed, for we live and are saved by the sure hope of what is to come. Our little Octavia is gone to her mother.[1] She was the young light of her grannie's eyes, but she takes comfort that our time is not, cannot be, so far away. ...

1. MacDonald's granddaughter Octavia died in February 1891. Her mother, Caroline Grace, had died in 1884.

To His Wife   Huntly,
July 13th, 1891

Dearest,

... I have just returned with James[1] from the churchyard where the bodies of all my people are laid — a grassy place, and very quiet, in the middle of undulatory fields and with bare hills all about.[2] But I see the country more beautiful than I used to see it. The air is delicious, and full of sweet odours, mostly white clover, and there is over it much sky. I get little bits of dreamy pleasure sometimes, but none without the future to set things right. "What is it all for?" I should constantly be saying with Tolstoi, but for the hope of the glory of God. ...

1. MacDonald's cousin, who was in possession of The Farm, Huntly.

2. Drumblade churchyard, Huntly, where members of the MacDonald family are buried.

To His Wife   [July 1891]
Huntly

I have been out for a few miles' drive — to the old church of Ruthven, of which only the gable and belfry remain, with a beautiful old bell, looking quite new, though I think the date on it is 250 years ago, with the legend in Latin "Every kingdom against itself [shall] be laid waste." Right at the foot of the belfry the fool of my story[1] is buried, with a gravestone set up by the people of Huntly telling about him, and how he thought that bell, now above his body, always said, "Come home, come home." Close to him, in a place chosen by himself[,] lies the Dr. Grant whose violin I bought. They are the only two lying there. I had never been there before. James made his man and another go up and take a rubbing of the legend on the bell. They could climb up the edge of the gable on the corbel-steps of it. . . .

1. "The Wow o' Rivven," in *The Portent and Other Stories* (London: Fisher Unwin, 1909). William Raeper notes: "The ruin stands in a small silent churchyard, and at the foot of the wall lies John McBey, the fool of MacDonald's story, whom he must have known from his boyhood" (*George MacDonald* [London: Lion Publishing Co., 1987], p. 361).

To Miss O'Neill   The Farm, Huntly,
Aberdeenshire,
July 16, 1891

Dear Miss O'Neill,

Only this morning have I received your letter. I am sorry, for you will be thinking I have neglected it. Please put the note in an envelope for me, and address it to Mr. Severn, for I have not one that will do.

Please tell your father that I have the hope of being able to send him an Edinburgh Burns[1] soon, for I have one in view. That edition is very scarce now.

I shall be in London, I believe, on the 25th or 26th of this month, for which two days my address will be 3, Orme Square, Bayswater, London W. On the Monday following, I shall be returning to our summer quarters in Stock Rectory Station, Billericay, but post town, Ingatestone Essex, an hour from Liverpool street. We shall be there till the end of September.

I hope this will reach you before your father leaves. Tell him I am as idle here, where I have been and shall be for a few days — till the 24th in fact — as a cat in the sun. It is my native place.

With love to your mother and all of you, including the dear little fellow, to whom I shall send a few words very soon.

Yours affectionately

GEORGE MACDONALD
p.t.o. [Please Turn Over]

[Note on back of letter:] I have not the least notion whether your father will be likely or not to see Mr. Ruskin.

1. An edition of the poetry of Robert Burns.

To A. P. Watt[1]

Stock Rectory,
Essex
August 8, 1891

Dear Watt,

Will you be at home in the beginning of the week after next which commences tomorrow, I want to bring you my new volume of sermons. I think of calling it the *Gospel of Hope*.[2]

Best thanks for the *House of the Wolf*. It is a very good and very well written story. The name has hardly root enough in it though. That is a small thing, however.

Yours always,

GEORGE MACDONALD

1. MacDonald's friend and literary agent.
2. *The Hope of the Gospel* (London: Ward, Lock, Bowden & Co., 1892).

To Messrs. K. Paul[1]   Stock Rectory
                                                            August 29, 1891

Dear Sirs,

As the sheets you mention of the reprint of *There and Back* have not arrived, do not take the trouble to send them; for the variations of which I should have to complain, judging from the past, would be so small and so numerous, that it would be impossible to make the alterations. It is not of blunders I complain: they can hardly be helped, and are not often serious; but of small impertinences of wilful alteration. I presume the printers are so accustomed to the indifference of writers who are anything but English scholars, that they think they know better than all authors, and cannot imagine that some writers weigh not merely their words, but their points and capitals every one. It is mainly in the substitution of their capitals for my lower case letters that I find myself aggrieved.

I send by this post a few more sheets of "The Flight of the Shadow," which themselves illustrate what I mean. How much trouble, more to themselves than me, it would save, if they would but follow copy in little things!

Yours truly

GEORGE MACDONALD

1. Publishers of *There and Back* (1891) and *The Flight of the Shadow* (1891).

To Henry Sutton   October 5, 1891

My very dear Henry Sutton,

I cannot look you in the face without having written to you, and I have the hope of seeing you again before long, as I shall be preaching at Iale next Sunday. It is to myself strange that all my good intentions of writing to you after the receipt of your precious letter, should have come to nothing. But the good delight to pardon. I read your poem to my Sunday night gathering — I need not say, only the printed part of it. Your part to myself is very dear to me. I am lecturing constantly. I may say every night but Saturdays till into the beginning of November.

My people are all gone home earlier than usual because Lily is very ill. In the spring she nursed her dearest friend till she died, and seems to have herself taken her complaint — though it is in our own family as well, as you know. But one door is as good as another to go through into the higher world and we shall all go soon. In haste,

Your loving friend,

George MacDonald

To His Wife   85 Harley Street, W.,
November 5, 1891

. . . This is your birthday, dearest. I hope you are full of hope in it. Though the outer decay, the inner, the thing that trusts in the perfect creative life, grows stronger — does it not? God will be better to us than we think, however expectant we be. . . .

Dearest, my love to you on this your birthday — a good day for me. I thank God for you.

Your loving
Husband

To His Wife   85 Harley Street,
November 6, 1891

. . . I may as well use this paper which wrapt my last lecture-fee to write my next to last letter to you. . . .[1] My work is done and I am better now than when I began it — 48 lectures in 58 days. . . . I hope I shall be able to help you in the nursing. I think I might manage to feed her fire for her in the night for one thing.[2] Greville says neither of the girls is strong enough to bear being disturbed in their sleep. . . .

. . . On Sunday afternoon Mr. William Nicholl came to sing to me. . . . He sang *Comfort ye,* and I have not heard it anything like so well rendered since you.

G. [Greville] says I have 15 or 20 years' work in me yet. The doctors say a man's age is the age of his arteries, and there is no decay, no age in mine. He says there is not an unsound spot in me. . . .

1. Greville MacDonald notes: "This lecture was literally his last: he never spoke again in public for any fee" (*George MacDonald and His Wife*, p. 525).

2. Referring to MacDonald's daughter Lilia, whose condition was deteriorating. On November 22, 1891, at the age of thirty-nine, she died in her father's arms.

To Helen MacKay Powell   Bordighera,
                                                     April 16, 1892

Dearest Helen,

I send you herewith a letter which will perhaps interest you a little.

You will hardly know that my cousin James, the last left of the family, who lives at the old place, has quite distinguished himself amongst Scotch antiquaries by a book on the Place-names of Strathbogie. In preparation for this he taught himself Gaelic, whence he became interested, for the [?] of our side of the family in the question with which his letter is concerned. I was able to tell him quite enough to satisfy him, but I cannot help wishing he had a little letter from you on the subject of our dear uncle's labours. There would seem to be or to have been some jealousy at work about that dictionary! I daresay you know more about that than I do.

I send you also a wee booky, which, as there is nothing or none to working of my own in it, I may be allowed to say I am sure you will like. You would hardly believe how much labour it cost me. I have nothing to do with putting the portrait there, which I do not believe in.

We are all pretty well. Louisa has been ill but is better, and hopes to be at her organ on Monday when we have an interesting wedding in the church.

How have you stood the winter? Our spring has been rather trying. We are not going to England this year, but are on the verge of taking a nice house we have heard of at Vallombrosa for the hot months. We hope this way to get some rest, of which there is little to be had here in the winter or in England in the summer.

I think we feel — Louisa and I at least — as if we were getting ready to go. The world is very different since Lily went, and we shall be glad when our time comes to go after our children. I hope and trust more and more as I grow older. The boys are no anxiety to us — except that Ronald suffers much. But he is very brave and diligent, and has the quaintest darling of a child — odd and pretty like her name, Ozella.[1]

I should like to have James's letter again if you did not mind the trouble of sending it back. If Lou [Louisa] were by me she would send her love.

Your loving cousin

GEORGE MACDONALD

1. The daughter of Ronald and his first wife, Verinda Blandy.

To W. Carey Davies[1]   Bordighera,
                                                                 June 15, 1892

. . . I have no impulse toward public work this year. I do not think I should feel at all sorry if I were told I should never preach or lecture again. Somehow I have very little of feeling of doing good that way. But let everything always be as our Father wills. I hope, with you, I shall not have to change much in my new edition of Poems.[2] It is very troublesome, but one cannot let wrongness of any kind willingly pass. It will be in two volumes and complete — all except the Diary, Translations, and the Poems in *Phantastes*. . . . I have just finished a story called *Heather and Snow*. . . .

1. Davies acted as MacDonald's secretary.
2. *Poetical Works,* 2 vols. (1893).

To W. Carey Davies   Bordighera,
                                                        October 15, 1892

My dear Davies,

Tennyson is gone to his peers, and I do not mourn much for any of the dead. God be with us here and there — that is all. We shall soon join them. . . . I feel as if I should never lecture more. I have no impulse to do so. If I am willed to do it, the impulse will wake. . . . I am certain I have greatly improved many of my poems. I was much displeased with them. But the first way of a thing sticks to you against reason somehow. . . .

I like your taking Renan's[1] part, but really the chatter of the world, that is the newspapers, is not worth minding. They, the newspapers, are becoming more and more impudent. . . .

1. Joseph Ernest Renan, the French historian and philologist.

To the Treasurer, Middle Temple   Bordighera, Nov. 20, 1892

Sir,

Allow me to lay before you some of the grounds on which I judge the Rev. A. T. Carlyle remarkably fitted for the honourable office of Reader to the Temple.

He reads quite unusually well — simply, clearly, articulately, and intelligibly, without any show, and with a dignity plainly unconscious. His style is quiet, intelligent, and impressive, without anything of false or forced emphasis. His voice, not powerful in tone, owes its influence to the just modulation of a pervading sympathy. In a word, his reading is, to my feeling, delightful — which may, however, owe not a little to the fact that, although deaf, I hear him.

He is a man of fine gifts, rarely cultivated. His knowledge of music seems great, while his rendering of it, whether on piano or organ[,] is much admired. On these points, however, I do not speak with authority.

His knowledge, especially of History, seems to me wonderful, and his conclusions seem wise, genuine, and unprejudiced. The largeness of his humanity claims its foundation in reverence for God and the truth. His justice, his love of fair-play, even where in opinion he is opposed, will, I think, make itself felt even upon a partial acquaintance.

His sense of duty is strong. In ordinary social relations he is open-hearted and responsive — a right man, cheerful because devout, and not the less but the more of a man that he is a clergyman.

In all the best ways he is distinguished. Therefore well fitted for the distinguished office to which his friends would gladly see him appointed.

> I am, sir,
> Your obedient servant,
>
> GEORGE MACDONALD

To Lady Mount-Temple

Casa Coraggio,
December 12, 1892

Dearest sister Georgina,

I hope you are daily getting stronger, though I fear it is but slowly. Best loving thanks for your dear letter. I cannot write one worth reading today. Last night's work has wearied me. But I am wonderfully well, and able on the whole to work hard — and hope no end.

I trust soon to send you a new edition of my poems,[1] with one little one that is your own private property if you will not disown it.

It is wonderful how you get over the hurts you give yourself! But I fear you have suffered much. I know how brave you are, but pain is an ugly thing.

My wife is wonderfully better, and enjoying her organ-work as usual. We have Lord & Lady Aberdeen at Bordighera for a few days, and much enjoy an occasional sight of them.

I think the last sermon in my volume will interest you.[2] I more & more think it sets forth the truth.

> Your loving & grateful brother
>
> GEORGE MACDONALD

---

1. *The Poetical Works of George MacDonald*, 2 vols. (London: Chatto & Windus, 1893).
2. "The Hope of the Universe," in *The Hope of the Gospel* (1892).

To Mr. and Mrs. Henry Sutton   December 13, 1892

Dear Friends,

Thank you both heartily for remembering me so beautifully. I am just going to send the portrait to be framed that it may hang in my little private gallery among others of my very best friends' earthly likenesses. I know Henry did not send it, and I greatly dislike doing that same thing myself, but I thank Mary[1] for doing so.

I only heard just before the wife wrote, that the husband had been very ill. I hope he is now strong again, and able for work: The portrait looks like it. I do not doubt, dear friend, you have come out of the furnace with some of the gold always in it. We are getting nearer to the harbour, thank the ever Blessed!

I am growing very forgetful and cannot remember if I sent you a little bunch of gatherings from Sir Ph. Sidney.[2] If I did not just send a card with NO on it, and I will send it.

Pardon haste. My love to you.

Yours always,
George MacDonald.

My wife would send her love if she were by me.

1. Mrs. Sutton.
2. *A Cabinet of Gems, Cut and Polished by Sir Philip Sidney* (1891).

To Henry Sutton   Bordighera,
December 24, 1892

My dear Sutton,

Be this a good time to you and yours. The life is drawing nigh. Our redemption is nearer than when we believe.

I had done up the little book to send you. Then I could not find your wife's letter to get your home address. Then I thought I would consult my pocket book as to the impression I had that I had sent you the book months ago. The book says I did. I addressed it to the Alliance Office. Then I bethought me that you were ill at that time, and it might have been laid aside in the office and be somewhere acceptable still: would you mind asking a question or two about it in the hope of its turning up, and please let me know? The book lies by me with your two names on it ready to send if this inquiry should fail, for I do want you to have it, only it will do for some one else if you should have it already.

Did I tell you I am hard at work on a two-volume edition of my poems up to date? I am getting tired of it, but it is nearly done. It is a great sedative of conceit to be disgusted with past work! So much that is imperfect slips through in the train of what one thinks will do! But I do think I shall have it decent now.

My love to you both, and am sorry to trouble you.

Yours always,
George MacDonald

To W. Carey Davies   Bordighera,
January 22, 1893

I gather from your last letter that you are now fifty years of age. I am nearly twenty years your senior — not very far from 70 now, but if I do not in all things, I do in all essential things feel younger than when I was a child. Certainly I am happier and more hopeful, though I think I always had a large gift of hope. It has been the one constitutional power of life in me — none of my making surely!

. . . Have you seen that Greville is made a Physician to King's College Hospital. We are all very much pleased. You have known him ever since he went to school at King's — a choir boy. . . .

I am rather driven with work, I think sometimes; but if my faith were stronger, as I hope it is on the way to being, I should never feel that.

To A. P. Watt   Haxted House,
                                                                       Edenbridge,
                                                                    June 11, 1893

Dear Watt,

I can't do it, even to oblige you. . . . I never have and never will consent to be interviewed. I will do nothing to bring my personality before the public in any way farther than my work in itself necessitates. Pardon my brevity. I have begun again to work, but writing takes all the strength I have to spend. . . . My memory plays me sad tricks now. It comes of the frosty invasion of old age — preparing me to go home, thank God. Till then I must work, and that is good. . . .

To Mr. Reid   Haxted House, Edenbridge
                                                                    July 23, 1893

Dear Mr. Reid,

The printers have sent me proof of the little essay, if such it can be called, on the fantastic imagination,[1] but they have sent me no *copy*, which entails more work, and I am so busy, I avoid all that is unnecessary. I am looking for the reprint of the Shelley essay too, which I must go over again with the copy also.

> In haste and yours very
> truly
>
> GEORGE MACDONALD

1. "The Fantastic Imagination," in *A Dish of Orts: Chiefly Papers on the Imagination and on Shakespeare* (1893), enlarged edition.

To Mr. Reid   Haxted House, Edenbridge
                                                                    August 1, 1893

Dear Mr. Reid,

I am afraid I must ask for revises of these, for, in the Shelley most, I found several betterments possible. I would also ask you to let me have a few copies of each, for which I should be grateful. I find that I cannot write a few words of preface without seeing the preface I have already written. Would you kindly send me a copy of the book.

How would this do for the new title:

Essays and Other Papers, formerly called *Orts,* with corrections and an added Essay?[1]

Yours very truly

GEORGE MACDONALD

1. The volume was entitled *A Dish of Orts. Enlarged Edition* (1893).

To Mr. Reid   Haxted House, Edenbridge
                                              August 5, 1893

Dear Mr. Reid,

I return you for press both papers, and would be glad of a few copies of both. I return also the preface, with a few added words. I send another proposed title, which, I fear, is the best I can do. You see we cannot leave out *Orts* because it would make some naturally suppose that it was a new book. The title I send would explain the book.

Yours very truly,

GEORGE MACDONALD

I like my [latest] proposed title myself, and think it would do. I think you were right in not liking the last I sent you.

To Lady Mount-Temple[1]   Bordighera,
                                              October 22, 1893

Dearest sister Georgina,

At home while the others are at church, I sit down to have a little talk to you. Except that you trust me, you must be wondering that I have not yet written you a word about the lovely gift you have sent me. But the time had not come when I could say anything worth saying to you. The same day, it is true, I wrote these lines, but did not think them good enough to send. I only set them down now to show I was not taking the gift lightly. I have altered them a little — yet in themselves they are hardly worth sending.

His snowdrop I will wear outside and in me —
    Yet may not keep the gift that love has given me;
But when, with him, in God I home and heaven me,
    Golden and blue it still to him will pin me.

So far I wrote on Sunday, and now it is Wednesday. So day glides after day till the blessed morning come. We have just heard that dear old Mr. Wyld is gone home. Now he knows something at least of what lay so mysteriously hidden from him all his long life. It seems strange to us to know so little of the only event in our lives of which we can be certain before it comes. But *He* will justify himself to the love and hope of his children! The story of the Son makes me hope infinitely from both the Father and the Son. If we are not the little ones of a perfect love, I can see no sense in things. Not only can there be for me no religion, but I do not care for any; and as for philosophy, there is no room for any. If God is, all is as well as a perfect imagination could desire — and divinely better. If there be no God, then is the universe a mockery. But what mocking Power could have invented such a world!

But there is the second dinner-bell, and I am stopped again!

Nov. 3. Yesterday we had a letter from Alice Wyld, from Edinburgh, to tell us that her dear good old father was gone home. What a little way it is across the shadow of this life to the more light beyond! A little while ago the old man wondered with us what was coming: now it has begun to come, and he to know! How the good people there must sometimes talk! And by and by we shall talk with them — not as here so many talk, "of who is in and who is out," but of what was and ever will be, and is making our hearts burn within us.

The cause that we have an ever unsatisfied idea in our hearts is that he through whom the Father made all things, is in our hearts, and is, whether we know it or not, that ideal. Not until we know the Lord, that is, have seen him with the inward eyes, can we be glad that we live. Those eyes nothing can open but the real presence and a heart hungry with conscious blindness.

Now I must stop my piecey letter. My love to you. The morning is on its way.

Ever your grateful and
loving brother,

GEORGE MACDONALD

1. This typewritten letter was written over a period of several days, which explains the repetition in it.

•

To an Unidentified Woman   Bordighera, Italy,
November 5, 1893

Dear Madam,

Would you kindly send me Mrs. McKinnell's address. Long before the volume was out, I meant to send a copy of "The Hope of the Gospel" to her, but I could not find her address which I had mislaid.

But as to an interview of the kind you ask for, that I would not give to anyone. I could not consent to send abroad my opinions through another, and especially by means of the Newspapers. What I have written you have a right to use as you see fit, but I cannot have anything to do with what you say about it.

I quite sympathize with your desire to see justice done to our brothers and sisters in lower kind. I do not think much can be done, however, save by helping men and women, and especially children, to see into the life and feeling and thought of animals, so as to recognize their real being. And I think the worst enemies of the lower animals are those that instead of teaching and raising them, spoil and pamper them, as doubtless they would children if they had them, until they are a nuisance.

Yours very truly,

GEORGE MACDONALD

FOR MY DEAREST SISTER CHARLOTTE GODWIN[1]

CHRISTMAS, 1893

Twilight is near, and the day grows old;
    The spiders of care are weaving their net;
The night will be blowing and rainy and cold;
    I cower at his door from wind and wet.

He sent me out the world to see,
    Drest for the road in a garment new;
It is clotted with clay, and worn beggarly —
    The porter will hardly let me through!

I bring in my hand a few dusty ears;
    Once I thought them a tribute meet!
I bring in my heart a few unshed tears;
    Which is my harvest — the pain or the wheat?

A broken man, at the door of his hall
    I sit and hear it go merry within!
It sounds as of birthday festival!
    Hark to the trumpet, the violin!

I know where they sit, glad but not gay,
    Sit on a bench where no one upbraids:
Make a little room for me, I will say,
    Dear publicans, sinners, and foolish maids.

Some one is hearing my heart forlorn!
    A step comes soft through the dancing din!
Oh Love eternal! oh woman-born!
    Son of my Father, to take me in!

GEORGE MACDONALD

---

1. Unpublished Christmas poem, written by MacDonald for his wife's eldest sister, Charlotte Powell Godwin.

To a Friend[1]   Casa Coraggio
                                                 Bordighera, Italy
                                                 January 1, 1894

My dear old friend,

I am going to write by this same post to send you for a New Year's remembrance a copy of my Hamlet, which if you have time to read it, I think you will in the main agree with, although it does not go with the general notion. Please read the preface. I send you also herewith a little poem I have written for my friends.

I hope you are feeling pretty well. I am put on half-time because of my years but am yet able to get through a good deal.

We shall get home to our father & elder brother before very long — at least we shall somehow get a little nearer to them. But the Father of Jesus Christ lives and we shall *know* that he lives because he is more than with us, he is in us. Love to your wife.

                                                 Always lovingly yours,

                                                 GEORGE MACDONALD

1. Possibly Henry Sutton.

To Susan Scott[1]   Bordighera
                                                 June 1, 1894

My dear Susan,

What *can* you be thinking of me that I have never yet written to you! And my explanation will seem strange, as indeed it is. Only yesterday, when clearing some letters from my table, did I come upon one from the Suttons which contained the sad news.[2] I had but partly read it. One portion was type-written; the other, from Mr. Sutton, I had partly read, had been interrupted and had postponed reading the rest till another time, and so forgotten it, which I attribute in part to my being in some trouble at the time, and to my mental condition being a good deal affected by the influenza, especially my memory.

So you are left alone of all that bright company! I have been a good deal with your father lately in reading some of the precious teachings he has left, and have been learning from him afresh. Surely if anyone ought to have patience and strength to endure the night and the lonesomeness, it is his daughter! The morning is at hand, as I feel more than ever, when we shall all go to our own. Blessed be the Father of our Lord who has given us such a lively hope. Even in my worst times I am able to look forward to the glory to be revealed. Be comforted, dear friend. Surely *he* comes nearer to you than ever who alone can comfort. It seems as if he threw a veil of sorrow over us sometimes, in order that in its shadows he might get nearer to our hearts. But what can I say to you that you do not know! The blessed influences of your family have never left me or my wife. And surely they have only grown in power with you! I cannot be wrong in thinking that we have as yet but the faintest glimmer of the splendour of the future that is at hand for those who shall see God and in him all the lovely and loved who have vanished for a time. You must have had a sore time — one after the other taken from you! But when we are brought low, he cometh nigh to us. The world seems full of dark and strange things, which drive me more and more to believe that he orders all things in a way that we can but partially understand because of its goodness. For my own part I know that I have needed to be afflicted, and yet need it, but at the last I shall say it was well to be afflicted.

My wife joins me in dear and true love to you. We begin to hope that some day you will come and see us here. We are now on the wing for the neighbourhood of Florence for a few months, where our address will be

Nilletta Demidoss
Pratolino
Firenze

Perhaps you may feel moved to write and say you can understand my strange behaviour. I have done no work for some months, but hope the change now at hand may revive me in some measure. Perhaps I had been working too hard, but how is one to know.

Affectionately yours as of
old,

GEORGE MACDONALD

1. Daughter of the MacDonalds' old friend A. J. Scott.
2. Perhaps the death of her brother John.

To A. P. Watt   Villetta Demidoff,
                                                              Pratolino, Italy,
                                                              June 18, 1894

. . . I am a little better, I think, and begin to imagine it possible I should one day begin another book. But I continue very weak mentally. I am only able to read and understand books worth reading, mixed with a good story now and then. . . . We are in a most lovely place with a big park all about us and fine weather, not at all too hot to enjoy it in. . . .

I am buried in Villari's *Life and Times of Savonarola,* and that wants so much thinking that the fact of its being in Italian hardly makes me longer in reading it. . . .

To J. S. Blackie[1]   Bordighera,
                                                              November 11, 1894

My loved and honoured old friend,

I was glad to have your letter, and would have written sooner but have been much occupied. I am sorry to hear of your suffering. I know what asthma is, but that, with all other troubles of the breathing apparatus[,] has long left me.

The shadows of the evening that precedes a lovelier morning are drawing down around us both. But our God is in the shadow as in the shine, and all is and will be well: have we not seen his glory in the face of Jesus? and do we not know him a little? Have we not found the antidote to the theology of men in the Lord himself? I may almost say I believe in nothing but in Jesus Christ, and I know that when life was hardest for him, he was still thoroughly content with his father, whom he knew perfectly, and to whom he has laboured and is labouring to make us know. We do know and we shall go on to know him. This life is a lovely school time, but I never was content with it. I look for better — oh, so far better! I think we do not yet know the joy of mere existence. To exist is to be a child of God; and to know it, to feel it, is to rejoice evermore. May the loving Father be near you and may you know it, and be perfectly at peace all the way into the home country, and to the palace home of the living one — the life of our life.

Next month I shall be 70, and I am humbler a good deal than when

I was 20. To be rid of self is to have the heart bare to God and to the neighbour — to *have* all life own, and possess all things. I see, in my mind's eye, the little children clambering up to sit on the throne with Jesus. My God, art thou not as good as we are capable of imagining thee? Shall we dream a better goodness than thou hast ever thought of? Be thyself, and all is well with us.

It may be that I shall be able to come and see you, if you are still within sight next summer. But the hand of age is upon me too. I can work only four hours a day, cannot, only I never could, walk much, and feel tired. But all is not only well, but on the way to be better.

I need hardly tell you how truly I am in sympathy with the sonnet you were so good as to send me. It seems to me that the antidote to party-spirit is Church history, and when the antidote itself has made you miserably ill, the cure is the gospel pure and simple — the story and words of Jesus. I care for no church but that of which every obedient disciple of the Lord, and no one else, is a member — though he may be — must be learning to become one. Good bye for a little while anyhow. I have loved you ever since I knew you, for you love the truth. Please give my love to your wife — from of old time also.

Yours always,

GEORGE MACDONALD

1. John Stuart Blackie, who had held the Chair of Greek at Edinburgh.

To Lady Mount-Temple   Casa Coraggio, Bordighera, Italy,
                                                            December 28, 1894

Dearest sister Georgina,

We thank you lovingly for your very welcome letter, and for the beautiful portrait. I fancy the mouth not quite right, but wife will not agree with me. She thinks it as like you as it is lovely, while I do not think it quite so lovely as you. But the day of our beauty is at hand I hope. Do not be in haste to get home before us. "Pazienza!" as the Italians say so often.

It came to me the other day how God seems not to mind that his Jesus was sorely troubled, and yet Jesus never thought it was really so. We must remind ourselves of that, and be on God's side against our own foolish fancies. If you could but see into God's mind, and understand what he was thinking you would be content for the whole world. We thank God that your Juliet is such a comfort to you. We too have great comfort now in both our little ones, not little by any means now, but good children and growing more and more of children — as they grow bigger.

Wife has been much better this winter. I am very well, only my capacity for work gets much less, and the doctors will not let me work more than four hours a day. I seem to be able to think as well, but not for so long together. I often doubt if I shall write another book. There is one in the printers' hands now, which, however, I fear you may not quite like.[1]

So many dear ones have gone through the straits before us, that we must not fear to follow them. Till then, like scholars too backward to be taught together, some of us are having much personal attention from the master. Gradually we are shut in from the public, then the social relations are narrowed, then some, thank God, are shut up to their dear ones, and when[,] as so often is the case, there are no dear ones, on this earth, then we are alone with the living one, and have to take spoonfuls of life from his own hand; and there are some, doubtless, who call and think it, only nasty medicine. Let us take it willingly and lovingly. But it is so much easier to *say* when I am well, than to *do* when I am ill.

> Pardon this hasty scribble
> from your
> loving older brother,
>
> GEORGE MACDONALD

1. *Lilith* (1895).

To Henry Sutton   Morning, July 14, 1895
                                                              [London]

My very dear old friend,

I have been in London for a week and ought to have taken your welcome letter with me, in order to answer it sooner.

Your friend Miss Layard may well be congratulated on waking the so hearty approval of such a judge as yourself. I had glanced into the little volume she sent me, but not really made acquaintance with it. Now, after your letter, I hope when I go home to make a better acquaintance with it. At the same time it was enough to incline me to acknowledge her kind gift by sending her a vol. of my own — or mainly my own,[1] seeing I find myself no more inclined to write letters than ever. There is no occasion, however, for her to write or show me more courtesy than I have shown her. I had hoped that she would understand and take it as an acknowledgment of her book, which it was meant to be.

We are hoping to see Miss Scott somehow before she leaves this neighbourhood, where I have heard she is — from Mrs. Godwin[2] who met her accidentally. We all much enjoyed her visit to us in the spring, and my wife & I especially, for the sake of old times, and those who are now beyond the region & influence of time. To those dear friends and many more we are now drawing nigh. May we meet in the love of the perfect Father, and the grace and tenderness of the one man.

My book is delayed by necessary arrangements with America, but will be out in September.[3] I have no doubt about your liking it, but much as to the reception, for which in itself I care next to nothing, of what they call the Public, which is long-eared, and long-tongued embodiment of the cumulative imagination. N.B. I do not demand your intelligent reception of this unintelligible sentence.

I am this week hoping to begin a new story, but much fear my day is over for this world. If only it be all as God wills!

Please give my love to your wife, and take much to yourself from your loving & old friend

                                                      GEORGE MACDONALD

1. Probably *A Threefold Cord: Poems by Three Friends,* edited by MacDonald (1883) and printed privately.

2. Charlotte Powell Godwin, Louisa MacDonald's eldest sister.

3. *Lilith* (1895).

To Messrs. Sampson Low, Marston   The Nook,
                                        Dorking, July 26, 1895

Mess. Sampson Low, Marston, Publishers
Dear sirs,

I have just received, after a delay for which I alone am responsible, your very kind and handsome gift of the new issue of my books in your possession. Among the many, however[,] I do not find a single copy of *The Vicar's Daughter,* of which indeed I had one copy a long time ago, I think, but am not sure. If it would not be troubling you too much, I should be glad to have a copy or two of this to give away. I am sorry it had got parted from the other preceding two, "The Annals," and "Seaboard Parish," with which it formed a trilogy, so to say, but with the fortune of my books I have had but little to do.

> With renewed thanks
> Yours very truly
>
> GEORGE MACDONALD

To Henry Sutton   Casa Coraggio, Bordighera, Italy
                                        March 14, 1897

Dearly loved old friend,

I have received your welcome letter — but have been delayed in answering it by the pressure of another story hurrying to get out.[1]

It is very considerate of you not to give Mrs. Bailey a note of introduction at once, but be sure any friend of yours will be welcome to us both. My wife will be very glad to see her; only she must find us out, by which I mean that we cannot go and search the hotels for her, for they are now, alas! numerous. But most people in Bordighera know our house, and Mrs. Bailey will easily find it.

I am getting old & feeble, but have still good heart and better hope, and look for the life to come. I have not seen "Great Thoughts"[2] and perhaps am a little prejudiced against it by the fact that the editor asked me about myself!! of which, as is my custom, I took no notice. I daresay I could help you a little, I mean only as to my intent about this or that in *Lilith,* if I were to see you; but it seems to me that there is nothing very obscure in it that is worth finding out; though I hope there are some things in it not therefore shallow.

My wife joins me in love to you & yours.

Is there no chance of your coming this way? It might revive you both greatly — but perhaps it would be better to use it for escape from worse weather than it is likely to be now. Still be sure of a hearty welcoming if you should see a way to coming. We shall probably be in London before very long.

Hurriedly but lovingly yours.

GEORGE MACDONALD

I find the paper Great Thoughts has arrived, sent by you; but that I did not care to look at it, and so my wife did not bring it to my notice, knowing I cared little or nothing to see such things & generally was better pleased not to see them.

1. *Salted with Fire* (1897).

2. An article consisting of selections from MacDonald's writings. Presumably the editor had asked MacDonald for biographical information.

To Mrs. W. Carey Davies[1]   Casa Coraggio,
                                                                 Bordighera, Italy
                                                                 Good Friday, 1898

Dear Mrs. Davies,

. . . I have been indeed unable to think, and still more to know what I was thinking. Indeed I feel sometimes as if I were about to lose all power of thought. But when I find Carey again, he will help to set me right. Ah, you will be glad when you go to him, and find him all right and well and happy! Surely our Lord meant no less for us! He is in joy and peace with Him.

I am drawing nearer to the time I shall have to go. I do not think it will be just yet, and it is a good thing we should not know when the call will come, but may He give me what readiness he pleases. I should like to be as ready as your husband. I do not think I can ever be more ready than he.

Write to me again although I do not deserve it. . . .

1. W. Carey Davies, who had recently died, had acted as MacDonald's secretary.

From Irene MacDonald   Casa Coraggio, Bordighera, Italy,
to Lady Mount-Temple   January 3, 1900

My dear Lady Mount-Temple,

Mother asked me to write to you some time ago to tell you she was going to write herself as soon as ever she could and to thank you for your lovely letter & tell you how very much she was delighted in having it.

It has been a very busy and happy time as we have had Greville and still have Winifred & her husband[1] and so I have found it very difficult to get the time to write.

Father is fairly well and better in some ways. He was able to come upstairs to see our Christmas tree which we had for the children & was able to speak to a few of our friends.[2] Mother reads to him a great deal which he enjoys very much.

I do hope you have not had such a very wet Christmas as we have. There was hardly one fine day while Greville was with us.

I hope soon to have another pair of slippers ready for you (I wish they were ready now) which I make with so much love to you dear Lady Mount-Temple.

Your loving,
IRENE MACDONALD.

Please give my love to Juliet.

1. Winifred MacDonald had married Charles Edward Troup; in 1897 he had become Sir Edward Troup, K.C.B.
2. MacDonald had suffered a stroke in 1898.

From Louisa MacDonald   Casa Coraggio, Bordighera, Italy
to Lady Mount-Temple   Tuesday March 16 [1900?]

Our most beloved Lady Lily,

I am always longing to say something to you. It's always love, we want to say — *There* it is, living & longing & now & then it must break out. We wish fortune or providence or best & highest name of *Our Father —*

may send us to see you before long — but then we don't know — do we, what's coming?

The other day, I came upon a quaint as I thought — little hanging bottle — & its little crown supported by angels — made me think of you. I thought perhaps you would use it some-times for love of George & me — because we both wanted to send it you. Your crown is a crown of glory & your ministering angels are in high heaven — but many loving hearts are still longing for a sight of you — here — *ici Ires.* It was lovely, most lovely, to see your dear note to Winifred — your own precious hand writing — that has golden cords of love & all that is beautiful & highest Romance! In days gone — by — holding us still & filling past, . . . [incomplete]

From Louisa MacDonald to Lady Mount-Temple   Casa Coraggio,
                                                      Bordighera
                                                      Saturday night
                                                      December 16th [1901]

Our beloved Sister Georgina,

How lovely to have from your own dear heart, a picture of the dwelling that holds you & where we last saw you. A *seeing* for which I can't express my gratitude. Your Bordighera brother, dear, is still but sadly — not always, and I believe rarely is the sadness deep down in his heart — but he has not had much power to converse with *it* — his heart — the fearful irritation of the nerves, prevents *comfort* — but I know nothing could stir the absolute obedience of the will to the Lord Divine — the Will of God — still it is only by a few words here & there & by the lovely smile & the pressure of the hand that we see the peace behind all the disturbance of nerves.

I send you a snap that I think perhaps you will like — & if you like you will love it. I mean if it is not too painful for you if the questioning rather distracted look in which perhaps comes a shade of dread is not too much, you will see in him, I think still the mystic. The see-er. The doubt is only material born of want of nerve power.

You — almost our oldest — oldest in Love certainly *the* oldest friend — of those days — left — will like to see him perhaps as he was taken in his fur coat in a garden chair, last June. But I feel so sure the public would not read him aright in it that I have forbidden the . . . [incomplete][1]

1. The photograph here mentioned is reproduced in *George MacDonald and His Wife* (p. 553) with the caption "The Golden Wedding, 1901."

From Louisa MacDonald to Lady Mount-Temple   Casa Coraggio
                                                  [1901]

I've been trying to get time ever since we came back to write to you, you who were the heart of — the seed that grew into this dear lovely home ought to know what a refuge it is now he is so still & sad. All the glory & glow of the house seems gone, but there's an indwelling I think going on back as he would have — — — — —

I have been wandering on too much. But I should so very much like to know how you are — if you are able ever to go out — or if your Wonderland is still the gate of heaven to you.

Our love to you — he is going to give you his love in his name[1] about all he can do but it means much. I wish you could have seen his face when I asked him "yes, yes." It looked as if he had just really seen you.

> We are your loving
> loving
>
> George MacDonald
> & Louisa MacDonald

1. MacDonald wrote "loving" and signed his name to the letter.

Afterword

The wayward landscape of the mind begins its planting early. Good or bad, whatever takes root will all too likely live with you for a lifetime. So I have found. At the age of eight or so I had the luck to discover *The Princess and the Goblin* and *At the Back of the North Wind.* Already I owned (from Grimm) glass mountains and forests with silver leaves (the forest itself has been an abiding image) and all the parts of the journey into the Snow Queen's glittering region, north of north. Now, in my personal lanscape, there were mountains, castles, stairs (ah, yes), and a wondrous godmother fairy, as young as she was old, with the golden thread of assurance for every reading child. And there was North Wind, with whom (and also by way of the essential Arthur Hughes pictures) the same child might range the midnight sky, the midnight world. These things may change as you change, but they do not go.

The MacDonald we know best today belongs to that phenomenal period in the later mid-nineteenth century when a number of individual writers, mostly known for their work in adult fields, suddenly turned to producing marvels of magic and fantasy for the young. Every approach was different. Kingsley, in *The Water Babies,* boldly commandeered the sea for his realm. MacDonald took earth (those goblins), air, sky, and night (North Wind). Carroll — in advance of his day — chose the human mind, quirkily viewed through various glasses, one of which was a looking glass. All wrote works of genius, but the most personal in their gifts to the reading young were surely the two MacDonald books.

It is largely forgotten, though, that MacDonald was chiefly known (and especially admired in America) as an adult novelist. His output in fiction was prodigious. And yet, not one of these novels is in general currency today. The letters offer many curious facts — for instance, that a Civil List Pension was organized for MacDonald, who, with his large household, was always dismally short of funds. But what is tantalizing about the letters is that, while they tell much about MacDonald the man, whose joys were all too often balanced by sorrows — so many births! so many deaths! — of his battle with dogma yet endless need for religious faith, about the writer or the works there is scarcely a word. Yet the one is not complete without the other.

There is a fine selection of further reading in Sadler's section here on critical studies. And you might try something else. If, unlike Glenn Sadler, you do not own the "other" MacDonald books, find a library that possesses them (such libraries do exist) and read behind the letters as you go. A secret man, but as writer he left a key.

NAOMI LEWIS

Principal Works of George MacDonald

1851	*Twelve of the Spiritual Songs of Novalis.* Arundel.
1855	*Within and Without: A Dramatic Poem.* London: Longmans.
1857	*Poems.* London: Longmans.
1858	*Phantastes: A Faerie Romance for Men and Women.* London: Smith, Elder.
1863	*David Elginbrod.* London: Hurst & Blackett.
1864	*Adela Cathcart.* London: Hurst & Blackett.
1864	*The Portent: A Story of the Inner Vision of the Highlanders Commonly Called the Second Sight.* London: Smith, Elder.
1865	*Alec Forbes of Howglen.* London: Hurst & Blackett.
1867	*Dealings with the Faeries.* London: Strahan.
1867	*Annals of a Quiet Neighbourhood.* London: Hurst & Blackett.
1867	*The Disciple and Other Poems.* London: Strahan.
1867	*Unspoken Sermons.* First Series. London: Strahan.
1868	*Guild Court.* London: Hurst & Blackett.
1868	*Robert Falconer.* London: Hurst & Blackett.
1868	*The Seaboard Parish.* London: Tinsley Brothers.
1868	*England's Antiphon.* London: Macmillan.
1870	*The Miracles of Our Lord.* London: Strahan.
1871	*Works of Fancy and Imagination.* 10 vols. London: Strahan.
1871	*At the Back of the North Wind.* London: Strahan.
1871	*Ranald Bannerman's Boyhood.* London: Strahan.
1872	*The Princess and the Goblin.* London: Strahan.
1872	*Wilfrid Cumbermede.* London: Hurst & Blackett.
1872	*The Vicar's Daughter: An Autobiographical Story.* London: Tinsley Brothers.

1873	*Gutta Percha Willie: The Working Genius.* London: Henry S. King.
1875	*Malcolm.* London: Henry S. King.
1875	*The Wise Woman: A Parable.* London: Strahan.
1876	*Thomas Wingfold, Curate.* London: Hurst & Blackett.
1876	*Exotics: A Translation of the Spiritual Songs of Novalis, the Hymn Book of Luther, and Other Poems from the German and Italian.* London: Strahan.
1876	*St. George and St. Michael.* London: Henry S. King.
1877	*The Marquis of Lossie.* London: Hurst & Blackett.
1879	*Paul Faber, Surgeon.* London: Hurst & Blackett.
1879	*Sir Gibbie.* London: Hurst & Blackett.
1880	*A Book of Strife in the Form of the Diary of an Old Soul.* London: Unwin Brothers.
1881	*Mary Marston.* London: Sampson Low, Searle & Rivington.
1882	*Weighed and Wanting.* London: Sampson Low, Searle & Rivington.
1882	*Castle Warlock: A Homely Romance.* London: Sampson Low, Marston, Searle & Rivington.
1882	*The Gifts of the Christ Child and Other Tales.* London: Sampson Low, Marston, Searle & Rivington.
1882	*Orts.* London: Sampson Low, Marston, Searle & Rivington.
1883	*Donal Grant.* London: Kegan Paul, Trench.
1883	*The Princess and Curdie.* London: Chatto & Windus.
1883	*A Threefold Cord: Poems by Three Friends.* Ed. George MacDonald. London: Unwin Brothers.
1885	*The Tragedie of Hamlet, Prince of Denmark: A Study of the Text of the Folio of 1623.* London: Longmans, Green.
1886	*Unspoken Sermons.* Second Series. London: Longmans, Green.
1886	*What's Mine's Mine.* London: Kegan Paul, Trench.
1887	*Home Again.* London: Kegan Paul, Trench.
1888	*The Elect Lady.* London: Kegan Paul, Trench.
1889	*Unspoken Sermons.* Third Series. London: Longmans, Green.
1891	*A Rough Shaking.* London: Blackie & Son.
1891	*There and Back.* London: Kegan Paul, Trubner.
1891	*The Flight of the Shadow.* London: Kegan Paul, Trench, Trubner.
1892	*A Cabinet of Gems Cut and Polished by Sir Philip Sydney,*

Now for the More Radiance Presented without Their Setting by George MacDonald. London: Elliot Stock.

1892   *The Hope of the Gospel.* London: Ward, Lock, Bowden.

1893   *The Poetical Works of George MacDonald.* 2 vols. London: Chatto & Windus.

1893   *Heather and Snow.* London: Chatto & Windus.

1893   *Scotch Songs and Ballads.* Aberdeen: John Rae Smith.

1893   *A Dish of Orts: Enlarged Edition.* London: Sampson Low, Marston, Searle & Rivington.

1895   *Lilith: A Romance.* London: Chatto & Windus.

1897   *Rampolli: Growths from a Long-planted Root. Being Translations New and Old, Chiefly from the German, along with a Year's Diary of an Old Soul.* London: Longmans, Green.

1897   *Salted with Fire.* London: Hurst & Blackett.

1899   *Far Above Rubies.* New York: Dodd, Mead.

1920   *Fairytales by George MacDonald.* Ed. Greville MacDonald. London: George Allen & Unwin.

For further information, see my dissertation "The Cosmic Vision: A Study of the Poetry of George MacDonald" (Ph.D. diss., Aberdeen University, 1966). See also John Malcolm Bulloch's "A Bibliography of George Mac-Donald," *Aberdeen University Library Bulletin* 30 (Feb. 1925): 679-747; reissued as *A Centennial Bibliography of George MacDonald* (Aberdeen: Aberdeen University Press, 1925). For a critical review of Bulloch's bibliography, see Muriel Hutten, "Sour Grapeshot: Fault-finding in *A Centennial Bibliography of George MacDonald*," *Aberdeen University Review* 41 (1965): 85-88. See also Raphael Shaberman's *George MacDonald's Books for Children: A Bibliography of First Editions* (London: Cityprint Business Centres, 1979) and *George MacDonald: A Bibliographic Study* (Detroit: Omnigraphics, 1990).

Recommended Reading

Since the publication of C. S. Lewis's *George MacDonald: An Anthology* in 1947 (Macmillan) there has been a steady interest in the writings of George MacDonald. In 1961 Robert Lee Wolff's *The Golden Key: A Study of the Fiction of George MacDonald* (New Haven: Yale University Press), a somewhat dubious contribution, launched an academic and popular rediscovery of MacDonald's writings that continues to the present. Louis MacNeice's extremely helpful *Varieties of Parable* (Cambridge: Cambridge University Press, 1965) sparked critical interest in MacDonald's parable-writing talent, even as Lewis had pointed out MacDonald's mythopoeic genius, and Richard Reis offered in *George MacDonald* (New York: Twayne Publishers, 1972) the first modern biographical study of MacDonald.

The notable biographical and critical studies that have appeared in recent years are too numerous to mention here, but some should be cited. William Raeper's biography *George MacDonald* (London: Lion Publishing Company, 1987) is a substantial contribution to biographical studies of MacDonald and is the first major biography of MacDonald since Greville MacDonald's *George MacDonald and His Wife,* published in 1924. Elizabeth Saintsbury's *George MacDonald: A Short Life* (Edinburgh: Cannongate Publishing, 1987) offers a concise and personal treatment of MacDonald's life, as does Marion Lochhead in *The Renaissance of Wonder in Children's Literature* (Edinburgh: Cannongate Publishing, 1977). One of the finest short studies to appear recently on MacDonald as a Scottish writer is David S. Robb's *George MacDonald* in the Scottish Writers Series (Edinburgh: Scottish Academic Press, 1987). Two studies by Kathy Triggs—*George MacDonald: The Seeking Heart* (London: Pickering and Inglis, 1984) and *The Stars and the Stillness: A Portrait of George MacDonald* (Cambridge: Lutterworth, 1986)—are also warm tributes to MacDonald's genius.

Another noteworthy contribution is Michael R. Phillips's *George Mac-Donald: Scotland's Beloved Storyteller* (Minneapolis: Bethany House, 1987), which offers an informative and moving account of the major events in MacDonald's life.

Critical studies of MacDonald continue to appear. Although they are too numerous to list, some should be noted. Rolland Hein's *The Harmony Within: The Spiritual Vision of George MacDonald*, Masterline Series, vol. 2 (Eureka, CA: Sunrise Publications, 1982) offers the reader an insightful study of MacDonald's religious beliefs in the context of his works. A recent collection of essays of special note is Roderick McGillis's *For the Childlike: George MacDonald's Fantasies for Children* (Children's Literature Association and Scarecrow Press, 1992), which gives an impressive summary of critical thinking on MacDonald to date. C. N. Manlove's *Modern Fantasy* (Cambridge: Cambridge University Press, 1975) and *The Impulse of Fantasy Literature* (Kent, OH: Kent State University Press, 1983) are two excellent studies of MacDonald's talent as a writer of fantasy fiction. William Raeper's equally excellent collection *The Gold Thread: Essays on George MacDonald* (Edinburgh: Edinburgh University Press, 1990) is certainly worth reading. Another useful study is Karen Michalson's *Victorian Fantasy Literature: Literary Battles with Church and Empire* (New York: Edwin Mellen Press, 1990), which offers some interesting information on the Victorian religious and political climate and the works of MacDonald and other similar writers of the period.

Despite the recent outpouring of critical studies, there has yet to be a definitive study of George MacDonald's writings. His genius as a maker of myth and fantasies and his special talent for writing fairytale-parables have been repeatedly explored. But MacDonald's place as a Scottish novelist has yet to be fully determined. For the present, the best study of George MacDonald is to be found—as he wished it—in his books.

Register of Letters

The editor and publisher gratefully acknowledge permission to reprint letters from the following sources (letters are identified by source in the register that follows):

The Beinecke Rare Book and Manuscript Library, Yale University, New Haven, CT. (George MacDonald Collection, General Manuscript 103.)

The Bodleian Library, Oxford, England. (MS. Autogr. d. 34, fol. 63; MS. Eng. lett. c. 481, fols. 102-3.)

The Brander Library, Huntly, Scotland.

The British Library, London, England.

Department of Special Collections, University Research Library, University of California at Los Angeles (UCLA).

Dr. Williams's Library, London, England.

George MacDonald and His Wife, by Greville MacDonald. London: George Allen & Unwin, 1924. Reprinted by Unwin Hyman. Selected letters reproduced by kind permission of Unwin Hyman Ltd.

Henry W. and Albert A. Berg Collection The New York Public Library Astor, Lenox and Tilden Foundations

The Houghton Library, Harvard University, Cambridge, MA. Selected letters reprinted by permission.

The Huntington Library, San Marino, CA. Selected letters reprinted by permission.

The Marion E. Wade Center, Wheaton College, Wheaton, IL.

National Library of Scotland, Edinburgh, Scotland. Selected letters reprinted by permission of the Trustees of the National Library of Scotland.

The Tennyson Research Centre, Lincoln, England. Letter reprinted by permission of Lincolnshire County Council.

The University of Nottingham Library, Nottingham, England.

The University of London Library. (University of London A.L. 223.) Reprinted by permission of the University Librarian.

Abbreviations

ALS	Autographed Letter Signed
B	Brander Library, Huntly
BL	British Library
Bodleian	Bodleian Library, Oxford
GMAW	*George MacDonald and His Wife* by Greville MacDonald. George Allen & Unwin. London, 1924. Reprinted by Unwin Hyman.
Harvard	Houghton Library, Harvard University
Huntington	Huntington Library
LERG	*Letters of Emelia Russell Gurney*
London	University of London Library
NLS	National Library of Scotland
Nottingham	University of Nottingham Library
NYP	New York Public Library, Berg Collection
PC	Private Collection
Tennyson	Tennyson Research Centre
UCLA	The Research Library, University of California at Los Angeles
Wade	Wade Collection, Wheaton College, Wheaton, IL
Williams	Dr. Williams's Library, London
Yale	Beinecke Rare Book and Manuscript Library, Yale University

Part I

1. p. 5, Aug. 15, 1833 (ALS Yale)
2. p. 6, Aug. 1, 1834 (ALS Yale)
3. p. 7 [1836?] (ALS Yale)
4. p. 8, Jan. 5, 1841 (ALS Yale)
5. p. 9, Oct. 28, 1841 (ALS Yale)
6. p. 11, Nov. 8, 1845 (ALS Yale)
7. p. 12, Dec. 26, 1845 (ALS Yale)
8. p. 14, Feb. 10, 1846 (ALS Yale)
9. p. 15, Mar. 13, 1846 (ALS Yale)
10. p. 15, June 15, 1846 (*GMAW*, p. 94)
11. p. 16, Apr. 11, 1847 (ALS Yale)
12. p. 20, May 22, 1847 (*GMAW*, p. 109)
13. p. 21 [1848?] (*GMAW*, pp. 110-11)
14. p. 22, Highbury Testimonial (Williams)
15. p. 26, Oct. 23, 1848 (*GMAW*, p. 117)
16. p. 26 [1848] (ALS Yale)

17. p. 27, May 12, 1849 (*GMAW*, pp. 121-22)
18. p. 28, May 15, 1849 (ALS Yale)
19. p. 30, July 25, 1849 (ALS Yale)
20. p. 32, Feb. 23, 1850 (ALS Yale)
21. p. 33, Apr. 29, 1850 (*GMAW*, p. 131)
22. p. 33, May 24, 1850 (*GMAW*, pp. 131-32)
23. p. 34, May 31, 1850 (*GMAW*, p. 132)
24. p. 35, Oct. 4, 1850 (*GMAW*, p. 138)
25. p. 35, Oct. 16, 1850 (ALS Yale)
26. p. 38, Oct. 29, 1850 (ALS Yale)
27. p. 39, Nov. 7-8, 1850 (*GMAW*, p. 145)
28. p. 40, Nov. 15, 1850 (ALS Yale)
29. p. 41, Dec. 17, 1850 (ALS Yale)
30. p. 42, Dec. 27, 1850 (*GMAW*, pp. 148-49)

Part II

1. p. 49, Jan. 9, 1851 (*GMAW*, pp. 146-50)
2. p. 49 [Jan. 16, 1851] (*GMAW*, p. 150)
3. p. 50, Apr. 15, 1851 (ALS Yale)
4. p. 52, May 27, 1851 (ALS Yale)
5. p. 53 [July 5, 1852] (*GMAW*, p. 179)
6. p. 54, July 27, 1852 (ALS Yale)
7. p. 55 [Jan. 19, 1853] (ALS Yale)
8. p. 57, Apr. 5, 1853 (*GMAW*, pp. 172-73)
9. p. 58, Apr. 29, 1853 (ALS Yale)
10. p. 60, May 20, 1853 (ALS Yale)
11. p. 61, June 3, 1853 (ALS Yale)
12. p. 62 [July 1853] (ALS Yale)
13. p. 62, Sept. 7, 1853 (ALS Yale)
14. p. 65, Sept. 26, 1853 (*GMAW*, pp. 201-2)
15. p. 66, Sept. 27, 1853 (ALS Yale)
16. p. 67, Oct. 17, 1853 (ALS Yale)
17. p. 68, Nov. 16, 1853 (ALS Yale)
18. p. 71, Nov. 29, 1853 (ALS Yale)
19. p. 72, Dec. 6, 1853 (ALS Yale)
20. p. 74, Dec. 21, 1853 (ALS Yale)
21. p. 74 [Dec. 30, 1853] (*GMAW*, p. 206)

22. p. 74, Jan. 4, 1854 (*GMAW*, pp. 206-7)
23. p. 75, Feb. 6, 1854 (ALS Yale)
24. p. 75 [1854] (ALS Huntington)
25. p. 76, Feb. 23, 1854 (ALS Huntington)
26. p. 77, Mar. 17, 1854 (*GMAW*, pp. 208-9)
27. p. 78, Mar. 20, 1854 (ALS Yale)
28. p. 79 [June 1854] (*GMAW*, pp. 212-13)
29. p. 80, June 26, 1854 (ALS Yale)
30. p. 80, July 19, 1854 (*GMAW*, pp. 213-14)
31. p. 81, Sept. 1854 (ALS Yale)
32. p. 83 [Feb. 5, 1855] (*GMAW*, pp. 221-22)
33. p. 83, Feb. 8, 1855 (*GMAW*, pp. 222-23)
34. p. 85, Mar. 31, 1855 (ALS Nottingham)
35. p. 86, June 3, 1855 (ALS Yale)
36. p. 87 [July 2, 1855] (ALS Yale)

37. p. 88 [July 4, 1855] (*GMAW*, pp. 229-30)

38. p. 89 [July 4, 1855] (*GMAW*, p. 230)

39. p. 90, July 5, 1855 (*GMAW*, pp. 231-32)

40. p. 91 [July 8, 1855] (*GMAW*, pp. 234-35)

41. p. 92, July 10-11, 1855 (*GMAW*, pp. 235-36)

42. p. 93, July 13, 1855 (*GMAW*, p. 238)

43. p. 94 [July 14, 1855] (*GMAW*, pp. 239-40)

44. p. 94 [July 15, 1855] (*GMAW*, p. 241)

45. p. 95 [July 17, 1855] (*GMAW*, p. 242)

46. p. 95 [July 17, 1855] (*GMAW*, p. 242)

47. p. 95 [July 20, 1855] (*GMAW*, p. 243)

48. p. 96, July 20, 1855 (*GMAW*, p. 239)

49. p. 96, July 25-27, 1855 (*GMAW*, pp. 244-45)

50. p. 97 [July 28, 1855] (*GMAW*, pp. 245-46)

51. p. 98 [Aug. 6, 1855] (*GMAW*, p. 249, & ALS Yale)

52. p. 99 [Aug. 1855] (*GMAW*, p. 248)

53. p. 100 [Aug. 1855] (*GMAW*, p. 249)

54. p. 100 [Aug. 1855] (*GMAW*, pp. 250-51)

55. p. 101 [Aug. 1855] (*GMAW*, pp. 249-50)

56. p. 102 [Aug. 26, 1855] (*GMAW*, p. 241)

57. p. 102, Sept. 27, 1855 (ALS Yale)

58. p. 103, Dec. 30, 1855 (*GMAW*, p. 254)

59. p. 104 [1856] (ALS Huntington)

60. p. 105, Jan. 2, 1856 (*GMAW*, p. 254)

61. p. 105, Jan. 2, 1856 (*GMAW*, p. 255)

62. p. 106 [Jan. 1856] (ALS Huntington)

63. p. 106 [Jan. 21, 1856] (ALS Huntington)

64. p. 107, Jan. 21, 1856 (ALS Yale)

65. p. 107, Jan. 24, 1856 (*GMAW*, pp. 259-60)

66. p. 108, Feb. 18, 1856 (*GMAW*, p. 260)

67. p. 108, Feb. 19, 1856 (ALS Huntington)

68. p. 109, Feb. 27, 1856 (ALS Yale)

69. p. 109 [Mar. 1856] (*GMAW*, p. 262)

70. p. 110, June 5, 1856 (ALS Nottingham)

71. p. 111, June 17, 1856 (ALS Huntington)

72. p. 112, July 16, 1856 (ALS Yale)

73. p. 114, Aug. 29, 1856 (ALS Yale)

74. p. 115, Nov. 20, 1856 (ALS Huntington)

75. p. 117, Nov. 28, 1856 (ALS Huntington)

76. p. 118, Christmas Eve 1856 (*GMAW*, pp. 269-70)

77. p. 120, Jan. 12, 1857 (*GMAW*, pp. 268-69)

78. p. 121, Feb. 4, 1857 (*GMAW*, pp. 272-73)

79. p. 121, May 28, 1857 (ALS Huntington)

80. p. 122 [June 1857] (*GMAW*, p. 278)

81. p. 122 [July 1857] (ALS Huntington)

82. p. 123, Aug. 27, 1857 (*GMAW*, p. 281)

83. p. 124, Dec. 2, 1857 (ALS Yale)

84. p. 125, Jan. 2, 1858 (*GMAW*, p. 288)

85. p. 161, Undated (*GMAW*, p. 290)

86. p. 126, May 17, 1858 (ALS Huntington)

87. p. 127, May 20, 1858 (*GMAW*, p. 291)

88. p. 128 [June 1858] (*GMAW*, p. 292)

89. p. 129 [Aug. 28, 1858] (*GMAW*, p. 295)

90. p. 129 [Oct. 15, 1858] (*GMAW*, p. 295)

91. p. 130, Jan. 19, 1859 (*GMAW*, p. 303)

92. p. 130, July 2, 1859 (ALS Huntington)

93. p. 132 [Nov. 2, 1859] (*GMAW*, p. 311)

94. p. 133, Jan. 6, 1860 (*GMAW*, p. 325)

95. p. 133 [Jan. 1860] (*GMAW*, p. 326)

96. p. 134 [1861] (*GMAW*, p. 326)

97. p. 134, Mar. 7, 1861 (*GMAW*, pp. 326-27)

98. p. 135 [Apr. 1861] (*GMAW*, p. 327)

99. p. 136, Jan. 18, 1862 (ALS NLS)

100. p. 136, Aug. 9, 1862 (ALS NLS)

Part III

1. p. 142, Jan. 14, 1863 (*GMAW*, pp. 344-45)
2. p. 142, Sep. 7, 1863 (*GMAW*, p. 321)
3. p. 143, Mar. 29, 1864 (ALS Huntington)
4. p. 144 [1865] (ALS Huntington)
5. p. 145 [Aug. 1865] (ALS NLS)
6. p. 146, Aug. 17, 1865 (*GMAW*, p. 358)
7. p. 146 [Summer 1865] (*GMAW*, pp. 348-51)
8. p. 150, Aug. 25, 1865 (ALS Huntington)
9. p. 151 [To the Secretary of a North London Congregational Church] (*GMAW*, p. 367)
10. p. 151, Aug. 25, 1865 (ALS Tennyson)
11. p. 152, Nov. 5, 1865 (ALS NLS)
12. p. 152 [1865?] (ALS Huntington)
13. p. 153 [1866] [Unknown lady] (*GMAW*, pp. 373-74)
14. p. 155, Feb. 9, 1866 (ALS Huntington)
15. p. 156, May 6, 1866 (*GMAW*, p. 372)
16. p. 157, Oct. 28, 1866 (ALS NLS)
17. p. 158 [ca. 1866] (ALS NLS)
18. p. 158, May 20, 1867 (ALS NLS)
19. p. 159, July 11, 1867 (*GMAW*, pp. 318-19)
20. p. 159 [ca. 1868] (ALS NLS)
21. p. 160, Feb. 11, 1868 (ALS NLS)
22. p. 161, Feb. 26, 1868 (ALS NLS)

23. p. 162, June 24, 1868 (ALS Yale)
24. p. 163, June 28, 1868 (ALS Nottingham)
25. p. 164, July 15, 1868 (ALS UCLA)
26. p. 164, Nov. 18, 1868 (BL)
27. p. 165, Dec. 2, 1868 (BL)
28. p. 166, Mar. 7, 1869 (Wade)
29. p. 166 [Summer 1869] (*GMAW*, p. 391)
30. p. 167, June 1869 (*GMAW*, pp. 392-93)
31. p. 168 [June 1869] (*GMAW*, p. 392)
32. p. 169 [July 1869] (*GMAW*, p. 394)
33. p. 169, Aug. 3, 1869 (ALS NLS)
34. p. 171, Nov. 3, 1869 (ALS Yale)
35. p. 172, July 20, 1870 (ALS Yale)
36. p. 172, Dec. 5, 1870 (ALS Yale)
37. p. 174 [Feb. 25, 1871] (*GMAW*, pp. 411-12)
38. p. 174, Mar. 9, 1871 [ALS NLS]
39. p. 175, May 15, 1871 (ALS Yale)
40. p. 176, May 27, 1871 (ALS NLS)
41. p. 177 [July 26, 1871] (*GMAW*, p. 412)
42. p. 177 [Aug. 31, 1871] (ALS Harvard)
43. p. 178, Sept. 14, 1871 (ALS Bodleian)
44. p. 179 [Undated] (ALS Bodleian)
45. p. 180, Dec. 10, 1871 (*GMAW*, p. 414)
46. p. 180, Dec. 10, 1871 (ALS Yale)
47. p. 181, Dec. 10, 1871 (PC)

Part IV

1. p. 187, Feb. 7, 1872 (ALS Yale)
2. p. 187 [Feb. 12, 1872] (ALS Wade)
3. p. 188, Mar. 5, 1872 (ALS Huntington)
4. p. 189, Mar. 22, 1872 (ALS Huntington)
5. p. 189, Mar. 24, 1872 (ALS Yale)
6. p. 190, May 20, [1872] (*GMAW*, p. 418)
7. p. 191, June 8, 1872 (PC)
8. p. 192, June 21, 1872 (ALS UCLA)

9. p. 193, July 7, 1872 (*GMAW*, p. 416)
10. p. 193, Sept. 11, 1872 (ALS Yale)
11. pp. 195-203, 205-33 [letters from America, copied by Lilia Scott MacDonald] (Yale)
12. p. 204, Oct. 8, 1872 (ALS Harvard)
13. p. 233 [Dec. 1872] (ALS Yale)
14. p. 235, Dec. 22, 1872 (ALS Yale)
15. p. 236, Dec. 22, 1872 (ALS NLS)
16. p. 237, Mar. 20, 1873 (*GMAW*, p. 452)

17. p. 237, Apr. 12, 1873 (ALS Harvard)
18. p. 239, June 20, 1873 (ALS Yale)
19. p. 240, Jan. 5, 1874 (ALS UCLA)
20. p. 240, Aug. 13, 1874 (ALS NLS)
21. p. 241, Mar. 24, 1875 (*GMAW*, p. 380)
22. p. 241, May 9, 1875 (ALS UCLA)
23. p. 242, May 15, 1875 (*GMAW*, p. 468)
24. p. 243, May 30, 1875 (ALS Yale)
25. p. 244, Dec. 7, 1875 (ALS NLS)
26. p. 245, Feb. 15, 1876 (ALS BL)
27. p. 246, Apr. 17, 1876 (ALS NLS)
28. p. 246, Oct. 5, 1876 (ALS NYP)
29. p. 247, Oct. 11, 1876 (ALS UCLA)
30. p. 248, Dec. 21, 1876 (ALS Harvard)
31. p. 249, Mar. 4, 1877 (ALS NYP)
32. p. 250, Apr. 1, 1877 (ALS NLS)
33. p. 251, Apr. 23, 1877 (ALS NLS)
34. p. 252, May 3, 1877 (ALS NLS)

35. p. 253 [Aug. 4, 1877] (ALS NLS)
36. p. 254 [Autumn 1877] (*GMAW*, p. 475)
37. p. 254, Oct. 1877 (LERG)
38. p. 255, Oct. 1, 1877 (ALS NLS)
39. p. 256, Oct. 5, 1877 (ALS NLS)
40. p. 257, Oct. 7 for Oct. 8, 1877 (ALS NLS)
41. p. 258, Oct. 11, 1877 (NLS)
42. p. 258, Oct. 1877 (ALS NLS)
43. p. 259, Oct. 16, 1877 (ALS NLS)
44. p. 260, Oct. 18, 1877 (*GMAW*, p. 477)
45. p. 260, Oct. 29, 1877 (*GMAW*, p. 479)
46. p. 261, Nov. 2, 1877 (*GMAW*, p. 479)
47. p. 261, Christmas 1877 (NLS)

Part V

1. p. 268, Nov. 2, 1877 (ALS NLS)
2. p. 268, Nov. 3, 1877 (ALS NLS)
3. p. 269 [Nov. 1877] (ALS NLS)
4. p. 271, Nov. 12, 1877 (ALS NLS)
5. p. 273, Jan. 6, 1878 (ALS NLS)
6. p. 276, Feb. 17, 1878 (ALS NLS)
7. p. 278, Apr. 7, 1878 (ALS NLS)
8. p. 281, May 12, 1878 (*GMAW*, p. 484)
9. p. 281, May 12, 1878 (*GMAW*, p. 360)
10. p. 282, June 5, 1878 (*GMAW*, p. 487)
11. p. 283, June 19, 1878 (*GMAW*, p. 487)
12. p. 283, July 7, 1878 (ALS NLS)
13. p. 284, July 20, 1878 (ALS UCLA)
14. p. 286, Sept. 1, 1878 (*LERG*)
15. p. 287, Sept. 23, 1878 (ALS UCLA)
16. p. 288, Jan. 13, 1879 (ALS NLS)
17. p. 290 [Mar. 1879] (*GMAW*, pp. 492-93)
18. p. 291, Mar. 11, 1879 (*GMAW*, pp. 492-93)
19. p. 291, Mar. 19, 1879 (*GMAW*, pp. 489-90)
20. p. 292, Mar. 20, 1879 (ALS NLS)
21. p. 293, Apr. 9, 1879 (ALS NLS)

22. p. 295, June 15, 1879 (ALS UCLA)
23. p. 295, July 7, 1879 (ALS NLS)
24. p. 297, Aug. 8, 1879 (ALS NLS)
25. p. 298, Aug. 18, 1879 (*GMAW*, p. 504)
26. p. 298, Aug. 21, 1879 (ALS Harvard)
27. p. 299, Christmas Eve 1879 (NLS)
28. p. 301, Jan. 26, 1880 (ALS NLS)
29. p. 302, Jan. 28, 1880 (PC)
30. p. 303, Aug. 3, 1880 (Wade)
31. p. 304, May 13, 1881 (ALS NLS)
32. p. 304, June 16, 1881 (*GMAW*, p. 528)
33. p. 305, July 18, 1882 (ALS NLS)
34. p. 306, Jan. 19, 1883 (*GMAW*, p. 529)
35. p. 307, Mar. 11, 1883 (ALS UCLA)
36. p. 308, Apr. 3, 1883 [misdated — 1833?] (ALS Yale)
37. p. 309, Dec. 24, 1883 (PC)
38. p. 311, Apr. 6, 1884 (*GMAW*, p. 530)
39. p. 311, Nov. 7, 1884 (*GMAW*, p. 497)
40. p. 312 [Last Sunday of 1884] (*GMAW*, p. 531)
41. p. 314, Jan. 10, 1885 (*GMAW*, p. 541)
42. p. 314, Feb. 26, 1885 (*GMAW*, p. 541)

43. p. 315, Sept. 17, 1885 (ALS NLS)
44. p. 315, Sept. 30, 1885 (ALS NLS)
45. p. 316, Oct. 18, 1885 (ALS NLS)
46. p. 317, Mar. 28, 1886 (PC)
47. p. 319, June 23, 1886 (ALS UCLA)
48. p. 319, July 20, 1886 (ALS UCLA)
49. p. 320, Aug. 29, 1886 (*GMAW,* p. 534)
50. p. 321, Dec. 20, 1886 (ALS NLS)
51. p. 321, Christmas 1886 (*GMAW,* p. 535)
52. p. 322, Jan. 19, 1887 (*GMAW,* p. 535)

53. p. 322, Feb. 24, 1887 (*GMAW,* p. 513)
54. p. 323, Mar. 8, 1887 (*GMAW,* p. 535)
55. p. 324, Mar. 20, 1887 (*GMAW,* p. 514)
56. p. 324, Apr. 12, 1887 (PC)
57. p. 326, Sept. 7, 1887 (ALS UCLA)
58. p. 326, Oct. 6, 1887 (ALS NLS)
59. p. 328, Nov. 5, 1887 (B)
60. p. 329, Dec. 8, 1887 (ALS UCLA)
61. p. 329, Dec. 11, 1887 (*LERG*)

Part VI

1. p. 335, Jan. 21, 1888 (ALS NLS)
2. p. 336, Sept. 30, 1888 (ALS NLS)
3. p. 337 [Sunday night] (ALS NLS)
4. p. 338, Dec. 2, 1888 (ALS NLS)
5. p. 339, Dec. 9, [1888] (ALS NLS)
6. p. 340, Dec. 19, 1888 (ALS NLS)
7. p. 341, Jan. 20, 1889 (*GMAW,* p. 535)
8. p. 341, Mar. 3, 1890 (*GMAW,* p. 536)
9. p. 342, June 1890 (ALS NLS)
10. p. 343, Jan. 4, 1891 (*GMAW,* pp. 517-18)
11. p. 344, Mar. 1, 1891 (ALS Yale)
12. p. 344, July 13, 1891 (*GMAW,* p. 520)
13. p. 345 [July 1891] (*GMAW,* p. 521)
14. p. 345, July 16, 1891 (ALS UCLA)
15. p. 346, Aug. 8, 1891 (ALS UCLA)
16. p. 347, Aug. 29, 1891 (ALS NYP)
17. p. 347, Oct. 5, 1891 (ALS Nottingham)
18. p. 348, Nov. 5, 1891 (*GMAW,* p. 525)
19. p. 348, Nov. 6, 1891 (*GMAW,* p. 525)
20. p. 349, Apr. 16, 1892 (ALS Yale)
21. p. 350, June 15, 1892 (*GMAW,* p. 539)
22. p. 351, Oct. 15, 1892 (*GMAW,* p. 541)
23. p. 351, Nov. 20, 1892 (ALS BL)
24. p. 352, Dec. 12, 1892 (ALS NLS)
25. p. 353, Dec. 13, 1892 (ALS Nottingham)

26. p. 353, Dec. 24, 1892 (ALS Nottingham)
27. p. 354, Jan. 22, 1893 (*GMAW,* p. 542)
28. p. 355, June 11, 1893 (*GMAW,* p. 542)
29. p. 355, July 23, 1893 (ALS UCLA)
30. p. 355, Aug. 1, 1893 (ALS UCLA)
31. p. 356, Aug. 5, 1893 (ALS UCLA)
32. p. 356, Oct. 22, 1893 (ALS NLS)
33. p. 358, Nov. 5, 1893 (ALS NLS)
34. p. 359, Christmas 1893 (ALS NLS)
35. p. 360, Jan. 1, 1894 (ALS Nottingham)
36. p. 360, June 1, 1894 (ALS Huntington)
37. p. 362, June 18, 1894 (*GMAW,* pp. 542-43)
38. p. 362, Nov. 11, 1894 (ALS NLS)
39. p. 363, Dec. 28, 1894 (ALS NLS)
40. p. 365, July 14, 1895 (ALS Nottingham)
41. p. 366, July 26, 1895 (PC)
42. p. 366, Mar. 14, 1897 (ALS Nottingham)
43. p. 367, Good Friday, 1898 (*GMAW,* p. 545)
44. p. 368, Jan. 3, 1900 (ALS NLS)
45. p. 368, Mar. 16 [1900?] (ALS NLS)
46. p. 369, Dec. 16 [1901] (ALS NLS)
47. p. 370 [1901] (ALS NLS)

Index of People and Places

Index of Subjects